The Kovacs Guide to Electronic Library Collection Development

ESSENTIAL CORE SUBJECT COLLECTIONS, SELECTION CRITERIA, AND GUIDELINES

DIANE K. KOVACS and **KARA L. ROBINSON**

NEAL-SCHUMAN-PUBLISHERS, INC.
New York   London

THE KOVACS GUIDE TO ELECTRONIC LIBRARY COLLECTION DEVELOPMENT:

ESSENTIAL CORE SUBJECT COLLECTIONS, SELECTION CRITERIA, AND GUIDELINES

Diane K. Kovacs and Kara L. Robinson

Don't miss the companion Web site that accompanies this book at:

www.neal-schuman.com/elibrary.html

Login name: egreader
Password: neal2schuman

Published by Neal-Schuman Publishers, Inc.
100 William Street, Suite 2004
New York, NY 10038

The paper used in this publication meets the minimum requirements of American National Standard for Informational Sciences—Permanence of Paper for Printed Library Materials, ANSI Z39.48—1992.

Printed and bound in the United States of America.

ISBN 1–55570–483–2

Library of Congress Cataloging-in-Publication Data

Kovacs, Diane K. (Diane Kaye), 1962–

    The Kovacs guide to electronic library collection development: essential core subject collections, selection criteria, and guidelines / Diane K. Kovacs, Kara L. Robinson.
        p. cm.
    ISBN 1–55570–483–2 (alk. paper)

    1. Digital libraries—Collection development—United States. I. Title: Guide to electronic library collection development II. Robinson, Kara. III. Title

ZA4080.5.K685 2004
025.2'84—dc22   2003044256

CONTENTS

List of E-library Success Stories

LIST OF FIGURES AND TABLES

FOREWORD

In our role as professional information mediaries, we need to take full advantage of Web resources. If you are simply going to a Web search engine, and these days it is likely that you utilize the one that ends with "oogle," you are very likely missing out on many tools, resources, and potential answers from current, in-depth, and authoritative resources. Diane K. Kovacs and Kara L. Robinson's *The Kovacs Guide to Electronic Library Collection Development: Essential Core Subject Collections, Selection Criteria, and Guidelines* is a critical resource in adapting the key concepts of librarian collection development and applying them to openly available Web resources.

You can offer patrons more by integrating Web resources into your library's collection by evaluating, selecting, and organizing these resources, so patrons find the best information in all formats. It is important to stress that by no stretch of the imagination is the "open Web" a comprehensive source of quality information—far from it. You already know this, but unfortunately, some members of the public believe that this is the case. How much time is it taking you and your patrons to find what's available? Then, how much time is needed to evaluate the quality and currency of the material?

In this time of declining budgets, are you fully exploiting the free high-quality content that *is* available on the "open Web." It can be a virtual treasure chest of quality information, if you understand its limitations and have knowledge of what is and is not available. In other words, collection development of Web resources is crucial. Finding top-quality content, keeping current with what content is available, and then making these choice resources easily and quickly accessible for your patrons, may seem like a never ending challenge to you and your colleagues. It is certainly a challenge worth the effort. Let *The Kovacs Guide to Electronic Library Collection Development: Essential Core Subject Collections, Selection Criteria, and Guidelines* facilitate the process.

Creating collections saves time for patrons. Remember that an important principle in Raganathan's Five Laws of Library Science is to "save the time of the reader." Modernizing the meaning of "reader" to include users of electronic tools, this guide puts into action the fundamental librarianship concept of selectively collecting and making needed information resources available. With the massive amount of data on the "open Web" it is essential that we direct library patrons directly to the important tools and resources.

Few could argue that in our busy library environment today, saving the time of the librarian has also become a tacit guiding principle. Often it seems more efficient to tackle a research question by typing a few words into a search engine, hoping for the best, and then start browsing. Even then, how much time do you have to spend on reviewing what you find?

This guide encourages the library community to develop localized and personal collections of open-Web resources, while simultaneously having the information professionals become familiar with resources. Developing e-library collections that are customized for local users at the library and the personal level continues to be an excellent goal. Even if you do not develop a local e-library collection, having a working knowledge of key resources from the "open Web" will not only make you a more valuable member of your library's staff, but it will also give you some very marketable knowledge.

Usually, before selecting a new book—and certainly after physically arriving in the library—you take some time to "learn" the volume. What information does it contain? How current is it? How is the content organized? What does the volume offer that similar volumes don't? As a good reference librarian, you would "know" key tools in your collection and be able to guide patrons directly to them.

Now apply this model to Web resources. "Learning" a Web resource goes a great deal further than just knowing it is there. Reviews of Web sites can be valuable, but often just scratch the surface of what the site offers. Librarians need to spend some time evaluating, selecting, and categorizing the sites and creating direct links (one or two clicks away) to where potential answers lie. These days, a directory link to the top-level page of a Web site can leave the patron and busy librarian far away from where the potential answer lies.

In this edition, Kovacs and Robinson build and improve upon the original *Building Electronic Library Collections*. The authors not only identify core sites for library reference collections, in addition they discuss strategies for evaluating, selecting, collecting and organizing Web resources that utilize a librarian's existing skills and knowledge. Furthermore, the "E-Library Success Stories" illustrate how many libraries are streamlining the integration of Web resources into the library collection and reference process.

The Kovacs Guide to Electronic Library Collection Development: Essential Core Subject Collections, Selection Criteria, and Guidelines is a must-have guide for libraries who want to capitalize on the power of Web information to serve their patrons and encourage new patrons to make use of library services.

Gary Price, Editor
The ResourceShelf. Available: www.resourceshelf.com.
Library and Internet Research Consulting
gary@resourceshelf.com

PREFACE

The Kovacs Guide to Electronic Library Collection Development: Essential Core Subject Collections, Selection Criteria, and Guidelines shows how to develop and maintain an electronic library—e-library for short. Let's first define "e-library." It is a Web-published collection of Web-accessible information resources. An e-library may include a "digital library" collection—a collection of electronic documents scanned or transcribed from print or holographic primary documents or artifacts—and may include documents that were published originally in electronic format or published in multiple formats. It may also offer "virtual library" services through the Web. The e-library concept encompasses both the digital library and the virtual library.

Creating an e-library is an ambitious project for any library, because the process attempts to recreate the library collection and the library services—in virtual space. In its simplest form an e-library is a collection of Web-accessible information resources from a variety of resources, including freely available Web sites and fee-based Web-accessible databases. An e-library may also include access to virtual library services, such as reference, the library catalog, circulation, and other document delivery services. Often e-libraries are manifest as Web published linked html pages, or through Web-accessible database software. Most e-libraries are accessible to users through the Web, but some are accessible only through private company or organizational Intranets.

The Kovacs Guide to Electronic Library Collection Development: Essential Core Subject Collections, Selection Criteria, and Guidelines includes e-library builder success stories that illustrate the diversity of e-libraries and provide practical information about how their e-libraries were planned, created, managed, and grown. Learning from libraries who have developed strategies for collecting Web-accessible information resources and constructing e-libraries is a recurring theme throughout this book. The specific resources that are selected and how they are organized and made accessible will be unique for each library, but we can learn from sharing experiences.

The Kovacs Guide expands on *Building Electronic Library Collections* (Neal-Schuman, 2000). It explains and updates all of the essentials tools of that earlier title. It also addresses the shifting environment in which e-libraries are created and managed today. Major changes include:

- integration of the library catalog including the cataloging of Web-accessible resources;
- integration of library services, such as virtual reference (real-time as well as e-mail or forms based reference services), and document delivery;
- greater variety and scope of Web accessible fee-based databases, including full-text resource aggregators; and
- greater variety and scope of electronic journals and electronic books.

The Kovacs Guide to Electronic Library Collection Development: Essential Core Subject Collections, Selection Criteria, and Guidelines is intended for any librarian who wants to begin developing, expanding, or improving an e-library.

The authors have attempted to shape *The Kovacs Guide* as a "one-step" resource that tries to serve three distinct functions of electronic collection policies: to guide collection planning, to steer collection management, and to identify subject collection, criteria, and core electronic resources.

The first function provides librarians with a collection-planning guide specifically written for collecting, evaluating, and selecting Web-accessible information resources. A collection development plan is just as essential, if not more so, for creating a good e-library as it is for building a collection of print resources or locally accessible databases. Every collection plan must consider users' information needs, information seeking behaviors (and expectations), and establish selection criteria.

Collection management, the second function of *The Kovacs Guide*, addresses issues including integration of the e-library collection and the library catalog, library services integration, database management choices, and database licensing issues. It confronts—and answers—essential e-library collection management questions. How much will it cost? Who will have access? How will access be managed/limited/monitored? How will the information be archived or otherwise safeguarded for the future? How will the e-library be searched or made searchable?

The third function—the guide as collection development tool—is purely practical. What are good for e-library collection evaluation, selection, and collection (acquisition)? Which Web-accessible resources are "core" or essential in any given subject area?

ORGANIZATION

The Kovacs Guide to Electronic Library Collection Development is arranged in three parts. Part I, "Recommended Practices" explores all of the wide-ranging concerns of e-libraries. Part II contains "Recommended Evaluation Guidelines, Selection Criteria, and Core Collections For Major Subject Areas" to create or improve the collection. Part III, offers important "Web Collection Development Resources."

In Part I, Chapter 1—"General Collection Development Principles for Web-Accessible Resources"—assesses the e-library collection development literature and then presents a framework within which librarians can plan and develop e-libraries. It explores the questions to answer in creating a usable Web-accessible resource collection plan as well as planning for making that collection Web-accessible. The chapter recommends specific strategies for collecting, evaluating, and selecting Web-accessible information resources—including a checklist/interview for preliminary planning and organization as well as a checklist/interview for creating a good E-library collection development plan individualized for each library's needs.

Chapter 2—"Integrating the Physical Library and the E-Library"—explores the most critical e-library collection management issues. Specifically the authors review the creation of MARC records for Web resources in the OCLC Connexion service and other forms of Web resource cataloging including the Dublin Core metadata project and how it affects library catalogs and making Web resources searchable. This chapter briefly discusses the creation of local digital collections, virtual reference services, and document delivery integration into the e-library.

Chapter 3—"Licensing Basics" addresses the various arrangements made and issues involved in licensing or purchasing Web-accessible databases.

In Part II: Recommended Evaluation Guidelines, Selection Criteria, and Core Collections for Major Subject Areas, nine separate chapters are each devoted to collection development and core resources collections for a specific subject area. These subject areas embrace the following categories of Web-accessible resources:

- ready-reference information,
- business information,
- jobs and employment information,
- medical information,
- legal information,
- biological sciences information,
- physical sciences, engineering, computer sciences, and technology information,
- social sciences and education information,
- readers' advisory information,
- resources for collection development activities.

Each chapter identifies specific evaluation criteria and recommends a core collection within the subject area of focus as well as recommending specific collection development tools.

Part III, "Web Collection Development Resources, provides up-to-date sources for collection development related discussion lists, newsgroups and blogs, evaluation guides, and multiple subject resource collection tools.

"E-Library Success Stories," including virtual reference services, are employed in each chapter to illustrate the diversity and creativity of e-library builders. Literally thousands of e-libraries might have been included, but these case studies are representative of the best. Peter Scott's LibDex (add URL) lists more than 18,000 library homepages, OPACs, and other library related Web sites. Michael Sauers' World Wide Web Library Directory lists nearly 9,000 library Web sites in 130 countries. Libweb edited by Thomas Dowling, includes nearly 7,000 library Web sites worldwide. The case study e-libraries represent different types of libraries including school, public, academic and special libraries, and regional library organizations. The scope of the case studies is international, but limited to English language sites or sites with an English version, such as the Biblioteca Digital de Catalunya-BDC.

Note: the Webliographies, bibliographies, and the core e-library resources for each subject area each chapter are available as frequently updated and revised Web pages on the companion Web site at www.neal-schuman.com/elibrary.html. This password-protected site is exclusively for readers of *The Kovacs Guide to Electronic Library Collection Development*. The login name and password are: *egreader*; *neal2schuman*.

Readers are encouraged to bookmark the companion Web site. It will frequently be updated as the sites identified in these print pages move or expire and new, even better sites are developed. Readers are also encouraged to send feedback on the sites chosen for inclusion in the core collection—and suggestions for expanding it—to diane@kovacs.com.

Librarians who create e-libraries are applying the best principles of traditional library collection development to Web-accessible resources. *The Kovacs Guide to Electronic Library Collection Development: Essential Core Subject Collections, Selection Criteria, and Guidelines* serves as a resource for clarifying how the collection development process translates to the Web environment, as a guide for planning collection management, and as a guide for developing selection criteria for specific subject areas, and as collection of carefully selected resources for starting or expanding an e-library collection.

ACKNOWLEDGMENTS

From Diane K. Kovacs:

Thank you very very much to Kara, my coauthor, especially for all the stress breaks with your family. Thank you to my husband Michael J. Kovacs who read and edited several versions of the manuscript. I appreciate how you nagged me just the right amount. My deepest appreciation to all of the individuals who responded to the case study interviews. Thank you especially, to the folks at the Science and Technology Department of the Cleveland Public Library, who let me be a real virtual reference librarian for an afternoon.

From Kara L. Robinson:

To Diane, my coauthor, for lots of reason—most of which have nothing to do with this book. Many thanks to my husband Bennett, my rock and roll man who seemed to know intuitively when not to disturb. Thanks also to my in-laws, the Crooks, for asking me what I was working on—all those questions helped me to clarify my ideas.

Both authors are grateful to Erica Lilly, Electronic Resources Coordinator, Kent State University for carefully and thoughtfully reading through the manuscript and providing her critique before we finalized the book.

Thank you also to Alli Shaloum at Neal-Schuman who edited Part II. As always, this book owes much to all the wonderful folks at Neal-Schuman, especially Charles Harmon and Michael Kelley.

PART I

RECOMMENDED PRACTICES

1: General Collection Development Principles for Web-Accessible Resources

"Concentrate on content. The bells and whistles of fancy software can cushion a lack of integrity of information, but the fact remains that content is the basis, and the final result, of any research. Whether beginning electronic collection development from scratch, or seeking to supplement existing resources, the process of selecting quality appropriate materials demands thorough investigation and attention to detail."

S. Brooks (2001: 316)

INTRODUCTION

Two unavoidable factors have made it imperative for libraries to build Web-accessible resource collections for their current and potential library patrons—the ubiquity of personal computers, and the publication of information on and through the World Wide Web. In the twenty-first century, being an effective librarian in any type of library (public, academic, or special) means expanding the range of resources that you provide for library patrons. Now libraries must include resources available in electronic format and make those resources accessible off site, outside of the physical library building.

Stephen Sowards's classic article clarifies why librarians should, do, and will create e-library reference collections:

- *Selection:* Users who can rely on reference Web sites save significant time by avoiding inefficient, inconclusive Web surfing.
- *Endorsement:* Librarians implicitly vouch for the quality of the linked sources: their relevance for solving a given problem, their consistent availability, and the accuracy and currency of their content.
- *Organization:* A well-designed site allows users to move rapidly and accurately among a large number of Web sites, finding a high proportion of relevant resources.
- *Cooperation:* These sites allow experienced librarians to share their knowledge of the Web with each other and with users, at all times of the day and irrespective of distance. (Sowards, 1998: 3)

Other benefits of building an e-library include:

- enhancing existing services for core user groups;
- providing new services to core user groups;
- attracting new library patrons; and
- providing new (or better) services to patrons who are reluctant (or find it difficult) to come into the physical library.

E-libraries extend the librarian's role as information intermediary to the Web. E-libraries can be designed to promote the library's overall service mission to their community of patrons. In order to survive, libraries and librarians must adapt to the information needs and respond to the information-seeking behaviors of their patrons. In part, librarians adapt to these needs and behaviors by building Web-accessible resource collections; or e-libraries, for short. We must also respond to changes in how current and potential library patrons seek information. In the twenty-first century, information is portable. Information comes to the user through the Web, cell phones, PDA's, and other portable electronic storage devices. On the Shifted Librarian Web log (hereafter, blog) (www.theshiftedlibrarian.com/stories/2002/01/19/whatIsAShifted Librarian.htm), Jenny Levine, describes this process as "information shifting." People are now very likely to be receiving information rather than pursuing it. Physically visiting a library is no longer an option for a growing number of our potential patrons. Jenny Levine describes the need for librarians to shift with the information-seeking behavior changes of our patrons to become shifted librarians:

> "To my mind, the biggest difference is that they expect information to come to them, whether it's via the Web, email, cell phone, online chat, whatever. And given the tip of the iceberg of technology we're seeing, it's going to have a big impact on how they expect to receive library services, which means librarians have to start adjusting now. I call that adjustment 'shifting' because I think you have to start meeting these kids' information needs in their world, not yours. The library has to become more portable or 'shifted'.…Therefore, a 'shifted librarian' is someone who is working to make libraries more portable. We're experimenting with new methods, even if we find out they don't work as well as we thought they would. Sometimes, we're waiting for our colleagues, our bosses, and even the kids to catch up, but we're still out there trying. And please don't think I don't love books and print, because I do. No amount of technology will ever replace them, and libraries will always be a haven for books. It's the extras that I'm concentrating on, especially as we try to serve our remote patrons.

The pattern of our professional activities is still recognizable although our tools have changed. We still collect, evaluate, organize, and facilitate our patron's search for information resources. Our roles as librarians are being redefined and focussed on providing patrons with the information they need, when they need it, where they need it, and organizing that information for logical access by our patrons. Whether we are reference librarians, collection development librarians, bibliographers, or catalogers, our jobs are much more proactive with patrons than they have ever been. We are becoming "Shifted Librarians."

Libraries may choose to incorporate the selection and acquisition of electronic resources into the routine collection development responsibilities of librarians, or they may choose to create positions specifically for electronic resource librarians. In either case, these new responsibilities require technical training and experience. Librarians must also reach consensus about, and receive training in, two critical issues: (1) the specific selection criteria for electronic resources, and (2) ensuring that those electronic resources are accessible by patrons.

In the early days of the Internet, online resources might be accessed through Gopher, FTP, Telnet, Usenet Newsgroups, or Web. Now the Web is the dominant access interface. Although Gopher, FTP, Telnet, and Usenet still exist, users generally access them through the Web via Web browser software.

Electronic resources librarians can develop their collection of Web-accessible information resources (shortened to Web resources hereafter) based on the same basic collection policies articulated by libraries for print and electronic resources accessed locally. Most libraries have devoted considerable time in developing collections of materials that best serve their communities of patrons. Of course, some unique criteria do exist, related to the collection of Web resources. Selection is a process of comparing individual resources against criteria defined in a library's collection development policy, evaluating the quality, determining the relevancy of the resource to the information needs of your patrons, and deciding whether the library can afford to provide access to a given resource. While patrons may access many Web resources free of direct costs, many others are fee-based and require some kind of subscription or licensing arrangement. Fee-based databases that were previously—and may still be—available through telephone dial-up, published on CD-ROM or other computer storage media are frequently Web-accessible. Web-accessible versions—e-books and e-serials—of reference sources and serials previously available only in print are among selection choices. E-books and e-serials may be just as expensive as print versions, if not more so. Some may require that the print version be acquired to gain access to the electronic version. Even free Web resources may require expenditure of staff time for evaluation, cataloging, link maintenance, and user training; thus, what is "free" may actually cost the library something.

The proliferation of Internet access around the world, especially access to and through the Web, has led to increased access to many types of information resources that were previously difficult or expensive to obtain. Current news and information is quickly delivered through the Web. Information sources, such as newspapers, newsletters, journals, books, dissertations, specialized bibliographic or full-text databases, statistical datasets, and even television and radio transcripts and video or audio transmissions, are being made accessible through the Web. Some content is even published directly to the Web instead of, or in advance of, print versions. Stored or streaming audio or video is accessible through the Web, as well. Maps, photographs, and other graphic images are accessible through the Web individually and in digitized collections. Resources in a variety of media formats, and once only available locally in libraries or agencies, are now accessible globally: information from local and national governments, nongovernmental organizations, industry trade organizations, community or campus specific information, and the list goes on.

Library catalogs—OPACs—are among the most valuable resources made accessible by the Web outside the physical library. On the Web, Jon Udell's "LibraryLookup homepage" (http://weblog.infoworld.com/udell/stories/2002/12/11/librarylookup.html) takes creative advantage of Web database standards to make it possible for users to search OPACs, in addition to searching online booksellers. Library patrons, searching online booksellers that adhere to Web database standards, can look up whether their local library owns a copy of the book they are thinking of buying.

The Web also makes possible the sharing of resources among libraries so that the expenses of maintaining individual library OPACs, licensing databases, and creating digital library collections can be shared. Some have argued that the accessibility of information through the Web obviates the need for libraries or librarians (do a search on Google for the phrase "no need for librarians"). We could argue convincingly to the contrary. The sheer volume and diversity of information made available through the Web creates a need for librarian intermediaries who will evaluate, organize, and simplify access for information patrons.

The Web makes a significant quantity of information available to users. Web search tools are easy to use and can be downloaded for free. The real problem for our patrons is not finding information on the Web, but finding information on the Web that is of high quality, reliable, and authoritative. Through the efforts of librarians, our e-libraries can be collections of the best—the highest quality, most reliable and authoritative—resources for our patron's information needs.

We might also say that the Web is both the shelves and the "books." That is, the Web is an information storage and organization mechanism, as well as the source or supplier of information products. The important word is library, whether we call it the e-, virtual-, or digital-library. Libraries are not collections of books and other resources. Rather, libraries are service organizations that fulfil the information needs of their community of patrons.

Keller, Reich, and Hercovic (2003) explore the question, "What is a library anymore, anyway?":

> "Ignoring the physical, technological underpinnings for now, we assert that the library is, at root, a collection of information selected for use of, and made useable for, a particular community. That community may be large or small, physically proximate or not, present or future, homogeneous or not, but it is essential that it be identified and at least partially understood. That is, proverbially like politics, all collections are local." (Keller, Reich, and Hercovic, 2003)

As discussed in the Preface, e-library success stories are used in each chapter to illustrate different phases of e-library creation and subject area collection development. We draw these e-library case studies from public and academic libraries; special libraries, school libraries, as well as uniquely Web library projects, and regional library organizations.

DEFINITIONS AND WORD CHOICES: AN E-LIBRARY VOCABULARY

The e-library vocabulary is still evolving. Much word and phrase choice is based on consensus understanding or local usage. The e-library vocabulary situation is analogous to that of the car as it developed over time. At times what in American English we now refer to as a "car," was called "auto" or "automobile," and was historically named a "horseless carriage." Some refer to a car by its make or model, for example we (the authors) refer to our family cars as the "Focus," the "Taurus Wagon," the "Del Sol," and the "Subaru." In that same vein, some librarians refer to their library's Web collections and/or Web-accessible services as an e-library, a virtual library, or a digital library or less frequently as "the library Web site." Many other words and phrases are used interchangeably that ultimately refer to the e-library or some individual piece of the e-library.

In an attempt to use the consensus vocabulary that will be the most meaningful to the most librarians, we informally surveyed library related discussion lists, asking librarians to share the words and phrases they used to describe e-library concepts. They were also asked to choose the terms they use to refer to the people who use their libraries. Table 1.1.1 reports the overall findings and scope of this survey. The survey itself is online at www.kovacs.com/votelibraries.html.

A majority of librarians, 54.5 percent, who responded to the survey, refer to the users of their libraries as "patrons." 34.1 percent of librarians who responded to the survey chose the phrase "electronic library" or "e-Library" to mean "a Web-published collection of Web-accessible information resources, that may include a 'digital library' collection or 'virtual library' services." However, a nearly equal percentage, chose either the phrase "digital library" (26.8 percent), or "virtual library" (21.3 percent). 17.8 percent offered alternatives, such as "electronic resources," "Web sites/Web pages," or "databases." Librarians use these phrases interchangeably. In this book we've chosen to use "electronic Library or e-Library," for the sake of consistency. We will also refer to the people who use libraries as "library patrons" or "patrons." In referring to reference services that are offered through the Web, we'll use the phrase "virtual reference," although many libraries use the phrase "digital reference" instead. "Digital libraries" is used specifically to refer to "a collection of electronic documents scanned or transcribed from print or holographic primary documents or artifacts and may include documents that were published originally in electronic format or published in dual format." 53.8 percent of the survey respondents concurred with this definition.

Table 1.1.1. Library Vocabulary Survey Results

751 Response—Query sent to:
Govdoc-l@lists.psu.edu
LawLibRef@lists.washlaw.edu
Libref-l@listserv.kent.edu
LIS-LINK@JISCMAIL.AC.UK
Medlib-l@listserv.acsu.buffalo.edu
Nettrain@listserv.acsu.buffalo.edu
Oplinlist@oplin.lib.oh.us
Publib@sunsite.berkeley.edu
Web4lib@sunsite.berkeley.edu

Which word do you use most frequently to refer to the people who use your library?

Patron	54.5%	409
User	23%	173
None of these*	17.7%	131
Client	4.8%	36

*Other Terms used:

Student(s) (faculty,teachers, etc)	7.1	53
Customer(s)	6.7	50
Reader(s)	1.5%	11

Which library type best describes the library you work in/for/with?

Academic (with Graduate Programs)	34%	254
Public (All sizes)	28.8%	216
Special Library (Business, Corporate, Law, Government, Research, Non-profit, etc.)	17.2%	129
Academic (4 year)	6.1%	46
School Libraries (K-12)	5.6%	42
Academic (2 year)	4.4%	33
Special (Hospital)/Medical/Health, etc.	4.4%	33
Other type of library	3.6%	27

Which phrase means to you "a collection of electronic documents scanned or transcribed from print or holographic primary documents or artifacts and may include documents that were published originally in electronic format or published in dual format" My answer: Digital Library

Digital Library	53.8%	404
Electronic Library (e-library)	25%	187
None of these*	16.8%	126
Virtual Library	4.7%	35

*Other Terms used:

Database(s)	2.3%	17
Electronic Resources/E-Resources	2.5%	17
Electronic Collection/E-Collection	1.1%	8
Digital Collection/Archive	1.1%	8

Which phrase means to you "a Web-published collection of Web-accessible information resources." An ... may include a "digital library" collection or "virtual library" services." My answer: Electronic Library (e-library)

Electronic Library (e-library)	34.1%	256
Virtual Library	26.8%	201
Digital Library	21.3%	160
None of these*	17.8%	134

*Other Terms used:

Electronic Resources	2.1%	16
Web site/Web page	1.7%	13
Database(s)	1.3%	10

All other terms had much fewer than 1%.

Which phrase means to you "... refers to the offering of library services through the Web." My answer: Virtual Library

Virtual Library	44%	330
Electronic Library (e-library)	25.4%	191
None of these*	22.3%	168

Digital Library	8.3%	62
*Other Terms used:		
Online Reference/Service	3.5%	26
Web Service/Web-based Library Service	2%	15
Library Service(s)	1.2%	9

When the phrase "Internet resources" is used, it refers to resources accessible through Internet services other than and including the Web; e.g., Gopher, FTP, Telnet, e-mail, Usenet, and RSS feeds (blogs). "Web resources" refers to any information product that is published through or on the Web.

Librarians may understand and use vocabulary quite differently from library patrons. Librarians' vocabulary choices may be confusing for many current and potential patrons. John Kupersmith has published "Library Terms That Users Understand" (www.jkup.net/terms.html), based on a survey of terminology used on library Web sites. His intention is to provide usability data, as well as "best practices" on which terms are most effective, "most users can understand them well enough to make productive choices," as labels for library resources and services. It may make sense to us to refer to online databases, but the patron may find "Search Electronic Journals" or "Research by Subject" more understandable. John Kupersmith's analyses will help e-library builders make word choices and descriptions that better communicate information types and research functions for their current and potential patrons. Our goal is to integrate library collections and services with the Web at the point of contact with our patrons. We must shift to meet the information needs and information-seeking behavior of our patrons regardless of what terms we used among ourselves to describe the shifting of the library to the Web. Ook! (www.co.uk.lspace.org/books/whos-who/librarian.html).

THE E-LIBRARY COLLECTION DEVELOPMENT LITERATURE

In 1994 and 1995, when the Internet first became accessible to the general public, Demas, McDonald, and Lawrence; and Piontek and Garlock, were some of the first librarians to discuss practical guidelines for collection development of Internet resources as opposed to the mainly theoretical discussions of previous publications.

A main theme of the discussion initiated by Demas, McDonald, and Lawrence (1995) is that collection of Internet resources can and should use the same collection criteria as more traditional resources. Johnson (1997) echoes and expands on this theme. Subsequent researchers have utilized the "Taxonomy of Internet Resources" introduced by Demas, McDonald, and Lawrence and it serves as a practical guide to many librarians. The taxonomy is adapted later in the "Developing a Collection Plan for the Web-accessible E-Library" section of this chapter. Demas, McDonald, and Lawrence also clarify the analogous relationships between Web and other Internet resources and other publications forms.

Yochelson et al. (2003, 1997), Miller (2000), Thornton (2000), Coutts (1998), Norman (1997), and Fedunok (1997), have all thoroughly reviewed the literature relating collection development of electronic resources in general and Internet resources in particular. Rather than duplicate the literature reviews provided by these authors, this section will mention specific articles that discuss issues central to this guide.

Yochelson et al. (2003, 1997) is a handbook for Library of Congress "Recommending Officers." Yochelson and others review the practical literature up to 1997 and also describe the collection tools that were extant for use in collecting Internet resources. Links in the handbook were updated in 2003.

Miller's article covers electronic resource collection development literature from 1980–2000. It is interesting to read the forecasts made in the early years and then to see how the situation has evolved.

Thornton explores the literature on the impact of electronic resources on resource sharing in libraries and the role of librarians and library consortia. Coutts has written a "state of the profession" report on collection development and electronic resources for research collections in the United Kingdom.

Norman's article is particularly interesting as he not only surveyed libraries on their handling of commercial electronic resources, such as CD-ROMs, but also on their procedures for acquiring and processing Internet resources. Another useful aspect of his study is that Norman used the definitions and recommendations made in the classic 1995 article by Demas, McDonald, and Lawrence to guide his survey.

Norman also asked whether libraries were training their subject specialists to use the Internet for collection development. Seventy-three percent reported that they were training specialists and the rest either reported that they planned to or did not answer the question. He also found that ninety-three percent of the libraries surveyed had developed a taxonomy of electronic resources similar to the one described by Demas, McDonald, and Lawrence.

In addition to her excellent review of the literature prior to 1997, Fedunok (1997) also provides a synthesis of eighteen library electronic resource collection policy statements.

Jasco (2001) makes a well-reasoned case for libraries to create locally tailored e-libraries as a way to promote the library's overall service mission.

Holleman (2000) reaffirms and updates the librarian's role in collecting electronic resources and the ongoing discussion of the changes and current challenges in practical collection development and selection:

> "Librarians continue to collect materials with adequate scope and depth of coverage that are relevant to their communities of users. Other criteria remain valid in concept but have changed markedly in application. Cost questions and differences in physical characteristics have evolved from relatively simple comparisons to a labyrinth of considerations. To some degree, however, there are entirely new questions for librarians in the electronic world." (Holleman, 2000: 698)

Intner (2001) reports an informal study on how the Internet has changed the work of collection development librarians, bibliographers, and directors. The respondents to her study, consistently reported that their selection of electronic resources followed methods identical to those used for collecting other types of resources. All respondents noted that collection of electronic resources must include financial and contractual relationships as well as archiving.

Baldwin (2000), Blake and Surprenant (2000) reiterate and expand on the concept that collection of Web resources requires good collection development policy and planning. Blake and Surprenant define collection development as collection planning, selection, and the creation of collection policies. They effectively argue that because the "consequences of ignoring the burgeoning digital revolution are far higher than the grudging accommodation made for media in the 1970s and 1980s," librarians need to receive more comprehensive education in collection development and management in library schools, as well as more continuing education.

Joyce Latham (2002) makes an articulate argument for requiring a collection development policy for all e-library collections. Especially for public libraries or libraries that are publicly funded, the collection development policy will not only guide the collection process but it may protect the library from legal difficulties, if some entity with a Web site demands to have their site linked. If the collection policy clearly states the scope of types of site and types of information that will be collected, then the library may defend itself from such demands.

Duranceau (2002) and Bryant (1997) present good discussions of the need for training specifically in e-resource collection development, and they ask and propose answers to the questions: Who will work in the library of the future? What will they be doing? Duranceau (2002) reports the results of an informal survey of library staffing trends, which indicates that staffing for e-resource collection management and the need for staff training is reaching a critical level.

Baldwin (2002) supports the need for e-library collection development planning especially in terms of how the collection will be organized and made accessible. This article provides clear discussions of various taxonomies for organizing e-libraries, including Dewey, Library of Congress, Dublin Core Metadata, and other options.

Guarino (1998); Tennant (1998); Rioux (1997); Morville and Wickhorst (1996); and Rosenfeld, Janes, and Vander Kolk (1995) all argue well for the role of librarians, especially subject bibliographers, in mediating access to Web resources for patrons through building e-libraries.

Guarino draws attention to the need for technical training of library staff in selecting and evaluating Web resources vis-à-vis authority, credibility, and accessibility. Librarians should attempt to optimize the use of Web resources for reference use, by tailoring the collection to community information needs.

Rioux's metaphor for e-library collection development as "hunting and gathering in cyberspace" is an amusing way to think about the process of free Web resource collection. She says:

> "Over the centuries librarians have pretty much gotten a handle on building collections of resources in the physical media like print and film. There are review journals, the publishing industry is well-organized, and subscription agents are always happy to help keep things neat and tidy. It's a little like agriculture, where the farmer/librarian goes into a well-tended field to harvest a crop of known type and quality. Developing a collection of Internet, especially World Wide Web, resources is another situation altogether. It's much more like foraging in the jungle; a trackless, vine-tangled wilderness full of unknown species, some of which look appetizing but may be poisonous and others of which look drab and unappealing but may well be the most nourishing. The librarian collecting electronic resources is not a harvester of cultivated crops but a hunter and gatherer of wild fruits and other treasures." (Rioux, 1997: 130)

Tonta (2001), Kuny and Cleveland (1998), and Kopp (1997), discuss the literature and general issues in creating and sustaining interlibrary cooperation in building and maintaining e-libraries. Libraries, and librarians, must work cooperatively with each other, with library organizations, and with the political entities that affect and support libraries.

Tonta (2001) discusses both the need for and the possibilities for interlibrary cooperation through the Web. Tonta describes the keys to successful interlibrary cooperation including a commitment to cooperation, patience, as well as skills in planning, organization, and administration.

Lord and Ragon (2001), discussing cooperation between health sciences libraries, conclude that a collection planning document is essential for good interlibrary cooperation:

> "Clearly written guidelines not only help us with selecting materials, but also serve as a guide to effectively promoting these resources to library users...an effective policy should include how your library plans to handle the licensing, technical support, and group purchasing of electronic resources." (Lord and Ragon, 2001: 42)

Learning from what other e-library builders have already done is a good strategy to follow in planning an e-library project. At this stage in the development of e-libraries there is no need for anyone to try to create their e-library from scratch. Pitschmann (2001) has synthesized the selection criteria and collection development policies of more than fifty e-libraries (called gateways by him). The full Web-accessible report "Building Sustainable Collections of Free Third-Party Web Resources" is cited at the end of this chapter. Pitschmann (2001) outlines the following selection criteria:

- Context: origin or provenance, content, relationship with other resources (e.g., aggregates);
- Content: validity (authorship, authority, credibility), accuracy, authority, uniqueness, completeness, coverage, currency, and audience;
- Accessibility (form/use): composition and organization, navigational features, adherence to standards, user support, terms and conditions of access; system integrity (stability and accessibility of the hosting system); and

- Process or technical: information integrity (security, maintenance), site integrity (stability of the site over time).

Sweetland (2000) compared the criteria used by academic librarians and by *Choice* in evaluating Web sites and found that there was some agreement that the provenance (origin, location, and related information), authority, content, currency, and functionality were all important. These criteria were at times inconsistently applied.

Walters et al. (1998) reviewed the criteria libraries use to select aggregated electronic resources (e.g., e-journals, e-books, database bundles). They identify three core criteria: content, coherence, and functionality.

Schneider (2002) discusses the biggest and best of the e-libraries exploring the idea of a cooperative of e-library projects. The INFOMINE (http://infomine.ucr.edu/projects), LII—Librarian's Index to the Internet (www.lii.org), MeL—Michigan Electronic Library (www.mel.org), BUBL (http://bubl.ac.uk), and other e-library projects have been involved. They are exploring a cooperation that would streamline the process of developing and maintaining these large collections. It would be a kind of "meta-cooperative." If the LOOK (previously called Fiat Lux) cooperation is implemented it will mark a giant step forward, because it:

"represents a 'best of the Internet' collection of over 110,000 records, the participation of 280 skilled librarians and information professionals, a cumulative 44 years of service provision and experience, and support of close to 9 million searches from the learning community annually." (Schneider, 2002)

Collection development of all kinds of materials is discussed in the e-book *Collection Development Training for Arizona Public Libraries* (www.dlapr.lib.az.us/cdt/index.htm).

"Collection development (also known as collection or materials management) involves the identification, selection, acquisition, and evaluation of a collection of library resources (e.g., print materials, audiovisual materials, electronic resources) for a community of users. While it is the goal of collection development to meet the information needs of everyone in a user community, this is not usually realized due to financial constraints, the diversity of user information needs, and the vast amount of information. Nonetheless, public libraries strive to provide the greatest number of library resources to meet the information and recreational needs of the majority of their user community within the confines of fiscal realities."

PRELIMINARY PLANNING

The first step is, of course, to decide if and why you want to build an e-library. Before beginning to plan for Web resource collection, there are some preliminary questions and issues to address. Planning ahead and mapping out the resources you have available will simplify the process. For the most part the preliminary planning questions relate to the time and commitment of personnel to the task of e-library construction. Basic technology, status, access, and availability questions will need to be answered. Other than general considerations and discussion in the e-library success stories, the specific software and hardware used for e-libraries is outside the scope of this book. *D-Lib Magazine* (www.dlib.org), as well as some of the other publications mentioned in the references and webliographies, cover e-library technical issues in more depth. The discussion list Web4lib@sunsite.berkeley.edu—with archives available at http://sunsite.berkeley.edu/Web4Lib/archive.html—serves as the primary in-depth, Web-accessible e-library technical information source for many librarians.

The most important preliminary planning questions are:

1. Is an Internet-connected computer running Web server software already available through your organization?
2. Will computer hardware and Web server or other e-library software need to be purchased or otherwise acquired? What will it cost? How will it be funded?

3. Are personnel available who have the technical skills and subject area knowledge to produce and maintain an e-library by collecting, evaluating, and selecting resources and incorporating them into a Web site?
4. How much time do you estimate that responsible individuals will be able to commit to planning, collecting, evaluating, and selecting Web resources, in addition to constructing and maintaining the e-library?
5. How many people will be available to plan, collect, evaluate, and select Web resources, and then to maintain the e-library?
6. What kinds of training will responsible individuals need in order to produce and maintain an e-library?

IS AN INTERNET-CONNECTED COMPUTER RUNNING WEB SERVER SOFTWARE ALREADY AVAILABLE THROUGH YOUR ORGANIZATION?

Just ask. If your organization has a systems department, ask them. If your organization is affiliated with a library system, consortia, or other regional organization, you might ask them about using any Web server that they make available. Most of the libraries in our e-library case studies had organizational access to an Internet-connected computer running Web server software. Many e-library projects have been developed without the need for additional support or funding, because the library already has access to a Web server through the institution that they serve or through an organization in which they participate. The San Bernardino County Library's e-library, for example, is hosted on the San Bernardino County government's Web server. Other examples include BUBL, which is hosted by the Centre for Digital Library Research at Strathclyde University. Other libraries may make arrangements with commercial Internet Service Providers (ISPs) to host their e-library. Some may decide to purchase, install, and maintain their own computer hardware, network services, and server software.

WILL COMPUTER HARDWARE AND WEB SERVER OR OTHER E-LIBRARY SOFTWARE NEED TO BE PURCHASED OR OTHERWISE ACQUIRED? WHAT WILL IT COST? HOW WILL IT BE FUNDED?

If you determine that your library will need to purchase computers, an Internet connection, server software, or other related hardware and software, you'll need to investigate costs and funding. Many states are providing grant money to schools and public libraries for Internet projects. A U.S. federal agency, the Institute of Museum and Library Services (IMLS) also makes grants for a variety of library services, including electronic library projects, available through state libraries. Several types of grants are available, but the Library Services and Technology Act (LSTA) funding is the best known. The IMLS publishes a list of the chief officers at each state library with contact information at www.imls.gov/grants/library/gsla_cos.htm. At the Community of Science site (www.cos.com), a person can search for other library grant funding agency sites and companies that provide funding to support school and library Internet projects and other projects. The American Library Association, Public Program Office (www.ala.org/ Content/NavigationMenu/Our_Association/Offices/Public_Programs_Office/Grants_and_Events /PPO_Grants_and_Events.htm) regularly announces library grants opportunities. If you have at least a basic Internet connection you can use Web search tools to search for other sources of grants and funding information. A good strategy is to look at other e-libraries and learn what kinds of funding and support they have. For example, LII is hosted by the University of California at Berkeley's SunSITE project, which is funded in part by Sun Microsystems (http://sunsite .berkeley.edu).

ARE PERSONNEL AVAILABLE WHO HAVE THE TECHNICAL SKILLS AND SUBJECT AREA KNOWLEDGE TO PRODUCE AND MAINTAIN AN E-LIBRARY BY COLLECTING, EVALUATING, AND SELECTING RESOURCES AND INCORPORATING THEM INTO A WEB SITE?

The people who collect, evaluate, select, and organize the links will require basic and advanced Web searching and resource evaluation skills (see the "General Evaluation Guidelines" section of this chapter). Knowledge of simple HTML elements and the URL format will be helpful for them, as well. Those who create the Web pages will need to know how to author Web pages with HTML or an HTML editor, or they may need to be trained on how to input link information into a Web accessible database.

Several previously cited authors have pointed out that the collection of Internet resources will be more efficient, if the individuals chosen to collect resources in particular subject areas have some background in those subjects. Subject expertise will will demonstrate its value when the resources are evaluated and selected for inclusion in the e-library. Nearly all of the e-libraries described in the e-library case studies identified or recruited individuals with subject expertise to select appropriate resources.

Depending on your choice or the availability of a computer platform, Web server software and Web site design may require qualified computer professionals, who are able to administer the computer system, Web server, and database software. In some cases you'll want a computer professional, or other trained individual who is able to create CGI (Common Gateway Interface) scripts in Perl, C, or other programming languages. Database programmers may also be necessary. Programmers will not be needed for simple HTML-based Web sites. However, if your e-library will access databases in response to searches, or will offer certain other types of interactivity, you will need a programmer with at least basic programming skills.

HOW MUCH TIME DO YOU ESTIMATE THAT RESPONSIBLE INDIVIDUALS WILL BE ABLE TO COMMIT TO PLANNING, COLLECTING, EVALUATING, AND SELECTING WEB RESOURCES, IN ADDITION TO CONSTRUCTING AND MAINTAINING THE E-LIBRARY?

Constructing e-libraries is very time consuming. Do you have staff who can spend time planning, implementing, and maintaining the e-library? Will you seek volunteers to assist in its construction and maintenance? Will you do all the work yourself? Will individuals be able to use paid "on-the-job" time or will they have to complete the work on unpaid personal time? Will you need to hire additional staff to support the e-library? The Taft Middle School e-library was created during unpaid personal time, but maintenance took place during librarian Deb Logan's working hours. Now that she is working at a different school, maintenance occurs sporadically. MeL is maintained by eleven paid subject librarians and coordinated by Rebecca Cawley, Statewide Database Administrator, for fully half of her work time. The Cyberstacks project was created and maintained under tenure-track conditions, where Gerry McKiernan was using research and personal time to develop and maintain the project.

Obviously, the more comprehensive you intend your e-library collection to be, the more time it will require. A small subject-focused e-library collection might take only a few hours. For example, for an article on collecting consumer health resources on the Web, one of the authors created a "Consumer Health Web Ready-Reference Collection." The focus patron group was librarians serving healthcare consumers. The collection consisted of Web resources that would be immediately useful for the kinds of medical ready-reference questions that are asked by health care consumers and fielded by librarians in many types of library. Using a set of frequently asked consumer health ready-reference questions to define the scope of resources, this mini e-library took about two hours to plan and outline, four hours to collect, evaluate, and select the consumer health information resources, and four more hours to create the Web page with this collection. (See the "Core Web Medical Reference Collection" in Part II, Chapter 4, section 4.7.)

How many people will be available to plan, collect, evaluate and select Web resources and then to maintain the e-library?

The number of people needed to work on the e-library, will depend on the scope of the e-library.

One person working with computer systems staff can do most small or very focussed projects. One health sciences librarian maintains the Health InfoNet of Alabama e-library. Larger comprehensive projects, such as BUBL, INFOMINE, and MeL, require the participation of many subject librarians and technical support personnel.

WHAT KINDS OF TRAINING WILL RESPONSIBLE INDIVIDUALS NEED IN ORDER TO PRODUCE AND MAINTAIN AN E-LIBRARY?

The answer to this question will vary depending on the staff you have available and the technical infrastructure of your e-library. However, any staff member who works on the e-library will benefit from solid training in four basic areas:

- Knowledge of Web collection development tools and strategies
- Detailed understanding of selection criteria and evaluation of information
- Basic technology skills: Web browsing, search tools, and e-mail
- Knowledge of subject discipline pattern of publication and user information-seeking behavior.

Additional technical training may be appropriate for some staff members depending on the kinds of support the e-library will require.

DEVELOPING THE COLLECTION PLAN

If you have thoughtfully made your decisions in the planning stage, constructing an e-library can be a routine part of overall library collection development. A collection development plan is essential in guiding the selection of Web resources that will be included in the e-library. Several authors cited in the literature review provide some very fine overviews of good collection development planning. The Infopeople Project (www.infopeople.org) workshop, "Using the Web for Collection Development," developed by Laura Lent and Cathy Nyhan also includes a particularly clear and comprehensive section titled, "Elements of a Good Collection Development Plan" (www.infopeople.org/training/past/2002/web_collection_dev).

This checklist of questions for Web resource collection development planning is a synthesis of the authors' working experience in building e-libraries and learning from the experiences of other e-library builders.

1. What purpose will your e-library collection serve? Why do you want to build an e-library?
2. What subject areas will you include? How will you decide? Will the e-library support distance learners? How? Who?
3. Who is the intended audience/user group for your e-library; e.g., academic faculty/students (multiple subject specialization), general public, citizens of the county/state/country?
4. What types of Web-accessible resources will you link to through your e-library? Fee-based or free?
5. How will you organize resources in your e-library? By subject? By resource type? By type of library service under which they might fit? Using a database back end? Will you catalog Web resources?
6. Will you plan to provide virtual reference services through your e-library? E-mail, Web form *(asynchronous)*, or chat *(synchronous)*? What other library services would you like to provide through your e-library? Why?

WHAT PURPOSE WILL YOUR E-LIBRARY COLLECTION SERVE? WHY DO YOU WANT TO BUILD AN E-LIBRARY?

These questions are closely related. The purpose any library collection serves is contingent on the community of patrons for which it is collected. The subject areas that will be included are defined by the purpose the library will serve for the intended community of patrons. Every library will have its own answer to these questions.

Will your patrons use the e-library for current awareness and recreational information? Research? Homework help? Business support? Legal research? How will an e-library collection benefit your patrons? Most libraries will find that an e-library collection greatly extends the scope and access of their available collection. Web resources are not always the best resources, but when smaller or isolated libraries can mediate Web access to their patrons, they can often provide access to information they might not have been able to afford in print or stand-alone database formats. For example, every library regardless of size and location can have access to the full-text of their own or any other U.S state's law code or statutes, the full-text of the U.S. Revised Code, numerous international legal codes, as well as many other full-text legal information documents through the Legal Information Institute Web site (www.law.cornell.edu). Even libraries that can't afford to purchase the large multivolume print set and updates, or to purchase Lexis/Nexis access, can provide their patrons with access to this information. Lexis/Nexis is an excellent Web-accessible legal and business research tool; however, it possesses more information and searching power than many libraries need, and it is very expensive.

Every library can now provide their patrons with a searchable full-text and image database of patents and trademarks courtesy of the U.S. Patent and Trademark Office (www.uspto.gov) and the European Patent Office (www.european-patent-office.org). No longer is it necessary for everyone to pay for commercial patent database access, or to purchase and maintain an expensive microform collection of patents. Granted, the USPTO patent and trademark databases do not allow the complex reporting and searching options that many special and academic libraries will need (commercial patent databases do provide the searching and reporting power required), but for everyone else the free patent search Web sites are invaluable.

WHAT SUBJECT AREAS WILL YOU INCLUDE? HOW WILL YOU DECIDE? WILL THE E-LIBRARY SUPPORT DISTANCE LEARNERS? HOW? WHO?

In what subject areas do your patrons need information? Nursing? Medicine? Business? Legal issues? Literature? Computer science? Reader's advisory? Recreational information? Music? Using existing collection development plans is an efficient way to decide. The University of Canterbury, Biblioteca Digital de Catalunya (BDC), INFOMINE, and many of the other e-library case studies in this book used their existing library collection development plans as the basis for e-library collection planning, rather than developing completely new plans just for Web resource collection.

Reviewing circulation and reference statistics, as well as current database-use data, can also inform the choice of subject areas and depth of subject that the e-library will include.

If your e-library will serve distance learners, it will be desirable to know what programs and courses the e-library will be supporting. Will the distance learners be home-schoolers in the general population? What grade levels of home-school students will be served? Will the distance learners be local but outside of the physical library, or will they be in distant locations (e.g., another state or country). Will the e-library need to include tutorials or instructions for using different resources? Will the e-library provide reference services or document delivery to distance learners? How?

WHO IS THE INTENDED AUDIENCE/USER GROUP FOR YOUR E-LIBRARY?

Are your patrons members of the general public? Healthcare consumers? Children doing homework? Hobbyists? What ages and educational levels do the patrons who will be using your e-library represent? Are you serving businesses? If so, what types? What kinds and levels of research will patrons be doing? Are they graduate students, faculty, or undergraduates?

The library patron population characteristics will define the scope of your e-library subject coverage, establish the complexity level of resources collected, and outline the areas of information that will be collected. Every library will need to decide individually what their patrons' information needs and levels are.

WHAT TYPES OF WEB-ACCESSIBLE RESOURCES WILL YOU LINK TO THROUGH YOUR E-LIBRARY? FEE-BASED OR FREE?

This taxonomy of Web resources is adapted from Demas, McDonald, and Lawrence. (1995: 288):

- Directories
- Dictionaries
- Abstracts, Indexes, and Table of Contents Services

- Encyclopedias and Almanacs
- E-Serials
- Bibliographies and Bibliographic Databases (See Web Sites Cited)
- News
- Key Primary Documents (such as, Annual Reports, Law Codes, or Statistical Sources)
- E-mail distributed (such as, Listserv, Majordomo, or Listproc)
- Usenet Newsgroups

Notice how closely the types of resources on the Web match the types of resources that we are also using in our libraries in print and stand-alone databases. There are both advantages and disadvantages to having these resources available through the Internet. In most cases the advantages outweigh the disadvantages, as McGeachin points out:

"Internet electronic materials have the advantage of supporting new information formats and new types of interaction with users. For example, a phone directory may include the ability to see a map of the location found and give driving instructions on how to get there from almost any place in the country. Another example is the ability to look at real-time weather data with maps showing the distribution and movement of clouds, rain, wind, and temperature. Multimedia encyclopedias and handbooks can include images, audio, and video to enhance and accompany the text. Many Internet chemical materials now include the option to view and interactively rotate and examine chemical compound images." (McGeachin, 1998: 3)

Will your e-library focus on Web resources that are free—or rather, without direct cost to your library—or will the collection include fee-based resources that your library must pay for, negotiate licenses for, or participate in a cooperative arrangement to gain access?

HOW WILL YOU ORGANIZE RESOURCES IN YOUR E-LIBRARY? BY SUBJECT? BY RESOURCE TYPE? BY TYPE OF LIBRARY SERVICE UNDER WHICH THEY MIGHT FIT? USING A DATABASE BACK END? WILL YOU CATALOG WEB RESOURCES?

In most cases, each library will answer this question differently, depending on their answers to the first question of what purpose its e-library will serve. Resource organization is partially a matter of style. The simplest and probably the most accessible information structure for patron access is simple broad-subject organization, categorized by resource types under each subject and subtopic umbrella heading. Or, a library might want to have an organization based on their library divisions, departments, or branches; for example, periodicals department, special collections, medical library, or a particular branch library.

Gerry McKiernan, builder of the Cyberstacks e-library, outlines a variety of different organizational structures for e-libraries in his Web site "Beyond Bookmarks: Schemes for Organizing the Web" (www.public.iastate.edu/~CYBERSTACKS/CTW.htm). BUBL uses the Dewey Decimal Classification (DDC) system.

Baldwin (2002) provides an overview of the many choices for organizing e-libraries, including Library of Congress, Dewey, unique taxonomies, as well as using the Dublin Core elements and Marc cataloging.

In *Information Architecture for the World Wide Web*, 2nd ed., Rosenfeld and Morville (2002) describe the importance of rigorous adherence to international standards, the need to design with the users clearly in mind, as well as the specific criteria for usability and accessibility. This book is strongly recommended for anyone planning for the organization of an e-library collection.

WILL YOU PLAN TO PROVIDE VIRTUAL REFERENCE SERVICES THROUGH YOUR E-LIBRARY? E-MAIL, WEB FORM (ASYNCHRONOUS), OR CHAT (SYNCHRONOUS)? WHAT OTHER LIBRARY SERVICES WOULD YOU LIKE TO PROVIDE THROUGH YOUR E-LIBRARY? WHY?

We'll explore some of these options in Part I, Chapter 2. In the planning process it will be helpful to consider what services you will offer, and to consider issues, such as, staffing, scope of service, costs of service, and other issues particular to your library and the patrons you will serve.

Once your collection plan is ready, collecting the resources is basically a research task. Search for or otherwise collect the sites that seem appropriate, then evaluate whether the sites are suitable for your library patrons and are of high quality, reliability, and timeliness.

IDENTIFYING AND COLLECTING WEB RESOURCES

The process of identifying and collecting Web resources is similar to that of identifying and collecting print or stand-alone electronic resources. In collecting free Web-resources, one difference is that frequently the acquisitions process requires no financial or contractual exchanges. Licensing of fee-based Web resources is discussed in Part I, Chapter 3. This section discusses the various tools on and off the Internet that you can use to identify and collect Web resources. In the discussion, we describe examples of useful Web resource collection tools. Webliographies of useful Web resource collection tools are included at the end of each chapter as appropriate, under "Web Sites Cited"; see also the Resource Lists in Part III at the end of this guide.

In general, you might use several types of collection tools, including:

- Web sites that review and evaluate Web resources: including other e-libraries or subject collection guides/webliographies
- Discussion lists and newsgroups where individual participants review and evaluate Web resources
- E-journals and e-newsletters that publish reviews and evaluations of Web resources
- Web logs, a.k.a. blogs, that publish reviews and evaluations of Web resource and other machine-assisted collection development tools.
- Print books and journals that review Web resources

WEB SITES THAT REVIEW AND EVALUATE WEB RESOURCES: INCLUDING OTHER E-LIBRARIES OR SUBJECT COLLECTION GUIDES/WEBLIOGRAPHIES

The first place to look for Web resources to collect is in other highly selective e-libraries or directories. This strategy is analogous to searching other libraries' catalogs, OCLC Worldcat (www.oclc.org/worldcat), RLIN Eureka (www.rlg.org), or using subject bibliographies to identify print resources that other similar libraries with similar patron communities have selected. The BUBL, MeL, INFOMINE, University of Canterbury, and Taft Middle School e-libraries all include annotations. LII staff and volunteers review each resource individually. Initials and contact information for the reviewer are included with the annotations. All of the e-libraries mentioned above, as well as many others, are included in Part III, Resource List 3: Multiple Subject Resource Collection Tools. Additional specific subject collections and webliographies are included with each subject chapter in Part II.

DISCUSSION LISTS AND NEWSGROUPS WHERE INDIVIDUAL PARTICIPANTS REVIEW AND EVALUATE WEB RESOURCES

A second successful identification and collection strategy is to have each person responsible for collecting resources in a particular subject area subscribe to the core discussion lists and newsgroups related to that subject area. This strategy is analogous to asking colleagues in your library or subject specialists (e.g., faculty, researchers, physicians) through conversation in-person, telephone or postal mail for their opinions of library materials.

Discussion lists and newsgroups are easy to find. Choosing which discussion lists and newsgroups will be most appropriate for a given subject can be difficult. Specific discussion lists (a.k.a. listservs) will be recommended in subsequent chapters. For example, the Net-Happenings (www.edu-cyberpg.com/Community/NetHappenings.html) and Hot5 Library (http://listserv .classroom.com/archives/hot5.html) lists exist entirely for the purpose of reviewing and discussing Web sites and Internet-related events.

Other discussion lists may be located by searching CataList—the official catalog of Listserv® Lists (www.lsoft.com/lists/listref.html)—that provides information about nearly one hundred thousand public discussion lists. Private or confidential lists are not listed. NewList announces new discussion lists and you may search the archives (www.edu-cyberpg.com/Community/newlist.html). FreeLists (www.freelists.org), and Yahoogroups (www.yahoogroups .com) host hundreds of discussions on as many topics.

The Directory of Scholarly and Professional Electronic Conferences (www.kovacs.com/directory) is a selective directory of discussion lists, newsgroups, mailing lists, chats, and MUDs (online meeting software known as multiuser dimension) that have a scholarly or professional topic.

E-JOURNALS AND E-NEWSLETTERS THAT PUBLISH REVIEWS AND EVALUATIONS OF WEB RESOURCES

Many print journals and newsletters are now publishing electronic versions on the Web. These are discussed under the "Print books and journals…" section below. There are thousands of e-serials that publish reviews of Web resources. E-serials are those published only on the Web or distributed through e-mail.

NewJour distributes e-mail announcements of new electronic journals and newsletters to subscribers. The NewJour project archives (http://gort.ucsd.edu/newjour) are a searchable directory of online journals and newsletters based on the NewJour distributions. Other collections of e-journals can be searched in JSTOR—The Scholarly Journal Archive (www.jstor.org)—or the Directory of Open Access Journals (DOAJ) from the Budapest Open Archive Initiative (www.doaj.org). The SPARC Institutional Member Repositories (www.arl.org/sparc) are a good source of e-journals and other e-texts. The OPCIT (The Open Citation Project—Reference Linking and Citation Analysis for Open Archives; http://opcit.eprints.org/explorearchives.shtml) site provides links to other e-journal and e-text archives.

One particularly useful Internet e-newsletter is *The Scout Report*, which has been published through e-mail weekly since 1994 and is archived at http://scout.wisc.edu.

"The Internet Scout Project is located in the Department of Computer Sciences at the University of Wisconsin-Madison, and is sponsored by the National Science Foundation to provide timely information to the education community about valuable Internet resources. Daily and weekly updates are offered for K–12 and higher education faculty, staff, and students, as well as interested members of the general public. Organizations are encouraged to link to this page from their own Web pages, or to receive the HTML version of the Report each week via email for local posting at their site." (http://scout.wisc.edu/about)

The Internet Scout Project team collects and reviews Web resources and publishes the reviews in a weekly e-newsletter that is distributed through e-mail as well as published on their Web site. Different versions of *The Scout Report* are available for free subscription: *The Scout Report* includes resources of general education and research interest, as well as other reports: The NSDL Scout Report for the Life Sciences, The NSDL Scout Report for Math, Engineering, and Technology, and The NSDL Scout Report for the Physical Sciences (see http://scout.wisc .edu/archives/previous.html).

D-Lib Magazine (www.dlib.org) features a digital collection of other Web resources each issue.

Another good example is the *Internet Tourbus* e-newsletter published on Tuesdays and Thursdays by Patrick Douglas Crispen and Bob Rankin. The *Internet Tourbus* is a "virtual tour of the best of the Internet, delivered by e-mail." (www.tourbus.com)

WEB LOGS, A.K.A. BLOGS, THAT PUBLISH REVIEWS AND EVALUATIONS OF WEB RESOURCES AND OTHER MACHINE-ASSISTED COLLECTION DEVELOPMENT TOOLS

Web logs, more commonly called blogs, are a good source of library-related news and resource reviews. Using a technology called Rich Site Summary (RSS) feeds:

"users can have content from web sites delivered to (and constantly updated) via a news aggregator, a piece of software freely available via the web (or purchased for more options), specifically tailored to receive these types of feeds." (Cohen 2002)

LISFEEDS (www.lisfeeds.com) lists library and information science related blogs and provides complete access information, as well as instructions for setting up your own RSS feed. LibDex also includes a directory of Library Weblogs (www.libdex.com/weblogs.html). Webreference (www.webreference.com/authoring/languages/xml/rss) publishes tutorials, articles, and lists and discusses the many collections that are available. Gary Price's ResourceShelf (www.resourceshelf.com), Tara Calishain's ResearchBuzz (www.researchbuzz.com), Peter Scott's Library Blog (http://xrefer.blogspot.com) and John Hubbard's Library Link of the Day (www.tk421.net/librarylink) are four blogs that will be useful for anyone collecting Web resources. LII's "New This Week" is also available through an RSS feed (http://lii.org/search/ntw). LIS-News, published by Blake Carver, is a favorite blog of the authors as it publishes a bit of everything that is happening in the library world (www.lisnews.com).

Other machine-assisted collection development tools—a.k.a. electronic resource management tools—have evolved. A list of locally-developed and commercial options is available at "A Web Hub for Developing Administrative Metadata for Electronic Resource Management" (www.library.cornell.edu/cts/elicensestudy/home.html). The iVia Open Source Virtual Library System (Mitchell et al., 2003.) and the Scout Portal Toolkit (available at the Scout Project Web site, http://scout.wisc.edu) are two that stand out.

iVia was developed by the INFOMINE project with support from the IMLS and in cooperation with Librarian's Index to the Internet and BUBL, as well as other projects and individuals. This system combines the e-library collection, database access, maintenance, and management in one tool. The collection tool is a "virtual library crawler" that searches an index of more than 1,300 "authoritative hubs" or e-library collections identified by INFOMINE project personnel. In other words the software automates the task of checking other similar e-library collections and searches the Web to identify the resources that those other collectors have deemed to be of high quality and usability. INFOMINE librarians review and verify the software's choices.

"It estimates the 'worth' of a an academic Internet resource by counting how many times the resource has appeared in this set of expert-vetted, high quality virtual libraries. In essence, this approach counts the 'votes' that the community of expert-created virtual libraries cast for a resource by virtue of its inclusion in their collections...metadata content and full-text are generated from the Internet resource itself, not extracted from the virtual libraries." (Mitchell et al., 2003).

The Web resources collected and identified by the iVia crawler are then further screened by expert librarians for inclusion in the database. Fortunately, the Web crawler iVia can be customized for local access by each individual e-library that uses it.

Print Books and Journals that Review Web Resources

In the last few years, dozens of books have been published that are essentially annotated webliographies. Because print sources quickly fall out of date, only the most recent, or publications that cover general reference sources, or collection development tools, will be mentioned here. Additional titles may be included in each of the subject-oriented chapters in Part II.

The Information Specialists Guide to Searching and Researching on the Internet and the World Wide Web. 2nd ed., by Ackermann and Hartman (2000), is an outstanding source. It not only identifies many of the same Internet collection development tools that are included in this book's webliographies, it also annotates and evaluates them as search tools.

Que's Official Internet Yellow Pages, by Joe Kraynak (2002), and *Harley Hahn's Internet Yellow Page*, by Harley Hahn (2002), both attempt to categorize and list high quality Web sites in a variety of subject areas.

Reference Sources on the Internet: Off the Shelf and Onto the Web, edited by Karen R. Diaz (1997), is a collection of articles focused on the collection of Internet reference sources in different subject areas. Although some of the online sources mentioned are already moved, replaced, or defunct, the strategies for Internet resource collection planning are still valid.

Reference and Collection Development on the Internet: A How-To-Do-It Manual, by Elizabeth Thomsen (1996), was the first book of its type. At this writing, most of the practical collection strategies discussed in Thomsen's book are obsolete (FTP, WAIS, Gopher), but the discussion of the raison d'être for electronic reference collections remains a stimulating and useful one.

Many journals in library science as well as other subject areas are now carrying regular columns or special issues that review a variety of Web resources. Many of these print journals are archiving their Web resource reviews—and other selected portions of the parent publication—for free access on the Web. In the library profession, *Choice: Current Reviews for Academic Libraries* has been a standard collection development tool for all materials. *Choice* publishes Web resource reviews for resources in many general and specific subject areas. The reviews from previous years are archived on their Web site (www.ala.org/acrl/choice). *Booklist* also publishes a "Reference on the Web" review section in each issue and archives the previous year's reviewed sites on their Web site (www.ala.org/booklist). The journals *College and Research Libraries, College and Research Libraries News, American Libraries, Library Journal,* and others, have also been publishing articles that evaluate and describe Web resources. One of the most useful and interesting is the "Internet Librarian" column in *American Libraries*. The column features discussions of different valuable, controversial, or otherwise interesting aspects of librarians' interactions with the Internet. The "Internet Librarian" columns and other articles from the *American Libraries* journal are available at the *American Libraries Online* Web site (www.ala.org/alonline). *College and Research Libraries News* publishes Web resource reviews on their Web site (www.ala.org/acrl/c&rlnew2.html). Each issue features reviews of Web resources in some subject area.

GENERAL EVALUATION GUIDELINES

We all use the basic criteria for evaluating information every day. In evaluating Web information it will be helpful to make those basic criteria explicit and to apply them consistently and rigorously. The real key is to know how to find the information that we need in order successfully to evaluate Web information. We may also need to teach our patrons about Web information evaluation. In fact our role vis-à-vis Web information should be one of evaluating and endorsing high quality sites.This section will discuss basic evaluative criteria, but more importantly it will discuss the specific places to look for the information that will allow you to evaluate a Web resource based on that evaluative criteria.

In anticipation of our discussion, we would like to direct your attention to two valuable sources of information. First, see Resource List 2: Evaluation Guides, included in Part III with additional guidelines, tutorials, and workshops for evaluating Web resources. Second, Cooke (1999), *Neal-Schuman Authoritative Guide to Evaluating Information on the Internet* covers evaluation of Internet information quite thoroughly. This book will be a very useful tool for e-library resource evaluators and selectors.

To enable evaluation of Web information, we need to have or acquire three kinds of knowledge:

1. Nature—Awareness of the nature of Internet information: Stuff and good stuff on the Internet.
2. Problems—Awareness and understanding of basic problems with information obtained from the Internet.
3. Source Determination—How to acquire the information needed to determine the source. It is useful to remember the mnemonic PAST: purpose and privacy; authority and accuracy; source and security; and timeliness.

AWARENESS OF THE NATURE OF INTERNET INFORMATION: STUFF AND GOOD STUFF ON THE INTERNET

In order to apply information evaluation criteria to Internet information, it is necessary to understand the term "Internet information." A useful concept in explaining and teaching Internet information evaluation workshops is the concept of "stuff" and "good stuff." Most information on the Internet is just "stuff," irrelevant and sometimes unreliable. "Good stuff" is any of the information on the Internet that is relevant to the information needs of your patron, which meets basic quality-of-information standards.

Stuff on the Internet

In general, "stuff" on the Internet can be found on personal private Web pages where people are expressing their opinions, ideas, and tastes, and providing their personal information. Commercial advertising pages are often just simple statements of a commercial entity's existence. People just talking about recreational or personal matters using discussion lists or newsgroups (e.g., MUDs, IRC, or Web chat) also make up a great deal of the "stuff" on the Internet. It is important to keep in mind that a great deal of information on the Internet and Web is actually the transcripts—called archives—from discussion groups, newsgroups, and chatrooms.

Stuff on the Internet includes:

1. Personal Web pages that offer valuable educational, recreational, or entertainment information or one person's opinions.
2. Commercial pages that are just ads or that offer product support, directory services, tutorials, or other caluable customer support services
3. Government pages that provide government collected information of all sorts internationally.
4. Educational pages from universities, colleges, schools, museums, and other organizations with educational missions.
5. Discussion lists, blogs, and newsgroups with education, research, or professional intent or with recreational, entertainment, or opinion intent.
6. MUDS, IRC, or other Web chat that can be discussing any topic of interest.

Good stuff on the Internet

The reality is that one person's "stuff" might be another person's "good stuff." Personal pages and commercial pages can offer quality useful content, as can discussion lists, newsgroups, and chats and their archives on the Web. Internet information types have their analogies in print and other media: a program on TV can be something like "Entertainment Tonight," or "The News Hour with Jim Lehrer"; a newspaper might be *The New York Times* or the *National Enquirer*; a radio program might be *Diane Rehm* or *Don Imus*.

Personal private Web pages might only contain information about the opinions and personal life of an individual, or they might contain valuable educational or recreation information. Valuable, that is, for someone who is interested and needs the information they provide. For example, most of the good quilting pages are provided by quilters to share with other quilters on personal private Web pages. Some of the best music, books, and movie reviews can also be found on personal private Web pages. Commercial pages may simply be advertisements with no useful content, or they might provide access to product catalogs, technical support information, or even e-commerce. Organizational pages might provide information for recreational, research, or educational interests that is useful or interesting for one patron but not for another. Government Web pages generally provide information that is as good and sometimes better than governmental information provided in any other format. However, government Web pages may not include complete information or may restrict access to certain kinds of information.

The Internet information "stuff" and "good stuff" concepts are useful as a loose model for clarifying the problem of classifying Internet information. These concepts cannot help directly in solving the problems of evaluating Web resources as sources of information. This is because one person's "good stuff" might be another person's "stuff" or even another person's "bad stuff." Those assessing Web content simply cannot evaluate information based solely on the type of

Web site or the domain address of the information provider (the possible exception is that dot-gov sites are highly likely to provide accurate, timely, and potentially useful information). Librarians must explore other factors before they can render evaluative judgments.

We have discussed "stuff" and "good stuff," but as we all know, there is also "bad stuff" on the Internet. "Bad stuff" is anything that you, your patrons, or your community, consider criminal, evil, or otherwise unacceptable. For example, for many people, racist, sexist, hate-speech, violent anti-government, historical-revisionist, or pornography sites are "bad stuff." For some sociology, political science, or psychology researchers—especially where libraries, as opposed to private individuals, are concerned—these sites might be useful as sources for sociological, political, or economic research.

AWARENESS AND UNDERSTANDING OF BASIC PROBLEMS WITH INFORMATION OBTAINED FROM THE INTERNET

Some basic problems with information obtained from the Internet, or just about anywhere else for that matter, are listed below in order of their observed frequency on the Web:

1. Typos
2. Factual errors (accidental or deliberate)
3. Opinion stated as fact
4. Out-of-date information
5. Bias
6. Deliberate fraud

Typos

The information provided on the Internet comes from many sources. Typos are one of the most prevalent problems, because **anyone** can publish information on the Internet and often no editors or publishing agencies review the information. The two most likely causes of typos are: inaccurate typing because of the informality of the medium, and ignorance of the language. English is the 'lingua franca' of the Internet, but many varieties or dialects of English exist. Some typos may in fact be spelling variants, rather than errors. Ballard and Gunther (2003) "Typographical Errors in Library Databases" (http://faculty.quinnipiac.edu/libraries/tballard/typoscomplete.html) publish the results of their ongoing analysis of the typos that occur in library catalogs, Web sites, and other library related sources.

Factual errors (accidental or deliberate)

These usually happen because people simply are not checking, or sometimes are just recalling information from confused memories. During an Internet searching workshop taught in 1993, the only answer we could find on the Internet to the question "What was the year of the first Thanksgiving?" was 1676. According to the *Information Please: Online Dictionary, Internet Encyclopedia, and Almanac Reference* (www.infoplease.com), the actual year of the first Thanksgiving is either 1621, 1789, or 1863 depending on whether you mean the first celebration, or the year that it was declared a holiday by George Washington or Abraham Lincoln. The answer we found in 1993—at a site that no longer exists—was supplied by a sixth grader at a suburban Chicago school. This example is not meant to imply that sixth graders are always a source of inaccurate information. A sixth grader might publish accurate information if they acquire the facts from an authoritative source (teacher) and or document their source (encyclopedia, almanac, or Web site).

Opinion stated as fact

Throughout the Internet, users can find opinion stated as fact; this problem is very prevalent. Do you question the veracity of something *just* because of who published it? Where the Internet is concerned, yes, you must question the veracity of information based on who said it. You have to ask "Did the person/doctor/sixth grader have training or do research that gives them the authority to provide the information?

A related issue is the fact that the actual live person who publishes information on the Internet can create an online identity that looks good, but has no connection to the reality of the person's real life. This means that checking offline sources to verify authority and credibility is essential.

Can that person provide documentation/proof that what they say is accurate? What type of information is provided online to make these determinations? In the next section we'll discuss strategies for answering these questions about Internet information. We do the same kinds of evaluation when we work with print resources. Looking at the author of an article and finding their sources, research, training, and background before believing what they say or write. Editors evaluate the veracity of content, and the authors producing that content, at the acquisition stage of publishing, and libraries rely on a publisher's reputation in making their purchasing decisions. During the acquisitions process, librarians rationalize that if a particular publisher accepted and published a book or journal, then it must by association be of good quality. Internet research evaluation is more difficult. It involves more primary research than we are used to doing. One factor unique to the Internet is that much information on the Internet was originally part of a conversation. Discussion lists, newsgroups, MUDs, and chat transcripts may be text based, but they are really more akin to speech than to publications. The difference between speech and published information is primarily formality of the language. A three-judge panel, who heard the initial arguments in *ACLU vs. Reno* (521 U.S. 844; 117 S. Ct. 2329; 1997), found that on the Internet "tens of thousands of users are engaging in conversations on a huge range of subjects. It is no exaggeration to conclude that the content on the Internet is as diverse as human thought." Some transcripts of this worldwide conversation are literate and/or authoritative, and others are not.

Out-of-date information

Considering how easy it can be to update Web pages and other Internet information sources, the amount of out-of-date information online is surprising. But people don't always have the time or ability to update information, or to take it offline when it is obsolete. For example, student project Web sites might remain online long after the project is finished and the student graduates. Another problem is that so much information on the Internet is actually archives of discussion lists and newsgroups. It is important to check the dates of the individual postings in such archives, as well as on any other Web resource that might be included in your e-library collection.

Bias

Bias is a bigger problem with all sources of information than many people realize. Many Internet sites—as well as every other publication medium—provide slanted information to influence how people think about something. An illustrative example is the "Dihydrogen Monoxide Research Division" (DHMO.org. Available at www.dhmo.org). The DHMO.org site uses hyperbole, negative statistics, and words that are meant to scare and alarm people; e.g., dangers, alerts, truth, cancer, DHMO Kills. Not much documentation supports the claims made by the DHMO.org site. Yet, none of the information or facts are false. The bias used in presenting the information gives a skewed sense of the meaning of the information. Only when the user pauses to consider the identity of dihydrogen monoxide, does it become clear that this site is intended to illustrate the problems of bias. This site also illustrates the need for selection of resources that take into account educational attainment, reading level, and information needs. The reader needs to have at least some basic chemistry education. "Di-" (two-) Hydrogen atoms—H_2, plus mono- (one-) Oxygen atom—O, makes H_2O. The DHMO.org site is all about water.

Election campaign information is biased, almost by definition. For that matter, so is all advertising information. Probably every piece of information reflects bias of some kind, due to the subjectivity of writing. The degree, type of, and reason for bias must be considered in evaluating information.

Deliberate fraud

Deliberate fraud is a rapidly growing problem, given the ubiquity of the Web. Medical fraud on the Web has increased. Business or consumer frauds are also common. See D. K. Kovacs

(2003) for a recent discussion of the different types of medical and business frauds on the Web. The best defense is to know where to check to see if an offer or claim really is too good to be true. Medical claims made on Web sites might be checked out using the FTC: Operation Cure-All site (www.ftc.gov/bcp/conline/edcams/cureall) on which the Federal Trade Commission reports ongoing health fraud investigations and warnings, or the Quackwatch Web site (www.quackwatch.com). Business or consumer frauds may be verified by reviewing the U.S Secret Service Advisories (www.secretservice.gov/advisories.shtml) of business and consumer scams, frauds, and related crimes, as well as terrorist threats being investigated by the U.S. Treasury law enforcement divisions. Other valuable sources of information are Quatloos!—Cyber-Museum of Scams and Frauds (www.quatloos.com), Scam o Rama (www.scamorama.com), and Scambusters (www.scambusters.org).

HOW TO ACQUIRE THE INFORMATION NEEDED TO DETERMINE THE SOURCE, AUTHORITY, ACCURACY, TIMELINESS, PURPOSE, SECURITY, AND PRIVACY OF INTERNET INFORMATION

Quality of information varies on the Internet, because anyone can publish or communicate information on the Internet. In general, use the same criteria used to judge information from print or other media. We must also consider some additional factors in evaluating Web information.

Evaluation criteria for Internet information can be reduced to five key concepts:

1. Authority and credibility of the information source
2. Accuracy of the information
3. Timeliness of the information in reference to the information type and the needs of the patron
4. Security of the information: Is the site liable to be hacked and information altered? Does the site request patrons to submit personal or financial information?
5. Privacy of the patron when using the information

Or simpler still: The underlying concept is reputation. What do you know and what have you learned to expect from a person or organization? Reputation is based on what we know about the authority and credibility of the information source and the purpose for which the information is provided. In the discussion below these questions and strategies are clustered together because the strategies for finding the answers to the questions are similar or the same.

1. Who provided the information?
2. What is their reputation as an information provider?
3. Do they have the authority or expertise to provide information on that topic?
4. What is the purpose for which the information is being provided?
5. Is the information provided for current information or historical purposes?
6. Does currency affect the quality of the information? When was the last update of the information?

One problem with the Internet is that many information providers haven't had time to establish a reputation. In the United States, the general public has only had access to the Internet since around 1992. Reputation requires time and exposure to public opinion. Users can usually find out about the information provider and their authority, as well as about the purpose for which the information is provided and whether or not it is current. If you cannot at least find out who provided the information, however, then you cannot use it in a library, teaching, or research environment. All of us have been trained to cite a source when we answer a question. For example, earlier in this chapter we said: "According to the *Information Please: Online Dictionary, Internet Encyclopedia, and Almanac Reference* (www.infoplease.com), the actual year of the first Thanksgiving is either 1621, 1789, or 1863 depending on whether you mean the first celebration or the year that it was declared a holiday by George Washington or Abraham Lincoln."

To find that answer, we first read through Web pages associated with the site. In this case we clicked on the "Company" link at the bottom of the page and found that the publisher of this

Web site is the same company that publishes the classic *Information Please Almanac* and others. They have a fifty-year history behind them. Furthermore, they provided contact information so we can telephone or e-mail to talk to a person. This is a best case example. Some Web sites do not provide such easy access to the information provider's identification information.

To find the answers to these questions, the first thing you need to do is read through the Web site. Most usable Web sites will provide an "About," "Who we are," or contact information in some manner. You may need to read through two or more pages, but it is necessary to read thoroughly and carefully through the site. Recall the DHMO.org site we discussed earlier? Careful reading of the home page shows that at the very bottom just above the copyright statement that identifies the person responsible for the site is a notice: "Note: content veracity not implied."

In order to establish the authority and credibility of an information provider, the first step is to read through the Web site again to find out the education, experience, research background, or other authority which the information provider says they have. If the authority information is not on the Web site or if the information is critical, e-mail the person or organization identified as responsible and ask them to answer the questions about their education, experience, and research background. There should be an e-mail address, Web form, or other contact information on a well-designed Web page. Lack of contact information may also indicate that no one is willing to take responsibility for the content of the Web page.

If still you do not find attribution information, but the information is valuable enough or you have reason to believe that the attribution information was left out inadvertently, here are some other strategies:

- If you are a subject expert, use your own judgment, otherwise ask a subject expert to review the information.
- Find reviews of Web resources by qualified reviewers or use selective subject directory/e-library collections to identify resources.
- Use your Web browser options to look at the page or document info, or the page or document source, and choose or look for possible author identification and/or publication date in <Meta> tag field. For example, if you look at the "Page Source" for www.kovacs.com, you will see: <meta name="Author" content="Diane K. Kovacs">.

If you still cannot find contact information on the Web page, or in the page source, and if the content is valuable enough (or you have reason to believe that contact information was left off inadvertently), then try e-mailing: hostmaster@<the base domain from the URL> or postmaster@<the base URL>—where <the base domain from the URL> is the first part of the URL minus the "WWW" part. For example, if you want to find the contact for www.kovacs.com/eval/eval03.html and don't see an e-mail address on it, then try sending e-mail to: hostmaster@kovacs.com or to postmaster@kovacs.com.

When you are participating in or reading the archives of discussion lists and newsgroups, ask the writer to qualify himself or herself. There is nothing wrong with doing a search offline or in commercial databases to verify or validate the authority of an Internet information provider. You can search to see if they've published anything else in the area in print or other media, or you can search to verify that they are a licensed medical professional, member of a state bar association, or otherwise professionally qualified.

Verifying the security and privacy of Internet information

Security and privacy are important features of accessing the Internet, because in essence there is no privacy on the Internet. Controlling access to the information on the Internet, as well as information about the patron accessing it, is difficult to achieve. If a Web site is not asking for personal or financial information, then the patron's security is less of an issue. However, the fact that hackers can attack a Web site, and alter its content, directly impacts the user's ability to verify the information found there, and to protect his or her own user information.

If security of personal or financial information is important, then use your Web browser functions to verify security of a Web page. You can set most browsers to warn you when you are entering or leaving a secure page.

Secure Web servers ensure that only the intended recipient of your information can receive and use it. This is analogous to your calling an 800 number and ordering from a catalog. Putting your information into a form on an insecure Web page is analogous to giving out your credit card information over a cell phone or to someone who called you and solicited the information from you. Never include your credit card information or other personal financial information in an e-mail message. The one exception is if you are using some form of encryption on your e-mail.

A fascinating piece on computer hacking and Web sites appears on the CNN Web site at http://cnn.com/TECH/specials/hackers. Hackers have altered the information stored on a number of important Web sites including the CIA Web site. Hackers can get into most standard Web servers unless great care is taken to configure and maintain server security. True information security requires excellent server security and a reliable certification and authentication system between the suppliers of the information and the Web server. This helps to ensure that only individuals authorized by the information provider may add or change information on the Web site.

If privacy of information-seeking behavior is an important factor for you or your patrons, then the Internet might not be a good choice for you. There is no privacy on the Internet. When you transmit e-mail, your message passes through many servers and may be intercepted either accidentally or purposely. E-mail is easily printed or forwarded to others. When you connect to a Web page you can be counted and your movements through the site tracked. For example, look at Metacrawler's MetaSpy site (www.metaspy.com) to peek at what other people are searching for using the Metacrawler Search Engine. Also look at Privacy.Net (http://privacy.net) or Who Am I? (www.mall-net.com/cgibin/whoami.cgi?src=webcons). These latter two Web sites are tools to test the privacy or lack thereof provided by your particular connection to the Internet. The best strategy to ensure privacy is to use an Internet-connected computer available to the public at a library or Internet cafe. Then the only thing the Web site owners can discover about you is where you connected from and that someone there is interested in their site. However, patrons should be aware that certain actions—e.g., visiting certain types of Web site or sending e-mail or other messaging that seems to threaten a prominent individual or national security—may trigger law enforcement action to track them.

Another issue related to security and privacy is the use of "cookies" by Web sites to record your activities and to store information like logins and passwords for your personal connections to their site. A "cookie" is described at Netscape's Web site in the following terms:

> "This simple mechanism provides a powerful new tool which enables a host of new types of applications to be written for Web-accessible environments. Shopping applications can now store information about the currently selected items, for fee services can send back registration information and free the patron from retyping a user-id on next connection, sites can store per-user preferences on the patron, and have the patron supply those preferences every time that site is connected to." (http://wp.netscape.com/newsref/std/cookie_spec.html)

Cookies are the Web equivalent of the "frequent shopper card." In exchange for marketing information and a certain loss of privacy, the patron may receive benefits, such as, free and simple access to a site. However, use of browser cookies on public Internet computers can be problematic. If cookie-based registrations or logins are used at public Internet computers there is a danger that the next patron using that terminal will be able to access the private information of other patrons.

GENERAL SELECTION CRITERIA

Electronic resources, Internet, or other electronic formats may require unique selection criteria. Many Web collection development sites and print published articles reference Caywood's

"Library Selection Criteria for WWW Resources" (Caywood 1996). Caywood shares an excellent listing of criteria for assessing the value of Web sites for library patrons. The criteria are organized under three main concepts: access, design, and content. These are outlined and edited for currency and compatibility with the structure of this chapter in Tables 1.1.2, 1.1.3 and 1.1.4. Selection criteria for any kind of information resource are derived from the answers arrived at during the collection planning process. Therefore, the core content criteria will always be:

1. Does the resource meet some information need of the e-library's intended patrons?
2. Does the resource provide the information at a level and language suitable to the age, educational background, and subject interests of the e-library's intended patrons?
3. Does the resource provide information in a form that you want to include in your e-library (for example, encyclopedias, directories, e-serials, or e-commerce facilities)?

The core Web specific selection criteria are:

1. Access and design
2. Archiving
3. Cost/licensing/user access control

Does the resource meet some information need of the e-library's intended patrons? Does the resource provide the information at a level and language suitable to the age, educational background, and subject interests of the e-library's intended patrons? Does the resource provide information in a form that you want to include in your e-library

Does the content and scope of information on the Web site meet an information need of the library's community of patrons? If the collection plan has defined the intention and scope of the e-library, then use those factors to make individual Web site selections. What types of resource are you going to include? For example, do you want to include only those Web sites that are e-versions of traditional style encyclopedias or other reference tools? Do you want to include e-commerce sites? Is the resource stable and consistent over time?

Table 1.1.2. Access Criteria for Internet Resources

Adapted from Caywood (1996) (www6.pilot.infi.net/~carolyn/criteria.html)

- Is the site accessible for people with disabilities? Does the site adhere to Web accessiblity standards?
- Is it written in standard HTML, or have proprietary extensions been used?
- Does it use standard multimedia formats?
- Must you download software to use it?
- Do parts of it take too long to load?
- Is it usually possible to reach the site, or is it overloaded?
- Is it stable, or has the URL changed?
- Is the URL stated in the text of the Web page?
- Does the site use the words the average person would try in a search engine?
- Is it open to everyone on the Internet, or do parts require membership and/or fees?
- If there is a charge, can the library pay it on a subscription basis for multiple access points?
- Are any rules for use stated up front?

Table 1.1.3. Design Criteria for Internet Resources

Adapted from Caywood (1996) (www6.pilot.infi.net/~carolyn/criteria.html)
- Are the individual Web pages concise, or do you have to heavily scroll?
- Do essential instructions appear before links and interactive portions?
- Do all the parts work?

- Is using the site intuitive, or are parts likely to be misunderstood?
- Can you find your way around and easily locate a particular page from any other page?
- Is it obvious when you move to a new site, or does an outside link appear internal?
- Is the structure stable, or do features disappear between visits?
- Does it look and feel friendly?
- Are backgrounds or other visual elements distracting or cluttered?
- Is it conceptually exciting? Does it do more than can be done with print?
- If Java or ActiveX extensions, frames, or plug-ins are employed, do they actually improve the site? How will they affect users with older browsers, slower connections, behind firewalls, etc.?

Table 1.1.4. Content Criteria for Internet Resources

Selection Adapted from Caywood (1996) (www6.pilot.infi.net/~carolyn/criteria.html)
- Are the scope and limits clearly stated? Is the title informative? Does the content fit the stated scope?
- Does the content meet the standards for accuracy, authority, timeliness, security, and privacy tested for during the evaluation process?
- Is the content unique, or readily available elsewhere? Has copyright been respected?
- Does the content meet information needs of the client community you are collecting resources for?
- Are headings clear and descriptive, or do they use jargon unknown to the average user?
- Is text well-written with acceptable grammar and spelling? What is the quality of multimedia files?
- Is the content organized by the needs of the user, or does it reflect an internal hierarchy?
- If there is advertising, what is its relevance and proportion to the rest of the site?
- Are there reviews of the site? How many other sites link to this one?

Access and design

Can patrons use the search system easily? Is the search system adequate to locate information in the database? Does the resource display in the Web browser within a reasonable amount of time over the expected mode of access? Does the resource allow for access by disabled individuals who may need to use text-to-voice software or other enabling tools?

Bobby (http://bobby.watchfire.com) is a tool that allows you to submit the URL of a Web page and evaluates its accessibility to everyone regardless of physical handicaps. It is also an HTML compatibility checker. According to the Bobby site documentation, "Bobby also analyzes Web pages for compatibility with various browsers. Analysis is based on documentation from browser vendors when available."

Archiving

Not every electronic version of an information product is superior to the print version. This is especially true if back files of an index or database are not available or not archived on the Web.

Will the information provider provide "back issues" or archives of the resource? Will you need to make arrangements to store such information locally if needed? This is especially important in the case of e-serials or current information that will become valuable historical information over time. Most scientific research information will require some kind of archiving arrangements be made. The information may be archived in print publications, microform, on electronic storage media, or simply kept available on the Web for an indeterminate period as long as researchers are assured that it will be archived and available in the future. Obviously, researchers may prefer that it be archived in some format that is easily accessible. It is possible for libraries to negotiate licensing that includes the agreement that they may locally archive resources. The free Web may be more ephemeral. The Internet Archive Project (www.archive.org), Wayback Machine (www.waybackmachine.org), created by Brewster Kahle, attempts to archive free Web sites. For example, they have the American Library Association (ALA) site (www.ala.org) archived back to 1996, and has archived a different ALA site (http://ala8.ala.org) back to 1999.

Cost/licensing/user access control

Does the library have the necessary computer resources to provide access to the resource? Do the patrons have the necessary Internet connected computers? How will user authentication be achieved? Can the database be networked or be used with a locally developed end-user interface? What is the total cost of implementation?

Many Web resources are fee-based. If that is the case, as with, for example, the *Encyclopedia Britannica Premium* (www.britannica.com), the library will need to give consideration not only to the cost of the resource, but also to any licensing arrangements or user access control that must be exercised. For instance, will the resource only be accessible by users from within the library's domain, or can any library patron from any location access the resource by using a login and password or library card number?

A librarian can almost always justify fee-based licensed access to a Web resource that meets other core selection criteria, if funding is available, on the basis that:

> "When a library, university system, or consortium, acquires a Web-accessible product, it essentially provides multiple copies since the product can be widely distributed to a very large patron base. If the system components are spread over a large geographical area, this can provide much easier remote access to the materials. Increasing interest in distance education seems to be a trend at many educational institutions, and as a result, the need to supply library materials to distant locations is growing. Providing Internet access to full-text materials for remote users is one solution to this service issue." (McGeachin, 1998: 2).

BRINGING IT ALL TOGETHER: SOME GENERAL CONSIDERATIONS FOR CONSTRUCTING, ORGANIZING, AND MAINTAINING THE WEB ACCESSIBLE E-LIBRARY

Building a Web-based e-library is an ongoing process. This process will eventually include "weeding" and will always include "shelf-reading," link checking, and site verification in the Internet context. Hopefully, this book will give you the information and background you need to begin developing and maintaining your Web-based e-library collection.

The creation of a Web page with links and annotations for collected Web resources is very simple; all that is required is a basic knowledge of HTML and an editor program; many HTML editors are available. See The Internet Scout Project (http://scout.wisc.edu/addserv/toolkit/webtools/authoring.html) or The Web Developer's Virtual Library (http://wdvl.internet.com/Reviews/HTML) for reviews of free and fee-based HTML editing software. They all require knowledge of HTML to a greater or lesser degree in order to be used effectively, which is not to say that you couldn't cobble something together with them even if you knew nothing of HTML. This book's companion Web site (www.neal-schuman.com/elibrary.html) contains a tutorial for Web page and Web site creation with HTML, Netscape Composer, or DreamWeaver. The authors both use DreamWeaver with BBEDIT to work on the companion Web site. If you want to incorporate a more sophisticated option, such as, putting your e-library collection into a Web-accessible database program, you'll need to work with a computer programmer or select from the available e-library management systems available. BUBL and INFOMINE both utilize custom-programmed e-library software. InfoMine calls its iVia interface a virtual library management system. We referred to the Scout Portal Toolkit earlier in Chapter 1. The Library Web Manager's Reference Center (http://sunsite.berkeley.edu/Web4Lib/RefCenter) and the Web Hub for Developing Administrative Metadata for Electronic Resource Management (www.library.cornell.edu/cts/elicensestudy/home.html) under Documents/Projects: Local e-Resource Management Systems list other e-library system management tools.

You may also choose to make your e-library available on a standalone computer or internal LAN or Intranet (intra-organizational TCP/IP network). The Roetzel & Andruss e-library case study, in Part II, Chapter 5, describes both of their e-libraries. The librarians at Roetzel & Andruss make their Law Links publicly available on the Web (www.ralaw.com), but their internal e-library collection is only available on the company's Intranet, or on specific computers in the library.

E-LIBRARY COLLECTION MAINTENANCE AND MANAGEMENT

Since the publication of *Building Electronic Library Collections* in 2000, it seems less likely to find the same person—or persons—collecting, selecting, and evaluating e-library resources who also maintains the software and hardware through which the e-library is made accessible. This book emphasizes collection development of the e-library, rather than the selection of software and hardware on which to make the e-library available. For the most part, the maintenance and management of servers, databases, and hardware, are being handled by Web server administrators or other IT systems staff. The e-library case studies reported in this volume reflect that reality, as well. For example, the HealthInfoNet of Alabama e-library—case study in Part II, Chapter 4—is supported by non-librarians, "UAB computer staff supply technical support as needed."

Fowler describes the need for collection development librarians to work closely with systems staff, "This function now requires close cooperation between collection development personnel, including the subject bibliographers, the information technology (or systems) department and the electronic resources coordinator, if one is available." (2002: 17).

In this section, when we use the phrase "e-library collection maintenance and management," the focus is on "collection management," rather than technical Web server or database administration.

E-library maintenance involves maintaining the quality and content of the e-library collection. This does not mean the e-library collection manager does not need to know anything about the technology. We must be aware of many technical details, even if we are not fully qualified server or system administrators.

Here is a checklist that will help to guide you in planning and implementing e-library collection maintenance:

- Stay in touch with the Web server administrator regarding software updates and changes.
- Regularly review and check links in the e-library and/or select and use link checking software.
- Provide a mechanism for e-library patrons to evaluate and comment on the e-library Web site contents and organization; take their comments into consideration for maintenance activity.
- Review e-library Web site organization and reorganize as necessary.
- Review, update, and grow the contents of the e-library.

STAY IN TOUCH WITH THE WEB SERVER ADMINISTRATOR REGARDING SOFTWARE UPDATES AND CHANGES

When upgrading or installing software or hardware, Web server administrators may alter access to e-libraries by adding or deleting directories structures, changing input permission status for database access, and other related system changes. We saw some of these kinds of problems in the overhaul of the American Libraries Association Web site (www.ala.org) in Spring 2003. Developing and maintaining good communications with Web server administrators can ensure that you are not taken by surprise and that you will have input into any major changes that are planned.

Regularly review and check links in the e-library and/or select and use link checking software

Maintenance of your e-library requires that someone regularly checks the links to make sure they are current and working. Software is available to assist you with this type of maintenance. Subscribe to the Web4lib listserv, or search the archives to find recommendations for link-checking software. The e-library case studies include details about what link-checking software is used if it is used. The Open Directory List of Link Management Tools (http://dmoz.org/Computers/ Software/Internet/Site_Management/Link_Management) offers hundreds of choices.

However tedious it may be, you must also check links manually. This allows you to review and verify that the Web site not only still links properly, but that it still provides the same information that it did when you originally annotated and added it to your e-library collection. We recommend that you plan to check links manually as often as possible, because things really do change or go away. Imagine your surprise if a library patron discovers that the great kids' games and puzzles site you linked to is now a porn site. This really happened to one of the e-library builders, who wishes to remain anonymous. Fortunately, a responsible adult discovered the problem, before children were exposed to the changed site.

You can use link-checking software for regular link-checking. It saves time, but it will only reveal to you whether the links are working and not whether the Web sites have changed. For example, Not Just Cows (www.morrisville.edu/~drewwe/njc), the most excellent agriculture e-library created by Bill Drew, is not a dead link, but the site is no longer actually available. Visitors are notified of this, given alternative sites, and told that the archives of Not Just Cows are available on the Wayback machine (www.waybackmachine.org).

However you manage your links, check them frequently. Dead links mean frustration for your patrons and defeats the purposes of the e-library in providing good access to information.

Provide a mechanism for e-library patrons to evaluate and comment on the e-library Web site contents and organization; take their comments into consideration for maintenance activity

Minimally, a simple "mailto" link, which redirects and incoming message, or a Web form should be provided, so that patrons can comment on or evaluate e-library contents and organization. This kind of feedback will allow you to make informed decisions about how well your e-library is serving your patrons. "Mailto" links may attract spammers—spammers use software that spiders through Web pages looking for e-mail addresses to steal. Web forms may prevent this kind of problem. Table 1.1.5 reproduces the Perl CGI script used by the authors for the Web form they use on the companion Web site and Table 1.1.6 reproduces the a HTML code for simplified version of this Web form. You can see the actual form at www.kovacs.com/questions .html. You may use these if you keep the attribution information in place for the Perl CGI script. Contact the authors through the companion Web site if you would like an electronic copy of the Perl script.

Table 1.1.5. Perl CGI Script for Processing a Simple Web Form

```
#!/usr/bin/perl
#
# nsquestions.pl
#
# Created for Diane Kovacs by Marc Armstrong marmstro@marmstro.com 4/18/00
#

# get the CGI parameters - store them in %params
```

```perl
%params = getcgivars();

# IMPORTANT: MAKE SURE THESE TWO VALUES ARE SET CORRECTLY FOR YOU!
$mailprog= "/usr/lib/sendmail" ;
$recipient= "diane\@kovacs.com" ;      # make sure to \ escape the @
#$recipient= "marmstro\@mca-dlm.com" ;      # make sure to \ escape the @

# Open the mailing process
open(MAIL, "|$mailprog $recipient")
    || &HTMLdie("Couldn't send the mail (couldn't run $mailprog).") ;

# Print the header information
$ENV{'HTTP_REFERER'} || ($ENV{'HTTP_REFERER'}= "your Web site") ;
print MAIL "Subject: This can be changed\n\n",
        "The following data was entered at $ENV{'HTTP_REFERER'}:\n\n" ;


# Find length of longest field name, for formatting; include space for colon
$maxlength= 0 ;
foreach (keys %params) {
    $maxlength= length if length > $maxlength ;
}
$maxlength++ ;

# Print each CGI variable received by the script, one per line.
# This just prints the fields in alphabetical order.  To define your own
#   order, use something like
#     foreach ('firstname', 'lastname', 'phone', 'address1', ... ) {
foreach (sort keys %params) {

    # If a field has newlines, it's probably a block of text; indent it.
    if ($params{$_}=~ /\n/) {
        $params{$_}= "\n" . $params{$_} ;
        $params{$_}=~ s/\n/\n    /g ;
        $params{$_}.= "\n" ;
    }

    # comma-separate multiple selections
    $params{$_}=~ s/\0/, /g ;

    # Print fields, aligning columns neatly
    printf MAIL "%-${maxlength}s  %s\n", "$_:", $params{$_} ;
}

# Close the process and mail the data
close(MAIL) ;

$params{'07Goal Analysis'} =~ s/\n/<BR>\n/g ;
```

```
print << "__EOF__";
Content-type: text/html
<!doctype html public "-//w3c//dtd html 4.0 transitional//en">
<html>
<head>
    <title>Kovacs Consulting Questions Form - this can be changed</title>
</head>
<body text="#000000" bgcolor="#FFFFFF" link="#0000FF" vlink="#551A8B"
alink="#0000FF">
<b> You have submitted the following questions and contact information:</a></b><br>
<These can be changed - params values=text area, radiobutton, select, values.  Do not
change anything above or below the two _EOF_s >
$params{'00name'}<br>
$params{'01telephone'}<br>
$params{'02email'}<br>
</BODY>
</HTML>
__EOF__
```

```
#-------------- start of &getcgivars() module, copied in -------------

# Read all CGI vars into an associative array.
# If multiple input fields have the same name, they are concatenated into
#   one array element and delimited with the \0 character (which fails if
#   the input has any \0 characters, very unlikely but conceivably possible).
# Currently only supports Content-Type of application/x-www-form-urlencoded.
sub getcgivars {
    local($in, %in) ;
    local($name, $value) ;


    # First, read entire string of CGI vars into $in
    if ( ($ENV{'REQUEST_METHOD'} eq 'GET') ||
       ($ENV{'REQUEST_METHOD'} eq 'HEAD') ) {
        $in= $ENV{'QUERY_STRING'} ;

    } elsif ($ENV{'REQUEST_METHOD'} eq 'POST') {
        if ($ENV{'CONTENT_TYPE'}=~ m#^application/x-www-form-urlencoded$#i) {
            $ENV{'CONTENT_LENGTH'}
               || &HTMLdie("No Content-Length sent with the POST request.") ;
            read(STDIN, $in, $ENV{'CONTENT_LENGTH'}) ;

        } else {
            &HTMLdie("Unsupported Content-Type: $ENV{'CONTENT_TYPE'}") ;
        }

    } else {
```

```
        &HTMLdie("Script was called with unsupported REQUEST_METHOD.") ;
    }

    # Resolve and unencode name/value pairs into %in
    foreach (split('&', $in)) {
        s/\+/ /g ;
        ($name, $value)= split('=', $_, 2) ;
        $name=~ s/%(..)/chr(hex($1))/ge ;
        $value=~ s/%(..)/chr(hex($1))/ge ;
        $in{$name}.= "\0" if defined($in{$name}) ;  # concatenate multiple vars
        $in{$name}.= $value ;
    }

    return %in ;

}


#-------------- end of &getcgivars() module ------------------------

# Die, outputting HTML error page
# If no $title, use a default title
sub HTMLdie {
    local($msg,$title)= @_ ;
    $title || ($title= "CGI Error") ;
    print <<EOF ;
Content-type: text/html

<html>
<head>
<title>$title</title>
</head>
<body>
<h1>$title</h1>
<h3>$msg</h3>
</body>
</html>
EOF

    exit ;
}
```

Table 1.1.6. HTML for a Simple Web Form

```
<!DOCTYPE HTML PUBLIC "-//W3C//DTD HTML 4.01 Transitional//EN"
"http://www.w3.org/TR/1999/REC-html401-19991224/loose.dtd">
<html>
<head>
<title>Untitled</title>
<meta name="generator" content="BBEdit 6.0">
```

```
</head>
Question Form
<a href="#privacy"><i>**Privacy Statement:</i></a>
<form METHOD="POST" ACTION="http://yourURL/cgi-bin/questions.pl">
<table BORDER COLS=3 CLASS="form" width="80%" cellpadding="1" cellspacing="1"
align="center" bordercolor="#330066" >
<tr align="left"> <td VALIGN=TOP colspan="3">Your  Name (required) **<br>
<input TYPE="TEXT" NAME="00name" ROWS="1" size="50" WRAP></td></tr>
<tr align="left"> <td valign=TOP>Telephone  number(Where to contact you if you prefer)
<br>
<input type="TEXT" name="01telephone" cols="20" WRAP></td>
<td valign=TOP colspan="2">Your e-mail address (required): **<br>
<input type="text" name="02email" size="50" maxlength="80"></td></tr>
<tr align=LEFT valign=TOP> <td valign=TOP nowrap>In what country are you
located?<br>
<select name="03country">
<option selected>Country</option>
<option value="US">United  States  </option>
<option value="xx">List Other Countries in the Option List </option>
</select>
</td>
<td valign=TOP colspan="2" nowrap>If you are from the USA or Canada in what state,
territory <br>
or province are you located? <br>
United States
<select name="04state">
<option selected>State</option>
<option value="OH">Ohio  </option>
<option value="xx">List Other States/Provinces in the Option List</option>
</select>
<br>
Canadian Provinces
<select name="05canada">
<option selected>Province</option>
</select>
 </td></tr></table>
<font face="Times">Your Questions or Comments:<br>
<textarea NAME="06Comments" ROWS="2" COLS="80" WRAP></textarea><br>
<input TYPE="submit" VALUE="Click Here to Send your Question or Comment">
<input TYPE="reset" VALUE="Clear the Form and Start Over">
</form>
<p align="left"><a name="privacy"></a>**Privacy Statement: The information you provide
on this question form will be used strictly for the library to work with you via e-mail,
postal mail, and telephone, while you are taking the workshops you register for and for
notifying you of future information that might interest you. Your information will never be
provided to anyone outside of the library, unless they have a court order. In those  cases
you will be notified of the request before the information is provided.</p>
</body>
</html>
```

REVIEW E-LIBRARY WEB SITE ORGANIZATION AND REORGANIZE AS NECESSARY

E-libraries grow and the needs of patrons may change. It will be necessary to reorganize to accommodate both or either situation. It may be decided to reorganize the e-library with management/database software or to add search capabilities.

For example, a review of the OPLIN e-library Web site revealed a large number of resources under the broad category of "Business Information" under the subtopic of "International Business." Given the quantity of information, the staff decided to organize those resources further under subheadings by continent (www.oplin.lib.oh.us/business).

REVIEW, UPDATE, AND GROW THE CONTENTS OF THE E-LIBRARY

E-library content should always be reviewed regularly. The only limitation to the growth of an e-library collection are disk space, the time and energy of the collectors, and the library's budget for fee-based Web-accessible resources. Collection development tools for e-library collections continue to develop. New and better review sources, as well as new and better Web-based information sources, are made available literally every day. Limitations of time and cost inherent in publishing in the print medium have affected some of the specific review sources and resources discussed in the previous chapters. The Web itself provides a marvelous alternative. This book's companion Web site will continue to annotate and include new, or newly discovered, or recommended e-library collection development tools, as well as additions and corrections to the "Core Web Reference Collections," found in each chapter of Part II. You may also ask to be e-mailed when resources are added or updated.

Maintaining the Web-accessible e-library will also include ongoing collection and incorporation of new resources. Mainstreaming ongoing selection of Web resources into the collection development responsibilities of each staff member is another consideration. Staff members will need to be trained to use the Internet effectively (monitoring discussion lists, learning Web evaluation and searching skills). The computers they use during the collection process should provide adequate memory, Internet connection speed, and current Web browser and plug-in software to make evaluative selections of, for example, multimedia and high graphics resources. Staff members need to be made aware of selection strategies defined for each library, and need to be able to communicate with each other regarding resource selections. Someone should coordinate all collection and selection efforts to avoid duplication.

ONE MORE IDEA

Throughout this chapter we've referred to annotations or reviews of Web resources. For librarians doing collection development, the annotations that others publish for the Web sites in their own collections are very important. Patrons also appreciate these annotations. Writing brief, clear, communicative annotations for each Web resource will be worth the time it takes. In addition, you can use annotations as a content enhancement strategy to customize the collection for your community of patrons. Describe each resource in terms of how your intended patron will use it. Provide the information that they will need to decide if this is the resource they will want to use for their question or research.

A FINAL THOUGHT

Building a Web-based e-library may be the most important thing a library ever does. It demonstrates to our library patrons and our communities and organizations that we are committed to fulfilling their information needs. It also projects our willingness to change and progress as the technological infrastructure of our international communities and global economy shifts between the paper-based transmission and storage of information to the computer-based transmission and storage of information. (No, we do not expect to see a "paperless" library any time soon) The survival of libraries and the library profession is related to that willingness to progress and change. Maintaining high standards of selectivity and information quality and adhering to an underlying philosophy of education and service have made librarians an essential profession in the United States and around the world. Bringing that professionalism to the Internet, we will certainly be welcomed as citizens—netizens—in the international community of the Internet.

E-LIBRARY SUCCESS STORY

BUBL INFORMATION SERVICE

Centre for Digital Library Research
Strathclyde University
101 St James Road, Glasgow G4 0NS, Scotland
http://bubl.ac.uk

Contact: Dennis Nicholson, Director CDLR
d.m.nicholson@strath.ac.uk

BUBL—originally named the **BU**lletin **B**oard for **L**ibraries—was one of the first and is still one of the best current information and Web resource collection tools for librarians. It grew out of an experimental library and information services bulletin board set up as part of a project to train librarians in using JANET (Joint Academic NETwork), then an X.25 network but now the backbone of the Internet for the UK.

BUBL Information Service

LINK / 5:15 | Journals | Search | News | UK | Mail | Archive | Clients | Admin | Feedback

Free User-Friendly Access to Selected Internet Resources Covering all Subject Areas, with a Special Focus on Library and Information Science *

➡ **BUBL LINK / 5:15**
Catalogue of 12,000 selected Internet resources

➡ **BUBL Search**
Search BUBL or beyond

➡ **BUBL UK**
Directory of UK organisations and institutions

➡ **BUBL Archive**
Historical BUBL content

➡ **BUBL Journals**
Links to current LIS journals/newsletters

➡ **BUBL News**
Jobs, events, surveys, offers, updates

➡ **BUBL Mail**
Mailing lists and mail archives

➡ **BUBL Clients**
Pages of organisations hosted by BUBL

BUBL Admin: All about BUBL: contacts, feedback, usage statistics, FAQ, reports

BUBL Information Service, Centre for Digital Library Research, Strathclyde University, 101 St James Road, Glasgow G4 0NS, Scotland
Tel: 0141 548 4752   *Email:* bubl@bubl.ac.uk   *Submit URL:* Suggestions

* BUBL neither claims nor aims to be comprehensive as regards resources within any one subject area, but only to provide a quick, user-friendly lead into key resources in any major subject area for those who find this approach helpful.
BUBL is not funded by any external organisation. Click here to see the BUBL access statistics.

Figure 1.1.0. BUBL Information Service

When funding for the original project ended in 1991, a group of librarians from the Universities of Strathclyde and Glasgow, coordinated at Strathclyde by Dennis Nicholson, took on the task of turning BUBL into a service.

"This group saved it from extinction by their voluntary efforts. The service continued on this voluntary basis until early 1994, growing in popularity and attracting small amounts of sponsorship from commercial and professional organizations. By 1994, BUBL had moved its service from Glasgow to UKOLN in Bath, but it was still managed over the network by Strathclyde University."

In its embryonic experimental form, BUBL was a central place to post and share files extracted from mailing lists, job listings, and original news and discussion among librarians and library school students. By 1993, however, Gopher and Web servers with links to Internet resources of library and information science interest were in place and access to Internet resources beyond LIS was beginning to come on stream—the beginnings of the BUBL 'Subject Tree' and (in time) the BUBL LINK (LIbraries of Networked Knowledge) service.

BUBL received funding from the Joint Information Systems Committee (JISC) in 1994 and 1995. In January 1995, JISC began funding BUBL as a UK national information service offering an all-subject-areas approach to free Internet resources and a specialist service to LIS professionals.

As the Web became the dominant Internet service, the focus for BUBL reviewers shifted increasingly to Web resources and an experimental catalogue offering Web, Gopher, and Z39.50 access to a searchable catalogue was developed (1994–95). In 1996/1997 as part of the move from UKOLN to Strathclyde, Alan Dawson (now a Senior Researcher/Programmer at CDLR), developed embryonic LINK demonstrator as the initial basis for BUBL Link 5:15 which is now the searchable catalog used to organize and access the resources collected on BUBL.

BUBL has become an integral part of the CDLR at Strathclyde University and is now funded and maintained by the CDLR as part of its research activities. Original BUBL staff members Emma McCulloch and Andrew Williamson continue to work on BUBL as part of their work for CDLR. These two staff members, as well as the Director, spend approximately 1.5 days per week on BUBL. Staff who work on the BUBL site have degrees in library and information science, and have training in the cataloging procedures specific to BUBL. Staff members do what they can to support BUBL as they have time and other work for CDLR allows.

As other work at CDLR gathers momentum, the resources and services available to BUBL users is expected to expand. The key to this expansion is cooperation with a sister service called SLAINTE (www.slainte.org.uk) and the developmental work of a project called SPEIR (http://speir.cdlr.strath.ac.uk). SLAINTE (Scots Gaelic for 'cheers') stands for Scottish Libraries Across the INTErnet. This service, managed by Gordon Dunsire, CDLR Deputy Director, has also been around since the early '90s and has recently been moved to CDLR. SPEIR (an old Scots word meaning 'to ask' or 'to enquire') stands for Scottish Portals for Education, Information and Research. It is a new project, funded by the Scottish Library and Information Council (SLIC) and will develop a 'Scottish Cooperative Infrastructure' (SCI—see projected infrastructure diagram at http://speir.cdlr.strath.ac.uk/images/infrastructure.htm). Amongst other things, this will include a Scottish Distributed Digital Library, built initially around LINK and other resources and distributed cooperative cataloguing, and an LIS professionals support service based on BUBL and SLAINTE cooperation.

BUBL is also working—again in the context of SPEIR—with the cooperative of virtual libraries known as LOOK (Libraries of Organised Online Knowledge) and formerly known as "Fiat Lux" which includes INFOMINE, LII, MeL, and others.

Library staff expect that overall time contributed to BUBL will increase as participation in the SPEIR project develops.

BUBL will continue to provide high quality reviews and links to Web resources in multiple subject areas as part of these initiatives. Although, it does not currently offer virtual reference services, these may be developed in the future as part of the Scottish Cooperative Infrastructure.

BUBL is an essential e-library collection development tool for librarians.

"However, it soon became apparent that much of the information being made available on BUBL was of direct interest to the wider academic community and was being widely used by nonlibrarians. Consequently, BUBL has broadened its approach, and whilst a specialist service is still provided to the UK's library and information science community, the service has for some time been aimed towards the UK higher education academic and research community more generally. BUBL caters for all levels of academia throughout the world and selectively covers all subject areas. As it becomes an integral part of the Scottish Cooperative Infrastructure, BUBL will aim to extend its audience beyond HE and FE into the public and school library sectors and to support general public access for lifelong learners and other users of the UK 'People's Network'."

Although BUBL is not currently designed to support distance learners directly, future development is expected to support activities of the Graduate School of Informatics, which is associated with the Department of Computing and Information Sciences at Strathclyde where CDLR is based.

BUBL staff monitor mailing lists on which Web resources in various subject areas are announced. They also receive recommendations of new Web resources and search directly on the Web for new sites. They then link to the Web resource and review and evaluate it for inclusion in the BUBL catalog. On the BUBL site (http://bubl.ac.uk/admin) administrative details, articles, annual report, and the FAQ, provide information about the scope and selection process (http://bubl.ac.uk/admin/faq.htm). BUBL staff members collaborate to cover different subject areas. They prevent duplication by making updates on a regular monthly basis, and by maintaining regular communication between the staff members.

"Broadly speaking, we tend to look for websites with academic relevance, UK orientation, up to date information and completeness. We tend to avoid commercial and personal pages where possible. Initially, a broad spread of resources were added on a regular basis to ensure all subject areas were adequately covered. Now that the service is well established, additions tend to be more selective in that staff give consideration to the number and quality of resources already in a particular section. The 5:15 element of the service was designed with the idea that the optimum number of resources in any given area requested by a user is somewhere between 5 and 15. Typical users are thought to find less than 5 resources to be too few and don't often want to deal with more than 15. This is upheld where possible but isn't practical in all areas as some subject areas may comprise a definitive list eg. 'universities and colleges in Scotland' at http://bubl/link/u/universitiesandcollegesinscotland.htm currently has a list of 24."

BUBL staff select, evaluate, and collect resources continuously. Links are updated each month and announced at http://bubl.ac.uk/link/updates/current.html and through the Lis-Link discussion list (www.jiscmail.ac.uk/lists/lis-link.html). For each Web resource included in BUBL, staff create a catalog record. An initiative to contribute to and copy records from the OCLC Connexion service is developing under the SPEIR project and began on February 1, 2003. The OCLC Connexions subscription is paid for by SLIC.

Various staff members are all responsible for adding records to the BUBL catalog. They add each other's records to the catalog, in the interest of having an additional set of eyes checking each record for grammar, style, Dewey Decimal Classification, and keywords.

"The whole team is responsible for maintaining the Web site. Some of the time spent supporting BUBL involves link checking and reviewing subject sections. Whoever undertakes work therefore makes the appropriate changes. Some of the web pages eg. the A-Z of subject terms (http://bubl/link/terms.html) are cached. If new terms are added we run a macro on these cached files to update them. Other files eg. BUBL UK are stand alone html files so these would be updated individually. For example if a newspaper were to cease publication it would be removed from http://bubl/uk/newspapers.htm manually."

They use Linkbot 3.5 to run automatic checks for broken links as well as manual checks and fixes.

BUBL does not provide access to fee-based Web accessible databases directly and does not plan to do so in the future, because the BUBL mission is to provide free and high quality Web resources. The CDLR has created digital collections, which will in time be available via a BUBL view on CDLR resources, as well as via other user landscapes (see, for example, http://gdl.cdlr .strath.ac.uk).

BUBL staff value user feedback and give it high priority (http://bubl.ac.uk/admin/feedback .htm).

"Any messages (email/phone) received from users are dealt with as soon as possible. The majority of these are suggestions for inclusion in which case we would review their recommendation and add it to the database if appropriate. Any broken/erroneous links reported are dealt with immediately. More in depth feedback, perhaps relating to the organization of a particular subject area, will be taken on board and time set aside for a staff member to examine the point in detail."

BUBL organization is continuously reviewed. Each month's update cycle includes making any changes to the index and DDC menus that are seen as necessary. Staff members discuss all changes and the person who makes a suggestion generally implements the change.

"Involvement in the CDLR, which runs other services, such as, the Scottish cross-searchable catalogue service, CAIRNS (http://cairns.lib.strath.ac.uk), the SCONE (http://scone.strath.ac.uk/service/index.cfm) Scottish Collections Network database, and the Glasgow Digital Library Service, has brought review under this wider heading and much is expected to change in the coming months."

The BUBL Information Service is poised for many changes in its role vis-à-vis its funding and role in the Scottish Cooperative Infrastructure. In the context of SPEIR, the future of BUBL includes local, regional, national and international collaborative Web resource collection and cataloging. Working in cooperation with other e-library efforts and planning for support of distributed access to e-collections via local portals.

A key element in the SPEIR vision is the recognition that the SCI and subcomponents like BUBL and SCONE (named after the Scottish "stone of destiny" or "stone of SCONE" and pronounced "SKOON"), will not survive in a vacuum—that distributed digital libraries require coordination at a people and organization level. To quote Dennis Nicholson:

"There is an assumption that people interoperability is a prerequisite of technical and metadata interoperability in the distributed environment and a recognition that coherent distributed digital libraries are only possible if organizations collaborate to manage collection development and user and retrieval environments. This is why COSMIC, the Confederation of Scottish Mini-cooperatives (http://cosmic.cdlr.strath.ac.uk), is seen as central to the success of the SCI initiative—the means by which people and organisation level issues in Scotland's information landscape will be addressed and coordinated."

Another essential element of the vision is a belief that "the distributed information environment must grow as a single thing, and staff, user, and organizational cultures must grow with it if the end result is to be an integrated, user-responsive whole and that we must take a holistic approach to its development." As in the early days of BUBL, patrons and institutions recognize the vital role played by information professionals in coordinating this approach. In addition, everyone involved considers BUBL, SLAINTE, and international partners in LOOK to be important support services for those who seek to develop the global digital library of the twenty-first Century.

REFERENCES

Ackermann, E. C., and K. Hartman. 2000. The Information Specialist's Guide to Searching and Researching on the Internet and the World Wide Web. 2nd ed. London: Fitzroy Dearborn.

Baldwin, V. 2000. Collection Development in the New Millenium-Evaluating, Selecting, Annotating, Organizing for Ease of Access, Reevaluating, and Updating Electronic Resources. In Electronic Collection Management, ed. S. D. McGinnis, 67-96. Binghamton, NY: Haworth Information Press.

Blake, V. L. P., and T. T. Surprenant. 2000. Navigating the Parallel Universe: Education for Collection Management in the Electronic Age. Library Trends 48, no. 4 (Spring): 891–922.

Brooks, S. 2001. Integration of Information Resources and Collection Development Strategy. Journal of Academic Librarianship 27, no. 4 (July): 316–20.

Borgman, C. 2000. From Gutenberg to the Global Information Infrastructure: Access to Information in the Networked World. Cambridge, MA: MIT Press.

Bryant, B. 1997. Staffing and Organization for Collection Development in a New Century. In *Collection Management for the 21st Century*, ed. G. E. Gorman and R. H. Miller, 196–206. Westport, CT: Greenwood Press.

Buchanan, W. E. 2002. Developing library collections when everyone thinks the Internet is everything—and other challenges on the road to diversity. *Rural Libraries* 22, no. 1: 31–40.

Budd, J. M., and B. M. Harloe. 1997. Collection Development and Scholarly Communication in the 21st Century: From Collection Management to Content Management." In *Collection Management for the 21st Century*, ed. G. E. Gorman and R. H. Miller, 3-28. Westport, CT: Greenwood Press.

Caywood, C. 1996. Library Selection Criteria for WWW Resources. http://memorial.library.wisc.edu/wla/caywood.htm.

Cohen, S. M. 2002. RSS For Non-Techie Librarians. (June 2, 2002) www.llrx.com/features/rssforlibrarians.htm.

Cooke, A. 1999. *Neal-Schuman Authoritative Guide to Evaluating Information on the Internet*. New York: Neal-Schuman.

Coutts, M. M. 1998. Collecting for the Researcher in an Electronic Environment. *Library Review* 47, no. 5/6: 282–89.

Curtis, D. 2002. *Attracting, Educating and Serving Remote Users through the Web*. New York: Neil-Schuman Publishers.

Demas, S. G. 1994. Collection Development for the Electronic Library: A Conceptual and Organizational Model. *Library Hi Tech* 12, no. 3: 71–80.

Demas, S. G., P. McDonald, and G. Lawrence. 1995. The Internet and Collection Development: Mainstreaming Selection of Internet Resources. *Library Resources and Technical Services* 39, no. 3: 275–90.

Diaz, K. R., ed. 1997. *Reference Sources on the Internet: Off the Shelf and Onto the Web*. New York: Haworth Press.

Duranceau, E. 2002. Staffing for Electronic Resource Management. *Serials Review* 28, no. 4 (Winter): 316–20.

Fedunok, S. 1997. Hammurabi and the Electronic Age: Documenting Electronic Collection Decisions. *RQ* 36, no. 1: 86–90.

Fialkoff, F. 2001. The Hidden Costs of Online." *Library Journal* 126, no. 20: 97.

Gerhard, K. H. 2000. Challenges in Electronic Collection Building in Interdisciplinary Studies. In *Electronic Collection Management*, ed. S. D. McGinnis, 51–66Binghamton, New York: Haworth Information Press.

Gorman, G. E., and R. H. Miller, eds. 1997. *Collection Management for the 21st Century*. Westport, CT: Greenwood Press.

Guarino, H. 1998. Making the Internet a Part of the Library's Collection. In *Public Library Collection Development in the Information Age*, ed. A. K. Stephens, 91—100. Binghamton, NY: Haworth Information Press.

Hahn, H. 2002. *Harley Hahn's Internet Yellow Page*. Berkeley: Osborne Media/McGraw-Hill.

Harvey, R. 1997. The Preservation of Electronic Records: What Shall We Do Next? *Collection Management for the 21st Century*, ed. G. E. Gorman and R. H. Miller, 173–90.Westport, CT: Greenwood Press.

Hastings, S. K. 1998. Selection and Evaluation of Networked Information Resources. In *Public Library Collection Development in the Information Age*, ed. A. K. Stephens, 109—22.Binghamton, NY: Haworth Information Press.

Holleman, C. 2000. Electronic Resources: Are Basic Criteria for the Selection of Materials Changing? *Library Trends* 48, no. 4 (Spring): 694–711.

Jasco, P. 2001. Promoting the Library by Using Technology. *Computers in Libraries* 21, no. 8 (September): 58–61.

Intner, S. 2001. Impact of the Internet on Collection Development: Where are We Now? Where are We Headed? An Informal Study. *Library Collection, Acquisitions, and Technical Services* 25: 307–22.

Johnson, P. 1997. Collection Development Policies and Electronic Information Resources. *Collection Management for the 21st Century*, ed. G. E. Gorman and R. H. Miller, 83–104. Westport, CT: Greenwood Press.

Keller, M. A., V. A. Reich, and A. C. Herkovic. 2003. What is a Library Anymore, Anyway? *First Monday* 8, no. 5, http://firstmonday.dk/issues/issue8_5/keller/index.html.

Kopp, J. J. 1997. The Politics of a Virtual Collection. *Collection Management* 22, nos. 1–2: 81–100.

Kovacs, D. K. 2003. Web Scams and Frauds: Consumer Protection Information Web Sites. *OPLIN Business Bytes* 4, no. 5, http://oplin.lib.oh.us/index.cfm?ID=7-568-3007.

Kraynak, J. 2002. *Que's Official Internet Yellow Pages*. Indianapolis: Que.

Kuny, T., and G. Cleveland. 1998. The Digital Library: Myths and Challenges. *IFLA Journal* 24, no. 2: 107–13.

Latham, J. 2002. To Link, or Not to Link. *School Library Journal* 48, no. 5 (Spring): 20–23.

Lee, S. D. 2002. *Electronic Collection Development: A Practical Guide*. Neal-Schuman: New York.

Lord, J., and B. Ragon. 2001. Working Together to Develop Electronic Collections. *Computers in Libraries* 21, no. 5 (May): 40–45.

Lynch, C. 2001. What Do Digital Books Mean for Libraries. *Journal of Library Administration* 35, no. 3: 21–32.

McGeachin, R. 1998. Selection Criteria for Web-Based Resources in a Science and Technology Library Collection. *Issues in Science and Technology Librarianship* 18 (Spring), www.library.ucsb.edu/istl/98-spring/article2.html.

Metz, P. 2000. Principles of Selection for electronic Resources. *Library Trends* 48, no. 4 (Spring): 711–29.

Miller, R. 2000. Electronic Resources and Academic Libraries, 1980–2000: A Historical Perspective. *Library Trends* 48, no. 4 (Spring): 645–671.

Milnor, N. 1998. Cyberselection: The Impact of the Internet on Collection Development in Public Libraries. In *Public Library Collection Development in the Information Age*, ed. A. K. Stephens, 101—8. Binghamton, NY: Haworth Information Press.

Mitchell, S., et al. 2003. "iVia Open Source Virtual Library System. *D-Lib Magazine* 9, no. 1 (Spring), www.dlib.org/dlib/january03/mitchell/01mitchell.html.

Morville, P. S., and S. J. Wickhorst. 1996. Building Subject-Specific Guides to Internet Resources. *Internet Research: Electronic Networking Applications and Policy* 6, no. 4: 27–32.

Newman, G. L. 2000. Collection Development and Organization of Electronic Resources. In *Electronic Collection Management*, ed. S. D. McGinnis, 97–114. Binghamton, NY: Haworth Information Press.

Nisonger, T. 1997. The Internet and Collection Management in Academic Libraries: Opportunities and Challenges. In *Collection Management for the 21st Century*, ed. G. E. Gorman and R. H. Miller, 29–57. Westport, CT: Greenwood Press.

———. 2000. Introduction. *Library Trends* 48, no. 4 (Spring): 639–45.

Norman, O. G. 1997. The Impact of Electronic Information Sources on Collection Development: A Survey of Current Practice. *Library Hi Tech* 15, nos. 1–2: 123–32.

Okerson, A. 2000. Are We There yet? Online E-Resources Ten years After. *Library Trends* 48, no. 4 (Spring): 671–94.

Piontek, S., and K. Garlock. 1995. Creating a World Wide Web Resource Collection. *Collection Building* 14, no. 1: 12–18.

Pitschmann. L. A. 2001. Building Sustainable Collections of Free Third-Party Web Resources. Digital Library Federation, Council on Library and Information Resources. Washington, DC. www.clir.org/pubs/reports/pub98/pub98.pdf.

Poisson, E. H. 1998. Collection Development of Electronic Resources at the Science and Industry and Business Library (SIBL). In *Public Library Collection Development in the Information Age*, ed. A. K. Stephens, 123–30. Binghamton, NY: Haworth Information Press.

Quinn, A. 2001. Collection Development in the Electronic Library: The Future Isn't What It Used to Be. *DttP* 29, no. 3: 11–12.

Rabine, J. L., and L. A. Brown. 2000. The Selection Connection: Creating an Internal Web Page for Collection Development. *LRTS* 44, no. 1 (January): 44–49.

Ramirez, D., and S. Gyeszly. 2001. netLibrary: a new direction in collection development. *Collection Development* 20, no. 4: 154–64.

Rioux, M. 1997. Hunting and Gathering in Cyberspace: Finding and Selecting Web Resources for the Library's Virtual Collection. In *Pioneering New Serials Frontiers: From Petroglyphs to Cyberserials*, ed. C. Christiansen and C. Leathem, 129–36. Binghamton, NY: Haworth Press.

Rosenfeld, L, J. Janes, and M. Vander Kolk, eds. 1995. *The Internet Compendium: Subject Guides to Humanities Resources*. New York: Neal-Schuman.

Rosenfeld, L., and P. S. Morville. 2002. *Information Architecture for the World Wide Web*. 2nd ed. Sebastapol, CA: O'Reilly and Associates.

Schneider, K. G. 2002. Fiat Lux: a Yahoo with Values and a Brain. *American Libraries: Internet Librarian*. (April), http://archive.ala.org/alonline/netlib/il402.html.

Sowards, S. W. 1998. "A Typology for Ready Reference Websites in Libraries." *First Monday* 1, no. 14, http://firstmonday.dk/issues/issue3_5/sowards.

Stephens, A., ed. 1998. *Public Library Collection Development in the Information Age*. Binghamton, NY: Haworth Information Press.

Stewart, L. 2000. Choosing Between Print and Electronic Resources: The Selection Dilemma. *The Reference Librarian* 71: 79–97.

Stielow, F., ed. 1999. *Creating a Virtual Library: A How-To-Do-It Manual for Integrating Information Resources on the Web*. New York: Neal-Schuman.

Sweetland, J. H. 2000. Reviewing the World Wide Web—Theory versus. Reality" *Library Trends* 48, no. 4 (Spring): 748–68.

Tennant, R. 1998. The Art and Science of Digital Bibliography. *Library Journal* 123, no. 17: 28–29.

Thomsen, E. 1996. *Reference and Collection Development on the Internet: A How-To-Do-It Manual for Librarians*. New York: Neal-Schuman.

Thornton, G. A. 2000. Impact of Electronic Resources on Collection Development, the Roles of Librarians, and Library Consortia. *Library Trends* 48, no. 4 (Spring): 842–56.

Tonta, Y. 2001. Collection Development of Electronic Information Rresources in Turkish University Libraries. *Library Collection, Acquisitions, and Technical Services* 25: 291-98.

Walters, W., et al. 1998. Guidelines for Collecting Aggregations of Web Resources. *Information Technology and Libraries* 17, no. 3 (September): 157–61.

Yochelson, A., et al. 1997 (2003 update). Collection Development and the Internet: A Brief Handbook for Recommending Officers in the Humanities and Social Sciences Division at the Library of Congress. Available: http://lcweb.loc.gov/acq/colldev/handbook.html.

WEB SITES CITED

(Note that some sites are included in the resource lists and webliographies in subsequent chapters, and therefore are not necessarily duplicated in this section.)

ACLU vs. Reno Supreme Court Decision. Available: http://www.kovacs.com/ns/acluvsreno.html.

American Library Association, Public Program Office. Available: www.ala.org/Content/NavigationMenu/Our_Association/Offices/Public_Programs_Office/Grants_and_Events/PPO_Grants_and_Events.htm.

American Libraries Online. Available: www.ala.org/alonline.

Ballard, T., and T. Gunther. 2003. Typographical Errors in Library Databases. Available: http://faculty.quinnipiac.edu/libraries/tballard/typoscomplete.html.

Bobby. Available: http://bobby.watchfire.com.

Booklist. Available: www.ala.org/booklist.

Choice: Current Reviews for Academic Libraries. Available: www.ala.org/acrl/choice.

Collection Development Training for Arizona Public Libraries. Available: www.dlapr.lib.az.us/cdt/index.htm.

College and Research Libraries News Net. Available: www.ala.org/acrl/c&rlnew2.html.

Directory of Scholarly and Professional Electronic Conferences. Available: www.kovacs.com/directory.

DihydrogenMonoxide Research Division—DHMO.org—Tom Way. Available: www.dhmo.org.

FTC: Operation Cure-All. Available: www.ftc.gov/bcp/conline/edcams/cureall.

The InFoPeople Project. Available: www.infopeople.org.

Institute of Museum and Library Services (IMLS) Library Services and Technology Act (LSTA) funding contact information. Available: www.imls.gov/grants/library/gsla_cos.htm.

The Internet Archive Project. Available: www.archive.org.

The Internet Tourbus. Available: www.tourbus.com.

Kupersmith, J. 2003. Library Terms that Users Understand. Available: www.jkup.net/terms.html.

Lent, L., and C. Nyhan. 2002. Using the Web for Collection Development. Available: www.infopeople.org/training/past/2002/web_collection_dev.

The Librarian—The L-Space Web. Available: www.co.uk.lspace.org/books/whos-who/librarian.html.

LibraryLookup—Jon Udell: LibraryLookup homepage. Available: http://weblog.infoworld.com/udell/stories/2002/12/11/librarylookup.html.

MetaCrawler's MetaSpy. Available: www.metaspy.com.

Netscape's Web site Cookie description. Available: http://wp.netscape.com/newsref/std/cookie_spec.html.

OCLC Worldcat. Available: www.oclc.org/worldcat.

Open Directory List of Link Management Tools. Available: http://dmoz.org/Computers/Software/Internet/ Site_Management/Link_Management.

OPLIN—Ohio Public Library Information Network. Available: www.oplin.lib.oh.us.

Privacy.net. Available: http://Privacy.net.

Quackwatch. Available: www.quackwatch.com.

Quatloos!—Cyber-Museum of Scams and Frauds. Available: www.quatloos.com.

RLIN Eureka. Available: www.rlg.org.

Scam o Rama. Available: www.scamorama.com.

Scambusters. Available: www.scambusters.org.

U.S. Secret Service Advisories. Available: www.secretservice.gov/advisories.shtml.

Wayback Machine. Available: www.waybackmachine.org.

A Web Hub for Developing Administrative Metadata for Electronic Resource Management. Available: www.library.cornell.edu/cts/elicensestudy/home.html.

Web4lib archives. Available: http://sunsite.berkeley.edu/Web4Lib/archive.html.

Webreference on RSS. Available: www.webreference.com/authoring/languages/xml/rss.

Who Am I? Available: www.mall-net.com/cgibin/whoami.cgi?src=webcons.

SEE ALSO PART III: WEB COLLECTION DEVELOPMENT RESOURCES:

Resource List 1: Collection Development Related Discussion Lists, Newsgroups, and Blogs, for discussion lists, newsgroups, e-serials, and other resources cited in this chapter; and Resource List 2: Evaluation Guides

2: Integrating the Library and the E-Library: Virtual Reference, Cataloging, and Digital Collections

"Whatever their reasons, it is clear that fewer and fewer people are physically crossing the thresholds of research libraries. The forward-thinking librarian sees this as an opportunity, not a crisis—a chance to make online resources as complete and easy to use as possible, and to expand the number of people who actually make use of the library's services. Offering remote access is a chance to make libraries as essential in the electronic era as they were in the print era, only richer, and more complete, and more fun....If our users aren't coming to us, why don't we go to them?"

R. Anderson (2002: 15)

INTRODUCTION: INTEGRATING THE E-LIBRARY AND THE BRICKS AND MORTAR LIBRARY

Integrating the electronic (or virtual or digital) services of our libraries and the physical, a.k.a. "bricks and mortar" is inevitable. Evidence of this process is offered by the case studies throughout this text. In this chapter we include three virtual reference case studies. Each virtual reference case is from a different type of library organization: a public library system, a regional public library consortium, and an academic library project with information from both the individual campus and the consortia-wide experience.

In practical terms, library services must be offered where and when our patrons will use them. If library services are not present at the point in time and space where our patrons and potential patrons are seeking information, they will turn elsewhere for information mediation services. This chapter provides an overview of three areas in which library services are offered through the Web: reference services; including support for distance learners, cataloging; other database options for creating organized, standard, and unique records for Web resources; and the ongoing creation of digital collections.

VIRTUAL REFERENCE SERVICES

Virtual reference services, a.k.a. digital, electronic, or online reference, are a critical part of our evolution as shifted librarians. Virtual reference services attempt to provide information mediation at the point in space and time when patrons are seeking information. Since many of our patrons are using the Web to search for information they require, it would be ideal if reference librarians could be available on the Web to assist them. Throughout this discussion the term "patron" will refer both to our current patrons, and to our potential patrons, both those who use our services now and those who could do so in the future.

This section reviews the options, discusses some of the challenges, and describes procedures for answering virtual reference questions in the three basic modes of virtual reference service.

This chapter synthesizes information gleaned from case studies of the experiences of three virtual reference services projects. There are literally thousands of such projects, and there are Web tools for identifying other libraries that offer virtual reference services.

Gerry McKiernan maintains two directories, LiveRef[SM] and IDEALS[SM]. LiveRef[SM] (www .public.iastate.edu/~CYBERSTACKS/LiveRef.htm) lists libraries that are offering synchronous virtual reference services. IDEALS[SM]—A Registry of Emerging Innovative Augmented Digital Library Services—(www.public.iastate.edu/~CYBERSTACKS/IDEALS.htm) is a categorized registry of library services projects that are using emerging technologies or innovative service strategies.

Bernie Sloan maintains his Digital Reference Pages at http://alexia.lis.uiuc.edu/ ~b-sloan/bernie.htm. Many virtual reference cases, discussion, and research reports, are included in his Digital Reference Services Bibliography (www.lis.uiuc.edu/~b-sloan/ digiref.html).

The Teaching Librarian (www.teachinglibrarian.org) lists libraries that offer chat reference services, organized by library type, consortia, software used, and by country. The Virtual Reference Desk (VRD) Project (http://vrd.org) lists a variety of "Ask-A" services organized by subject area.

The MARS Ad Hoc Committee on Virtual Reference Guidelines Draft Guidelines" (www.ala.org/Content/NavigationMenu/RUSA/Our_Association2/RUSA_Sections/MARS/Our_ Section3/Committees14/Draft_Virtual_Reference_Guidelines.htm) has begun developing guidelines and standards for the implementation of virtual reference services.

Lipow (2002) and Meola and Stormont (2002) have written guides to how and why an individual library would go about setting up and managing a virtual reference service.

There are three basic modes of virtual reference service:

1. Ready-reference collections on the Web; as well as pathfinders, tutorials, guides, knowledge bases, and FAQs
2. Asynchronous reference—e-mail or Web-forms—through which reference librarians respond to questions within a certain amount of time, but not immediately
3. Synchronous reference—chat or telephone

READY-REFERENCE COLLECTIONS ON THE WEB; AS WELL AS PATHFINDERS, TUTORIALS, GUIDES, KNOWLEDGE BASES, AND FAQs

This mode for virtual reference service is usually the simplest. It does not require librarians to interact directly with patrons. However, librarians who build ready-reference collections on the Web, or create pathfinders, tutorials, guides, and similar resources, will have to anticipate the kinds of ready-reference questions that their patrons will ask. Most e-library collections include a ready-reference collection.

A knowledge base is a collection of the questions asked and the answers provided either through a virtual reference service or through in-person reference service. Gerry McKiernan maintains a directory of library knowledge bases at www.public.iastate.edu/ ~CYBERSTACKS/KBL.htm. An FAQ or Frequently Asked Questions type of guide is a form of knowledge base that extracts—obviously—the most frequently asked questions along with the answers provided. The Internet Public Library is an example of an e-library that provides some reference assistance through pathfinders as well as through an FAQ collection (www.ipl.org/div/askus). The San Bernardino County Web E-Library (www.sbcounty.gov/ library/homepage) also provides pathfinders. Some e-libraries have tried to organize ready-reference resources in such a way that patrons can easily locate the answers to certain types of questions or to frequently asked questions. Examples from the case studies include Cleveland Public Library (CPL) Links Library (www.cpl.org/LinksLibrary.asp?FormMode=DBNew) and Kent State University's Information Resources page (www.library.kent.edu) does this in a broad form by organizing resources by the types of question or by the type of resource. The Westchester Library System's firstfind.info project (www.firstfind.info) uses a branching structure to guide patrons to appropriate Web resources to answer basic questions. The firstfind.info project was created with the support of the Brooklyn Public Library, New York Public Library, Queens Borough Public Library, and American Library Association. It was funded also by an IMLS LSTA grant through the New York State Library.

ASYNCHRONOUS REFERENCE—E-MAIL OR WEB-FORMS

Asynchronous reference is the most direct and easiest virtual reference service to offer on the Web. Questions are received through e-mail or Web-forms. Librarians can take the time to answer the questions and reply through e-mail or other mechanism offered by the patron. The Internet Public Library offers one of the best known and longest running asynchronous virtual reference services (www.ipl.org/div/askus). Questions are answered by Internet Public Library volunteers, who may be located anywhere in the world (www.ipl.org/div/askus/refstaff.html).

Many libraries that offer asynchronous virtual reference services also make statements about how long it will be before a librarian responds to the question. For example, Kent State University's Ask-A-Librarian e-mail Web-form option advises, "This service enables you to ask short, factual questions and receive a response by e-mail. Most responses to questions will be sent within 2 working days."

The HealthInfoNet of Alabama e-library (http://hinfonet.lhl.uab.edu/asklibrarian.htm) offers a Web-form Ask-A-Librarian Service that explains: "We will work on your question and respond to you as soon as possible. We strive to answer all requests by the next business day." They ask people from outside of Alabama to contact their own local library for assistance.

Disadvantages and limitations of asynchronous virtual reference services are the delay in responding to the patron's question, the requirement that the patron provide contact information to receive an answer, and the difficulties in clarifying the question through a reference interview. The time delay in answering may or may not be a problem for the patron depending on the question. If the patron does not provide contact information then the librarian cannot give them an answer. If they do provide contact information then they lose a certain amount of privacy. It may be more difficult for a patron to ask a sensitive personal-type of question under these circumstances, whereas asking on the telephone—or through synchronous virtual reference—might be more private, and therefore easier, for the patron to ask. Going back and forth through e-mail to clarify a reference question can be slow and frustrating . It can work well if both parties to the interaction are quick to respond.

SYNCHRONOUS REFERENCE—CHAT OR TELEPHONE

The main advantage of synchronous virtual reference is interactivity. Librarians and patrons have the opportunity to engage in a clarifying reference interview. Other advantages may depend on the virtual reference software selected. Virtual reference service may be offered through simple chat options through the open Web (e.g., AOL, IRC, ICQ), or special software designed for virtual reference or Web customer service. The specialized software for synchronous communications frequently includes the functionality for pushing Web pages, sending files, or even interacting through audio so that patrons with visual difficulties or those who just prefer a voice can interact more easily. For example, the Mid-Illinois Talking Book Center (www.mitbc.org) uses the QuestionPoint software (http://questionpoint.org) developed by the Library of Congress and OCLC, with the voice over IP option (www.mitbc.org/ref.shtml).

The Chat with a Librarian service of OhioLINK (www.ohiolink.edu) uses the GroupZ software (www.groopz.com), which was designed as a customer-service software. The GroupZ software allows for a certain amount of co-browsing. That is, the librarian staffing the virtual reference desk can not only push Web pages to the patron, they can also "show" the patron what they are doing or need to do in locating an OhioLINK database and then searching it. Co-browsing depends on the Web browser and connectivity of the patron. Co-browsing is a function of other virtual reference software as well, including LSSI. One advantage of the GroupZ software is that librarians may install the software on their home computer, or at other remote locations (e.g., branch campuses or department offices) in order to work. Coauthor Kara L. Robinson staffed the Chat with a Librarian service from the office of coauthor Diane K. Kovacs at various times while they wrote this book. The software works on both Mac OS and Windows operating systems.

Many organizations and individuals have reviewed and evaluated virtual reference software. A Web search on "virtual reference software evaluation" retrieves reports from John W. Owen, III Baltimore County Public Library (BCPL) system (www.bcpl.net/~jowen/virtualref) and the Western New York Library Resources Council (www.wnylrc.org/vreferen/softcomp.pdf). Both organizations have posted their evaluations of virtual reference software including approximate pricing. The archives of the Dig_Ref discussion list (http://vrd.org/Dig_Ref/dig_ref.shtml, http://groups.yahoo.com/group/dig_ref) are also a good source of current evaluations, technical information, and pricing details.

Staffing virtual reference services requires that librarians be available during the hours that the synchronous reference is offered. Libraries may offer 24/7 reference service. For example, both the KnowItNow24x7 and the Ask-a-Pro cases in this chapter offer virtual reference service twenty-four hours a day, seven days per week. Both of these services use Library Systems and Services' (LSSI) Virtual Reference software (www.vrtoolkit.net) and pay for after hours staffing through LSSI Virtual Reference Center (http://vrs.lssi.com).

Libraries may choose to schedule coverage of virtual reference by staff dedicated specifically to this task, while others may choose to have staff at the reference desk (or center or other reference service physical location) also monitor the virtual reference service.

KnowItNow24x7 works with a mix of dedicated staff and reference staff multitasking. For example, when a patron requests a Science and Technology reference person, any librarian who is staffing the reference service area may respond to the query during Science and Technology division hours. Clevnet system libraries handle virtual reference service during scheduled time periods. Individual member libraries vary in whether reference staff are dedicated to the virtual reference service, or multitasking with the physical reference service. Ask-a-Pro is staffed during library hours by librarians, who are simultaneously staffing the reference service area as well.

Some libraries have staff scheduled to dedicated times, for example, OhioLINK's Chat with A Librarian service. Librarians at member institutions are scheduled to staff the service either at times dedicated to their own patrons (students, faculty, and staff), or at times when they are available to all OhioLINK member institution's patrons.

Disadvantages and limitations of synchronous virtual reference service identified by the case study participants included: the time lag between questions and responses, the lack of visual communication to let the patron know that the librarian is working on their problem, or conversely the librarian cannot see the patron to determine age/grade level of the materials required, the urgency of the question, or the patrons' reactions to responses. The reference librarian must specifically query the patron to know their response to the question. Another issue raised was that of patron privacy. The two public library virtual reference case study participants described in this chapter do not require patrons to identify themselves; however, that does make it difficult to provide follow-up after the interaction. If a patron provides a real e-mail address, the reference staff is able to e-mail them additional information. OhioLINK's Chat with A Librarian service requires that patrons identify themselves with their student ID barcode number.

In a discussion on Dig_Ref during July 2003 (http://vrd.org/Dig_Ref/dig_ref.shtml), someone asked, "What do patrons hate about virtual reference?" Some of the survey results and opinions posted during the discussion include:

- perception that the librarian was "mean"; attributing attitude because of lack of communication or the impersonality of the medium;
- long "silences" between the time the question is asked and the time someone affirms that the question is being answered; long "silences" while the librarian looks for an answer;
- slowness of response; also described as slow typing by the librarian;

- being told they have to come into the library to get certain information;
- librarian gave the wrong answer; sometimes this was when the patron didn't like the answer, was referred elsewhere for an answer, or told they'd need to come into the physical library to get an answer.

More than a dozen Dig_Ref subscribers participated in this discussion. Please see the Dig_Ref archives for the full-text of the discussion. Note that you must subscribe to the group in order to view the archives. However, it is an obvious conclusion that virtual reference providers need to be pro-actively responsive through the text-based communication medium. We need to make a special point of letting the patron know we are with them and remain with them as we work. The librarian must give constant updates, friendly greetings, and reassurances of the kind that we give in-person through our posture, facial expression, and verbal communication in words that we type into the system when we are providing virtual reference services.

STRATEGIES AND TRAINING FOR VIRTUAL REFERENCE

All three case study projects report that they rely on reference staff collaboration in much the same way as they do when offering in-person reference services. If one person cannot answer a question or is having difficulty finding supporting documentation, they refer to other staff members on duty, or in some cases are able to refer the patron to additional reference services. The KnowItNow24x7 staff may refer patrons to the Cleveland Law Library for law questions, the MetroHealthLine for medical questions, and also has Tutor.Com in assisting with homework questions. They also participate in the QuestionPoint and ExpertRef cooperative virtual reference projects.

Training for reference staff was provided to key staff members by LSSI in the case of KnowItNow24x7 and Ask-A-Pro. Those staff members then led training for other reference staff. Training involved workshops, as well as hands-on and one-on-one experience, in using the system. Critical factors in the training of reference staff include the ability to handle the essentially text based, real-time interface, operate the virtual reference software, use the scanner or otherwise cut and paste text from non-Web resources, and to be able to select and push appropriate Web resources to patrons.

In "Education for Digital Reference Services," Linda Smith (2002) explores the history and current state of virtual reference (digital reference) and the education and training that reference staff need to prepare to offer virtual reference services. This paper provides an excellent breakdown of the educational activities that may prepare reference staff for virtual reference services:

"1) formal sequence of courses as part of the master's degree; 2) on-the-job training; 3) continuing education (conferences, seminars, workshops, professional association programs, formal university courses, professional reading); 4) evaluation (self, peer, supervisor); and 5) acquisition of substantive, multidisciplinary knowledge." (Smith, 2002)

Professor Smith surveyed library schools concerning whether they had incorporated "digital reference services" into the curriculum, either as a separate courses or as part of other reference courses. They were also asked if they had taught either a specifically digital reference course or other reference course as a Web-based course. They were also queried about whether the library school had sponsored any continuing education programs related to digital reference service. Professor Smith's survey indicated that

"some attention is given to digital reference services in almost all of the basic reference course offerings, primarily through lectures, and readings, and occassionally through guest speakers involved in digital reference." (Smith, 2002)

A few library schools reported that they tried to give students practice in virtual reference, especially in asynchronous mode. Internet Public Library was mentioned as one tool used for this training. Faculty reported difficulties in giving students practice in the real-time tools because the software had not been readily available for such practice. Recently LSSI, QuestionPoint, and other software vendors have been providing training logins for students or demonstration software copies for practice, as well as evaluation. Very few schools offered

Web-based courses, although they did use Web communication tools as an adjunct to face-to-face instruction. Continuing education offerings in this area were also minimal. An important issue addressed in this paper is the relative importance of virtual reference skills in overall reference training and education. Increasingly, librarians will benefit by having basic virtual reference services training in library school. Professor Smith identifies some tools that educators and trainers might use in helping reference staff to prepare including "Transcripts...Knowledge bases...Manuals...and collaboration with vendors and service providers."

Many library school faculty members have begun covering virtual reference skills and knowledge in the curriculum or in continuing education or professional development programs. For example, The University of Maryland's College of Information Studies has begun offering "The Virtual Reference Workshop 1.0" (www.clis.umd.edu/ce/virtrefwork.html) on a regular basis as part of their distance learning program for professional development.

E-LIBRARY SUPPORT FOR DISTANCE LEARNERS

Virtual reference services are critical for distance learners, as well as for students who are working from off-campus. The OhioLINK Chat with a Librarian service in particular is designed to assist distance learners in using the excellent collection of Web-accessible scholarly databases and full-text journals and reference sources provided through the OhioLINK consortium (www.ohiolink.edu). That e-library collection also supports distance learners. With the virtual reference service, they can receive assistance in choosing an appropriate source, tutoring in searching or otherwise using one of the databases, or librarians can refer them to other resources on the Web and advise them when visiting a physical library will be essential.

Several of the e-library case studies in other chapters of this book are offering synchronous virtual reference services in addition to their e-library collection in support of distance learners. For example, the University of Canterbury Web E-library (http://library.canterbury.ac.nz) offers their AskLive service.

CATALOGING WEB-ACCESSIBLE INFORMATION RESOURCES

Libraries catalog books, videos, DVD's, maps, and a multitude of other information forms and artifacts in order to organize them so that the people who wish to read, consult, or view them can easily identify and retrieve these sources. Cataloging Web resources does not necessarily mean that libraries will keep trying to make the MARC record work in ways it was not designed to work (Tennant, 2002).

Librarians may use a variety of other flexible and powerful database tools to catalog Web resources. For example, in the BUBL case study, Dennis Nicholson describes BUBL as a catalog of Web links. The BUBL project developed "BUBL Link 5:15 which is now the searchable catalog used to organize and access the resources collected on BUBL" (BUBL Case Study in Part I, Chapter 1). Developers are exploring many alternatives, including XML, as well as ways to make the MARC record work with Web resource metadata.

In this section we will overview some of the issues related to cataloging Web resources with the MARC format, as well as point to examples and resources of other database creation options. Some method of cataloging Web resources will benefit libraries and their patrons.

Sanford Berman makes the best case for cataloging all of a library's resources in all formats. His credo for "Why Catalog?":

> "Cataloging should identify and make accessible a library's resources—in all formats. That identification and access should be swift and painless. The language and structure of catalog entries should be familiar and comprehensible. And catalogers should recognize that they do what they do not to please bosses and not to mindlessly adhere to rules and protocols, but to serve their information desk colleagues and the public. That's whom they're working for." (Berman, 2000: 11)

WHY DO SOME LIBRARIES INCORPORATE RECORDS FOR WEB-ACCESSIBLE RESOURCES IN THE LIBRARY CATALOG?

We asked this question in an interview with Margaret Maurer, Cataloging Manager, Libraries and Media Services, Kent State University, in April, 2003. She responded that:

"Web resources, both free and fee-based, represent robust sources of information for library patrons. Including catalog records for Web resources in the library OPAC accomplishes three important goals for libraries:

1. establishes a uniform user interface for searching for Web sites, books, serials, and other electronic resources that the library owns or has access to;
2. encourages the use of high quality Web resources;
3. encourages standards for Web resource quality and inter-accessibility."

Kent State University Libraries has a policy of cataloging Web resources, as does the OhioLINK consortium. They do not attempt to catalog every single Web resource, but rather choose carefully which Web resources to catalog. The key question is: Will cataloging a given Web resource add to the patron's access to the kinds of information they are looking for? Web-accessible databases licensed by OhioLINK are all cataloged, as well as being organized on the OhioLINK main Web site and each individual campus site.

Professor Maurer was asked to identify the criteria used to decide whether a given Web resource would be cataloged. In general, Web resources to be cataloged could be identified by a reference or technical services librarian or on occasion by students or faculty members. Copy cataloging of Web resources involves checking to see if a record is available in the OhioLINK system. Note that the central OhioLINK catalog does not display all of the "holding" libraries. The data entry field, number 856 is used to add electronic access information; that is, the URL. When a patron retrieves a Web resource record, they may link directly to the site from the catalog (www.ohiolink.edu). If a catalog record for the Web resource exists in OCLC, the decision may be made to download it to the catalog. If the Web resource will require original cataloging, catalogers look for the following criteria. Note that these are paraphrased from a long discussion of the concept:

- Unique content; content that is clearly identifiable and can be adequately described through cataloging.
- Contains metadata information or other clearly identifiable bibliographic information that can be extracted to create a catalog record.
- Clearly and easily identified information provider or source. Information analogous to "publisher" that includes detailed attribution and valid contact information.
- Credible documentation that the Web resource content will be stable or continue for a foreseeable future.
- Content up-to-date or otherwise clearly identified as historical; time-stamped.
- Authoritative content based on authoritative and credible information provider or source; content verifiable as factual, research-supported, or otherwise possessing scholarly value.
- Appropriate education level; since Kent State is an academic institution the resource must be intended for college students or faculty—other libraries would make similar decisions based on the educational level of the patrons they serve.
- Accessibility; the Web resource is easily navigated and follows the basic guidelines for accessibility
- Commercial aspect is minimal or otherwise does not affect the value of the content.

Some libraries may choose to create original MARC records for Web resources but many records are already available through OCLC (see OCLC Connexion below), WEB FEET (www.webfeetguides.com) and other catalog record vendors.

OVERVIEW AND INTRODUCTION OF DESCRIPTIVE CATALOGING OF WEB RESOURCES:

For the past decade, catalogers have been developing various strategies for cataloging Web and other electronic resources. OCLC has provided leadership in the assessment of Internet resources for cataloging, and the development of cataloging standards. They began a series of Internet resource cataloging experiments in 1992 based on the assumptions that the *AACR2*, 2nd edition, Chapter 9, "Computer Files" guidelines were adequate for creating cataloging records of Internet resources, and that Internet resources provided sufficient data for creation of minimal-level cataloging records (Dillon et al., 1993). In that pre-Web era, most Internet resources were downloaded as computer-readable files through FTP or Gopher or by logging in through a telnet session.

The advent of the Web added layers of complexity and problems of data uniformity that had to be addressed if Web resources were to be cataloged in the MARC format.

Nancy B. Olsen's pioneering work *Cataloging Internet Resources*, 2nd Edition (www.oclc.org/oclc/man/9256cat/toc.htm), was one of the first (1997), and is still one of the best, sources for catalogers who are doing descriptive cataloging for Web resources using the MARC format. *Cataloging Internet Resources*, 2nd Edition, was developed as part of an OCLC and U.S. Department of Education funded project called "Building a Catalog of Internet Resources." It is based on *AACR2*, 2nd Edition, along with OCLC's *Bibliographic Formats and Standards* (www.oclc.org/bibformats), and "Cataloging Electronic Resources: OCLC-MARC Coding Guidelines." (Weitz, 2002)

The 2002 *Anglo-American Cataloging Rules* (*AACR2* 2002) describes a new paradigm for cataloging Web resources. AACR2 refers to Web resources as "Integrating Resources" and addresses them in much the same way as loose-leaf serials or monographs that have continuous updates and supplements. (Maurer, 2003) However, AACR2 2002 fails to address the role of metadata or other related issues in describing Web resources.

In *Cataloging Nonprint and Internet Resources: A How-to-Do-it Manual for Librarians*, Mary Beth Weber (2002) addresses these issues and describes the cataloging of Web resources in a thoughtful and understandable manner. She introduces the key relationships between MARC and metadata and how they impact the cataloging of Web resources.

Dublin Core Metadata and cataloging Web resources

Catalogers are working with the Dublin Core Metadata project (Dublin Core for short) (http://dublincore.org) to develop Web resource data elements that can be used in the creation of MARC or other types of catalog/database records.

The Dublin Core consists of fifteen data elements that are determined by Web site builders/Web page creators, and placed in the HTML META tags in the <HEAD> of the Web page or pages that are the entry point of a given Web site. Search engines can use these metadata tags (http://dublincore.org/documents/dces) as a uniform source of information to index Web sites, as well as to establish standards that allow for interoperability between search tools, including library catalogs. Automated tools exist to aid in the creation of metadata and to aid in the conversion of metadata tags to MARC fields.

The Library of Congress Network Development and MARC Standards Office has published a "Crosswalk" for mapping between the fifteen Dublin Core data elements and the MARC21 bibliographic data elements (http://lcweb.loc.gov/marc/dccross.html).

OCLC CORC/Connexion

OCLC's Cooperative Online Resource Catalog (CORC™), began in 1999 as an attempt to combine high quality descriptive cataloging and the 15 elements of the Dublin Core Metadata in the MARC record. Hundreds of thousands of MARC records for Web resources were created by more than five hundred libraries in twenty three countries. The OCLC CORC™ service was integrated into the OCLC Connexion service in July 2002.

Other cataloging/database formats for Web-accessible resource records

MARC is a library-specific format. Only libraries use this format. It is rigid and obsolete. In short, it is not industry-standard in regard to current database technology.

What can libraries do? Some catalogers work to adapt MARC to modern database standards (see also OCLC Connexion above; IFLA, 1998). Others recommend that MARC be abandoned in favor of industry-standard database technologies, such as XML:

"Libraries exist to serve the present and future needs of a community of users. To do this well, they need to use the very best that technology has to offer. With the advent of the web, XML, portable computing, and other technological advances, libraries can become flexible, responsive organizations that serve their users in exciting new ways. Or not. If libraries cling to outdated standards, they will find it increasingly difficult to serve their clients as they expect and deserve." (Tennant, 2002)

XML is the eXtensible Mark-up Language. It is a mark-up language used to define electronic data records.

"XML is a markup language for documents containing structured information ....Structured information contains both content (words, pictures, etc.) and some indication of what role that content plays (for example, content in a section heading has a different meaning from content in a footnote, which means something different than content in a figure caption or content in a database table, etc.). Almost all documents have some structure...the word 'document' refers not only to traditional documents, like this one, but also to the myriad of other XML 'data formats'. These include vector graphics, e-commerce transactions, mathematical equations, object metadata, server APIs, and a thousand other kinds of structured information." O'Reilly XML.Com. What is XML. Available: www.xml.com/pub/a/98/10/guide1.html#AEN58.

Fianders (2001) discusses the application of XML to the bibliographic description that is the essence of a catalog record. In "Moving From MARC to XML," Lam (2001) provides a practical guide to converting MARC records to XML. Or, rather Lam has created an XML document type for MARC. He shows that by using XML:

- "we can create bibliographic records once and publish them in different formats;
- bibliographic records can (will) be directly viewed by the Web browsers, search engines, and potentially library systems without the need of further conversion;
- bibliographic records can be interchanged between XML and MARC without any data loss;
- many of the problems that were inherited with MARC format become insignificant, including those related to CJK, romanization and authority control." (Lam, 2001)

Miller (2000) presented a paper on the Medlane Project XMLMARC software at the MARBI/CC:DA joint meeting (http://laneweb.stanford.edu:2380/wiki/medlane/xmlmarc). XML-MARC is software that converts MARC records to XML, with some additional features. It was developed by librarians of Lane Medical Library, Stanford University Medical Center as one product of their Medlane Project. The Medlane Project is:

"an experiment by Lane Medical Library to investigate new methods for making library information available to the public. Current library information is segregated from other information resources on the World Wide Web due to its archaic communications and, often, storage format. The Medlane project is investigating recasting library information into a more universally accepted format, XML (the eXtensible Markup Language)." (Miller, 2000)

Other database options are also being explored and used. Currently, libraries have many technology choices open to them. The important issue remains our role as information intermediaries regardless of the technology choices we make.

MAINTAINING DIGITAL COLLECTIONS

Many individual libraries are creating digital library projects or are planning to do so. Such projects are labor intensive and complex. In this section we discuss some of the basics, as well as resources for learning more about the creation of digital collections that will be Web-accessible.

Creating digital collections may involved scanning, transcribing, retyping, photographing, or otherwise reproducing in electronic format full-text, data, images, maps, and other artifacts held by a library, data creator/provider, or other archival organization. Those digitized documents and other artifacts must also be organized in a database of some kind so that they can be searched and retrieved by users. The Digital Library Federation (DLF) (www.diglib.org) and the DSpace Federation (www.dspace.org) are both consortia of academic and research libraries that share standards and "best practices" for creating and managing digital collections in the networked environment. DSpace is developing a digital repository system. DLF members assist each other in creating and managing digital collections. The DLF Web site publishes standards and links to publications, such as the report of the IMLS, "A Framework of Guidance for Building Good Digital Collections" (www.imls.gov/pubs/forumframework.htm). DLF supports the Open Archives Initiative (OAI; www.openarchives.org) and plans to develop "Internet gateways through which users will access distributed digital library holdings as if they were part of a single uniform collection."

Some digital collections are preservation projects designed to ensure that fragile historical materials are available for future generations. Libraries participate in many local history projects and preservation projects. The American Memory Project (http://memory.loc.gov) digital collection created by the Library of Congress is one of the most comprehensive and best known of these kinds of projects. Many individual state library organizations have begun state level "Memory Projects"—e.g., the Ohio Memory Project (www.ohiomemory.org). The USGenWeb Digital Library (USGenWeb Archives™) (www.rootsweb.com/~usgenweb) project is an example of individual volunteers cooperating in digitizing historical documents and sharing them through the Web (www.rootsweb.com/~usgenweb).

Many guides and documents on the Web, and in print, aim to share standards and practices, assist libraries in creating their own digital collections, or to discuss the database software, metadata encoding and transmission or other technical issues (Cole, 2002; and Brancolini, 2002). Perhaps the best compilation of this type of information is Fred Stielow's *Building Digital Archives, Descriptions, and Displays: A How-To-Do-It Manual for Archivists and Librarians*, because it puts all the best information together in a clear and usable format.

E-LIBRARY VIRTUAL REFERENCE SUCCESS STORIES

ASK-A-PRO VIRTUAL REFERENCE SERVICE

Cuyahoga County Public Library
Maple Heights Public Library
Maple Heights, Ohio, USA
www.cuyahogalibrary.org/researchinfo/AskaPro/AskaPro.htm

> Contact: Nancy Pazelt, Regional Adult Services Manager, Maple Heights Regional Library
> npazelt@cuyahoga.lib.oh.us (e-mail and chat reference service)

Ask-A-Pro is staffed by reference librarians at the Maple Heights Regional Library, but serves all patrons of the Cuyahoga County Public Library (CCPL). The CCPL serves a population of nearly a million people with thirty-one locations in forty-seven Cuyahoga County (Ohio) communities. CCPL

> "is one of the 10 busiest library systems in the US and of these, has the highest per capita circulation. The Library has earned a national reputation for innovative programs and

services, many of which have become models for libraries across the nation." (www.cuyahogalibrary.org/aboutlibrary/about.htm)

"At the end of our first year, we will review and evaluate the Ask-A-Pro service to determine if it will continue to be handled by one regional or if the other three regionals will cover their own subject specialties."

Ask-a-Pro was created to serve patrons using CCPL's catalog and *remote* licensed databases. It also serves anyone with a Web connected computer who needs reference assistance. Nancy Pazelt reports that the service is very popular during the day when it is used by elementary and secondary school students, while they are doing their homework in study halls or other periods when they are in classrooms with Web connected computers.

"Ask-a-Pro uses the LSSI Virtual Reference software. They pay for use of up to 6 seats at one time and for six hundred after hours reference questions per year. This after hours reference service is staffed by the LSSI Virtual Reference center (http://vrs.lssi.com). We used 500 in the first seven months and most (1/3) of those came during two months when patrons were asking how to use our new catalog system."

On the Ask-A-Pro screen, patrons have the option to ask their questions *through virtual reference or e-mail*. The initial login screen requests the patron's name and e-mail address. Patrons are not required to use either their real name or a valid e-mail address, so they may choose to be anonymous. If the patron does supply a valid e-mail address they automatically receive a transcript of the reference transaction via e-mail.

Rather than assigning specific librarians to staff the virtual reference desk, all librarians take turns staffing. Some are more positive about virtual reference service than others, but all are learning and doing a great job. Five of the librarians staffing Ask-a-Pro went through formal LSSI

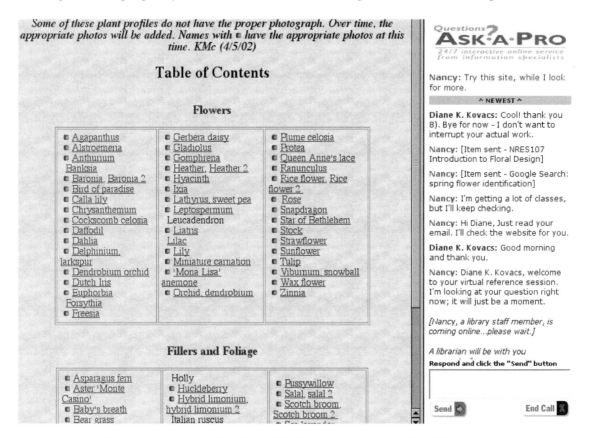

Figure 1.2.1. Ask-A-Pro Virtual Reference Service Session Windows

VRS training and the rest were trained one-on-one with an experienced virtual librarian. E-mail reference services are staffed in the same way—whomever is on reference duty at the time the question is received is expected to research and reply to the patron or refer the question as appropriate.

Ask-a-Pro librarians collaborate with each other in answering "tough" reference questions much the same way they do for in-person reference questions. If the librarian on duty with Ask-a-Pro needs to refer the question, he or she types in that information for the patron and then either asks another librarian to assist, or refers the patron to other sources of reference assistance. Particularly in the case of genealogy questions, librarians recommend that patrons contact the Fairview Park Regional Library and give them that library's telephone number. Similar policies exist for other subject areas that are challenging to answer remotely, such as medical, or legal questions. Ask-a-Pro reference librarians share a list of appropriate response messages for a variety of situations, including a response that politely advises the patron: "Reference librarians can answer many questions and direct you to other information sources, but we cannot give advice on this subject." Other messages include the offer to work with them on the telephone and techniques to cope with patrons who use obscene language. The latter has not been any more of a problem than it has been for telephone reference. Other messages convey that the patron may want to use e-mail or that the question may take a long time to answer.

Ask-a-Pro librarians share answers to frequently asked reference questions and current homework problems between them in much the same way as similar sharing takes place at the physical reference desk. Much information sharing takes place by making bookmarks or shortcuts on the reference desk computer. Plans for the future include doing this sharing more formally.

Librarians can display most free Web sites, and any Web-accessible databases with which the CCPL has a licensing arrangement that allows patron access outside of physical library locations. These sites are displayed in the patron's Web browser window in a frame adjacent to the chat interaction. Librarians are able to cut and paste information from electronic databases to the patron in the chat window. This has obvious advantages over telephone reference. Patrons who do not have printers or valid e-mail addresses will still have to take notes.

Ask-a-Pro librarians report the main limitation is the time lag between questions, responses, and answers when there is no visual communication to let the patron know that the librarian is working on their problem. From another point of view, the librarian cannot see the patron to determine age/grade level of the materials required, the urgency of the question, or the patrons' reactions to responses without asking specifically. A technical limitation is that the LSSI software requires that the patron go into their Web browser preferences and disable JAVA. For some, this would make access difficult.

Ask-a-Pro also keeps statistics on the times, and lengths of time transactions take place. Transcripts are analyzed to identify ways of improving services. Patrons (not librarians) have an opportunity to complete a survey on how they viewed the reference transaction and outcome. The Patron Satisfaction Survey (PaSS)™ comes on the customers screen after both parties logoff. It gives patrons an opportunity to evaluate the service and to suggest changes.

KnowItNow24x7

CLEVNET Library Consortium
Cleveland Public Library
Cleveland, Ohio, USA
www.knowitnow24x7.net

> Contact: Penny O'Connor, Assistant Head Science and Technology (poconnor@cpl.org); Tracy R. Strobel, Web Applications Supervisor (tstrobel@cpl.org); Nina Fried, Head of General Reference (Nina.Fried@cpl.org); and Bob

Murnan, Cleveland Research Center (robert.murnan@cpl.org) (e-mail and chat reference services)

KnowItNow24x7 celebrates its second birthday in 2003. Between June, 2001 and June, 2003, KnowItNow24x7 librarians have answered more than 45,000 reference questions for the patrons of CLEVNET library consortium members. (www.cpl.org/Locations.asp?FormMode =CLEVNETmap). Beginning in 2003, KnowItNow24x7 also serves patrons of the Worthington, Grandview Heights, and Upper Arlington Public Libraries in Central Ohio, as well as the Dayton Metro and Green County Public Libraries. Any patron of any of a member library may make use of the KnowItNow24x7 service by typing in the zip code of their community of residence into the opening page.

KnowItNow24x7 was created to serve library patrons using CLEVNET services remotely. It also serves anyone with a Web connected computer, who needs reference assistance.

> "KnowItNow24x7 is part of an integrated web presence. It reinforces the reference and research role of the Library. We are reaching out to a new group of users. HomeworkNow (www.HomeworkNow.net), Yread (www.yread.org), and the Tutor.com (www.tutor.com) projects are designed to reach future library patrons." (O'Connor, 2003)

Welcome to the CLEVNET Library Consortium's live online reference service, **KnowItNow24x7**. We unite the information expertise of librarians, the comprehensive resources of the CLEVNET libraries and advanced technology to meet your information needs whenever you need it, wherever you are.

Enter your zip code: [   ] CONNECT

KnowItNow24x7 serves Cuyahoga County, Ohio and the communities of the CLEVNET Libraries. Click here to learn about other participating Ohio libraries.

Now with Health & Medical Information from **The MetroHealth*Line*** !

Looking for homework help? Try **HomeworkNow**.

Click here to learn more about KnowItNow24x7.

Figure 1.2.2. KnowItNow24x7 Virtual Reference Service www.knowitnow24x7.net

CLEVNET includes thirty-one library systems (including the Cleveland Public Library) in nine counties throughout Northern Ohio. Since 1982, CLEVNET member libraries have cooperated in reciprocal borrowing, computer network sharing, and in combining their buying power for licensing online databases accessible to all library cardholders. CLEVNET serves 1.3 million library cardholders.

KnowItNow24x7 is staffed during the day by Cleveland Public Library subject specialists and staffed in rotation by librarians from eleven other CLEVNET libraries from 5:30–8:30 p.m. and on some weekday afternoons. After hours reference questions are handled by the LSSI Virtual Reference center (http://vrs.lssi.com).

Patrons may choose from available subject librarians or choose "General Reference." "Health and Medicine" questions may be transferred to registered nurses staffing the MetroHealthLine nurse service twenty-four hours per day seven days per week. MetroHealthLine nurses handle health questions that might be personal or require medical advice. MetroHealthLine has its own disclaimer and procedures for login.

Only the subject areas available at a given time are displayed as choices when a patron connects. Subject reference choices for the patron may include:

- General Reference
- Health and Medicine
- Science and Technology
- Cleveland Law Library (9 a.m.–5 p.m., Monday-Friday)
- Social Sciences
- Business, Economics, and Labor

Patrons beginning with "General Reference" may also have their questions referred to specialist librarians in specific subject area when these are available. Patron may also choose to connect directly to the HomeworkNow (www.homeworknow.net) service that is staffed by librarians specializing in helping with homework questions. HomeworkNow also offers live, online professional tutors from 2:00-10:00 p.m. seven days per week through Tutor.com (www.tutor.com). The Yread.org online book discussion for young adults is another option (www.yread.org). Tutor.com requires an additional login.

Cleveland Public Library (CPL) participates in the QuestionPoint collaborative reference service developed by the Library of Congress and OCLC (www.questionpoint.org/web/about). The Cleveland Research Center at CPL coordinates QuestionPoint referred questions, and it also refers questions to other QuestionPoint participants if needed. The Cleveland Research Center also serves as a resource library for ExpertRef, a fee-based service offered by LSSI

"QuestionPoint and ExpertRef questions come via e-mail to CPL. These are questions that were judged to need in-depth research or in-depth resources not available at the library where the question originated. That library sets a time frame on the question. The staff of Cleveland Research Center, Bob Murnan backed up by Pam Benjamin and Nina Fried in General Reference, receive these questions, decide to answer them or to pass them on to other libraries. QuestionPoint questions are filtered through a system which sends questions to resource libraries based on a collection profile."

KnowItNow24x7 uses the LSSI Virtual Reference software (www.vrtoolkit.net). They pay for a certain number of seats on the system per year and for after-hours reference service that is staffed by LSSI Virtual Reference center (http://vrs.lssi.com). KnowItNow24x7 librarians answer nearly four thousand questions per month during the school year and nearly two thousand questions per month during the summer. The number of questions varies by subject area and by time of day.

Between June, 2001 and Februrary, 2003 KnowItNow24x7 questions were answered by subject area and seat, as follows:

CPL—General Reference	24%
LSSI	23%
CPL—Science and Technology	17%
CLEVNET Member Libraries	15%
CPL—Social Sciences	13%
CPL—Business, Economics, and Labor	5%
Cleveland Law Library	2%
MetroHealthLine	1%

(O'Connor, 2003)

The number of questions answered by KnowItNow24x7 is growing but still represents a small part of member library reference question totals.

Patrons also have the option to ask their questions through e-mail, telephone, or are invited to visit their local library. The chat login screen (after the patron has typed in an appropriate zip code) requests the patron's name and e-mail address. Patrons are not required to use either their real name or a valid e-mail address, so they may choose to be anonymous. A patron who supplies a valid e-mail address automatically receives a transcript of the reference transaction via e-mail. If a librarian finds additional information, or if the question requires extended research, that information is forwarded to the patron (if the patron has supplied a valid e-mail address).

Sixty KnowItNow24x7 librarians received a week of training from LSSI staff, with support from Tracy Strobel and Pam Benjamin from CPL. This original group then provided training one-on-one with their coworkers. Librarians had a week of practice using the KnowItNow24x7 system before it went live. Refresher training, and training of new librarians is continuous. Specialized training is arranged for new services (e.g., Tutor.com). Future training will include development of guidelines for handling inappropriate patron behavior.

E-mail reference services are also offered. A librarian in the Automation or the Planning and Research Department reviews each e-mail and forwards to the subject departments as appropriate. Subject reference librarians try to respond within twenty-four hours.

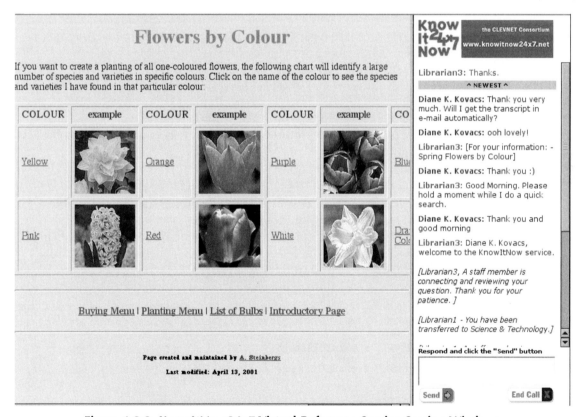

Figure 1.2.3. KnowItNow24x7 Virtual Reference Service Session Windows

KnowItNow24x7 librarians collaborate with each other in answering "tough" reference questions much the same way they do for in-person reference questions. If the librarian on duty with KnowItNow24x7 needs to refer the question, he or she types in that information for the patron, and then either asks another librarian to assist, or refers the patron to other sources of reference assistance. KnowItNow24x7 librarians informally share answers to frequently asked reference questions through shared bookmarks, e-mail, telephone, reference meetings, and the like. Plans for the future include doing this sharing more formally in a frequently asked questions type of knowledge base. The CPL and CLEVNET shared databases and Links Library serve as a knowledge base as well.

Librarians can display most free Web sites, and some proprietary Web-accessible databases if CLEVNET (or their local library) has a licensing arrangement, which allows patron access outside of physical library locations. These sites are displayed in the patron's Web browser window in a frame adjacent to the chat interaction (See Figure 1.2.3). Print reference sources are the best way to answer many questions and the system allows the librarian to display scanned images of print sources or to cut and paste information from print sources and from electronic databases to the patron in the chat window. This has obvious advantages over telephone reference. Patrons who do not have printers or valid e-mail addresses will still have to take notes.

Limitations of virtual reference service include:

- the time lag between questions, responses, and answers when there is no visual communication to let the patron know that the librarian is working on their problem.

- the librarian cannot see the patron to determine age/grade level of the materials required, the urgency of the question, or the patrons' reactions to responses without asking specifically asking.

The LSSI software requires that the patron go into their Web browser preferences and disable JAVA. For some, this would make access difficult. Another technical problem is what staff call "framebuster sites." These are Web sites that cause the chat session to close, lock up the patron's or the librarian's browser, or otherwise interfere with a smooth reference transaction.

From the librarian side of the transaction, each workstation is equipped identically. Workstations are equipped with an HP Scanjet Scanner. Each workstation is running Windows 2000, the LSSI Virtual Reference toolkit, Adobe Capture, Internet Explorer, as well as Netscape Navigator. This helps to ensure that technical and software training is consistent and that trouble-shooting of problems is consistent between KnowItNow24x7 libraries.

Reference librarians review and monitor transcripts for insight into how the patron interview and reference process is working.

The library has many plans for extending KnowItNow24x7.

"The future of KnowItNow24x7 includes the addition of ReadThisNow—Reader advisory Service and United Way's First Call for Help REFER database as a second tier referral, in the same way that MetroHealth, Cleveland Law Library, and Tutor.com are used. United Way's First Call For Help, Refer database can connect customers to more than 1,000 agencies, 4,000 programs, and 10,000 services. Other future projects include: Spanish version of KnowItNow24x7." (O'Connor, 2003)

KnowItNow24x7 is also planning for participation in a statewide service and extending marketing of the service. ReadThisNow, a 24x7 online readers` advisory service will also go online July 1, 2003.

ASK-A-LIBRARIAN/CHAT WITH A LIBRARIAN

Kent State University Libraries and Media Services/OhioLINK
Kent, Ohio, USA
www.library.kent.edu/reference/equest.html

> Contact: Leela Balraj, Information Services Librarian, lbalraj@lms.kent.edu (e-mail and chat reference services)

Ask-A-Librarian was created to serve students, faculty, and staff of Kent State University who use the library's services remotely. Kent State's Ask-A-Librarian is a gateway to the OhioLINK library consortium's Chat with a Librarian service. Any student, faculty, or staff member of any OhioLINK member library may make use of the Chat with a Librarian service by typing in their username, institution, and student or faculty identification number through either the OhioLINK main page or their own library's page. The Chat with a Librarian chat box is not visible until after a successful login.

Regional Campuses
Kent State University

Ask A Librarian:
8-Campus Reference Service on the Web

Have a question? Need help with a project? Here's how you can reach us...

 • **Live chat:** Check out our new online service - chat with a librarian online!
First time users click here...

• **By e-mail:** E-mail our librarians with your question and receive a response within 2 working days.

• **In person:** Visit our libraries at the Kent Campus, Branch and Regional libraries during reference desk hours.

• **By phone:** Call our librarians at the Kent Campus, Branch and Regional libraries during reference desk hours.

Figure 1.2.4. OhioLINK/Kent State University Virtual Reference Services
www.library.kent.edu/reference/equest.html

"The Ohio Library and Information Network, OhioLINK, is a consortium of Ohio's college and university libraries and the State Library of Ohio. Serving more than 500,000 students, faculty, and staff at 80 institutions, OhioLINK's membership includes 17 public universities, 23 community/technical colleges, 39 private colleges and the State Library of Ohio. OhioLINK serves faculty, students, staff and other researchers at member institutions via 120 campus-based library systems and networks, and the Internet." (www.ohiolink.edu/about/what-is-ol.html)

Chat with a Librarian is staffed by librarians from more than forty of the OhioLINK institutions, including Kent State University. Additional campuses will also staff the service in the near future. The GroopZ software is used for the interaction. Librarians may work from any location with an Internet connection. GroopZ software runs on both Windows and Mac OS. Currently the Chat with a Librarian service is staffed Monday-Thursday 9 a.m.–10 p.m., Friday, 9 a.m.–5 p.m., Saturday 1 p.m.–5 p.m., and Sunday 1 p.m.–10 p.m. during the academic year. If the service is not available the option will not display; alternative reference options are displayed instead.

Students, faculty, or staff members (patrons for short), also have the option to ask their questions through e-mail, telephone, or are invited to visit their local library.

Chat with a Librarian is an example of the shifted librarian concept discussed in Part I, Chapter 1. Librarians are shifting our services to where our patrons are looking for information.

"The advent of new technology has required today's librarians to adjust reference services to meet the needs of library users who no longer physically come into the library. Reaching out to off-site users includes the use of both synchronous and asynchronous modes of reference service. Kent State University Libraries has explored several methods of virtual reference services including Ask-A-Librarian e-mail services, video/audio conferencing and a statewide chat service initiative." (Balraj, 2003).

While the video/audio conferencing seemed like a neat idea it was very limited in how it could be used. The technology requirements were difficult to manage and training of librarians required a great deal of time and effort.

The GroopZ chat software, by contrast, has a very straightforward training requirement. In fact, the authors were able to download and install it using instructions from OhioLINK, and were able to staff the virtual reference service all within about fifteen minutes. Kara L. Robinson is a reference librarian at Kent State University, who did two shifts on the virtual reference desk while Diane K. Kovacs observed. From the librarian point of view it is possible to see who else is logged on as a librarian and to see where someone is connecting from when they click on the Chat with a Librarian link.

Librarians who respond to Chat with a Librarian inquiries collaborate with each other in answering "tough" reference questions, much the same way they do for in-person reference questions. If the librarian on duty with Chat with a Librarian needs to refer the question, he or she types in that information for the patron, and then either asks another librarian to assist, or refers the patron to other sources of reference assistance. Chat with a Librarian staff members informally share answers to frequently asked reference questions through e-mail, telephone, reference meetings, and the like. Plans for the future include doing this sharing more formally in a frequently asked questions type of knowledge base. The OhioLINK shared databases serve as a knowledge base as well.

Patrons are asked to complete an evaluation survey after the transaction. Patron feedback is used to assess and improve service. The OhioLINK chat survey is available at http://olc6 .ohiolink.edu/survey and Kent State's Email-A-Librarian survey is at http://ctlsilhouette.ctlt .wsu.edu/CTLSilhouette2_5/mode/respondent/takeHTMLsurvey.asp?s=zs9155.

Librarians can display most free Web sites, and any Web-accessible databases that OhioLINK has a licensing arrangement with for remote patron access. These sites are displayed in the patron's Web browser window in a frame behind the chat interaction. This has obvious advantages over telephone reference. The librarian can talk the patron through using the database since both can see the same screens. Limited co-browsing is available as well.

The reference interview is the most important skill required for Chat with a Librarian reference librarians. Training has included discussion of the skills required to search quickly and efficiently, but also to evaluate the reference interview as it moves along to respond effectively to the patron's question or make appropriate referrals. Other training has discussed the differences between in-person and virtual reference and some strategies for coping with these limitations, as well as making the most of advantages in each reference situation. Figure 1.2.5 is a transcript of session between one of the authors and Chat with a Librarian Reference Librarian Chris Sheetz, from Lorain County Community College, an OhioLINK member library.

Figure 1.2.5. Transcript of Chat with a Librarian Virtual Reference Session.

Following is the transcript of your interactive session with a librarian, as you requested.

Chris@Lorain: Hello, this is Chris from the Lorain County Community College. How may I help you?

Diane K. Kovacs: Good morning Chris, Is there a Web site I can use to identify spring flowers in my yard? (I'm writing about Ask-A-Librarian and am just stepping through the system—so stop me if you are busy—Thank you!

Chris@Lorain: Hi Diane! I admit, my stomach did a flip when I saw your name! I'm not busy, so I'll be happy to help.

Diane K. Kovacs: golly I don't want to inspire that kind of reaction ;).

Chris@Lorain: I'd try co-browsing with you, but it doesn't work reliably with Macs

Chris@Lorain: So instead I'll push you some pages

Diane K. Kovacs: Is it usual for people on Netscape /Mac to have trouble connecting? I switched to IE and it works now.

Diane K. Kovacs: Co-browsing isn't necessary. Leela Balraj warned me it was iffy.

Chris@Lorain: Actually, I think you are the first person I've helped who has been on a Mac

Chris@Lorain: I'm going to try to find you some web sites

Diane K. Kovacs: Ah 8). I know that some of the librarian's at Kent are working from Macs so I'll ask them. Thank you I'd like to see the push pages thingy.

Chris@Lorain: I'm going to "push" (send) a web page to your computer. It should appear in a separate window on your screen.

Chris@Lorain: Pushed <http://www.google.com/search?hl=en&ie=UTF-8&oe=UTF-8&q=wildflower+identification>http://www.google.com/search?hl=en&ie=UTF-8&oe=UTF-8&q=wildflower+identification

Chris@Lorain: Did you get that page? If you don't see it, it might have appeared in a window which is not your top window.

Diane K. Kovacs: Got it! This is neat—like the tool I use for Web teaching in WebCT

Chris@Lorain: The students love it — it is really neat to have the info suddenly appear.

Chris@Lorain: Co-browsing is even better, because I can take control of your machine, or you could take control of mine.—Kinda eerie!!

Diane K. Kovacs: This is fairly fast too…not a lot of lag even at this time of morning. Do you like doing reference this way?

Chris@Lorain: Love it! It really stretches my reference interview skills

Chris@Lorain: And when I get a call, I am totally absorbed—mentally (can't think fast enough!), physically (can't type fast enough!)

Diane K. Kovacs: My mom and dad in law are sort of students of yours. They are in some sort of seniors program with exercise etc. Though my Dad-in-law takes classes on and off. He'll love this.

Chris@Lorain: Send him on—I love the questions I get—you never know where they willtake you

Diane K. Kovacs: Sounds like regular reference—it is so easy to get caught up in the question—I miss reference myself. Teaching is almost the same at times but not really ;).

Diane K. Kovacs: Right now he's been doing tax preparation for seniors—he retired two years ago or so and he's now working just on stuff he likes to do.

Chris@Lorain: Reference still has the thrill of the hunt—and after several years at the desk with the same assignments, it feels good to get some new questions

Chris@Lorain: That's the life—only doing what you like to do !!

Diane K. Kovacs: Okay Let me test the system ;). I want to ask a question that has to use the fee databases... So can you tell me if there are any articles on Virtual Reference/Digital Reference full-text published this year and in peer-reviewed journals? Ignore if you get busy.

Chris@Lorain: OK, first off—are you on campus or at home now?

Diane K. Kovacs: or refer me as you would someone else asking the same question for real. I'm in my home-office—I can get to EbscoHost and LibraryLit (Kara Robinson and I are working ont his book together)

Chris@Lorain: What I would do for a student is push them the Academic Search Premier search page, like this ...

Chris@Lorain: Pushed <http://web2.epnet.com/search.asp?tb=1&_ug=dbs+0+ln+en%2Dus+sid+3FDF2C02%2DB249%2D4FC3%2DA4D9%2DA1BEA2F0D50F%40Sessionmgr6+53BD&_us=ex+default+hs+0+sm+ES+ss+SO+26D3&newsrch=1>http://web2.epnet.com/search.asp?tb=1&_ug=dbs+0+ln+en%2Dus+sid+3FDF2C02%2DB249%2D4FC3%2DA4D9%2DA1BEA2F0D50F%40Sessionmgr6+53BD&_us=ex+default+hs+0+sm+ES+ss+SO+26D3&newsrch=1

Chris@Lorain: let me know when you get it

Diane K. Kovacs: Got it! Thank you 8)

Diane K. Kovacs: Then you'd talk them through the search—Do you have to warn them that the GroopZ window will go behind at times? Is that a problem in general?

Chris@Lorain: Great! Now type "virtual reference" in the Find box

Diane K. Kovacs: ok

Chris@Lorain: Since you want full text, click the full text box

Diane K. Kovacs: ok

Chris@Lorain: and since you want "peer-reviewed", click the Scholarly Journals box—you may have to scroll down to see it below the full text box

Chris@Lorain: Then click on search—I found 8 articles

Chris@Lorain: How many did you get?

Diane K. Kovacs: ok found it—I found just 1 but I skipped ahead and put 2003 in the year box.

Chris@Lorain: Ah—you are a good student—most students wouldn't do that!!

Diane K. Kovacs: Thank you ;). I can see that you are Chris@lorain and I think I must know you? Would you be okay if I mention your name in the text when I talk about this?

Diane K. Kovacs: Or would it be okay to just say Chris@lorain? If you share an e-mail address I'll let you read the write-up—Leela Balraj will also review it as I'm using a lot from her NORASIST presentation.

Chris@Lorain: No I don't think you know me—but what librarian doesn't know of you! Feel free to use my name, I am Chris Sheetz and I'm at Lorain County community College. My e-mail is <http://csheetz@lorainccc.edu>csheetz@lorainccc.edu

Chris@Lorain: Also, when you leave, you will be sent an web-based survey about the service

Diane K. Kovacs: Thank you 8).. lI think the librarians in tech services at OSU think I'm a telemarketer ;).

Chris@Lorain: Would you like me to send a transcript of this chat session to you by e-mail?

Diane K. Kovacs: Thank you Chris, I really appreciate your time. I will complete the survey. Yes please I would like a transcript—does it come automatically?

Chris@Lorain: i have to tell it to be sent, I have your e-mail address as <http://diane@kovacs.com.> diane@kovacs.com. Is that correct?

Diane K. Kovacs: Yes that is correct.

Chris@Lorain: OK, watch your e-mail. It was fun chatting with you—I look forward to seeing the article!

Diane K. Kovacs: Thank you and Have a great morning! Bye.

Thanks for using our service.

REFERENCES

American Library Association. Joint Steering Committee for Revision of AACR. 2002. *Anglo-American Cataloguing Rules*. 2nd ed, 2002 revision. Ottawa: Canadian Library Association / London: Chartered Institute of Library and Information Professionals / Chicago: American Library Association.

Balas, J. 2003. Is the Reference Librarian Real or Virtual. *Computers in Libraries* 23, no. 4 (April): 48–51.

Balraj, L. 2003. Digital Reference in Action: Perspectives from Kent State. NORASIST presentation, April 3, 2003, at Kent State University School of Library and Information Science. Available: www.library.kent.edu/%7Elbalraj/norasist_files/frame.htm.

Berman, S. 2000. Why Catalog? *The Unabashed Librarian—Berman's Bag*. no. 116: 11. Available: http://web.library.uiuc.edu/ahx/ala/ccard/ALAControlCard.asp?RG=97&SG=1&RS=40.

Brancolini, K. R. 2002. Selecting Research Collections for Digitization: Applying the Harvard Model. *Library Trends* 48, no. 4 (Spring): 783–98.

Bromberg, P. 2003. Managing a Statewide Virtual Reference Service: How Q and A NJ Works. *Computers in Libraries* (April): 27–31, www.qandanj.org.

Cole, T. W. 2002. Creating a Framework of Guidance for Building Good Digital Collections. *First Monday* 7, no. 5, http://firstmonday.dk/issues/issue7_5/cole/index.html.

Curtis, D., ed. 2002. *Attracting, Educating and Serving Remote Users Through the Web*. New York: Neal-Schuman.

Digital Library Forum. 2001. A Framework of Guidance for Building Good Digital Collections. Institute of Museum and Library Services. www.imls.gov/pubs/forumframework.htm.

Dillon, M., et al. 1993. *Assessing Information on the Internet: Toward Providing Library Services for Computer-Communications*. Dublin, OH: OCLC Online Computer Library Center.

Fiander, D. J. 2001. Applying XML to the Bibliographic Description. *Cataloging and Classification Quarterly* 33, no. 2:17–28, www.catalogingandclassificationquarterly.com/ccq33nr2.html.

IFLA Study Group on the Functional Requirements for Bibliographic Records. 1998. Functional Requirements for Bibliographic Records. International Federation of Library Associations and Institutions (IFLA). www.ifla.org/VII/s13/frbr/frbr.htm.

Lam, K. T. 2001 (1998). Moving from MARC to XML. http://ihome.ust.hk/~lblkt/xml/marc2xml.html.

Lipow, A. G. 2002. *The Virtual Reference Librarian's Handbook*. Berkely: Library Solutions Press / New York: Neal-Schuman.

Manoff, M. 2002. Hybridity, Mutability, Multiplicity: Theorizing Electronic Library Collections. *Library Trends* 48, no. 4 (Spring): 857–76.

Maurer, M. 2003. AACR2 2002—The Year We Describe the Integrating Resource. *TechKNOW* 9, no. 1: 5–8, www.olc.org/pdf/Techknow_Feb03.pdf.

Meola, M., and S. Stormont. 2002. *Starting and Operating Live Virtual Reference Services: A How-to-do-it Manual for Librarians*. New York: Neal-Schuman.

Miller, D. R. 2000. XML and MARC: A Choice or Replacement? Presentation at the MARBI/CC:DA Joint Meeting, American Library Association, Chicago. http://elane.stanford.edu/laneauth/ALAChicago2000.html.

O'Connor, P. 2003. KnowItNow24x7—2 years of digital reference for CLEVNET. NORASIST presentation, April 3, 2003, at Kent State University School of Library and Information Science. Available: www.slis.kent.edu/~norasis/Penny.ppt.

Olsen, N. B. 2003. *Cataloging Internet Resources*. 2nd ed. Dublin, OH: OCLC Online Computer Library Center. www.oclc.org/oclc/man/9256cat/toc.htm.

Rosenfeld, L., and P. S. Morville. 2002. *Information Architecture for the World Wide Web*. 2nd ed. Sebastapol, CA: O'Reilly and Associates.

Schuyler, M. 2003. You Can't Disintermediate the Great Intermediaries. *Computers in Libraries* 23, no. 4 (April): 42–43.

Smith, L. C. 2002. Education for Digital Reference Services. White Paper prepared for the Digital Reference Research Symposium, Harvard University, Cambridge, MA, August 2–3.

Stielow, F. 2003. *Building Digital Archives, Descriptions, and Displays: A How-To-Do-It Manual for Archivists and Librarians*. New York: Neal-Schuman.

Tenant, R. 2002. MARC Must Die. *Library Journal Online* (December 15, 2002), http://libraryjournal.reviewsnews.com/index.asp?layout=article&articleid=CA250046&publication=libraryjournal.

Vizine-Goetz, D. 2002. Using Library Classification Schemes for Internet Resources. www.oclc.org/research/publications/default.htm or http://www.haworthpress.com/store/toc/htmv/J141v05n04_TOC.htm.

Weber, M. B. 2002. *Cataloging Nonprint and Internet Resources: A How-To-Do-It Manual for Librarians*. New York: Neal-Schuman.

Weitz, J. 2002. Cataloging Electronic Resources: OCLC-MARC Coding Guidelines. www.oclc.org/support/documentation/worldcat/cataloging/electronicresources.

WEB SITES CITED

(Note that some sites are included in the resource lists and webliographies in subsequent chapters, and therefore are not necessarily duplicated in this section.)

ALA/MARS—Draft Virtual Reference Guidelines. Available: www.ala.org/Content/NavigationMenu/RUSA/Our_Association2/RUSA_Sections/MARS/Our_Section3/Committees14/Draft_Virtual_Reference_Guidelines.htm.

American Memory Project. Available: http://memory.loc.gov.

Bibliographic Formats and Standards: Special Cataloging Guidelines. Available: www.oclc.org/bibformats/en/specialcataloging. Bibliographic Formats and Standards [OCLC—Support]. Available: www.oclc.org/bibformats/en.

Cataloging, Identifiers, Linking, and Metadata. Available: http://info.lib.uh.edu/sepb/rcat.htm.

Cataloging: Organizing Internet Resources: Non-Cataloging Approach. Available: www.itcompany.com/inforetriever/catinet1.htm.

Dig_Ref discussion list archives. Available: http://vrd.org/Dig_Ref/dig_ref.shtml, http://groups.yahoo.com/group/dig_ref.

The Digital Library Federation (DLF). Available: www.diglib.org.

DSpace Federation. Available: www.dspace.org.

Dublin Core/MARC/GILS Crosswalk. Available: http://lcweb.loc.gov/marc/dccross.html.

Dublin Core Element Set, Version 1.0—Reference Description. Available: http://dublincore.org/documents/1998/09/dces/#.

firstfind.info project. Available: www.firstfind.info.

LSSI Virtual Reference Center. Available: http://vrs.lssi.com.

LSSI's Virtual Reference software. Available: www.vrtoolkit.net.

MALVINE—Manuscripts and Letters via Integrated Networks in Europe. Available: www.malvine.org.

Medlane Project. Available: http://laneweb.stanford.edu:2380/wiki/medlane/overview.

Mid-Illinois Talking Book Center. Available: www.mitbc.org, www.mitbc.org/ref.shtml.

OCLC Scorpion project. Available: http://orc.rsch.oclc.org:6109.

OhioLINK. Available: www.ohiolink.edu.

Ohio Memory Project. Available: www.ohiomemory.org.

Open Archives Initiative (OAI). Available: www.openarchives.org.

O'Reilly XML.com, What is XML. Available: www.xml.com/pub/a/98/10/guide1.html#AEN58.

QuestionPoint software. Available: http://questionpoint.org.

The Teaching Librarian. Available: www.teachinglibrarian.org.

USGenWeb Digital Library (USGenWeb Archives TM) Project. Available: www.rootsweb.com/~usgenweb.

XMLMARC. Available: http://laneweb.stanford.edu:2380/wiki/medlane/xmlmarc.

SEE ALSO PART III: WEB COLLECTION DEVELOPMENT RESOURCES:

Resource List 1: Collection Development Related Discussion Lists, Newsgroups, and Blogs, for discussion lists, newsgroups, e-serials and other resources cited in this chapter, and Resource List 2: Evaluation Guides

3:   Licensing Basics

"All electronic resources a library offers must begin with a license agreement that identifies how the library and its users may use the content. Achieving the terms and services that best meet the needs of your users is fundamental to creating and maintaining a strong virtual library."

Metzinger Miller (2003: 20)

INTRODUCTION

Given that more and more of the content on the Web is being offered by commercial vendors for a fee, understanding licensing of that content is key in developing electronic libraries. Even free Web-accessible resources may require the library to agree to a license. In this environment, librarians who build e-library collections, even if they are not the individuals directly responsible for negotiating and signing the licenses, need to become familiar with licensure issues and terminology. Being able to identify the limitations and restrictions inherent in license agreements is essential in making selection decisions. Developing definitions for license terms, such as, "authorized user," helps greatly to clarify the needs of the library and the goals to be met by the electronic library.

In this chapter, we provide a basic introduction to licensing concepts that impact how you will make selection decisions. This chapter does not attempt to teach all of the intricacies of licenses and their negotiation, numerous resources already exist, which do a more thorough job of that. If you will be responsible for negotiating the contracts, as well as selecting the resources, please seek out additional information. Books such as *Interpreting and Negotiating License Agreements*, by Bielefield and Cheeseman (1999), and *Licensing Digital Content*, by Harris (2000), as well as *De-Mystifying the Licensing of Electronic Resources*, which is the video and accompanying workbook of a 1999 teleconference cosponsored by the Association of Research Libraries and Special Library Association. All of these are very good resources for more in-depth discussions of licensing. Consulting legal counsel is also advisable.

The American Heritage Dictionary of the English Language, Fourth Edition defines license as "Official or legal permission to do or own a specified thing" (http://dictionary.reference.com/search?q=license). Generally, the term license is used to refer to the agreement requiring commitment of time and/or money on the part of a licensee to use or access a resource, and on the part of the licensor to provide defined access to a resource with specific content and format. Any agreement between the licensee and a resource supplier (licensor) is, under this definition, a license. This agreement could be something as simple as the free registration required by some sites, the click-through agreement required before using new software or accessing a Web site, or something as complex as the contract between a large consortium with multiple users and sites and a major database vendor.

REVIEW OF RECENT LITERATURE ON LICENSING WEB-ACCESSIBLE RESOURCES

As the licensing of Web-accessible resources becomes commonplace, more and more is being published on the topic. Numerous books and articles have been written which serve as a solid introduction to the topic. Keep in mind that the majority of these resources are written for an audience that requires in-depth information regarding licensing, though a librarian who selects e-resources (a selector) may find something of interest in most of them.

Metzinger Miller's 2003 article, "Behind Every Great Virtual Library Stand Many Great Licenses," discusses how some of the most important characteristics of e-libraries can complicate license negotiations. Among the factors that a selector must consider are: "reaching a particular population...supporting distance education; and sustaining online education, including both web-based and web-enhanced courses." (Metzinger Miller, 2003: 20) Metzinger Miller takes examples of typical clauses in license agreements and uses them to demonstrate the questions that a library must answer, both in selecting a resource, and then negotiating for it. Of particular note for selectors are the samples that focus on "authorized users" and "remote sites." Both are key concerns and should be helping to drive any selection decisions.

In her book, *Licensing Digital Content*, Harris starts at the very beginning of the licensing process: when the librarian is selecting Web resources for an e-library. The first chapter revolves around the key question that every selector should ask when selecting a new resource: When to license? "Licensing comes into play when you want to use electronic or digital content such as a database or periodical, or when someone wants to use such content owned by your library." (Harris, 2002: 2) In Chapter 2, Harris points out twelve common misconceptions in the licensing process—misconceptions that librarians should be aware of when making selection decisions. Chapter 4 is extremely valuable, because it identifies and defines the key legal terms found in license agreements. In Chapter 7, Harris provides the equivalent of an FAQ for digital content licensing, including such common questions as, "What does 'third-party rights' mean?" and "May a license prohibit interlibrary loans?" (Harris, 2000: 104–5). An excellent glossary as well as a listing of additional resources to consult is provided.

Alford's article on "Negotiating and Analyzing Electronic License Agreements" (2002) also contains valuable content for both selectors and negotiators. Alford focuses on the licensing of legal information, though much of the content applies to nonlegal resources, as well. Selectors will find the "negotiating points" section useful for its identification and detailed analysis of topics that overlap the selection process. This section discusses issues such as price, users, access, types of use, and archiving. The article also includes a thorough discussion of the licensing principles endorsed by various groups, reviews of three different "standard" licenses and an introduction to UCITA, which is discussed in brief at the end of this chapter.

In *Selecting and Managing Electronic Resources*, Gregory (2000) provides a full and complete discussion of key issues for libraries selecting and managing electronic resources. Chapter 7 focuses entirely on the key issues of copyright and licensing agreements. This chapter makes an important distinction between "purchased" versus "licensed" content. This is a key issue when trying to determine the "fair use rights of the library purchaser, and regarding the library's long-term access to the material." (Gregory, 2000: 69) When making selection decisions, whether a purchase or a license would be of greater benefit to your institution is an essential question to answer. The list of best practice suggestions also provides a useful means of learning how other libraries are working through these issues. The parts of the chapter dealing with license negotiation, selecting a license negotiator and managing licenses are not essential reading, since they delve into administrative processes that may not pertain to the selecting librarian, but they do provide insight into the licensing process as a whole.

Metz (2000) discusses the transitions from the selection process to the licensing process. "In larger institutions, the move from the decision to collect to negotiations and the making of final arrangements signals a transfer of responsibility from the chief collection development officer to the head of library acquisitions. In smaller institutions, these roles are often combined in one person." (Metz, 2000: 718) Whether your role as a builder of electronic library collections also includes the negotiation of licensing agreements or not, this article will make you aware of the differences between how vendors define terms, such as, "authorized user," and how a particular library would. These issues can come into play during negotiations and can sometimes result in not being able to provide a resource you selected. Metz also discusses other areas of potential difficulty between vendor and library.

KEY TERMS

Librarians selecting Web-accessible resources will benefit from familiarity with some of the key terms that are standard in most licenses. Thinking of these legal terms in the context of your user population and needs is especially beneficial.

Authorized users—the individuals permitted within the scope of the license to use the resource. By preference, librarians will want this definition to be as broad as possible to permit access to the largest number of patrons; whereas, a vendor will be seeking a narrower range of users to limit access or will negotiate higher fees for broader authorized user definitions. For an academic institution, "users should at least include the current faculty, staff and students of the university. Distance education students, temporary researchers, and patrons walking into the library on campus should fall within the definition of 'users'." (Alford, 2002: 636)

Definitions—this is the most important clause in a licensing agreement, because it is where the agreed-to definitions of terms are spelled out. Though many selectors may not have a role in negotiating the terms of the license agreement, their input is still necessary to the process. Selectors must help identify the needs of the library's users as well as classifying those users. This process needs to begin long before any negotiations take place.

Fair Use—libraries will want to make sure that a license does not restrict Fair Use rights. "There should be no restrictions in the electronic license agreement that would be more restrictive than that provided under the copyright law for printed materials." (Alford, 2002: 636–37) In other words, if you select a resource, you want your patrons to be able to use it without having to worrying about excessive restrictions.

Rights Granted—this clause delineates which specific rights the library is granted as licensee. Printing and downloading are two of the rights that you should keep in mind when selecting. A Web resource that doesn't allow your users to print or download is probably not worth the effort to license.

Site—if dealing with a license where use is tied to a particular site (called a "site license"), the definition of this term is very important. Is it defined as a physical location, such as, a single building or a campus, or is it defined as an IP (Internet Protocol) address range or a geographical region; e.g., residents of a specific state (MeL) or of a zip code area (KnowItNow24x7)?

IMPORTANT LICENSE ISSUES

In addition to key terms, selectors must consider several other license-related issues.

Know your library's needs. Before selecting and licensing Web resources, establish and detail your library patron's information needs. "First ask yourself how you will be using this particular content in your library." (Harris, 2000: 12) Selectors should be asking that question about every resource chosen for an e-library, but it serves a double purpose when it comes time to negotiate a license. The answer to this question permits libraries to make certain that groups of users, such as, distance learning students, or types of use, electronic reserves for example, are not specifically excluded in the license agreement.

After selecting a resource, make "a list of all the things that you and your patrons might do with the journal or database." (Harris, 2000: 12) By doing so, you can arm the negotiator with the right type of knowledge. Remember that you selected the resource to make it available to your users. Creating a list makes it less likely you'll overlook rights and limits that are important to your users. For most libraries this list should include:

Archiving—what happens to licensed digital content when the license is concluded? "Archiving of materials previously licensed tends to decrease the amount of fees available under a license agreement." (Alford, 2002: 640) Not surprisingly, this is an issue where there is usually considerable disagreement between the library and the licensor.

Virtual Reference Service—can the resource be used to provide reference assistance to individuals who may not be physically present in the library?

Distance Learning Students—are there restrictions that might prohibit registered students from accessing the resource from off-campus?

E-Reserves—can the content be placed on reserve in either its electronic or print versions? A related question would be whether the material might be used in course packs.

Interlibrary Loan (ILL)—can the content from the resource be used to fill ILL requests?

Printing, Downloading, E-mailing—in what formats can the content be delivered for library patron use?

Examining licenses. It is likely that librarians may not be able to see in advance the license for a particular product. This is particularly true in the case of commercial resources where licenses are typically negotiated between the vendor and each individual institution. Since individualized negotiations are the norm, "numerous publishers include a nondisclosure provision in their contracts, especially in contracts negotiated with large institutions." (Alford, 2002: 630) They do this so that librarians at one institution cannot reveal the details of their deal to another. The selector must help the negotiator determine which are the "make or break" issues, a task complicated by not being able to see provisions in advance.

Click-through licenses. Some sites will have click-through licenses that librarians should review immediately and prior to completion of the click-through. A click-through agreement "requires users to affirmatively click on a button indicating their acceptance of the licensing agreement before they can install the software or view the information." (Harris, 2002: 126). If you select a resource that has a click-through agreement, be certain to take the time to know the provisions included with the license, as these are nonnegotiable. Once someone agrees, they are bound to the agreement as written. This is particularly necessary in libraries where Internet access is open. If a patron responds affirmatively to a click-through license, and then abuses the conditions therein, it is possible that the library may be held partially responsible.

OUTSIDE FACTORS THAT MAY AFFECT WEB-ACCESSIBLE RESOURCE LICENSES

When your library has selected a given Web resource and negotiated a workable license with the vendor, the process has only just begun. Other outside factors may change the content, format, or accessibility of the resource or change the legal status of the license after the fact. Librarians will want to be aware that this can happen and try to determine how such factors may affect the license or the Web resource. One example of an outside factor that changed the content and format of several Web resources was the court case *New York Times v. Tasini*. The case revolved around six freelance authors who sued the New York Times for licensing their articles to full-text vendors, such as LexisNexis, in violation of the authors' copyright. The court held that the authors were correct and as a result the articles in question were removed from a number of licensed resources.

Another outside factor capable of dramatically changing information sources is governmental action, either through policy or legislation. We have all seen this happen most recently through the government's decision to remove materials from their Web sites. In many of those cases, no alternative source of that information is available leaving an unfilled gap in many collections. Decisions to sell content that was previously available free of charge is another way in which the content, format, and accessibility of Web resources can change. Requiring libraries that had been getting materials for free to license them instead can dramatically modify the range of what a library can provide. The passage of legislation can have unexpected and problematic repercussions. Laws such as the Digital Millennium Copyright Act can transform a library's rights regarding information, while laws such as the USA Patriot Act can alter the relationship between libraries, their resources, and their patrons. All of these factors may affect the legal status of the license.

UCITA, the Uniform computer Information Transactions Act, is a proposed law, which if it is adopted more widely, will be a major source of headaches for libraries and others. "Librarians should be aware of how pervasive UCITA will be in their daily lives. Moreover, library administrators [and others] should be aware that there is a push in the digital information industry to have contracts control their products rather than copyright law." (Wyatt, 2002: 84) One of the problems of UCITA is that it would "allow software publishers to change the terms of the contract after purchase." (Computer Professionals for Social Responsibility www.cpsr.org/program/UCITA/ucita-fact.html) Even though UCITA has been adopted by only two states so far (Maryland and Virginia), it may affect some libraries' current licenses.

> "For example, many large software vendors and publishers are located in Virginia, and with UCITA's enactment in Virginia, its effects may be felt in states that have not passed UCITA through licensing contract provisions specifying the law of Virginia as being applicable to the license in question. If these 'choice of law' provisions become common and are ultimately upheld by the courts, many vendors and publishers could simply establish a presence in Virginia or Maryland (and any other state that adopts UCITA) in order to take advantage nationwide of the additional protections offered them by UCITA." (Gregory, 2001: 83)

Authors' Note: As this book was going to press, the National Conference of Commissioners on Uniform State Laws (NCCUSL) Executive Committee decided to discharge the UCITA Standby Drafting Committee and to stop spending any further resources in promoting the Act. (Press release: www.nccusl.org/nccusl/DesktopModules/NewsDisplay.aspx?ItemID=56) While this move does not eliminate the possibility of further adoption of UCITA by states, it may limit the chance for it to spread.

E-LIBRARY SUCCESS STORY

BIBLIOTECA DIGITAL DE CATALUNYA (BDC)

Consorci de Biblioteques Universitàries de Catalunya (CBUC)
Barcelona, Spain
www.cbuc.es

Contact: Núria Comellas, Librarian-Projects Assistant, ncomellas@cbuc.es, and Lluís Anglada, Director, langlada@cbuc.es

The Biblioteca Digital de Catalunya (BDC)—in English: Catalan Digital Library—is a shared, central e-library collection and union catalog for the eight academic library members of the Consorci de Biblioteques Universitàries de Catalunya (CBUC)—in English: Consortium of Catalan University Libraries. CBUC was formed in 1996 with an agreement between the eight Catalan academic libraries and the National Library of Catalonia to build a union catalog. As they implemented the union catalog plan, CBUC studied and demonstrated the potential benefits of purchasing equipment and central database licensing negotiation for the member libraries. In 1998, CBUC received initial funding from the Catalan government to begin building the BDC.

The BDC is designed so that each member library can either access shared resources from the CBUC page or link directly from the member library Web site to any of the shared resources. It is not designed for patron access but rather for the member libraries to incorporate shared resources into their e-library.

> "In fact it is mostly the name we've given to the abstract idea of licensing, in the mid-term , a core collection of remote (mainly commercial and fee-based) e-resources available for all Catalan academic libraries, but licensed through the consortium (because of

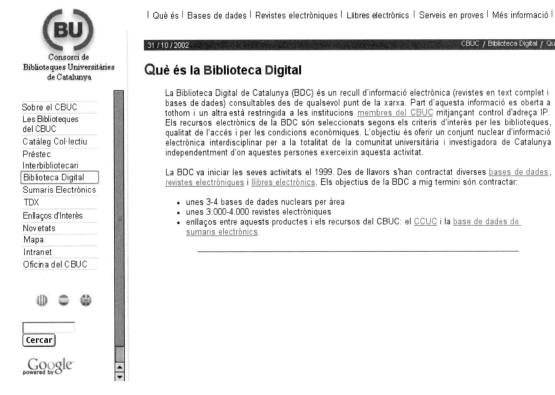

Figure 1.3.0. Biblioteca Digital de Catalunya (BDC) www.cbuc.es

the economic and managing advantages this means for the members). That is why BDC website is just an alphabetical list of CBUC licensed e-resources, mainly addressed to CBUC members librarians, so they can integrate the "consortium e-resources" with their "individual resources" in their own academic Web sites. You would have to go to each CBUC member's websites to find a more accurate (by subject, etc.) arrangement of e-resources. However, our union catalogue (CCUC) would be an example of integrating e-resources."

The CBUC members are:

- Universitat de Barcelona (www.bib.ub.es/bub/bub.htm, or www.ub.es)
- Universitat Autònoma de Barcelona (www.bib.uab.es, or www.uab.es)
- Universitat Politècnica de Catalunya (http://bibliotecnica.upc.es, or www.upc.es)
- Universitat Pompeu Fabra (www.upf.es/bib/index.htm, or www.upf.es)
- Universitat de Girona (http://biblioteca.udg.es or www.udg.es)
- Universitat de Lleida (http://www2.bib.udl.es or www.udl.es)
- Universitat Rovira i Virgili (www.urv.es/biblioteca/marcos.htm, or www.urv.es)
- Universitat Oberta de Catalunya (http://xina.uoc.es/cat/inici.html, or www.uoc.edu/web/cat/index.html)
- Biblioteca de Catalunya (www.gencat.es/bc)

Three CBUC staff members support the BDC, including one librarian-projects assistant who handles database licensing negotiations and access issues full time. Two staff members support the BDC part time.

The collection plan of the BDC is to provide

"a core collection of electronic resources that provides a homogeneous and interdisciplinary basis for all university members and researchers regardless of the institution to which they belong....E-resources in the CBUC E-Library are licensed for the 'natural' audience of its academic libraries: teaching staff, students, and administrative staff at member universities."

An English language version of the basic BDC collection policy is online at www.cbuc.es/angles/5digital/5mcdigital.htm.

Access to the BDC is restricted to authorized users. One of the member libraries supports a distance learning program. Licensing is negotiated to take those students into account.

CBUC evaluated the databases already in use by each member library and studied which databases would be of interest to the member libraries. The BDC collection is based on that examination of the needs of the member libraries. Essentially the plan follows the guidelines that databases and e-journals to which the most member libraries subscribed were acquired as a priority. When negotiating the licensing agreements CBUC requires that:

"any offer must accomplish the following three basic conditions:

1. Interest: licensed e-resources must be interesting to the main part of CBUC members, and the areas covered should be as interdisciplinary and broad as

possible;

2. Accessibility: they must also improve existent access conditions (from CD to online, more concurrent users, etc.);

3. Cost: a consortial offer must be 'cheaper' than the addition of individual prices, or it must have an affordable price increase balanced with additional advantages (more accesses, more information, cancellation or DDP for print subscriptions in the case of e-journals, etc.)."

Plans for expanding the CBUC collection include emphasizing resources that contain local information or that support new scholarly communications models (e.g., The Scholarly Publishing and Academic Resources Coalition—SPARC—www.arl.org/sparc).

Each member library has their own selection criteria and makes recommendations for adding new e-resources. The CBUC member library directors technical committee then decides on which e-resources to license. Free Web resources are selected by each individual member library. The CBUC Director signs the license agreements, and the Librarian-projects assistant sets up access, adds the link to the BDC, and informs libraries about the new resource.

CBUC negotiates prices and clauses in the licenses with reference to the needs of the member libraries. The CBUC pays database and e-book license fees from annual maintenance monies paid by the member libraries to the CBUC. Each CBUC member pays for e-journals directly to the publisher, based on an internal allocation formula calculated by the CBUC Office. The CBUC and member libraries also receive some funding from the Catalan government towards paying for databases and e-journals.

All CBUC licensed databases, e-books, and e-journals are cataloged in the union catalog (CCUC). Subject guides published on the Web by CBUC member libraries may also be cataloged and included in the CCUC. Free Web resources may be cataloged in the CCUC by individual member libraries but this is not done centrally. Usage is tracked for the licensed e-resources but not for the subject guides or free Web sites.

The CBUC e-collection includes several locally created databases including a Base de dades de sumaris electrònics (or electronic table of contents database http://sumaris.cbuc.es, details at www.cbuc.es/angles/6sumaris/6mcsumaris.htm), which includes tables of contents from more than ten thousand journals subscribed to by CBUC members.

The Tesis Doctorals en Xarxa (TDX) (www.tdx.cesca.es) is the CBUC maintained part of the Networked Digital Library of Theses and Dissertations (NDLTD) project (www.ndltd.org). Each member university is responsible for adding their own theses and dissertations to the database.

"We also act as a 'shop window' for some academic Catalan databases, created at universities or government agencies. You can see them at the bottom of page www.cbuc.es/5digital/52bases.htm)."

The BDC runs with the Apache Web server on Unix. TDX uses MySQL and free software from VTLS and the Sumaris electrònics database use locally created software. BDC initial startup hardware and software cost was approximately 260,000 euros. The Sumaris electrònics project startup cost was approximately 33,600 euros for hardware and software.

CBUC is studying the possibility of creating a portal for Catalan E-journals as well.

Interlibrary loan services are offered through the CCUC, but they do not currently offer virtual reference services.

Links are checked manually as they are used. Some member libraries use link checking software.

"In the end it seems it always requires 'human work' to find the correct new link."

CBUC publishes two e-mail addresses (info@cbuc.es and webmaster@cbuc.es) for user feedback, questions, suggestions for changes, improvements, or problems.

"We try to answer quickly, and we always learn something from the messages received."

The BDC is still in the process of building. The CBUC and member libraries review it as they build. Faculty from the University of Barcelona, School of Librarianship are evaluating e-journal usage statistics. CBUC staff plan to improve the integration and searching of e-resources and to upgrade or change the CBUC software to better manage e-resources. Currently it uses Classic VTLS. Providing uniform search capabilities for all the CBUC databases is a priority for the future.

REFERENCES

Alford, D.E. 2002. Negotiating and Analyzing Electronic License Agreements. *Law Library Journal* 94, no. 4: 621–44.

Association for Research Libraries and Special Libraries Association (Cosponsors). 1999. *Demystifying the Licensing of Electronic Resources*. VHS (Video and workbook). Recorded with permission on March 4, 1999 from a satellite transmission.

Bebbington, L. W. 2001. Managing Content: Licensing, Copyright and Privacy Issues in Managing Electronic Resources. *Legal Information Management* 1, no. 2: 4–12.

Bielefield, A., and L. Cheeseman. 1999. *Interpreting and Negotiating Licensing Agreements*. New York: Neal-Schuman.

Croft, J. B. 2001. Model Licenses and Interlibrary Loan/Document Delivery from Electronic Resources. *Interlending and Document Supply* 29, no. 4: 165–68.

Eonta, J. 2000. Defining Vendor Terminology. *Library Journal Net Connect* 125, no. 7: 33–34.

Fowler, D. C. 2000. Information Technology and Collection Development Departments in the Academic Library: Striving to Reach a Common Understanding. In *Electronic Collection Management*, ed. S. D. McGinnis, 17–36. Binghamton, NY: Haworth Information Press.

Gregory, V. L. 2000. *Selecting and Managing Electronic Resources*. New York: Neal-Schuman.

Gregory, V. L. 2001. UCITA. *Online* 25, no.1: 30–34.

Harris, L. E. 2000. Deal-Maker, Deal-Breaker: When to Walk Away. *Library Journal Net Connect* 125, no. 1: 12–14.

———. 2002. *Licensing Digital Content: A Practical Guide for Librarians*. Chicago: American Library Association.

"Licensing and UCITA." (2002). *Library Technology Reports* 38, no. 1: 104–10.

McGinnis, S. D. 2000. Selling Our Collecting Souls: How License Agreements Are Controlling Collection Management. *Journal of Library Administration*. 31, no. 2: 63–76.

Metz, P. 2000. Principles of Selection for Electronic Resources. *Library Trends* 48, no. 4: 711–28.

Metzinger Miller, K. 2003. Behind Every Great Virtual Library Stand Many Great Licenses. *Library Journal Net Connect* 128, no. 1: 20–22.

New York Times Co. v. Tasini, 533 U.S. 483; 121 S. Ct. 2381; 150 L. Ed. 2d 500; 2001 U.S. LEXIS 4667.

Pace, A. K. 2003. *The Ultimate Digital Library: Where the New Information Players Meet*. Chicago: American Library Association.

Pike, G. H. 2002. The Delicate Dance of Database Licenses, Copyright and Fair Use. *Computers in Libraries* 22, no. 5: 12–14, 63–64.

Tennant, R. 2000. Beg, Buy, Borrow, License or Steal. *LibraryJournal* 125, no. 11: 30–31.

Wiant, S. K., and S. McCaslin. 2002. UCITA and Fair Use: A Compatible or Combatable Relationship. *Serials Librarian* 42, no. 1–2: 79–88.

Wyatt, A. M. 2002. UCITA's Impact on Library Services. *Journal of Library Administration* 36, no. 4: 83–94.

WEB SITES CITED

(Note that some sites are included in the resource lists and webliographies in subsequent chapters, and therefore are not necessarily duplicated in this section.)

American Library Association. *UCITA*. Available: www.ala.org/washoff/ucita.

Association for Research Libraries. *Licensing Issues*. Available: www.arl.org/scomm/licensing.

Association of Learned and Professional Society Publishers. *Licensing and Related Initiatives*. Available: www.alpsp.org/htp_licens.htm.

Coalition for Networked Information. *Negotiating Networked Information Contracts and Licenses (Draft)*. Available: www.cni.org/projects/READI/guide.

Computer Professionals for Social Responsibility. *UCITA Fact Sheet*. Available: www.cpsr.org/program/UCITA/ucita-fact.html.

Demystifying the Licensing of Electronic Resources. Available: www.arl.org/scomm/licensing/resources.html.

Electronic Resources in Libraries list. Available: ERIL-L@listserv.binghamton.edu.

International Coalition of Library Consortia (ICOLC). *Statement of Current Perspective and Preferred Practices for the Selection and Purchase of Electronic Information*. Available: www.library.yale.edu/consortia/statement.html.

International Federation of Library Associations and Institutions. *Licensing Principles 2001*. Available: www.ifla.org/V/ebpb/copy.htm.

Kippel, C. Central Kansas Library System. *Licensing Digital Information*. Available: http://skyways.lib.ks.us/central/ebooks/licenses.html.

LibLicense-L List Archives. Available: www.library.yale.edu/~llicense/ListArchives.

Yale University. *LibLicense: Licensing Digital Information*. Available: www.library.yale.edu/~llicense/index.shtml.

SEE ALSO PART III: WEB COLLECTION DEVELOPMENT RESOURCES:

Resource List 1: Collection Development Related Discussion Lists, Newsgroups, and Blogs, for discussion lists, newsgroups, e-serials and other resources cited in this chapter, and

Resource List 2: Evaluation Guides

Part II: Recommended Evaluation Guidelines, Selection Criteria, and Core Collections For Major Subject Areas

PART II

RECOMMENDED EVALUATION GUIDELINES, SELECTION CRITERIA, AND CORE COLLECTIONS FOR MAJOR SUBJECT AREAS

1:   Ready-Reference Information Resources

"A 'reference Website' is an HTML-based page (or system of pages) that provides potentially useful information by assembling hot links to online tools (some sites also include citations to paper tools). Because Web site designers must assume that remote users will be working without direct human assistance or the opportunity to discuss subtle nuances, these sites emphasize factual material: reference information that addresses basic questions of the sort known to librarians as 'ready reference' questions.

S. W. Sowards (1998: 2)

1.1 DEVELOPING THE COLLECTION PLAN FOR READY-REFERENCE INFORMATION RESOURCES

When you begin providing reference service in a new library, or after your reference collection has been reorganized in someway—and sometimes as a library patron—what are the first things you look for? You look for the core ready-reference tools that you will need to assist patrons or to answer your own research questions. Both authors agree that we have a clear mental image of the contents and organization of the ready-reference service area at Kent State University Library. In our imagination we can reach back from the desk or walk over to a particular section and pull out the reference books we will use most often. Similarly, we have become familiar with the reference databases accessible from our reference computers or from remote locations when staffing a virtual reference service. Similarly, a good ready-reference Web collection will contain the resources that both librarians and patrons will use most often and be organized in such a way that we can easily locate those resources. Ready-reference tools are those books and databases that will answer quickly and accurately most single-fact, specific-search, simple-answer reference questions.

"Ready-reference and specific search queries presuppose specific answers and specific sources, which, with practice, the librarian usually can locate quickly." (Katz, 2001: 18)

In *Introduction to Reference Work: Basic Information Services,* 8th ed. vol. 1, William A. Katz (2001) assumes that the ready-reference collections of most libraries includes Web resources. Web resources are an integral part of basic information services.

Using a Web search engine or even a known Web resources may not be the best source of ready-reference answers. For patrons who are not physically in the library or for very up-to-date information it may be the first or only choice. Creating e-libraries with a good collection of high quality Web resources and making them available through the library Web site will increase the likelihood that patrons will choose the best ready-reference sources. This is also a good strategy for promoting the value of the library as information source for patrons. Some e-library builders even add information about equivalent print sources that are available in the library to their annotations for Web resources. "When is it best to use a digital or a printed ready-reference source? Answer: Use the source where the answers may be found quickly." (Katz, 2001: 279).

WHAT PURPOSE WILL YOUR READY-REFERENCE COLLECTION SERVE? FOR WHOM ARE YOU COLLECTING READY-REFERENCE WEB RESOURCES?

Ready-reference sources at the most basic level provides quick simple factual answers. Definitions of words, contact information for individuals, organizations, and companies, statistics from health, geography, politico-economic, business, and other areas of interest, and biographical information, are all frequently requested ready-reference types of information. A Web ready-reference collection will need to include resources that answer these questions with high quality answers. The librarian will need to pay some attention to the educational level of patrons using the ready-reference resources. Will your ready-reference Web collection serve students doing homework? Distance learners in a college program? Healthcare consumers looking for medical definitions? Will your patrons be looking for current awareness information such as news, weather, sports, theater and movie, celebrity information or similar kinds of information? Will your patrons be looking for statistical information of various kinds? As always each library will be guided by the needs of their patrons in deciding what to collect for their ready-reference e-library.

WHAT TYPES OF READY-REFERENCE WEB RESOURCES WILL YOU COLLECT?

Ready-reference Web resources tend to resemble closely the print resources on which they are based. There are eight core ready-reference tool types:

- Directories (phone books, association, business, and organization directories)
- Dictionaries (English as well as international language translation dictionaries)
- Abstracts, Indexes, and Table of Contents Services (including those with full-text of the journals and magazines indexed)
- Encyclopedias and Almanacs
- Full-text Databases (e-books, e-serials aggregations)
- Bibliographies and Bibliographic Databases
- News (Current Awareness) sources
- Key Primary Documents—such as Annual Reports, Law Codes, and Statistical Sources)

Directories are one of the most frequently used type of ready-reference tool. Every subject chapter in this book includes discussion of specific directories for that subject. The Web has enhanced the scope and currency of directory information as well as access to more information. Gale Publishing, for example, has a Web site where authors, scholars, and organizational representatives, can input their current information (www.gale-edit.com) for *American Men and Women of Science, Biography Resource Center, Contemporary Authors and Something about the Author, Directory of American Scholars, Encyclopedia of Associations, and How Products Are Made*. The Hoovers Online directory has similar current information for companies.

There are few abstracting and indexing tools that are freely available on the Web. However, nearly all the standard indexes are fee-based Web accessible databases. For example, the *Consumer Index* (www.consumerreports.com) has partially free indexing, and the *Reader's Guide to Periodical Literature* (www.hwwilson.com). An important thing to consider when using these Web-accessible indexes is that the backfiles may not yet be in electronic form. *Reader's Guide to Periodical Literature* is one that does have the back files from 1890–1982 in the databases searchable through the WilsonWeb database collection.

Dictionaries are essential ready-reference tools. Searching Web dictionaries can be very convenient when no print dictionary is available. However, it is often faster to reach over and pull a print dictionary off the shelf. The other issues to be aware of in using Web dictionaries are the identity of the publisher and the source of the dictionary information. Several sites with "dictionaries" amount to no more than some individual's glossary of terms; so, evaluate carefully.

Encyclopedias and almanacs are also frequently available on the Web. Many excellent titles are available, either for free or partially free. For example, the *Information Please Almanac* contents are available through www.infoplease.com. *Encyclopedia Britannica* (www.britannica.com)

offers some basic information for free, though premium full-text access is only available for a subscription fee.

Bibliographies and bibliographic databases have established a new and powerful existence on the Web. Sites such as Amazon.com not only sell books, but they also provide the opportunity for individuals to post their bibliographies on a variety of themes. Many individual and organizational sites publish bibliographies of particular authors or genres. Two of the authors' favorite bibliography sites are the L-Space Web (www.co.uk.lspace.org/about-terry), which features the works of Terry Pratchett (compiled by The L-Space Librarians), and George Simenon's Maigret (www.trussel.com/f_maig.htm), which exclusively features Simenon's works about Inspector Maigret. (as compiled by Steve Trussell). Many similar kinds of bibliographic resource exist on the Web for both recreational reading and academic scholarship—e.g., the Eudora Welty bibliography at www.olemiss.edu/depts/english/ms-writers/dir/welty_eudora/bib.html and the Winston Churchill bibliography at www.winstonchurchill.org.

News, weather, entertainment, and sports information in a current and interactive form that has never been available in the past, is now available on the Web. For example, we can get transcripts of breaking news (http://news.bbc.co.uk, or www.cnn.com), play-by-play baseball games at ESPN Sports Zone (www.espnsportszone.com), and celebrities from P.O.D., to The Dixie Chicks, to the Cleveland Orchestra maintain Web pages with their current information. The weather information (www.weather.com, www.nws.noaa.gov, or www.wunderground.com, and others) was one of the first types of current awareness resource to be made available through the Web. Whenever we travel, we check the weather report for where we're going by connecting to the weather reports on the Web.

The Web is without peer in terms of its ability to deliver up-to-the-second news and popular culture information. Interview transcripts, song lyrics, or photographs are readily available through the Web. This is one type of information for which the need is the same for all types of libraries. Everyone—from child to adult—who uses a library—may need or desire current awareness information. A current awareness collection can be very broadly inclusive with listings of newspapers online and access to the online sites of television news services. Or it can be focused on current awareness in a narrower subject field, such as business, law, or medicine.

Primary documents or electronic copies of primary documents are available through the Web to an extent never possible with print publication. Law codes and court documents are available now through the Web to everyone with an Internet connected computer. We discussed the Legal Information Institute (http://law.cornell.edu) in Chapter 1, and other law reference tools are discussed in Chapter 7. Annual reports information about publicly traded companies is available full-text through the Securities and Exchange Commission Edgar database (www.sec.gov).

How will you organize your Ready-reference Web resources?

Some e-libraries organize by ready-reference source type. For example the San Bernardino County Web Library organizes by type under the main category "Reference." Other libraries organize by the kind of question answered—e.g., Biography, Business contact information. For example, MEL "Best of the Internet" collection is organized by kind of question or data need under the main category "Reference Desk." The best way to organize is so that your patrons and staff can find the information they need quickly and easily.

1.2 Identifying, Collecting, and Selecting Ready-Reference Resources

The difficult part of identifying, collecting, and selecting Web ready-reference resources will be choosing from the plethora of resources and evaluating the quality of information each resource provides. This process can be simplified by making use of the resources that review ready-reference Web resources.

WEB SITES THAT REVIEW AND EVALUATE WEB RESOURCES: INCLUDING OTHER E-LIBRARIES OR SUBJECT COLLECTION GUIDES/WEBLIOGRAPHIES

The Internet Public Library (www.ipl.org) is an excellent ready-reference Web resource collection tool as is the LII (www.lii.org). Both sites provide high quality, carefully selected Web sites under the category of ready-reference.

Most of the Web sites included in the core collection were found in one or more of the case study e-libraries under their "Ready-Reference," "Reference Desk," or "Reference" collection headings. MEL, BUBL, and InfoMine were most useful.

Gary Price's ResourceShelf (www.resourceshelf.com) and John Hubbard's Library Link of the Day (www.tk421.net/librarylink) are published as RSS feeds, but are also Web sites that review and evaluate ready-reference Web resources regularly and archive those reviews.

Peter Jasco reviews reference Web sites and databases on Peter's Digital Reference Shelf (www.galegroup.com/free_resources/reference/index.htm). His reviews are careful, thorough, and frequently critical. Jasco's reviews provide details that some other reviewers might skim over such as search tool functionality, archiving of backfiles, availability of source information and more.

DISCUSSION LISTS AND NEWSGROUPS WHERE INDIVIDUAL PARTICIPANTS REVIEW AND EVALUATE READY-REFERENCE WEB RESOURCES

Essentially any library reference related discussion list will at times discuss ready-reference Web resources. Monitoring your favorite discussion or browsing the archives will be fruitful. Libref-L, Publib, and Dig_Ref were very useful in the process of writing this book.

E-JOURNALS AND E-NEWSLETTERS THAT PUBLISH REVIEWS AND EVALUATIONS OF READY-REFERENCE WEB RESOURCES

Interestingly many of the Web sites and RSS feeds discussed previously in this chapter and in Chapter 1, also have e-newsletter subscription options. For example, ResourceShelf invites subscription to a weekly reminder and highlights e-newsletter via e-mail each Thursday.

PRINT BOOKS AND JOURNALS THAT REVIEW READY-REFERENCE WEB RESOURCES

All of the library related journals will at some time review ready-reference Web resources. All of the books cited in Chapter 1 under this section heading include discussion of ready-reference resources. Many of the subject specific books, mentioned in other chapters, do address ready-reference sources.

1.3 EVALUATION GUIDELINES

Any ready-reference resource is only as good as the information provider or new source. The best rule of thumb for evaluating ready-reference resources is to look for publishers or news organizations that you know and recognize for having a good reputation. Look for source attributions, contact information, and the mission or intention in providing the information. Follow the evaluation guidelines discussed in Chapter 1 in evaluating any ready-reference Web resource for inclusion in your e-library collection.

Be especially careful in evaluating current awareness sites. If the site declares that the information is provided "for entertainment purposes only" its value as a source for facts is questionable.

Accepting the evaluation of a high quality collection, such as LII, is a reasonable strategy. Check the selection criteria of each e-library collection you browse for resources. You cannot always assume that if any given library has included a resource in their e-library collection that they have carefully evaluated it, or in fact evaluated it with the same quality standards as you have determined for your own e-library collection.

1.4 Selection Criteria

In October 2002, as a follow-up to previous surveys done in 1998 and 1999, we posted the questions reproduced in the following survey results box to several library reference discussion lists. Ten reference databases (CD and Web) were clear favorites and these are also listed in the survey results box. Fifteen core print reference tools were also identified. We also surveyed some subject specific discussion lists with slightly different questions. The results for each subject area will be discussed where appropriate in subsequent chapters. The clear results for the core ready-reference tools, both print and electronic, make an excellent guide for Web ready-reference resource selection. In other words, if you can find Web ready-reference resources that are similar to the core ready-reference tools in print and other electronic forms you have the framework for a great Web-based core ready-reference collection.

Table 2.1.1. Core or Essential Reference Tools Survey

Posted to publib@sunsite.berkeley.edu, libref-l@listserv.kent.edu, & oplinlist@oplin.lib.oh.us.

1. What are the top 3-5 print reference books that you can't work without?
2. What are the top 3-5 CD-ROM, Tape or Online databases that you can't work without?

Table 2.1.2. Core or Essential Reference Databases

1. EbscoHost (Academic Search Premier, Business Source Premier, Health Source, and Novelist mentioned specifically). Available: www.epnet.com.
2. Gale Databases (Group Literature Resource Center, Gale Ready Reference, Gale General Periodicals, Gale General Reference Center Gold mentioned specifically). Available: www.galegroup.com.
3. Reference USA. Available: www.referenceusa.com.
4. InfoTrac. Available: www.galegroup.com.
5. Proquest Databases. Available: www.proquest.com.
6. Lexis-Nexis/Academic Universe. Available: www.lexisnexis.com, and http://support.lexis-nexis.com/academic/default.asp.
7. Worldcat. Available: www.oclc.com/worldcat.
8. Electric Library/Elibrary. Available: http://ask.elibrary.com and Books in Print. Available: www.booksinprint.com/bip.
9. Google. Available: www.google.com.
10. Amazon.com. Available: www.amazon.com.
11. Masterplots. Available: www.masterplots.com, and ERIC. Available: www.askeric.org/Eric, and MLA International Bibliography Online. Available: www.mla.org, and Psycinfo. Available: www.psycinfo.com.

URLs provided are for the publisher's Web site.

Table 2.1.3. Core or Essential Print Reference Tools

1. *World Book Encyclopedia*. Available: www.worldbook.com.
2. *World Almanac* and *Book of Facts: World Almanac Education*. Available: www.wae.cc.
3. Any good dictionary
4. Any almanac
5. *Encyclopedia of Associations*. Available: www.galegroup.com.
6. Local telephone books
7. *Oxford English Dictionary*. Available: www.oed.com.

8.　NADA car guides. Available: www.nada.com.
9.　Any atlas
10.　Statistical Abstract of the United States. Available: http://bookstore.gpo.gov.
11.　*Gale Encyclopedia of Medicine*. Available: www.galegroup.com.
12.　*Consumer Reports Index*. Available: www.consumerreports.org.
13.　Chilton's auto repair manuals. Available: www.chiltonsonline.com.
14.　City directories
15.　Haines Criss+Cross Directories. Available: http://haines.com/ccdir1.htm.
16.　Contemporary Literary Criticism/Contemporary Authors. Available: www.galegroup
　　　.com.

These received 2 votes each:

• Any unabridged dictionary
• Style guides: *St. Martin's Handbook, Publication Manual of the American Psychological Association, The Chicago Manual of Style, MLA Handbook for Writers of Term Papers, Electronic Styles* (Li).
• *Physician's Desk Reference* . Available: www.pdr.net.
• *Directory of Corporate Affiliations*. Available: www.nationalregisterpub.com.

We created the Core Web Ready-Reference Collection in this chapter using the survey results as a model collection. The intended patrons are librarians who will need a quick, easy, high quality, and reliable collection of core ready-reference Web resources. The access and design of all these core ready-reference Web resources are based on standards of simplicity, international Web accessibility standards, and no special software required for access. Most of them are free of direct cost. Some have special fee-based products or services.

1.5 E-Library Success Story

Michigan eLibrary (MeL)

The Library of Michigan
http://mel.org

Contact: Rebecca E. Cawley, Statewide Database Administrator, Library of Michigan, rcawley@michigan.gov

Way back in 1992 in the middle of the night, Sue Davidsen, woke up thinking about creating an e-library of Internet resources organized by subject using Gopher. That gopher evolved into the original Michigan Electronic Library (MeL) "Best of the Internet" collection. Now called the Michigan eLibrary (MeL), this original project has grown and has a bright future planned.

The Michigan eLibrary (MeL) is now a function of the Library of Michigan, an agency within the Michigan Department of History, Arts and Libraries.

"The Library of Michigan serves the legislature, the Executive and Judicial branches of state government and libraries throughout Michigan by meeting information needs, providing administrative, developmental and technical assistance, and functioning as a statewide resource for individuals and agencies."

In addition to the "Best of the Internet" collection, MeL currently includes public access for Michigan residents to e-journals, e-books, and other specially selected fee-based databases.

"In Sept 1999 Michigan libraries held a "Preferred Futures Conference" that brought together close to 100 librarians from public, school, college and special libraries to talk about the needs they saw for libraries in Michigan for the next 10 or so years. One of the needs identified was to expand on our collection of Internet resources and commercial databases in order to create our version of a statewide virtual library. The components to

MeL Internet
"Best of the Internet" Selected by Librarians

MeL Weather

Timely Topics in the News   _Michigan Authors & Illustrators_

Arts & Humanities
Electronic texts, Genealogy, Michigan arts, more...
Business, Economics & Labor
Automotive, Michigan business, Small business, more...
Children & Young Adults
Animals, Countries, Science, TV shows, more...
Education
Home schooling, Lesson plans, Michigan education, more...
Government, Politics & Law
Michigan government, Statistics, Taxes, more...
Health Information Resources
Diseases, Food safety, Michigan hospitals, more...
The Internet & Computers
Myths & hoaxes, Online safety, Viruses, more...

Libraries & Information Science
Books, Intellectual freedom, Michigan libraries, more...
Michigan
History, Sports, Travel, more...
News, Media & Periodicals
Cartoons, News indexes, Radio, TV, more...
Recreation & Leisure
Food, Movies, Music, Pets, Restaurants, more...
Reference Desk
Addresses, Biography, Dictionaries, more...
Science & the Environment
Astronomy, Horticulture, Weather, more...
Social Issues & Social Services
Aging, Diversity, Parenting, more...

About MeL Services

This service is funded in part by the State of Michigan through the Library of Michigan.
Additional project support comes from the federal Library Services and Technology Act (LSTA)
via the Institute of Museum and Library Services (IMLS).
http://mel.org/melindex.html
This page was last modified:03/20/03

Michigan.gov Home | HAL Home | MeL Internet | MeL Magazines and eBooks | Search MeL
Accessibility Policy | Privacy Policy | Link Policy | Security Policy

Figure 2.1.0. Michigan eLibrary (MeL) http://mel.org

be added were: a statewide catalog and interlibrary loan system (these exist regionally but not statewide) a collection of digitized local resources, a portal to pull these resources together, and a statewide library delivery system."

The MeL "Best of the Internet collection" includes selective coverage of free Web resources collected, annotated, and published on the Web by eleven subject expert librarians who work under the Library of Michigan. These skilled selectors collect in the following subject areas:

- Arts and Humanities
- Business, Economics and Labor
- Children and Young Adults
- Education
- Government, Politics and Law
- Health Information
- The Internet, Computers and Technology
- Libraries and Information
- Michigan
- News, Media and Periodicals
- Recreation and Leisure
- The Reference Desk
- Science and the Environment
- Social Issues and Social Services

The collection policy is online at http://mel.org/about/melcollection.html. The "Best of the Internet" collection includes more than 29,000 free Web sites. Many of the selectors have worked on the MeL project from the beginning. They use their subject expertise and experience, site reviews from print and e-journals, as well as other electronic collection development tools to select the "best" freely accessible Web sites in their subject areas.

> "Selectors spend about 10 hrs per week on their sections. Some sections such as 'Government, Politics and Law' and 'Health Information' change frequently. Selectors are charged to delete as well as add sites and to check for dead or rerouted links. There are times when most of their effort goes to maintenance. MeL Internet includes about 29,000 links and grows at the rate of several thousand links per year. Our goal is not to be large; it is to be selective."

For Michigan residents, the Michigan eLibrary provides access to databases with more than 7,500 full-text popular, business, and health magazines and newspapers from GALE, OCLC, SIRS, ProQuest, and LearnATest and a collection of nonfiction e-books from netLibrary. Login requires a Michigan state driver's license or state issued identification.

Rebecca E. Cawley, Statewide Database Administrator, spends about fifty percent of her time on the current and future MeL. The Library of Michigan contracts with the Michigan Library Consortium (MLC) for training and help desk services. One full-time and one part-time person are needed to handle IP registration, database use questions, work with database vendors, and to create training packages. Along with two part-time Web application managers, MeL also contracts for as many as thirty part-time trainers.

Eight statewide library committees have worked on design for the next phase of MeL. The RFP writing process for the new MeLCat was contracted out.

> "From the beginning MeL's audience has been multitype Michigan libraries and their users both in the library and remotely. The MeL goal has been to 'level the playing field' for information seekers statewide by providing a core set of resources available anywhere, anytime. MeL has such diverse content that it truly caters to all audiences including students, professionals, teachers and the amateur researcher. Selection criteria for the MeL commercial databases grew through a process of focus group discussions with all types of libraries in the state. Database topic priorities recommended by the focus groups were used to help select resources from database vendor RFP responses."

LSTA funding and some state appropriations are used to pay for the commercial database subscriptions.

MeL has no official role in supporting distance learning but is acknowledged as an important support resource for other state institutions, organizations, and individuals (e.g., home-schoolers, virtual university participants).

> "Distance learners often rely on local public libraries for research materials. Using MeL, all students no matter the size of their local library have access to a core set of substantive materials. With the addition of a statewide catalog and interlibrary loan service students will also have access to materials in all the state's library collections."

MeL is reviewed continually. Feedback from users, as well as statistics on current database usage are used to make decisions about future resources to be added or changes to be made in the collection.

> "Recently a group of health sciences librarians selected and used grant funds to purchase health related titles from netLibrary to add to the state collection. They chose materials that would serve the needs of the general user as well as the health care student and professional. Since libraries repeatedly express the need for quality, up-to-date health information accessible to the general user, selection by these experts was very valuable."

Web sites are not cataloged, but MeL has made MARC records for the netLibrary e-book titles available for individual libraries to include in their catalog. When the statewide catalog is available it will include these records as well as MARC records for the e-journal titles.

By Fall 2003 the MeL "The Best of the Internet" collection will be migrated from a collection of links to Web pages to a Web-accessible database.

"For the new MeL Internet collection database, the MeL Internet directory is a web accessible database, which is maintained using a web-based administration interface. Selectors (collectors) access the maintenance tools from any computer using a web browser. The MeL Internet directory is being created at a cost of $126,900, including design, software development, data conversion, implementation, and the first year of support. Hardware and network costs are an additional cost.... Once converted the new MeL Internet directory will run on a pair of servers running Redhat Linux version 8, using MySQL for the database and Apache for the web server. The MeL directory application is written in Java and is hosted by the open-source java application server JBoss."

Selectors will use the new software interface to add and revise links. Currently link checking is done entirely manually. The new interface will include automatic link checking as well.

"The new MeL database application will include a custom, integrated link checking service that runs on the server. It executes at a defined interval (customizable by the administrator), and reports changes in content and whether the target site is dead, has moved, or is otherwise unavailable. In addition, the link checker will always check a problem site twice before reporting the problem to avoid false positives or incorrectly reporting temporary conditions."

Digitized collections will be a very important part of the future MeL.

An IMLS funded project "Making of Modern Michigan" (http://mmm.lib.msu.edu) is developing digitization standards, and will create digitization centers around the state, as well as train library staff in digitization techniques. A LSTA mini-grant program has been established to encourage libraries to participate in training and to help them begin digitization projects using defined standards.

MeL will soon offer a portal that brings all the resources, including MeL Internet, the commercial databases, digitized local collections and the statewide library catalog, interlibrary loan and document delivery service, together and makes them searchable from one cross-database search tool. Virtual reference services are planned for future development.

"Our belief is that when seeking information, users don't care where it comes from as long as it is reliable and accessible. Right now we ask patrons to use different methods to obtain information from the Internet or from a magazine database or from a library catalog. We think they would like to have the option to search across these resources to retrieve the information they need."

1.6 REFERENCES AND WEB SITES CITED

(Note that some sites are included in the resource lists and webliographies in previous chapters, and therefore are not necessarily duplicated in this section.)

Katz, W. A. 2001. *Introduction to Reference Work: Basic Information Services.* 8th ed. Vol. I. Boston: McGraw-Hill.

Sowards, S. W. 1998. A Typology for Ready Reference Websites in Libraries. *First Monday* 1, no. 14, http://firstmonday.dk/issues.

Amazon.com. Available: www.amazon.com.

Books in Print. Available: www.booksinprint.com/bip.

Cleveland Orchestra. Available: www.clevelandorch.com.

Dixie Chicks. Available: www.dixiechicks.com.

EbscoHost (Academic Search Premier, Business Source Premier, Health Source, and Novelist mentioned specifically). Available: www.epnet.com.

Electric Library/Elibrary. Available: http://ask.elibrary.com.

ERIC. Available: www.askeric.org/Eric.

Gale Databases (Group Literature Resource Center, Gale Ready Reference, Gale General Periodicals, Gale General Reference Center Gold mentioned specifically). Available: www.galegroup.com.

Gale Publishing online update form. Available: www.gale-edit.com.

Google. Available: www.google.com.

InfoTrac. Available: www.galegroup.com.

L-Space Web (compiled by the L-Space Librarians). Available: www.co.uk.lspace.org/about-terry.

Lexis-Nexis/Academic Universe. Available: www.lexisnexis.com and http://support.lexis-nexis.com/academic/default.asp.

Masterplots. Available: www.masterplots.com.

MLA International Bibliography Online. Available: www.mla.org.

P.O.D. Available: www.thesouthtown.com.

Peter's Digital Reference Shelf. Available: www.galegroup.com/free_resources/reference/index.htm.

Proquest Databases. Available: www.proquest.com.

Psycinfo. Available: www.psycinfo.com.

Reference USA. Available: www.referenceusa.com.

Simenon's Maigret (compiled by Steve Trussell). Available: www.trussel.com/f_maig.htm.(

Weather Reports. Available: www.weather.com, www.nws.noaa.gov, or www.wunderground.com.

Worldcat. Available: www.oclc.com/worldcat.

1.7 THE CORE WEB READY-REFERENCE COLLECTION

(Special Subject Reference sections added specially on the recommendations of all the reference librarians who took the May 20, 2003 CAMLS workshop)

CONSUMER INFORMATION/GENEALOGY REFERENCE/DIRECTORIES

Anywho Directory

www.anywho.com

AT&T Labs sponsored 800/888 toll free directory, reverse lookup, white pages, and yellow pages telephone directory information.

Zip Code Look-up and Address Information

www.usps.gov

United States Postal Services Web site lets you search for any zip code in the United States as well as links to postal rate information and related services.

Moviefone Movielink

www.moviefone.com

Searchable movie theater schedules for many cities in the United States. Search by zip code or major city, by theater, movie title, movie actor, or time of showing. Also includes synopses of movie plots.

TV Guide

http://listings.tvguide.com

Full television (broadcast, cable, and satellite) listings for the United States and Latin America. Listings are retrievable by zip code, major network, or satellite linup.

Yahoo! People Search

http://people.yahoo.com

E-mail and telephone book information search database.

DICTIONARIES

Dictionary.com

http://dictionary.reference.com

Single search through high-quality full-text dictionaries on line.

Dictionary of Units of Measurement

www.unc.edu/~rowlett/units/index.html

> Created by Russ Rowlett, Director, Center for Mathematics and Science Education, University of North Carolina at Chapel Hill, this dictionary contains detailed definitions about units of measurement. Middle-school and up should find this fascinating and potentially very useful; e.g., "Zhubov scale—a scale for reporting ice coverage of polar seas."

OneLook Dictionaries, The Faster Finder

www.onelook.com

> Meta search engine for nearly 500 Web-based dictionaries in multiple subject areas.

The Language Hub

www.cetrodftt.com/translate.htm

> Directory of language dictionaries and translation tools on the Web.

AltaVista/BabelFish Machine Translation

http://babel.altavista.com/tr?

> Use this site like a dictionary to look up words in French, German, Italian, Portuguese, or Spanish, and translate them into English or vice versa.

YourDictionary.com

www.yourdictionary.com

> Collection of high quality specialty online dictionaries in English and other languages. Some fee-based access.

ABSTRACTS, INDEXES, AND TABLE OF CONTENTS SERVICES

Free Journal Indexes and Databases

http://library.wustl.edu/subjects/life/free.html

> Washington University Libraries has compiled this annotated collection of journals, publishers, and vendors who provide some free access indexes, tables of contents, abstracts, and some search capabilities for the journals they publish or aggregate. Encyclopedias and Almanacs.

Biography.com

www.biography.com

> Searchable database of over 25,000 biographies provided by A&E.

Encyclopedia Britannica

www.britannica.com

> Although this is a fee-based resource, it must be considered core to any collection. Individuals as well as libraries can subscribe, and individual subscriptions can be monthly or daily. The "Year in Review" allows historical and chronological searching of international news events from 1993–1997. Some portions of the encyclopedia are free.

InfoPlease: Online Dictionary, Internet Encyclopedia and Almanac Reference

www.infoplease.com

> Searchable collection of online almanacs, atlases, dictionaries and the sixth edition of the *Columbia Encyclopedia* online.

The Internet Movie Database

www.imdb.com

> Online filmography of nearly 200,000 titles with nearly three million filmography entries. It is expanding continuously. This site is sponsored by Amazon.com. It includes biographical information about actors, links to reviews by other

users, from film related newsgroups as well as external reviews by professional film reviewers.

Music Resources—Sibelius Academy

www.siba.fi/Kulttuuripalvelut/music.html

Huge list of music sites that not only links "you to jazz, blues, rock, and pop pages but covers famous composers, gospel, instruments, research, theory, and opera as well."

FULL-TEXT DATABASES (E-BOOKS, E-SERIALS AGGREGATIONS)

Audible.com

www.audible.com

License or buy e-books (audio) through Audible.com. Amherst (Ohio) Public Library (www.amherst.lib.oh.us) is one of the first libraries to make licensing arrangements with Audible.com.

Bartelby.com

www.bartelby.com

Reference e-books (text) for downloading fee and free resources. Many reference text full-text free online; e.g., *Roget's Thesaurus*, *Bartlett's Familiar Quotations*.

Gutenberg Project

http://gutenberg.net

Since 1971, Michael Hart has coordinated volunteers who are transcribing the text of public domain books into electronic format. Nearly 7,000 e-books are available free through the Project Gutenberg Web sites.

Bibliographies and Bibliographic Databases

Note: Use any Web search engine to locate bibliographies for any author, genre, or other detail.

Amazon.com

www.amazon.com

Online bookstore that has searchable database of over 2.5 million books in-print and out-of-print.

NEWS (CURRENT AWARENESS) SOURCES

BBC News

http://library.wustl.edu/subjects/life/free.html

Full-text version of the BBC World news television and radio news productions. Continuously updated with searchable archives.

CNN

www.cnn.com

Full-text version of the CNN news reports and features. Updated continuously. Searchable archives.

Editor and Publisher Online

www.editorandpublisher.com/editorandpublisher/index.jsp

E&P Online offers daily headlines, in-depth features, and exclusive columnists. News is focused on the news and publishing industry. Only selected stories from the weekly print edition are available for free online. The entire contents of each week's print edition are available in the online archives for a fee.

MSNBC.com

www.msnbc.com/news

Besides giving the lead stories of the day, links are provided to consumer news on health, technology, business, sports and more. Easy links to local news, sports and up-to-the minute local weather are also provided. Also links to Newsweek online.

Time.com
www.time.com/time

Provides news stories, links to breaking stories via the newswires, and special Web features that relate current stories to historical coverage in time.

U.S. News Online
www.usnews.com/usnews/home.htm

Includes a news section with top stories, education section with news about colleges including their famous rankings, and a consumer section with health, technology and travel information.

NewsDirectory.com
www.newsd.com

This is a free directory of newspapers, magazines, and other periodic literature. Newspapers can be browsed geographically and magazines geographically and by subject.

New York Times Online
www.nytimes.com

Searchable full-text online version of the New York Times. Requires free registration.

Open Directory Project—News
http://dmoz.org/News

The Open Directory Project is a human selected and organized Web directory. The news section is very thorough collection of newspapers, magazines, and other media outlets on the Web. Searchable and browseable by geographic area.

KEY PRIMARY DOCUMENTS
(Annual Reports, Law Codes, Statistical Sources)
See also these resources in each subject reference collection.

Statistical Abstracts of the United States (Selected Data)
www.census.gov/statab/www

Summary statistics and a full-text collection of state rankings on such factors as population, poverty, age groups, crime rate, teen pregnancy, and employment, as well as, frequently requested tables including: Bankruptcy cases by state, Employment by industry, Crimes and Crime Rates

See the Legal Information Institute www.law.cornell.edu site to identify the specific law codes for your state and region.

See the subject reference core collections for business, law, medical and other sources you would add here.

SPECIAL SUBJECT READY-REFERENCE

CONSUMER INFORMATION

Better Business Bureau Online
www.bbb.org

Check businesses for their status with the BBB, or report problems.

Best Places to Live in America
http://money.cnn.com/best/bplive

Search on city name and receive ratings based on more than sixty rating criteria with detailed information about each city. Also search for a city that meets individual criteria and compare costs of living.

Homefair.com

www.homefair.com

> Various calculators, research information, and reports (schools, crime) all relating to relocating.

EConsumer.gov

www.econsumer.gov/english

> The consumer protection agencies from seventeen countries have cooperated to create this site through which consumers may file complaints about frauds and scams, both in-person and through the Web or e-mail. News and warnings about ongoing frauds and scams are posted here as well as news about successful prosecutions of scammers and spammers.

Kelley Blue Book

www.kbb.com

> Online version of the *Kelley Blue Book* provides new and used automobile, truck and motorcycle pricing as well as automobile and truck reviews, and overview of insurance rates and services.

GENEALOGY REFERENCE

Social Security Death Records

www.ancestry.com, or www.rootsweb.com

> The Social Security Administration makes a computer file of their Death Master Index available for sale. The Index is searchable on several Web sites including Ancestry.com and RootsWeb. Social Security information about birth and death dates, and last known address are available in the index. The original Social Security application or benefits requests (in certain cases) may be ordered from the SSA. This is a good starting point for genealogical research.

Vital Records Information for All States and Territories of the United States and International

www.vitalrec.com

> Comprehensive listing of Vital Records sources and access guidelines for site on the Internet or otherwise. Collected and maintained by Elizabeth Orsay vital-records@usa.net.

RootsWeb Genealogical Data Cooperative

www.rootsweb.com

> The Oldest and most comprehensive Web site for genealogy resources. Sponsors and links to the USGenWeb, WorldGenWeb, GenConnect, and many other volunteer projects. Also sponsors and hosts Cyndi's List.

USGenWeb Project

www.usgenweb.com

> All volunteer coordinated state by state/county by county projects to put full-text genealogy materials online. Including: cemetery records, census data, family histories, newspapers, diaries and more. This is where most of the state genealogical and historical societies Web pages can be located.

Ellis Island Records database at the American Family Immigration History Center

www.ellisislandrecords.org

> Use this search tool to locate ancestor's known to have emigrated to the United States between 1892 and 1924 through Ellis Island. Remember that this database does not contain all of those records as some were lost or unavailable. Many people also came to the U.S. prior to or after these dates. Still more came through other U.S. ports of entry or across the Canadian or Mexican borders.

See the NARA Web site www.nara.gov/genealogy for information about retrieving those records if there are any.

FamilySearch

www.familysearch.org

This is the LDS church's (Mormon) searchable full-text collection of family history records and materials and links to helpful genealogical research. Includes assistance in How to Do a Family History and List of Where to find (LDS) Family History Centers

Ancestry.com

www.ancestry.com

Commercial site which provides many full-text databases for free, the Social Security Death Records, for example, as well as a subscription service for Web access to census images and many other databases. Magazine format provides instructional articles and tips. Searchable index to family history Web pages registered with this site.

GENDEX—WWW Genealogical Index

www.gendex.com/gendex

Gendex was the first tool which indexes and searches family history Web pages. Search using a surname or the soundex equivalent. The family history Web pages that are indexed are specially formatted GEDCOM files. This is a standard computer format for genealogical charts. You may read more about them on the GENDEX site.

Cyndi's Genealogy Homepage

www.CyndisList.com

The most comprehensive genealogical metasite on the Web.

NARA National Archives and Records Administration Genealogy Page

www.archives.gov/research_room/genealogy/index.html

This is a marvelous site with great potential. The genealogy page provides information for genealogical researchers about what is in the NARA collections, how to order documents, which forms are required for Immigration records, Census Records, Military Records, and more. The site publishes articles explaining the limitations and information requirements for obtaining certain kinds of records as well. Limited full-text information online as of this writing.

SPECIAL REFERENCE SEARCH ENGINES/SERVICES

NoodleQuest

www.noodletools.com/noodlequest

Database advisor for the general Web. Complete the form and NoodleQuest will advise which search engines or directories are best for your search.

1.8 READY-REFERENCE RESOURCE COLLECTION TOOLS

See also Part III: Web Collection Development Resources
See also the Core Web Ready-Reference Collection

Eurekalert!

www.eurekalert.org

Science news organized by subject. "Reference Desk" Collection of scientific dictionaries, glossaries, and special statistical resources in each subject area. This is a project of the American Society for the Advancement of Science.

www.eurekalert.org/links.php

Earlham College Libraries—Web Searching

www.earlham.edu/%7Elibr/more

> Graphic-free, General and Reference Section; now includes a Web search and subject directories.

Internet Public Library—Ready Reference Collection

www.ipl.org/div/subject/browse/ref00.00.00

> Huge "Annotated collection, chosen to help answer specific questions quickly and efficiently." This directory includes links to other topics than basic reference material.

netLibrary

www.netlibrary.com

> OCLC subsidiary company that licenses/sells e-book (full-text) collections to libraries

Peter's Digital Reference Shelf

www.galegroup.com/free_resources/reference/index.htm

> Peter Jasco's column on the Gale Web site. Reviews reference sites, databases, and similar resouces. Very critical and frequently provides details that other reviewers skim over; e.g., search tool functionality.

Quick Reference

www.indiana.edu/~librcsd/internet

> Alphabetic listing of both reference databases and academic databases, which is searchable.

Reference Shelf—University of Pennsylvania Libraries

www.library.upenn.edu/cgi-bin/res/sr.cgi

> Most-used reference sources (links) displayed first and annotated; other reference resources (some relating just to the college) are listed at side bar.

The Gateway to Information: Titles of Useful Resources

www.lib.ohio-state.edu/gateway

> Searchable alphabetic and subject directory of reference titles. The title is annotated if it is online or physically in one of their libraries.

Reference Collection—University at Albany

http://library.albany.edu/reference

> Not only is a directory of all types of references, also includes a link to other reference Metasites.

Reference Sources—Longwood University Library

www.longwood.edu/library/ref.htm

> Librarian selected directory of links to ready-reference sources—Abstracts to Zip Codes.

Reference Review Europe

www.rre.casalini.com

> "Over 1000 European reference book reviews online, full-text searchable, updated quarterly."

Virtual Reference Collection (M.I.T.)

http://libraries.mit.edu/research/virtualref.html

> Each reference category is listed with its corresponding sites.

2:   Business Information Resources

"The U.S. Bureau of Labor Statistics has predicted a net increase of more than 10,000 information professionals in the U.S. labor force by the year 2006....As demand for information-sorting expertise has grown, the role of the special librarian has evolved....The corporate librarian "no longer stacks shelves and archives company information," said SLA Executive Director David R. Bender. "Today's corporate librarians are technologically savvy information professionals who use the latest information technology to proactively gather, analyze and disseminate knowledge for strategic decision making."

A. Katz-Stone (2000)

2.1 DEVELOPING THE COLLECTION PLAN FOR BUSINESS INFORMATION RESOURCES

Business resources are some of the common and numerous on the Web. In an effort to attract customers (both consumer and business to business) and investors to their Web sites businesses are sharing an unprecedented level of information. Company Web sites often contain product catalogs, technical support information, company financial data, annual and quarterly reports, and other information. Traditional business information sources are building on this trend by publishing their directories on the Web. Advertisers have always been the main source of revenue for most publishers of business directories and company, industry, and financial news. The Web opens a whole new source of advertising revenue for them. As a result, many such publishers have been steadily expanding versions of their products onto the Web.

Government collectors of business information are using the Web to make this information available to the public and also requiring businesses to use the Internet to submit their required "paperwork" to government agencies. For instance, the U.S. Securities and Exchange Commission requires public companies to upload required reports such as 10K (annual reports) or 10Q (quarterly reports) to the Edgar database via FTP. Business and financial news is also being published directly to the Web. This type of information is especially sensitive to security issues and quality considerations because it frequently involves financial or private information. Business information on the Web is primarily found in the form of directories of businesses and industries, stock market quotations and analysis, and business and financial news. Web business directories, such as Hoovers Online (www.hoovers.com), contain business listings along with industry, product, competitors, financial status, contact information, and other basic data. Thomas Register Online (www.thomasregister.com) in addition to the contact information and basic industry and product data, includes direct links to company catalogs, Web sites, and other e-commerce options. Stock and commodities market information is also available online in real-time or delayed time (15–20 minutes). Many people make stock and commodity trades through the Web in almost real-time. Such trades are never instantaneous and may be delayed by network connection speeds, or server loads. Other kinds of business information include currency and exchange rates, consumer information, small business support resources, product information, catalogs, and customer support services. Electronic commerce (e-commerce) sites where patrons can purchase products, services, transportation, make investments, do banking, and many other business transactions through the Web are numerous.

What purpose will your Business information collection serve? For whom are you collecting Business information Web resources?

Who is asking business information questions? Business people (owner, manager, employee, researcher, broker, financial analyst), potential small business owners, job seekers, students (high school and college), or marketing company? What are they asking?

Ready-reference/single source for answers:

- I have a job interview with Company X—how can I learn more about the company?
- Where can I find a supplier/vendor of X product in the US?
- Where can I get contact addresses to create a mailing list for marketing my product/business/services in the US?

In-depth/multiple sources for answers:

- Is this U.S. company a good risk for investment (or job security)?
- Where can I get marketing and demographic data for a marketing plan to start a business in the x country? (e.g., U.S., Canada, UK, EU, China, Brazil, Mexico, or anywhere)
- How do I get money to start a business in x country?
- How do I write a legally binding contract with my client in the x country/state/province?

Will the library encourage or allow patrons to engage in e-commerce activities? Will the library primarily provide access to product catalogs and consumer information (price comparison sites, for example). Will storefronts and stock and commodity trading sites be included directly in the e-library?

Public libraries will want to provide resources focused on the needs of local businesses as well as for potential small business owners, students and jobseekers. They may find that either, or both, small businesses or local major companies are their primary business information patrons and will want to collect resources to support those businesses. Many academic libraries may need to gather a collection of archived historical business information such as annual reports, historical stock market data, and other materials used in academic business studies or business research. Academic libraries will be collecting for students engaged in business studies defined by their parent university or college programs, as well as for faculty and researchers. The collection scope for their business e-library will be defined by the programs offered and the supporting information required by those programs and by research needs of faculty or graduate students. Special librarians will be collecting resources to support the business in which they work. For example, the library for a company in the petro-chemical industry would need resources related to the production and use of petro-chemicals, vendor and customer Web sites, professional organizations, datasets, safety guidelines, and so on. The business librarian will almost always need to have access to some of the fee-based Web resources that provide very current and detailed research reports, statistics, and financial information. School libraries may need to look carefully to find age appropriate business information depending on the age of the children the library serves, and the curriculum that the library supports. Some excellent business information resources exist that were designed for teenagers. One example is the "I Don't Flip Burgers" (http://library.thinkquest.org/C0114800/about/index.php) site, which is a guide to books and Web sites to assist students in achieving entrepreneurial success. The site also features a small business simulator program in which the student plays the role of an entrepreneur.

Geographical coverage is also an important consideration. A library may wish to provide in-depth support for local, state, provincial, district, regional, or international business interests. In fact, any modern library may find, in our global economy, that their local businesses, students, and other business information patrons need access to international business information.

WHAT TYPES OF BUSINESS INFORMATION WEB RESOURCES WILL YOU COLLECT?

Business Web resources take forms that can be described in terms of traditional reference source types. An annotated "Core Web Business Reference Collection" at the end of this chapter lists essential business information Web reference tools chosen from these reference source types. Business reference sources may be books, databases, or Web sites, but basically they fall into these seven types.

- Business Reference Metasites
- Business Directories (business contact, government contact, customer contact, grants and development information)
- Business News, public financial data, statistics, and other related types of data
- Business Legal and Regulatory Compilations
- Abstracts, indexes, and table of contents services for business serials
- Key primary documents such as annual reports, stock, commodities, and industry reports

On the Web, business metasites may include full-text of or links to all of the different types of business reference source. For example, Hoover's Online provides a directory, publishes news and financial data, links to statistics and other data, as well as including key primary documents. Much of this is only available in the subscription version but a significant amount of information is provided without charge.

In business reference, sources of current news, financial, statistical, or other business or industry related data are critical and are frequently included in business reference collections.

Abstracts and indexes for business serials are generally not freely available on the Web. Although, many commercial services provide subscription access through the Web.

Key primary documents such as stock and commodity reports, financial and statistical reports, marketing reports, and annual reports are also a core part of the business reference collection.

HOW WILL YOU ORGANIZE YOUR BUSINESS INFORMATION WEB RESOURCE COLLECTION?

This question is always going to be answered differently by each library depending on their answers to the first two questions in the collection planning discussion. Some libraries will organize business resources by subject and subtopics. Some might choose to organize by the resource types identified above. A good combination of these two organizational structures can be very accessible. The British Library—Business Sources on the Net (www.bl.uk/services/information/bislinks.html) collection is organized by both subject and resource types, for example.

2.2 IDENTIFYING AND COLLECTING BUSINESS INFORMATION RESOURCES

Business information Web resources were some of the first to be collected and organized by librarians. In 1994, our colleague Leslie Haas—now head of the general reference department at the J. W. Marriott Library, University of Utah—began compiling the first "Business Sources on the Net" collection. Mel Westerman, business librarian at Pennsylvania State University (now retired), had asked for volunteers from the Buslib-L discussion group to collect and annotate the resources in the many different subtopic areas of business. Hope Tillman, Director of Babson College libraries, was one of the key volunteers. Leslie Haas volunteered to coordinate the volunteers and publish the list on the Internet. This list was then organized and published on the Kent State University Gopher server and FTP server, which are now defunct. With the advent of the Web, many of "Business Sources on the Net" volunteers and other business librarians began collecting business Web resources and organizing them on their own Web sites. The business Web resources identification and collection strategies that the original Buslib-L volunteers used involved monitoring and searching with some of the same types of Web resource collection tools described below.

WEB SITES THAT REVIEW AND EVALUATE BUSINESS INFORMATION WEB RESOURCES: INCLUDING OTHER E-LIBRARIES OR SUBJECT COLLECTION GUIDES/WEBLIOGRAPHIES

Many excellent business Web resource collections, metasites, and e-libraries are included in the Business Resource Collection Tools webliography at the end of this chapter. Some of the most valuable sites in terms of thorough annotations, evaluations, and scope of subject coverage are the Louisiana State University Library's Business Web collection (www.lib.lsu.edu/bus/index.htm), The New York Public Library Science, Industry and Business Library (www.nypl.org/research/sibl/index.html), and Jeanie M. Welch's VIBES—Virtual International Business and Economic Sources (http://library.uncc.edu/display/?dept=reference& format=open&page=68).

DISCUSSION LISTS AND NEWSGROUPS WHERE INDIVIDUAL PARTICIPANTS REVIEW AND EVALUATE BUSINESS INFORMATION WEB RESOURCES

The core discussion lists and newsgroups related to business Web resources for business libraries is Buslib-L. Buslib-L is a moderated discussion list that addresses all issues relating to "the collection, storage, and dissemination of business information within a library setting—regardless of format." Subscription information and archives are available at http://listserv .boisestate.edu/archives/buslib-l.html. Search the archives for information about individual business Web resources or subscribe for ongoing discussions. For example, search for "Thomas Register" to find out what Buslib-L subscribers think about *Thomas Register Online*.

E-JOURNALS AND E-NEWSLETTERS THAT PUBLISH REVIEWS AND EVALUATIONS OF BUSINESS INFORMATION WEB RESOURCES

Many of the business resource metasites included with this chapter also publish e-newsletter or e-journals as part of their basic service. The Dow Jones Business Directory (http:// businessdirectory.dowjones.com) and the bizjournals.com (www.bizjournals.com/bizresources) sites both publish reviews of business-related Web sites, as well as organizing and linking to many sites. Several of the business metasites included in section 2.8, the Business Resource Collection Tools: Metasites, E-library collections webliography list business e-serials. For example, the OPLIN Business Information subtopic Business News (http://oplin.lib.oh.us/index .cfm?id=7-262). The Business Reference and User Services Section (BRASS) of ALA publishes two e-newsletters that review business Web resources. *Academic BRASS* (www.ala.org/ Content/NavigationMenu/RUSA/

Our_Association2/RUSA_Sections/BRASS/Publications8/Academic_BRASS/Academic_BRA SS.htm) and Public Libraries Briefcase (www.ala.org/Content/NavigationMenu/RUSA/Our_ Association2/RUSA_Sections/BRASS/Publications8/Academic_BRASS/Academic_BRASS.htm)

PRINT BOOKS AND JOURNALS THAT REVIEW BUSINESS INFORMATION WEB RESOURCES

Several excellent books have been published recently that provide assistance in identifying good business information Web sites. The Global Guides to Internet Business Resources series published by Greenwood Publishing Group (www.greenwood.com/search/series_search .asp?Listing=List&series_title=Global**Guides**to**Internet**Business**Resources) includes *Internet Resources and Services for International Finance and Investment* (2001), by Q. G. Jiao and L. G. Liu, *Internet Resources and Services for International Marketing and Advertising—A Global Guide* (2002), by J. R. Coyle, *Internet Resources and Services for International Real Estate Information—A Global Guide* (2001), by S-Y. Y. Chao, and The *Internet Resources and Services for International Business: A Global Guide* (1998), by L. G. Liu. These books review and annotates hundreds of business-related Web sites.

Essential Business Websites: You Need to Use Everyday (2000) is also a good book to look for business Web resources.

Most business journals and newsletters frequently include reviews of Web resources either as articles or, in the same section, as book reviews. *Barrons, Inc.*, *Fortune*, and *The Wall Street Journal*, feature Web resource reviews in nearly every issue. The Special Libraries Association,

Business and Finance Division publishes a quarterly bulletin that includes Web resource reviews.

2.3 EVALUATION GUIDELINES

Evaluating business information found on the Web requires answers to the same basic questions that should be asked about any source of information. Business, medical, and law information are especially sensitive. Quality of information on these subjects can affect the financial and physical well-being of library patrons. Therefore, it is particularly important to very carefully evaluate any source of information in these subject areas. Evaluation of medical Web resources is discussed in Chapter 6. Evaluation of law Web resources is discussed in Chapter 7.

The quality and currency of business information may affect the financial success or failure of individuals, businesses, and organizations. Therefore, accuracy, timeliness, and security are of great importance.

WHO PROVIDED THE INFORMATION? WHAT IS THEIR REPUTATION AS AN INFORMATION PROVIDER? DO THEY HAVE THE AUTHORITY OR EXPERTISE TO PROVIDE INFORMATION ON THAT TOPIC?

The reputation of any provider of business information is very important in business decision making. Information obtained from MorningStar (www.morningstar.com) or Valueline (www.valueline.com), has more credibility and authority than information obtained from "some guy" on a Usenet newsgroup or Web chat. The only way to determine the source of information provided on the Internet is to read through the Web site, e-mail message, or newsgroup posting, and look for an attribution. For example, Information obtained from Yahoo Finance! (http://finance.yahoo.com) is supplied by Reuters, Ameritrade, TD Waterhouse, CyberTrader, Scottrade, and others. Links to each source are provided.

If you cannot easily determine the source and publisher of business information, then it is best not to use it. The reputation of a business information source is usually based on their record of successful projections and analyses as well as their record in terms of ethical business practices.

DOES THE BUSINESS INFORMATION PROVIDER HAVE THE AUTHORITY OR EXPERTISE TO PROVIDE INFORMATION ON THAT TOPIC?

In business, authority and expertise go hand in hand. Providers of business information are expected to have both education and experience in researching and analyzing financial, economic, and other business data. Education is not necessarily as important as experience and the information provider's record of successful predictions, analyses, and ethics. Use the same strategy to find this information as you did in determining who provided the information. Again, if it is not clear to you that the information provider has the requisite experience and expertise, do not use the information. When in doubt about the authority of an individual source, ask. Any legitimate broker, business or financial advisor, will be more than willing to supply you with their credentials and references. It is wise to monitor the scam information sites discussed in Chapter 1 and to check the Better Business Bureau Online (www.bbb.org) before doing business.

IS THE INFORMATION PROVIDED FOR CURRENT INFORMATION OR HISTORICAL PURPOSES? DOES CURRENCY AFFECT THE QUALITY OF THE INFORMATION? WHEN WAS THE LAST UPDATE OF THE INFORMATION?

Much business information, especially financial information, needs to be as current as possible. Stock and commodities prices, currency exchange rates, news about current events which affects business, agriculture and other commodities reports are very time sensitive. Publication on the Web, potentially, implies that this source of business information is the most current information available. Sites such as CNNmoney (http://money.cnn.com) can provide all the types of information described above, and provide them with a date and time stamp so that the information user knows precisely the time at which the information was gathered and published.

Yahoo Finance! (http://finance.yahoo.com) also provides time and date information about currency exchange rates, stock quotes, and related financial information.

Other sources and types of business information are actually historical in nature. Economic trends, changes in an industry over time, stock values over time, as well as changes in the products, personnel, and mission of individual companies are historical information. Read carefully through Web sites and e-serials to verify times and dates of publication. Decide also if the site is intended to provide historical information.

Is security important in interacting with a given business Web site? Is a site likely to be hacked and information altered? Will personal or financial information be requested from patrons?

Security of business information on the Web is extremely critical from both the site security and patron security perspectives. These two security questions are very different. The information user needs to feel that the information that they might find on the Web, has not been altered by an agent other than the original information provider. They also need to know that the Web site in question is actually published by the organization it seems to be published by. See the discussion of Web site hacking in Chapter 1.

When engaging in e-commerce, the patron needs to feel secure in giving their personal and financial data to a company through their Web site. Personal and financial information should never be submitted through un-encrypted e-mail or Web forms. Always use Web browser functionality to determine the security certification of any Web site, which requests personal or financial data. Never send personal or financial information through e-mail, unless you are using an e-mail encryption tool.

Is privacy an important factor for you or your patrons?

Some business research requires privacy in order to ensure information security. Industrial espionage is a very real problem in our modern global economy. If a competitor learns that a given company is researching along a certain line, that knowledge may give them a competitive advantage in developing or marketing a product, obtaining a contract, or recruiting desirable personnel. The fact that there is no privacy on the Internet may be a problem for many businesses. For example, a friend of ours used to be a librarian for a high-tech, research and development division of a Fortune 100 company. That friend would call our academic library and ask us to research certain things on the Internet rather than doing the research from their own Internet connection. That way it just looked like someone at Kent State University was researching in a particular area rather than someone from that company's competitor. Public libraries may find that business people are using their Internet services for the same reason. Researching on the Web from a public library computer is relatively anonymous. All anyone can find out is that someone at a particular library is researching a particular topic. Overall, this is a positive trend, as it means librarians also have the opportunity to prove their value to the businesses in their communities. It also may result in increased research assistance to those businesses when they are using the library or need to do research and fax, e-mail, or report the results over the telephone. For example, KnowItNow24x7 serves businesses in Northern Ohio through virtual reference service. Patrons may elect to ask questions directly to the Business and Finance Librarians (www.knowitnow24x7.net). The Web links collection and business databases in the Clevnet system e-library (www.clevnet.org) are resources the librarians can use to assist those patrons.

2.4 Selection Criteria

In October 2002, we surveyed librarians on Buslib-L, PubLib, Libref-L, and OPLINLIST about their core or essential business reference tools. The questions asked and the results generated thereby are reproduced in the following survey box.

Table 2.2.1. Survey Results: Essential Business Reference Tools

Question Posted to publib@sunsite.berkeley.edu, libref-l@listserv.kent.edu, and oplinlist@oplin.lib.oh.us:

- What are your 2–5 most used reference tools for Business Questions?

Question Posted to buslib-l@listserv.boisestate.edu:

- What are the top 5–8 print reference books that you can't work without?
- What are the top 5–8 CD-ROM, Tape or Online databases that you can't work without?

Table 2.2.2. Essential Business Reference Tools

1. Standard & Poors Surveys, Directories, Reports. Available:www.standardandpoors .com.
2. Harris Directories. Available: www.harrisinfo.com, and
   Thomas Register. Available: www.thomasregister.com, and
   ValueLine. Available: www.valueline.com.
3. Morningstar. Available: www.morningstar.com, and
   Dun & Bradstreet's Million Dollar Directory. Available: www.dunandbradstreet.com.
4. Brands and Their Companies. Available: www.galegroup.com.
5. Reference USA. Available: www.referenceusa.com.
6. Hoovers Online. Available: www.hoovers.com, and Lexis-Nexis. Available: www.lexisnexis.com.
7. ABI/Inform and other Proquest Databases. Available: www.proquest.com.
8. International Directory of Company Histories. Available: www.galegroup.com, and
   Business Source Premier. Available: www.epnet.com, and
   Ward's Business Directory of U.S. Private and Public Companies. Available: www.galegroup.com.
9. MergentOnline/FIS Online. Available: www.mergentonline.com.
10. Access to company Web pages.
11. Directory of Corporate Affiliations. Available: www.nationalregisterpub.com, and
    Encyclopedia of American Industries. Available: www.galegroup.com, and
    Hoover's handbooks. Available: www.hoovers.com, and
    Wall Street Journal. Available: http://online.wsj.com.

URLs provided are for the publisher's Web site.

It is interesting to observe that many of the core business reference tools identified in this survey are Web-accessible. In fact most respondents who specified a choice, preferred the Web-accessible versions to the print version.

This model core collection was used to choose business reference resources for the "Core Web Business Reference Collection" at the end of this chapter and on the companion Web site.

Additional selection criteria for business information resources can be derived from the answers arrived at during the collection planning process.

The "Core Web Business Reference Collection" was compiled with these criteria in mind. The intended patron group is librarians working with patrons who might be interested in basic business reference information regardless of their educational level. All these core business reference Web sites conform to international standards for Web accessibility, with no special software required for access. At least some information provided by each of these sites is free of direct cost. Many have additional special fee-based services such as detailed datasets, document delivery, or more advanced search options. Several require registration. The registration serves as a marketing research tool for the information provider. Many Web sites are funded by advertising. The information provider uses the information obtained during the registration procedure to count their "circulation" demographics. This is the same principle used by newspapers and magazines. They sell advertising based on the circulation rate and demographics that they can guarantee to advertisers. However, registering on Web sites may result in having your e-mail address included in spam e-mail lists. Most reputable sites will provide an opportunity for you to opt out of such lists. Read carefully the privacy policies that should be posted on each site to decide if you will use them.

2.5 E-LIBRARY SUCCESS STORY

SAN BERNARDINO COUNTY LIBRARY WEBLIBRARY

San Bernardino, California, USA
www.sbcounty.gov/library/homepage

> Contact: Richard Watts, Web Librarian, rwatts@lib.sbcounty.gov, Nannette Bricker-Barrett, Electronic Resources and Training Coordinator nbricker@lib.sbcounty.gov, and Susan Erickson, Youth Services Coordinator, serickson@lib.sbcounty.gov and Kristin Lane, Library Assistant. (Youth Services), klane@lib.sbcounty.gov

The San Bernardino County library's e-library Web site was conceived by County Librarian Ed Kieczykowski as a way to provide selected library services to a large community of users.

> "Our primary target audience is the residents of San Bernardino County. The county is the largest in the United States, covering 20,131 square miles (51,961 square kilometers) and with a 2000 population of 1,709,434. About 90 percent of the county is

Figure 2.2.0. San Bernardino County Library Team: From left: Dani Cinquemani, Graphics Technician; Ed Kieczykowski, County Librarian; Richard Watts, Technical Services; Rick Wright, Automation Services.

located in the Mojave Desert; the remainder consists of the San Bernardino Valley, lying on the eastern outskirts of metropolitan Los Angeles, and the San Bernardino Mountains, a popular resort area. The San Bernardino County Library serves over 1,000,000 county residents through 28 branches and an administrative headquarters. Six cities in the county support independent city library systems." RW

It has grown and evolved from a basic Internet links collection and pathfinders that existed in 1999 to include four completely redesigned information areas, including the WebLibrary, Children, Teens, and general Internet.

"The Director of the Library wants to use our limited financial resources in the manner which will provide the greatest accessibility—so rather than buying individual reference books which are only available in certain libraries at certain times he wants us to offer information more universally to our patrons. For that reason we are spending less money on paper reference resources and more on electronic resources that are available to our patrons" NBB

The San Bernardino County E-library was created primarily by Richard Watts, who is currently the Technical Services Coordinator and Webmaster, but other library personnel also provide ongoing development and maintenance of the site is also provided by other library personnel.

Nannette Bricker-Barrett maintains the WebLibrary area. The Children and Teen area is developed by Youth Services Librarian, Susan Erickson, and her assistant Kristin Lane. Richard Watts continues to develop the OCLC pathfinders. Graphic Artist, Dani Cinquemani, works on the graphics for the Children and Teens areas. Automated Systems Technician Rick Wright provides expertise in Web site structure and development, Javascript, Active Server Pages, and patron authentication for the project.

"When the new version of the home page was under development, 60–70% of staff time was not unusual. Now that the site is basically complete except for "Teens," 1–10% is more typical. The graphic artist is still heavily involved in finishing the "Teens" section, and the Webmaster is still involved at a 30–40% level." RW

San Bernardino County Library chose personnel who had education and training that qualified them for their tasks in the e-library. The Children and Teen area developers attended an Infopeople Project (www.infopeople.org) workshop for basic curriculum subject areas and related links. They used what they learned to create the basic design and content.

The WebLibrary (www.sbcounty.gov/library/WebLibrary) debuted in 2001 and is a collection of annotated and organized Web sites, as well as links to licensed fee-based database that are intended for adults. It is:

"a library you can use anytime of the day or night 365 days of the year from any computer with Internet access. Use these databases and links to Internet sites to find answers to your questions, help with homework assignments, decide what to read next, check out electronic books and more."

The WebLibrary was created with the citizens of San Bernardino County in mind. No formal e-library collection policy was created although the San Bernardino County Library does have a general policy for collections.

"When given the assignment to come up with a virtual library (webLibrary) I started by looking at other libraries' sites to see what they had to offer. We knew that we wanted to combine our subscription databases (e.g., Gale products) and reviewed general interest websites. The websites would all be "end" sites—that is not portals that took you in circles to other portals or rings, but sites that would provide information on the topic. As I developed the subject areas and sites the Adult Services department looked over the offerings making suggestions for additions and deletions and then the site went to a Committee that had formed to overhaul the entire Library website." NBB

Staff evaluate all sites for authoritative source of information, currency, accuracy, as well as information content desirable to San Bernardino County Library patrons. Of the resources used by the San Bernardino County Library, some sources of potential sites to add include Librarian's Index to the Internet (www.lii.org) and Internet Scout Report (http://scout.wisc.edu).

"WebLibrary content is one of my projects—the time I spend on it varies. In development it was about 4 months solid time; revisions again can take chunks of time (days)—for example we're getting together Spanish language sites to put on a Spanish page and the gathering of sites took me several days; those sites are now being reviewed by Spanish speaking staff. Once the sites are up then I spend time coordinating access—taking complaints/problems from staff/public and contacting vendors and/or Automation department to keep the databases up and running. A staff member in Adult Services keeps the Hot Topics section going as part of her duties—spending probably 2 hours a week (content typically changes monthly.) To keep WebLibrary up and running also involves Community Services (graphics and design), and the Automation and Technical Services departments." NBB

Licensed databases include ten Gale Group products including Business and Company Resource Center, History Resource Center, and others, as well as The Facts on File, LearnaTest, World Book, OnLine Book Clubs, and the netLibrary e-books product.

With the potential of library budget cuts some databases may be renegotiated for number of simultaneous users or cancelled based on usage statistics.

"We use Gale Group's Infotrac Total Access for cross-database searches. Searches can include 10 Gale products, Yahoo, Google, GPO Access, and the library's online catalog." RW

All of the databases except Mitchell 1's ondemand5.com (automotive manuals) are remotely Web-accessible by San Bernardino County Library patrons with a library card number or other ID.

The Children or "Kids Page" (www.sbcounty.gov/library/children/New%20page/Main_page.htm) debuted in 2003. The "Kids Page" is designed for children twelve and under and includes Web sites specially selected by library staff to assist children in doing their homework, having fun, and learning more about books, parents and teachers, and other libraries' "Kids Pages." The "Kids Page" includes a collection of Spanish language Web sites.

"Children's sites are selected in alignment with the California State Dept. of Education's curriculum areas. Sites from the InfoPeople Workshop "Surfing the Curriculum" form the bulk of the content in this area" SE

The Children and Teens area developers identify new and appropriate sites from:

"recommended Web sites by other libraries posting to various listservs, and we subscribe to various web site review services, such as: Berit's Best Sites for Children (www.beritsbest.com), Librarian's Index to the Internet (www.lii.org), and Neat New Stuff I Found On the Net This Week (www.marylaine.com/neatnew.html)." KL

The "Teens" (www.sbcounty.gov/library/teens/main.htm) page is currently being developed.

The Internet area provides links to major search engines and Web research tutorials. The pathfinders—guides to different subject research areas are hosted by OCLC.

All areas are reviewed continually and changes and updates are made as they are discovered. New sites are chosen by subject specialists: Dani Cinquemani creates the html pages, and Richard Watts adds the new links and annotations to the Web site.

"The site is mounted on San Bernardino County's server (www.sbcounty.gov). It is a Dell, operating under Windows NT 4.0 and IIS 4.0. It is located in the County's Information Services Division building, located several miles from the library administration building. Rick Wright uses Frontpage 2000 for most of his development work. Dani Cinquemani uses Macromedia Dreamweaver 4.0 and Fireworks 4.0. Richard Watts uses Dreamweaver 4.0." RW

San Bernardino County Library has offered an e-mail reference service for the past four years. Recently they began to offer virtual reference to patrons with 24/7 Reference offered through the Tierra Del Sol Regional Library Network (www.inlandlib.org/ Library%20of%20California/TDS%20pg.htm). San Bernardino County Library provide reference librarians to staff the 24/7 Reference service for several shifts. Patrons can access by clicking on the "Ask A Librarian" option from the main library home page.

San Bernardino County Library participated in the original OCLC CORC project to catalog Web resources. (Incorrect. We use CORC records, but we were not participants in the CORC project.)

"The library's earlier lists of cataloged Web resources were transformed into OCLC Pathfinders when the new lists of categorized links were mounted. Those pathfinders were parsed against the OCLC Resource Catalog with OCLC's Connexion software. All relevant OCLC catalog records (mostly from the CORC project) have been added to the catalog using copy cataloging. Unique links from "webLibr@ry," "Children" and "Teens" will receive similar treatment in the near future. No original cataloging of sites not found in OCLC's Resource Catalog has been performed. Use of these records is not yet tracked." RW

Figure 2.2.1. San Bernardino Web E-library www.sbcounty.gov/library/homepage

Maintenance of the e-library is done as needed. They use Xenu's Link Sleuth (http://home.snafu.de/tilman/xenulink.html) to check links every four months or so and then they follow up with a manual check of links to catch any content or redirect changes.

"Link Sleuth is used to check an entire list of links in batch, followed by a manual second check. The price is right (freeware), and we do not have direct access to the Web server for such checking. The software does an excellent "quick and dirty" job of checking on and reporting dead and redirected links (as long as the redirect is encoded at the old URL). "RW

The San Bernardino County Library solicits feedback from e-library users via an e-mail link on the home page and a user suggestion link in the online catalog. A "What I like about the library's new home page" essay contest when the WebLibrary debuted generated a lot of positive feedback.

Future developments of the San Bernardino County e-library are planned by the Site Review Committee.

> "the County Librarian, the Assistant County Librarian, 2 staff members from the Automation Dept., 1 branch manager, 2 members from the Community Services Dept., the Coordinator of Technical Services, the Electronic Resources and Training Coordinator from the Adult Collection Development Dept., and 2 staff members from the Youth Services Dept. The team meets when any major changes are to be made to the homepage." RW

2.6 REFERENCES AND WEB SITES CITED

(Note that some sites are included in the resource lists and webliographies in subsequent chapters, and therefore are not necessarily duplicated in this section.)

BF bulletin / Business and Finance Division. New York: Special Libraries Association (ISSN: 1048–5376). Available at: www.slabf.org.

Chao, S-Y. Y. 2001. *Internet Resources and Services for International Real Estate Information—A Global Guide*. Westport, CT: Oryx Press.

Coyle, J. R. 2002. *Internet Resources and Services for International Marketing and Advertising—A Global Guide.* Westport, CT: Oryx Press.

Global Guides to Internet Business Resources series, published by Greenwood Publishing Group. Available: www.greenwood.com/search/series_search.asp?Listing=List&series_title=Global**Guides**to**Internet**Business**Resources

Jiao, Q. G., and L. G. Liu. 2001. *Internet Resources and Services for International Finance and Investment*. Westport, CT: Oryx Press.

Katz-Stone, A. 2000. Web Overturning Image of Book-filing Librarian. *Washington Business Journal* http://washington.bizjournals.com/washington/stories/2000/04/03/focus4.html?t=printable

Liu L. G. 1998. The *Internet Resources and Services for International Business: A Global Guide*. Westport, CT: Oryx Press.

Welch, J. 2002. Hey! What About Us?! Changing Roles of Subject Specialists and Reference Librarians in the Age of Electronic Resources. *Serials Review* 28, no. 4 (Winter): 283–86.

ABI/Inform. Available: www.proquest.com.

Business Source Premier. Available: www.epnet.com.

Lexis-Nexis. Available: www.lexisnexis.com.

MergentOnline/FIS Online. Available: www.mergentonline.com.

Morningstar. Available: www.morningstar.com.

Reference USA. Available: www.referenceusa.com.

Standard & Poors Surveys, Directories, Reports. Available: www.standardandpoors.com.

ValueLine. Available: www.valueline.com.

Wall Street Journal. Available: http://online.wsj.com.

2.7 THE CORE WEB BUSINESS REFERENCE COLLECTION

BUSINESS REFERENCE METASITES
(See also Business Resource Collection Tools)

Hoovers Handbook
www.hoovers.com

The Hoovers Handbook provides company profiles for five hundred major corporations indexed by type of industry, geographical location of headquarters, by names of people included in the profiles, and by company name and products. Hoovers online provides searchable free basic data from Hoover company profiles; the complete profile is available for a fee. Links are provided to EDGAR and individual company Web sites where available. The Hoovers Online site also links to the Datek Online stock quotations site and the Standard & Poors Rating Services online as well as other Internet Business directories.

Infoplease.com
www.infoplease.com/bus.html

Searchable collection of business and economics information from online almanacs, dictionaries and the sixth edition of the *Columbia Encyclopedia* online.

BUSINESS DIRECTORIES (BUSINESS CONTACT, GOVERNMENT CONTACT, CUSTOMER CONTACT, GRANTS AND DEVELOPMENT INFORMATION)

Associations on the Net: Business and Economics (Internet Public Library)
www.ipl.org/div/aon/browse/bus00.00.00

Business associations are a major source of high quality information. The Internet Public Library project has organized hundreds of key associations in this section of their excellent e-library collection.

Community Foundations Directory
www.foundations.org/communityfoundations.html

This directory of community foundations, which may be a source of business or other types of grants, is published online by the Northern California Community Foundation, Inc.

CorpTech
www.corptech.com

Searchable database of in-depth profiles for more than fifty thousand public and private high-tech companies. Partially international in scope.

Federal Grant Resources
www.sba.gov/expanding/grants.html

This listing of links to federal grants information sites is provided by the Small Business Administration. Some state grants sites are also listed.

Foundations and Grantmakers Directory
www.foundations.org/grantmakers.html

This directory of corporate and private foundations which may be a source of business or other types of grants is published online by the Northern California Community Foundation, Inc. Includes the Community Foundations Directory

GrantsWeb
www.srainternational.org/newweb/grantsweb/index.cfm

The Society of Research Administrators. Federal and international goverment resources plus some private foundations.

Hierarchies.org: Who Owns Who
www.hierarchies.org

Volunteer/community-based project to gather and make available information about corporate ownership. Subsidiary and Parent companies are searchable and browseable. Editors verify the accuracy of the information.

Inter-Agency Electronic Grants Committee—IAEGC
www.iaegc.gov

Committee that is working on interagency electronic grant compatibility and inter-networking. Includes link to state and local efforts.

Online Chambers of Commerce HomePage

http://online-chamber.com

> Directory of international, national, state, and local Chamber of Commerce Web sites. This is not a comprehensive directory, but rather a list of those Chambers of Commerce with an Internet presence. This is a commercial site—meaning it is a dot-com URL—but doesn't seem to sell or promote anything.

Small Business Investment Companies

www.sba.gov/hotlist/sbic.html

> This listing of links to small business investment companies (venture capital sources) is provided by the Small Business Administration.

Thomas Register

www.thomasregister.com

> Thomas Register is a thirty-three volume directory of U.S. vendors of fifty thousand products manufactured by one hundred twenty-five thousand U.S. companies. It is indexed alphabetically, geographically, and by trademark/brandnames. The Internet version is better in many ways. It takes up less space and actually covers more companies and products. It requires registration but provides free company and product information for nearly one hundred sixty thousand companies. Searchable by brandname, company name, or by product or service. Links directly to company online catalogs, product support, or other Web sites are provided where available. See "The Thomas Register Online" OPLIN Business Bytes 2(1) May 2000 http://oplin.lib.oh.us/index .cfm?ID=2450

Thomas Register Regional

www.thomasregional.com

> Industry information and news by region as well as the information in the full Thomas Register online. Option for weekly industry information e-mail newsletter.

Thomas Global Register Europe (TRG Europe)

www.tipcoeurope.com

> The venerable and trusted publisher of the Thomas Register publishes this directory as well. This is a six-language directory of two hundred ten thousand manufacturers and distributors from seventeen European countries, classified by ten thousand five hundred products and services categories.

Thomas Register of Indian Manufacturers (TRIM)

www.thomasindia.com

> The venerable and trusted publisher of the Thomas Register publishes this directory as well. The Web site lists companies from all regions of India in six Indian regional languages.

BUSINESS NEWS (INCLUDING PUBLIC FINANCIAL DATA, STATISTICS, AND OTHER RELATED TYPES OF DATA)

CNNmoney

http://money.cnn.com

> CNN and Money Magazine financial network Web site. Contains full-text transcripts of CNN's financial news stories and links to financial and other data. Access to quotes and stock analysis. International and local in scope.

Conference Board Business Cycle Indicators

www.tcb-indicators.org

> This is a membership organization providing free access to the leading economic indicators and archives. Includes a tutorial on the importance and meaning of

economic indicators. The business cycle indicators database requires fee-based subscription

Forbes
www.forbes.com

Full text of articles from *Forbes*, *Forbes FYI*, and *Forbes ASAP*. Searchable and updated daily.

Inc.
www.inc.com/home

Full text searchable site of selected *Inc.* magazine stories. Monthly with archives.

Value Line Publishing
www.valueline.com

Requires registration, but has many free articles and reports as well as research from the Value Line investment publications. Also provides subscription access to Value Line publications.

Yahoo! Finance
http://finance.yahoo.com

Current Stock market quotes, currency and exchange information, market and company analysis. Other sites provide this information, but Yahoo! Finance provides it in simple format suitable for the general public. Provides links to tutorials on stock and investment terminology and procedures. Yahoo! Finance site links to most of the major suppliers of national and international business news that have a Web presence.

BUSINESS LEGAL AND REGULATORY COMPILATIONS
(See also Core Web Legal Reference Collection)

Internal Revenue Service
www.irs.gov

Searchable site that also has full-text publication, forms and information for business taxes.

Juris International
www.jurisint.org

Collection of full-text legal documents and guidelines. In English, Spanish, and French. This collection is intended for lawyers and legal counsels in business and economic development.

Uniform Commercial Code—Legal Information Institute
www.law.cornell.edu/uniform/ucc.html

"This locator links to state statutes that correspond to Articles of the Uniform Commercial Code."

U.S. Patent and Trademark Office
www.uspto.gov

Information on how to file either a patent or trademark, as well as searchable database of existing patents and trademarks.

ABSTRACTS, INDEXES, AND TABLE OF CONTENTS SERVICES FOR BUSINESS SERIALS
(See Core Web Ready-Reference Collection)

Key primary documents such as annual reports, stock, commodities, and industry reports

Stat-USA

www.stat-usa.gov

Fee-based access to current economic, financial, and other statistical documents provided by the U.S. Department of Commerce Security and Exchange Commission (SEC) Edgar.

Security and Exchange Commission

www.sec.gov

Publicly traded companies must file all required reports including 10K, 10Q directly to Edgar. The SEC makes the Edgar database full-text available for searching by the general public. This is the complete annual reports information for publicly traded (traded on the stock exchange) companies doing business in the United States. It does not include international companies unless they have a presence in the U.S., which is traded on a stock exchange: e.g., Kobe Steel.

Swain Library: Patent and Technology Transfer Databases

http://www-sul.stanford.edu/depts/swain/patent/patdbases.html

Stanford University, Swain Chemistry and Chemical Engineering Library collection of patent and technology transfer tutorials, Web sites, and databases, both fee and free. This site is thorough in reviewing each resource collected. This site will be useful for both business and science and technology librarians.

2.8 BUSINESS RESOURCE COLLECTION TOOLS

See also Part III: Web Collection Development Resources
See also Core Web Business Reference Collection: Business Reference Metasites

Academic BRASS

www.ala.org/Content/NavigationMenu/RUSA/Our_Association2/RUSA_Sections/BRASS/Publications8/Academic_BRASS/Academic_BRASS.htm

E-newsletter published by the Business Reference and User Services Section (BRASS) of ALA. Includes reviews of key business Web resources, as well as other resource reviews, news, and articles. This e-journal is intended for academic business librarians. See Public Librarian's Briefcase in this same list.

Binghamton University Libraries—Business and Economics Resources

http://library.lib.binghamton.edu/subjects/business/index.html

Annotated and updated Business resources of accounting and tax, economics, finance and investment, international business, management, marketing, and social science data, with subdivisions. Includes an annotated gateway to online business resources.

Biz/ed

www.bized.ac.uk

Compiled for business and economics teachers and researchers. This is "a searchable and browsable catalogue of over 4300 quality checked Internet resources," that is international in scope.

British Library—Business Sources On The Net

www.bl.uk/services/information/bislinks.html

Collection of business information Web sites selected and evaluated by the librarians of the British Library.

Competitive Intelligence—Internet Intelligence Index

www.fuld.com/i3/index.html

Internet resources for competitive intelligence research. Compiled by Fuld & Co.

CyberNavigator—New York Times
(Business Connections, and similar links)

www.nytimes.com/ref/technology/cybertimes-navigator.html

This collection is used by journalists writing for the New York Times. The Business Connections section contains hundreds of Business Reference sites of all types. The links are organized, annotated, and proven practical.

Gary Price's List of Lists

www.specialissues.com/lol

Collection of sites with lists of companies, industries, organizations, meeting different criteria; e.g., the "Best Companies to Work for in America" list.

Librarian's Index to the Internet—Business, Finance, and Jobs

http://lii.org/search/file/busfinjobs

Librarian selected, reviewed, and annotated collection of business information Web sites.

New York Public Library Science, Industry and Business Library

www.nypl.org/research/sibl/index.html

Includes guides written by NYPL library staff on small business information, international business, and other topics, as well as a collection of high quality annotated Internet business site links.

Louisiana State University—Business

www.lib.lsu.edu/bus/index.htm

Internet subject guide of databases and resources for business.

Public Libraries Briefcase

www.ala.org/Content/NavigationMenu/RUSA/Our_Association2/RUSA_Sections/BRASS/Publications8/Academic_BRASS/Academic_BRASS.htm

A publication of the BRASS Business Reference in Public Libraries Committee with reviews of business Web resources, news, articles, and other resources.

VIBES—Virtual International Business and Economic Sources

http://libweb.uncc.edu/ref-bus/vibehome.htm

Jeanie M. Welch, a librarian at the University of North Carolina has created this collection of high quality reviewed international and U.S. business and economic Web sites. This is one of the best metasites for business information.

3:   Jobs and Employment Information Resources

3.1 DEVELOPING THE COLLECTION PLAN FOR JOBS AND EMPLOYMENT INFORMATION RESOURCES

Jobs and employment resources are some of the most popular on the Web. Users can access job advertisements and offers from all over the world, and sometimes they may even apply for jobs through the Web. Thousands of Web sites list job opportunities. There are sites for every kind of job, in every country, state, and region. Many sites allow individuals to post their resumes in public resume databases. Job seekers may post their resumes on sites such as Monster.com or Careerboard.com and employers can peruse them. Posting resumes to these services will not be a useful job-seeking tool for all types of job. According to Richard Bolles, author of *What Color is Your Parachute, the Net Guide* (www.jobhuntersbible.com), in his "The Resume Fairy Godmother Report" (www.jobhuntersbible.com/resumes/fgmresumes.shtml), employers actually view very few resumes posted on the Web. It is more likely that the resumes of accountants, computer programmers, engineers, nurses, and other high demand professions will generate success from posting on public resume sites. For other professionals, putting a resume online—preferably on their own Web site—and then referring to their online resume site in print cover letters or attaching the resume to e-mailed cover letters can be a good strategy. For individuals applying for a job in which some Web or other computer skills are required, this strategy demonstrates that they have some basic knowledge of both.

WHAT PURPOSE WILL YOUR JOBS AND EMPLOYMENT COLLECTION SERVE? FOR WHOM ARE YOU COLLECTING JOBS AND EMPLOYMENT WEB RESOURCES?

A Jobs and Employment e-library collection might serve two obvious purposes: access to job listings and application information for job seekers; and information about career choices and vocational/educational preparation for different careers. School, academic, and public libraries are likely to need to provide e-library resources that support both purposes. Students eventually graduate and need to find jobs. A library patron may be seeking a job at any time. Furthermore, students, new graduates, or individuals looking for a career change will find the information about career choices and vocational/educational preparation invaluable. Special business libraries are unlikely to want to collect resources for job seekers. They may, however, support their personnel departments in recruiting employees by maintaining awareness of some of the sites where resumes are posted.

WHAT TYPES OF JOBS AND EMPLOYMENT WEB RESOURCES WILL YOU COLLECT?

The "Core Web Jobs and Employment Reference Collection" at the end of this chapter lists essential Internet reference tools organized by these reference source types:

- Jobs and Employment Metasites
- Encyclopedias of Occupational, Careers and Employment Information
- Jobs and Employment Listings and News

Jobs and employment metasites include both of the other reference source types. News and current information resources are the most important information sources for job seekers and employers. In this area the Internet supplies tools which are without peer in the print world. Some of the most global jobs and employment information and "want-ads" sites are listed in the core reference collection presented later in this section.

How will you organize your Jobs and Employment Web resources?

Jobs and employment information might be organized by job type or subject area, depending on the intention of the collecting library.

3.2 Identifying and Collecting Jobs and Employment Information Resources

Web sites that review and evaluate Jobs and Employment Web resources: including other e-libraries or subject collection guides/webliographies

One guide to jobs and employment resources on the Internet stands head and shoulders above any others: The Riley Guide: Employment Opportunities and Job Resources on the Internet (www.dbm.com/jobguide). It is the ultimate source for these types of information on the Web and through the Internet. For many libraries, providing a link to the Riley Guide and links to local jobs sites may be sufficient for their jobs and employment e-library collection. Margaret Riley Dikel has been compiling the Riley Guide: Employment Opportunities and Jobs Resource on the Internet since 1996 (www.rileyguide.com). It is the ultimate metasite for these types of information on the Web. The Riley Guide contains a comprehensive collection of job advertisement and opportunity listing Web sites organized by type of job, by local, state, or international location, and other criteria. In addition, it contains a collection of employment and career information and advice Web sites.

Discussion lists and newsgroups where individual participants review and evaluate Jobs and Employment Web resources

There is no single discussion list or newsgroup for all jobs and employment resource discussions. A number of discussion lists and newsgroups related to jobs and employment Web resources for specific occupations can be found using the discussion list and newsgroups finding tools discussed in Chapter 1.

Print books and journals that review Jobs and Employment Web resources

Margaret Riley Dikel and Francis Roehm's *Guide to Internet Job Searching, 2002–2003* reviews the best Web sites and strategies for job seekers. One other book, *Jobsearch.Net* (1998), all though specific site information may be dated, guides readers through the process of researching jobs and employment information on the Internet.

Plunkett's Employers' Internet Sites With Careers Information (2001), profiles hundreds of Web sites where major employers list job openings, salaries/benefits information, and provide opportunities to apply online.

3.3 Evaluation Guidelines

Evaluation of jobs and employment information is highly idiosyncratic. One person's good job information is definitely not everyone's idea of good job information. Some job seekers may be looking for professional positions that require experience and education, or creativity and communications skills, and others may be looking for jobs for beginners or that do not require experience or more than minimal education. Jobs and employment information needs to be accurate and current. The strategies for evaluating resources described in Chapter 1 work exceedingly well for jobs and employment information. It is very unlikely that a legitimate jobs and employment information Web page will not have full attribution and contact information. After all, how else will they expect the job seeker to contact them and apply for their positions?

Let patrons know that any site requiring a "fee" should be carefully investigated. There are a number of employment scams on the web. Review the scam and hoax sites discussed in Chapter 1.

In the case of general employment information, such as resume guides, employment outlook reports, cost-of-living, and salary surveys, the prime criteria must be the source of the data provided. For example, the *Occupational Outlook Handbook* is published by the U.S. Bureau of Labor Statistics (www.bls.gov/oco) based on data they have gathered from employers and other sources.

3.4 SELECTION CRITERIA

Selection criteria for jobs and employment Web resources are derived from the answers arrived at during the collection planning process. Again, we'll use the survey results for core Jobs and Employment reference tools identified by subscribers to Libref-L, Publib, and OPLINLIST. The survey question and the subsequent results are reproduced in the following box.

Table 2.3.1. Core or Essential Jobs and Employment Reference Tools Survey

Question Posted to publib@sunsite.berkeley.edu, libref-l@listserv.kent.edu, and oplinlist@oplin.lib.oh.us:

- What are your 2–5 most used reference tools for Jobs and Employment Questions?

Table 2.3.2. Core or Essential Jobs and Employment Reference Tools

- Occupational Outlook Handbook/Web site. Available: www.bls.gov/oco.*
- Encyclopedia of Careers and Vocational Guidance, 4-volume set (print) 10
- Local newspaper classified sections**
- Monster.com. Available: www.monster.com.
- JobBank Series. Available: www.adamsmedia.com.
- Resume books***
- Federal Jobs Digest. Available: www.jobsfed.com.
- The Riley Guide: Employment Opportunities and Jobs Resource on the Internet. Available: www.dbm.com/jobguide.
- CareerBuilder.com. Available: www.careerbuilder.com.
- Jobstar.org. Available: www.jobstar.org.

Almost every respondent selected the Occupational Outlook Handbook as a core reference tool.
**To find local newspaper's online search the Open Directory Project (http://dmoz.org/News/Newspapers/Regional)*
***"all my resume books get stolen, so I link to online sites and refer students to the career center"*
"Resumes That Knock 'em Dead is a favorite here." (www.adamsmedia.com)
"What Color is Your Parachute?" (www.jobhuntersbible.com)

The Core Web Jobs and Employment Reference Collection included below was compiled with this core collection in mind. The intended patron group is librarians who work with job seekers who might be interested in looking for a job or learning about employment opportunities. The educational level tends to be postsecondary, because the jobs that are advertised on the Web tend to be professional or academic-level jobs. All Web sites chosen for this collection conform to international standards for Web accessibility and other design standards. Most of them are free of charge for job seekers. Several have special fee-based services for employers or recruiters listing their positions. Several require registration, but not a fee. The registration serves as a marketing research tool for the information provider as described in the previous section. Be sure to read carefully any privacy statements made on a given site.

3.5 E-LIBRARY SUCCESS STORIES

PINAKES: A SUBJECT LAUNCHPAD

Heriot-Watt University
Edinburgh, United Kingdom
www.hw.ac.uk/libWWW/irn/pinakes/pinakes.html

Contact: Roddy MacLeod
R.A.MacLeod@hw.ac.uk

"The name Pinakes comes from ancient Greece: In ancient times, the Library of Alexandria was seen as a universal store of human knowledge. As the Library grew in size, however, it became increasingly difficult to locate relevant material. The poet Callimachus solved the problem by compiling a catalogue called The Pinakes. On a far smaller scale, the Pinakes Web pages hope to provide a similar function for Internet resources, by linking to the major subject gateways."

Pinakes: A Subject Launchpad, is intended as a starting point for subject searching for Internet resources. Roddy MacLeod with the support of the Heriot-Watt University Library administration developed Pinakes as a small but high quality Internet resource collection tool.

Pinakes is designed as a great access point for subject searching, and has proved very popular. It now includes fifty-five subject area gateways.

Roddy MacLeod didn't produce a written collecting plan, but his overall idea was "to provide a top level entry point for subject based enquiries, and to publicize the fact that several excellent subject based gateways exist."

Pinakes consists of two simple Web pages that require very little maintenance. They are published on the Heriot-Watt University's Web server. There was no direct hardware or software cost and the personnel cost was minimal. Roddy MacLeod and Dave Bond maintain the pages as part of their regular duties. They are mainly pointing to specific high-quality subject directories of Internet resources. Future developments will include some updating and expansion.

3.6 REFERENCES AND WEB SITES CITED

(Note that some sites are included in the resource lists and webliographies in previous chapters, and therefore are not necessarily duplicated in this section.)

Krannich, R. L., and C. R. Krannich. 2002. *The Directory of Websites for International Jobs: The Click and Easy Guide.* Click and Easy Series. Manassas Park, VA: Impact Publications.

Plunkett, J. W. 2001. *Plunkett's Employers' Internet Sites with Careers Information.* Houston: Plunkett Research.

Riley-Dikel, M., and F. E. Roehm. 2002. *Guide to Internet Job Searching, 2002–2003.* Lincolnwood, IL: VGM Career Horizons / Public Library Association.

"I Don't Flip Burgers." Available: http://library.thinkquest.org/C0114800/about/index.php.

Subject List   About

Featured in the BBC Web Wise guide to the Internet, and many other online and print publications.

Hosted by Heriot-Watt University, Edinburgh, Scotland.

ADAM: art, design, architecture and media

AERADE: aerospace and defence studies

AGRIGATE: agriculture, forestry, environment, food science, horticulture

AHDS: arts and humanities

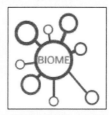

ALTIS: hospitality, leisure, sport, tourism

Biogate: biological sciences

BIOME: health and life sciences

Biz/ed: business and economics

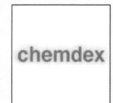

BUBL: library and information science

CAIN: conflict studies

ChemDex: chemistry

EdWeb: educational reform and information technology

Figure 2.3.0. Pinakes: A Subject Launchpad www.hw.ac.uk/libWWW/irn/pinakes/pinakes.html

3.7 THE CORE WEB JOBS AND EMPLOYMENT REFERENCE COLLECTION

JOBS AND EMPLOYMENT METASITES
(See also Jobs and Employment Resource Collection Tools)

ENCYCLOPEDIAS/DIRECTORIES OF OCCUPATIONAL, CAREERS, AND EMPLOYMENT INFORMATION

Career Guide to Industries

www.bls.gov/oco/cg/home.htm

"The Career Guide to Industries provides information on available careers by industry, including the nature of the industry, working conditions, employment, occupations in the industry, training and advancement, earnings and benefits, employment outlook, and lists of organizations that can provide additional information."

Monthly Labor Review
http://stats.bls.gov/opub/mlr/mlrhome.htm

> Publication of the U.S. Federal government that reports employment trends and statistics.

Occupational Outlook Handbook
www.bls.gov/oco

> "The Occupational Outlook Handbook is a nationally recognized source of career information, designed to provide valuable assistance to individuals making decisions about their future work lives. Revised every two years, the Handbook describes what workers do on the job, working conditions, the training and education needed, earnings, and expected job prospects in a wide range of occupations."

JOBS AND EMPLOYMENT LISTINGS AND NEWS

America's Job Bank
www.ajb.dni.us

> Information from the U.S. Department of Labor for both job seekers and employers; links to Talent Bank, Career Infonet, and Learning Exchange.

CareerBuilder.com
www.careerbuilder.com

Federal Jobs Digest
www.jobsfed.com

Jobstar.org
www.jobstar.org

Monster.com
www.monster.com

> Job listings for seekers, create a resume, search companies, and information for recruiters.

NationJob
www.nationjob.com

> Comprehensive listings of jobs available by field/position, and/or location, and/or education. Profile and search for companies that meets your criteria.

Overseas Jobs Express
www.overseasjobs.com

> This site "features international job opportunities for professionals, expatriates and adventure seekers." Information for employers, too.

USA Jobs
www.usajobs.opm.gov

> "This is a United States Office of Personnel Management web site. USAJOBS is the Federal Government's official one-stop source for Federal jobs and employment information."

CareerBuilder.com
Jobstar.org

MISCELLANEOUS JOBS AND EMPLOYMENT-RELATED

Homefair.com
www.homefair.com

> Various calculators, research information and reports (e.g., schools, crime) all relating to relocating.

3.8 JOBS AND EMPLOYMENT RESOURCE COLLECTION TOOLS

See also Part III: Web Collection Development Resources

The Riley Guide

www.rileyguide.com

This comprehensive guide compiled by Margaret F. Dikel, is more than job listings. Provides links to specific occupation databases of job listings or use the new A-Z guide for specific career positions, fields, and locations.

What Color is Your Parachute—The Net Guide

www.jobhuntersbible.com

Collection of career development resources on the Internet by Richard Bolles the author of the popular *What Color is Your Parachute* books.

4: Medical Information Resources

MEDLINEplus is designed to help you find appropriate, authoritative health information. To do this, we provide access to information produced by the National Library of Medicine and the National Institutes of Health, such as searches of MEDLINE, our database that indexes medical literature, and ClinicalTrials.gov, the database of research studies from the National Institutes of Health. We also provide you with a database of full-text drug information, an illustrated medical encyclopedia, a medical dictionary, interactive health tutorials, and the latest health news...In addition, MEDLINEplus contains pages that link to other Web sites. For example, we have Health Topic pages on over 600 diseases and conditions from Alzheimer's Disease to West Nile Virus. We focus on organizing the full-text publications produced by the NIH Institutes and other federal government organizations. We also link to other Web sites.

From MEDLINEplus Selection Guidelines
(http://medlineplus.nlm.nih.gov/medlineplus/criteria.html)

4.1 DEVELOPING THE COLLECTION PLAN FOR MEDICAL INFORMATION RESOURCES

Medical information resources on the Web support the information needs of healthcare consumers, healthcare professionals, and medical researchers. The Internet has proven to be a convenient way to deliver medical information to both consumers and healthcare professionals. Healthcare consumers expect to find quality in-depth medical information on the Web. Kovacs (2003) discusses in detail the need for clear selection criteria, evaluation of information quality, as well as for educational level of healthcare consumers. Collection of medical Web resources for healthcare professionals obviously requires careful attention to information quality, currency, subject knowledge of specialties and medical research areas, as well as selection criteria based on the information-seeking behavior of healthcare professionals. For example, sources that require a lot of time reading, researching and analyzing might be suitable for a medical student or researcher but will not benefit the physician who needs clinical guidelines during or very close to them time when communicating with patients.

Lord and Ragon (2001) confirm that a good collection plan is needed for collecting medical Web resources. They describe their own experiences in defining the user groups, identifying full-text resources, and maintaining local databases on CD versus Web-accessible databases.

"What we've learned...a well-written electronic collection policy proved to be a very effective blueprint for building a digital library. Clearly written guidelines not only help us with selecting materials, but also serve as a guide for effectively promoting these resources to library users...an effective policy should include how your library plans to handle the licensing, technical support, and group purchasing of electronic resources." (Lord and Ragon, 2001: 42)

WHAT PURPOSE WILL YOUR MEDICAL E-LIBRARY COLLECTION SERVE? FOR WHOM ARE YOU COLLECTING MEDICAL WEB RESOURCES?

An e-library developed for a medical school library might support medical education for physicians, nurses, and other healthcare practitioners. For example, the Hardin Meta Directory (www.lib.uiowa.edu/hardin/md/index.html) is a comprehensive e-library collection intended for medical school students selected by the librarians of the Hardin Library for the Health Sciences, University of Iowa. Medical researchers will also find valuable Web resources that assist in the dissemination and accumulation of medical research knowledge. The real value in Web access to medical information is for the practicing healthcare professional and for the healthcare consumer, because it is available at the desktop. Hospital and clinic libraries, whether serving healthcare professionals or consumers, will find plenty of high quality medical Web resources— both free and fee-based. Public libraries and academic libraries may also choose to collect for both healthcare professionals and consumers, as well as for medical or allied health students and faculty. The resources for healthcare professionals may overlap with those intended for consumers. Healthcare consumers, however will need medical dictionaries and frequent referral to a healthcare professional. Librarians must be very careful to not give medical advice. Looking up a word is one thing, translating or interpreting might be dangerous. Take the word "idiopathic," for example. A patron asks the reference question: "My Doctor says I have idiopathic. I need to find some books about this." The librarian might properly respond by starting with a medical dictionary. MedlinePlus medical dictionary is the Merriam Webster Medical Dictionary. It gives the definition of idiopathic as "arising spontaneously or from an obscure or unknown cause: PRIMARY <idiopathic epilepsy> <idiopathic hypertension> <idiopathic thrombocytopenic purpura>." At this point, the librarian will want to refer the patron back to his or her healthcare professional for more information. The question is: what disease or problem do they have, that is arising spontaneously or from an obscure or unknown cause? Only a healthcare professional can answer that question.

WHAT TYPES OF MEDICAL RESOURCES WILL YOU LINK TO THROUGH YOUR LIBRARY?

Medical Web resources range from basic diagnostic and support information about diseases to pharmaceuticals and treatments for consumers, to continuing medical education, clinical guidelines, and research information for healthcare professionals.

Some medical Web resources take forms that can be described in terms of traditional reference source types. Many medical Web resources are actually metasites or Web sites that provide multiple types of reference tool including medical encyclopedias, dictionaries, directories, bibliographies, e-serials, as well as collections of additional links.

Medical metasites include original publications on a variety of health topics, searchable medical encyclopedias, dictionaries, and pharmaceuticals information, as well as selective collections of links to other, more specialized, medical information Web sites.

The "Core Web Medical Reference Collection" at the end of this chapter includes core Web reference tools organized by these reference source types:

- Medical Metasites
- Directories of medical information, such as hospital and healthcare-professional contact information or licensing status, and drug information
- Medical dictionaries
- Abstracts, indexes, and table of contents services for medical serials such as PubMed and other electronic versions of the Medline database
- Encyclopedias of health and medical information
- Medical e-serials and full-text databases (e.g., MDConsult, UpToDate, MayoClinic)
- Medical news
- Key primary documents such as medical and pharmaceutical research data, statistics, clinical trials, and clinical guidelines

Medical metasites often include all of these reference resource types in a single Web site. Medical metasites that include links to other medical Web resources are good tools to identify other medical Web resources to collect. Many of the medical metasites also provide some indexing and/or abstracting, table of contents services, and some full-text access to print and medical e-serials.

Several collections of full-text medical journals exist on the Web. For example, PubMed Central (www.pubmedcentral.nih.gov), which is free and unrestricted access to the U.S. National Library of Medicine's growing "digital archive of life sciences journal literature."

Free e-mail or Web table of contents services are offered by most medical journals with Web sites. For example, Psychiatric Services (http://ps.psychiatryonline.org/subscriptions/etoc.shtml) a journal of the American Psychiatric Association offers the "eTOC" service.

HOW WILL YOU ORGANIZE YOUR MEDICAL WEB RESOURCES?

Some consideration might be made for dividing Web resources intended for healthcare professionals from those intended for healthcare consumers. In the "Core Web Medical Reference Collection" we have not done so, but include details about the intended audience in the annotations. Medical Web resources can sometimes be efficiently organized by disease or injury. However, many medical Web resources provide information for multiple diseases or injuries. Many medical e-libraries organize by the medical field, specialty, or using a formal structure such as the MeSH® medical subject headings created and maintained by the National Library of Medicine for its health and medical information products (www.nlm.nih.gov/mesh). The OSF St. Francis Medical Center Library and Resource Center organizes their e-library by the patron groups served: clinicians, pharmacists, nurses, managers, consumers, and librarians.

4.2 IDENTIFYING AND COLLECTING MEDICAL INFORMATION RESOURCES

WEB SITES THAT REVIEW AND EVALUATE MEDICAL WEB RESOURCES: INCLUDING OTHER E-LIBRARIES OR SUBJECT COLLECTION GUIDES/WEBLIOGRAPHIES

We include several medical subject collections, metasites, and e-libraries in this chapter's webliography. The most promising sites in terms of annotations, evaluations, and scope of subject coverage are the Hardin Meta Directory (www.lib.uiowa.edu/hardin/md/index.html) and HealthWeb (http://healthweb.org). The Hardin Meta Directory collects directories and e-library collections of medical resources for medical and allied health students and researchers. The HealthWeb site collects directories, e-library collections, and individual medical resources. HealthWeb emphasizes quality of information and collects for healthcare consumers and professionals. HealthWeb is a project of the Greater Midwest Region of the National Network Libraries of Medicine. The Consumer and Patient Health Information Section of the Medical Library Association (CAPHIS) (http://caphis.mlanet.org/consumer) collects a core one hundred high quality sites for healthcare consumers and organizes them by general health categories.

DISCUSSION LISTS AND NEWSGROUPS WHERE INDIVIDUAL PARTICIPANTS REVIEW AND EVALUATE MEDICAL WEB RESOURCES

The core discussion list for medical Web resources for libraries is MEDLIB-L, the Medical Libraries Discussion List. CAPHIS-L, the discussion for the Consumer and Patient Health Information Section of the Medical Library Association, is also an active and useful discussion. Another valuable health resource discussion list is MedWebMasters-L where webmasters who create and manage medical Web sites discuss their concerns regarding quality of information, quackery, as well as design, access, and content issues. Some examples of discussion lists that review medical specialty Web sites include P-SOURCE Psychiatry Resources List and ACCRI-L. The former discusses reviews of psychiatric Web sites and other resources, and the latter discusses reviews of anesthesia and critical-care Web sites and other resources.

There are medical subject specific discussion lists for almost every possible disease or medical specialty. There are also literally thousands of discussion groups for patient and family support. Use the tools for finding discussion lists in Part III, Resource List 1: Collection Development Related Discussion Lists, Newsgroups, and Blogs, or on the companion Web site, to identify additional discussion lists or newsgroups. Another strategy to locate patient support discussions is to search MedlinePlus for the disease, injury, or other problem in which the patron is interested. Choose one of the organization Web sites that MedlinePlus links to and look through the organization site for information about patient support discussion lists. This strategy works well for healthcare professional support discussion lists on specific topics. For example, a recent reference question was asked by a patron who has a relative who has a history of depression and has been taking anti-depressants for a long time. The question relates to the news that the relative is now pregnant and the patron is looking for information in addition to that which her relative is giving her. The patron doesn't know what drugs the relative is taking, or anything else; e.g., she might be taking anti-psychotic as well as anti-depressant drugs. Searching MedlinePlus for "depression pregnancy support" and also for "psychiatric drugs pregnancy support" retrieves about a dozen organizations that provide information as well as hosting support discussion lists or Web forums for patients, family, and healthcare professionals.

E-JOURNALS AND E-NEWSLETTERS THAT PUBLISH REVIEWS AND EVALUATIONS OF MEDICAL WEB RESOURCES

JMIR: Journal of Medical Internet Research (www.jmir.org) is a peer-reviewed e-journal, indexed by Medline that publishes reviews and articles about the quality and use of medical Web resources. JMIR is free and provides full-text access on the Web. It is the official journal of the Internet Healthcare Coalition (www.ihealthcoalition.org). Another good example of this kind of collection tool is Medicine on the Net (www.corhealth.com). Although it is fee-based, Medicine on the Net provides news and basic information, including a table of contents service, for free on their Web site. Medicine on the Net is available in print as well. This e-journal is used by many librarians in reviewing medical Web sites to include in their own e-library collection or to use for reference service. Other e-serials that review Web resources—specific to hundreds of diseases and treatments and intended for healthcare consumers or healthcare practitioners—can be found by searching PubMed Central (www.pubmedcentral.nih.gov), or on of the other full-text medical serials archives listed in the "Core Web Medical Reference Collection" in section 4.7 below, and on the companion Web site. Searching the NewJour archives (http://gort.ucsd.edu/newjour) for medical e-journals is also a good strategy.

PRINT BOOKS AND JOURNALS THAT REVIEW MEDICAL WEB RESOURCES

Many books on the market list medical Web resources. Several titles published since 2001 are listed in section 4.6, "References and Web Sites Cited." Medical Economics/PDR Publications (www.PDRbookstore.com) has begun publishing a series of eMedguides™ or Medical Internet Resource Guides from PDR® in a number of medical specialties. These are compiled by medical specialists and include reviews and annotations for thousands of specific Web sites. The descriptions indicate that these will be useful for hospital, clinical, and medical research libraries.

The *Journal of Consumer Health* on the Internet (previously Health Care on the Internet) (www.haworthpress.com) publishes reviews of medical Web sites, articles about medical Web sites, e-library collections and anything related to consumer health information and the Internet.

Many print medical journals including BMJ: *British Medical Journal* (http://bmj.com), JAMA: *The Journal of the American Medical Association* (http://jama.ama-assn.org), and *The New England Journal of Medicine* (http://bmj.com) review medical Web resources. Additional print medical journals that review Web resources may be found by doing a search on PubMed (www.ncbi.nlm.nih.gov/entrez/query.fcgi?db=PubMed) for "Web sites reviews" or "Web review." Click on "LinkOut" to see if full-text of the review articles might be available on the Web.

Popular family magazines such as *Women's Day* or *Family Circle* frequently feature reviews or articles about useful Web sites for family health issues. These may be found by doing a *Reader's Guide to Periodical Literature*, *Infotrak*, or *Magazine Index* search in the print, CD-ROM, or online database version of these indexes.

4.3 EVALUATION GUIDELINES

Steven L. MacCall, Ph.D., of the Clinical Digital Libraries Project, University of Alabama, School of Library and Information Science, has compiled a bibliography of publications concerning the quality of medical information on the Internet. Many of the publications cited are also linked to full-text or abstract of the articles. The Web Quality Bibliography (For Medical Information) is available at http://bama.ua.edu/~smaccall/qualitybib.html.

Kim et al. (1999), reviewed the published criteria for specifically evaluating health-related information on the Web. They found significant consensus on the key criteria for evaluating medical Web sites. The most frequently identified criteria were content quality, authority and disclosure of information source, currency of information, and accessibility of the Web site.

The Internet Healthcare Coalition (www.ihealthcoalition.org) and Health on the Net Foundation (HON) (www.hon.ch) both attempt to guide critical thinking and quality assurance of medical Web sites. HON publishes a code of conduct that medical Web masters may choose to follow. The Internet Healthcare Coalition also publishes a code of ethics and encourages critical thinking by both healthcare consumer and professionals in using Web resources.

Medical Web sites may voluntarily agree to the HON Code guidelines and place a logo on the site. Because adherence is voluntary and is not verified, the presence of HON logos on a Web site is a clue to the quality of the information on the site. It will still be necessary to review and evaluate the site carefully before selecting it.

Although evaluating health and medical information found on the Internet requires answers to the same basic questions as any other kind of information in selecting health and medical resources, quality must be a major criteria. Health and medical information quality may affect the life, health, and safety of human beings. It is, therefore, of great importance that it be extremely accurate and complete, or refer the healthcare consumer or professional to more in-depth information sources—or to advise them to consult a specialist. Library staff should not even give the appearance of providing health or medical advice to library patrons. They must, however, be knowledgeable enough to select the very highest quality resources to provide to their patrons. E-library resource collectors should evaluate each possible selection very carefully using the criteria described in Chapter 1 or other good published evaluation criteria.

WHO PROVIDED THE INFORMATION? WHAT IS THEIR REPUTATION AS AN INFORMATION PROVIDER? DO THEY HAVE THE AUTHORITY OR EXPERTISE TO PROVIDE INFORMATION ON THAT TOPIC?

When evaluating medical information on the Web these three questions should be answered at the same time. If a medical Web resource has no provider attribution—and this must include the information provider's qualifications and educational attainments—it is unusable in a library, educational, clinical, or research setting. The WebMD metasite (www.webmd.com) illustrates good examples of the attribution information to expect from quality medical information Web sites. WebMD Health is intended for healthcare consumers. Medscape from WebMD is intended for healthcare professionals. Medscape from WebMD requires registration and that you establish two basic facts: 1. You understand that this site is intended for healthcare professionals. 2. You are a healthcare professional or you work with healthcare professionals.

Reading carefully through the WebMD Health home page, notice the menu option—currently in the left near the end of the menu—"Who We Are" with two links: "About WebMD," and "Privacy and You." These two pages provide detailed information about the WebMD company and the WebMD staff, as well as their privacy protection policies. The WebMD staff description contains a further link for a "See Who We Are" page, which includes pictures of all contributors, authors, and editors along with their names and links to their biographical information. All of the medical editors are medical doctors (M.D.'s) although some of the writers are journalists. For example, the education and qualifications of Dr. Charlotte E. Grayson, Senior Medical Editor, who is responsible for "ensuring the quality and accuracy of WebMD's consumer health content," are clearly detailed:

"Dr. Grayson is an internist who completed her internal medicine residency at the Medical University of South Carolina, attended the Boston University School of Medicine, and received her undergraduate degree from Spelman College in Atlanta, where she was a National Achievement Scholarship winner and graduated cum laude. She graduated with a bachelor of science degree in chemistry and distinguished herself by an acceptance into Boston University School of Medicine in their Early Medical School Selection Program during her sophomore year." (http://my.webmd.com/content/biography/7/1756_50193_)

Even if the WebMD site changes between the time of this writing and the time of reading, the qualifications of the WebMD staff will be easy to find and clearly stated on the site. Medscape from WebMD is intended for healthcare professionals. In addition to the description of WebMD staff, each individual news piece or article are carefully dated and signed by the medical researchers who authored them. The authors' credentials are supplied with the article as well. Credentials include not just their degrees but also the clinic, hospital, or university where they are working. This information doesn't guarantee that the contents of the news and articles are always going to be good, but it does indicate that the information came from credible and authoritative sources.

IS THE INFORMATION PROVIDED FOR CURRENT INFORMATION OR HISTORICAL PURPOSES? DOES CURRENCY AFFECT THE QUALITY OF THE INFORMATION? WHEN WAS THE LAST UPDATE OF THE INFORMATION?

These questions should be very easy to answer on a high-quality medical Web site. Although some sites do provide history of medicine materials, most sites try to provide current medical information. MedHist (www.medhist.ac.uk) collects free Web resources for medical history research.

Verifying the dates and currency of a site can be critical to the healthcare consumer or healthcare practitioner using the information from the site to inform a medical decision. For example, some new research (www.nlm.nih.gov/medlineplus/news/fullstory_13577.html) on breast cancer treatments discusses the use of genetic analysis of the breast cancer tumor by healthcare professionals to guide decisions about which chemotherapy or surgical options will be most successful. It is important for both patient and physician to have the most current research available. Some research shows that some breast cancer treatments are more or less successful depending on the genetic pattern of the tumor cells.

Another recent case in point is the report on central nervous system toxicity (resulting in seizures and serious insomnia) side effects of the antibiotic "Floxin." A healthcare professional must have the very latest information about a drug in order to prescribe it safely. Using the Drug Info search in Medscape by WebMD (www.webmd.com), which was created for healthcare professionals, search for information on the drug "Floxin." Do the articles discuss the central nervous system toxicity effect? What are the dates of the articles? Try this test with some of the other medical resources listed in the "Core Web Medical Reference Collection" in this chapter and on the companion Web Site.

IS SECURITY IMPORTANT IN INTERACTING WITH A GIVEN BUSINESS WEB SITE? IS A SITE LIKELY TO BE HACKED AND INFORMATION ALTERED? WILL PERSONAL OR FINANCIAL INFORMATION BE REQUESTED FROM PATRONS?

Security is essential to ensure high-quality medical information on the Web. It is difficult to verify that security measures are in place without contacting the Web site owners directly and asking them.

It is unlikely that patrons will be asked for their financial information when accessing a medical information site—unless it is also a storefront. It is possible to purchase prescription and over the counter drugs, herbs, health devices, alternative medical treatments, and dietary supplements, among other things, through the Web. Always use your browser settings to verify a secure server before you input financial or personal information.

It is possible that patrons will be asked for financial and personal information when they access a medical Web site that is actually a storefront or is a fee-based database or e-journal.

For example, when you register for Medical Matrix (www.medmatrix.org), you must provide your name, professional, and other personal data as well as a credit card number. MerckMedicus (www.merckmedicus.com) requires personal and professional information, including licensure status, for registration, although it requests no financial information. This is used to guarantee to the database providers that the appropriate users are registering and using the system. MerckMedicus provides free access to several fee-based medical databases and services to healthcare professionals who register.

IS PRIVACY AN IMPORTANT FACTOR FOR YOU OR YOUR PATRONS?

This is frequently an important factor for healthcare consumers who are suffering from diseases, such as genetic disorders, AIDS, Asthma, or Cancer, that might inspire others to persecute, discriminate against them, or fear them, or that might cause insurance companies to drop them from coverage. Great care should be taken, if possible, to warn patrons that personal information is not private on the Internet.

Healthcare professionals also need to be careful of the privacy of their patients when searching or asking questions on the Web. They may feel that their e-mail to a colleagues is private, but this assumption may not fit the reality.

For example, if a patron visits a site that asks them to register for a personalized self-diagnosis or calculator type program, will that site keep that personal information private? What is their privacy policy? Will they turn around and sell the patron's personal information to telemarketers or spammers?

Look carefully at how privacy and security issues are addressed in the Web site. For example, are privacy guidelines available? Are they ethical? Do they meet privacy requirements of HIPAA—specifically the Federal Health Privacy Rule integral to the Health Insurance Portability and Accountability Act of 1996. The HIPAA Federal Health Privacy Rule became effective in the U.S., in 2001, as part of the implementation of the Health Insurance Portability and Accountability Act of 1996. Information about the privacy rule is available at http://aspe.hhs.gov/admnsimp/pl104191.html, as well as articles, reports and summaries that will give additional perspective on privacy of medical information specifically. The site also provides links to research and analysis of evaluation criteria and self-regulation of privacy protection on medical Web sites.

4.4 SELECTION CRITERIA

Selection criteria for any format in which you find medical information resources are derived from the answers arrived at during the collection-planning process. As with previous reference subjects, a survey was sent to Medlib-L, Libref-L, Publib, and OPLINLIST asking librarians to identify their core or essential medical reference tools. The questions and their responses are reproduced in the box following this paragraph. As with the business reference core tools, the medical reference core tools are frequently both print and Web-accessible. When a preference was expressed librarians preferred the Web-accessible versions, except in the cases of the medical dictionaries. Although we were not surprised at the popularity of MedlinePlus (#3 on our list of Essential Medical Reference Tools), we were surprised that Google was counted in the top ten core medical reference tools. This is possibly because Google actually searches the deep contents of some of the high quality medical metasites including MedlinePlus and Mayo Clinic.

Table 2.4.1. Core or Essential Medical Reference Tools Survey

Question Posted to publib@sunsite.berkeley.edu, libref-l@listserv.kent.edu, and oplinlist@oplin.lib.oh.us:

- What are your 2–5 most used reference tools for Medical Questions? (Books, CD, Online and Web Databases)

Question Posted to medlib-l@listserv.acsu.buffalo.edu:

- What are the top 5–8 print reference books that you can't work without?
- What are the top 5–8 CD-ROM, Tape or Online databases that you can't work without?

Table 2.4.2. Core or Essential Medical Reference Tools

1. Physicians' Desk Reference (PDR). Available: www.pdr.net; consumer version free/professional version fee-based.
2. Medline (Ovid). Available: www.ovid.com, or Ebscohost (see #6 below).
3. Medlineplus. Available: www.medlineplus.gov.
4. PubMed. Available: www.ncbi.nih.gov/PubMed.
5. Gale Encyclopedia of Medicine. Available: www.galegroup.com, and The Merck Manual of Diagnosis and Therapy. Available: www.merck.com.
6. EbscoHost-All Health/Medical Databases. Available: www.epnet.com, and Stedman's Medical Dictionary. Available: www.stedmans.com.
7. CINAHL (Ovid). Available: www.ovid.com, or www.cinahl.com, and Professional Guide to Diseases. Available: www.lww.com/nursing/?kw=springhouse.
8. American Hospital Formulary Service Drug Information. Available: www.ashp.org.
9. Cecil Textbook of Medicine. Available: www.us.elsevierhealth.com, Dictionary of Medical Syndromes. Available: www.lww.com, Harrison's Principles of Internal Medicine.* Available: http://books.mcgraw-hill.com), Netwellness. Available: www.netwellness.com, OmniGraphics Sourcebooks Health Reference Series. Available: www.omnigraphics.com, and Taber's Cyclopedic Medical Dictionary. Available: www.fadavis.com.
10. PsycINFO (Ovid). Available: www.ovid.com, Gale Group Health Reference Center Academic. Available: www.galegroup.com, WebMD. Available: www.webmd.com, Dorland's Illustrated Medical Dictionary.* Available: www.us.elsevierhealth.com, and Google. Available: www.google.com.

*Available on MerckMedicus. Available: www.merckmedicus.com/pp/us/hcp/hcp_medical_library.jsp.
Additional sites received two votes each. Contact the authors for that list.
URLs provided are for the publisher's Web site.

The "Core Web Medical Reference Collection" included below was compiled with these core medical reference tools in mind. The intended patron group is librarians working with English-speaking healthcare consumers and professionals. These patrons might want either ready-reference type consumer health or medical information, or more in-depth, diagnostic, pharmaceutical and treatment information on a quick-response basis. The access and design of all these core medical Web resources are based on standards of simplicity, international Web accessibility standards, and no special software required for access. Most of them are free of direct cost—free except for the cost of Internet access—with some having special fee-based services including document delivery.

4.5 E-LIBRARY SUCCESS STORIES

ARCTIC HEALTH AND ASIAN AMERICAN HEALTH WEB SITES

http://arctichealth.nlm.nih.gov and http://asianamericanhealth.nlm.nih.gov
National Institutes of Health, National Library of Medicine, USA

> Contact: Lucie Chen, Office of Outreach and Special Populations, SIS/NLM/NIH
> CHENL@mail.nlm.nih.gov

The Arctic Health (http://arctichealth.nlm.nih.gov) and Asian American Health (http://asianamericanhealth.nlm.nih.gov) sites are the first two in a planned series of special population health e-library collections. The series began with the Arctic Health site conceived in 2000, by Dr. Phil Chen, National Institutes of Health, Senior Advisor to the NIH Director of Intramural Research when he was serving as U.S. representative to the Arctic Council. Unites States was the Chair of the Arctic Council from 1999–2001, and wanted to leave a legacy for this arctic region.

Dr. Chen asked Lucie Chen at the Specialized Information Services, NLM to develop a Web site collection or database that focused on health issues specific to the arctic region. The original plan was to provide an information portal that focus on special population health information

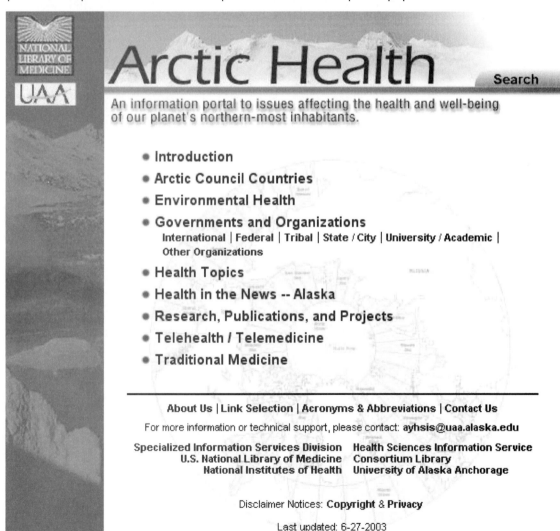

Figure 2.4.0. Arctic Health Web Site http://arctichealth.nlm.nih.gov

needs for this arctic region. National Library of Medicine management expanded the concept to include development of series of collections Web sites specific to other special populations such as Asian American Health, American Indian Health, African American Health and Hispanic American Health.

The intended audience is the general public, however, the most likely audience for these are probably healthcare information providers who work with members of special populations, or the special populations themselves.

The Arctic Health collection is built around an introduction (http://arctichealth .nlm.nih.gov/intro.html), which describes the populations of people in the Arctic regions of the U.S. and other areas of the world and an overview of the health issues that affect them. The general areas of the Web site include chronic diseases, traditional medicine, behavioral issues, general health resources and environmental (pollution) factors. Each category lists key Web resources. The collection makes good use of information on chronic disease and health information provided by other government agencies including links to specific information through MedlinePlus.gov For example, under "Traditional Medicine," links include the Alaska Native Knowledge Network (www.ankn.uaf.edu/index.html) and the Traditional Knowledge and Native American Information (www.pmel.noaa.gov/bering/pages/traditional.html) sites among others.

The Asian American Health collection also begins with an introduction, which clarifies who Asian-Americans are and what kinds of special health issues affect them. Categories of

Figure 2.4.1. Asian American Health Web site http://asianamericanhealth.nlm.nih.gov

information include an overview of Major Asian American related Web sites, health and diseases, Web sites that cover Asian-American cultural and behavioral issues, complementary and alternative medicine, pacific rim Web Links, and health organizations.

Although currently the two available e-libraries do not specifically support any distance learning programs, in the future they could be part of professional continuing education programs that NLM can offer.

There is no written collection plan other than the general guidelines that each e-library should include free Web accessible sites and databases that are of high quality—from authoritative, credible sources—support health information needs of each special population in some discernable way.

Lucie Chen collected the resources for both sites with the support from an NLM staff programmer who handled the HTML coding.

"I would estimate about 1/2 of the two staff time for six months to start the process and finish populating the Web sites."

Aspens Systems was contracted by NLM for the design of the Web sites.

The URLs were sent to volunteer focus groups that represented each special population to evaluate the Web site for sensitivity issues and with regard to the content and usability of each site.

The University of Alaska at Anchorage, Health Sciences Library was contracted in 2002 to update and maintain the Arctic Health Web site once it was designed and created by Lucie Chen. It is planned to make a similar arrangement for the Asian American Health and the other special population Web sites.

The University of Alaska contractor checks the Arctic Web site links regularly and plans are in the works to revise the Web site. Usability studies are planned as well for all of the special population sites.

There are no plans to catalog Web sites for inclusion in the NLM catalog, nor are there any plans for offering virtual reference services. The future of these sites will involve concentration on building the content to better serve the health information needs of special populations.

HEALTH INFONET OF ALABAMA

Public Libraries of and Jefferson and Shelby Counties and the Lister Hill Library of the
    Health Sciences of the University of Alabama at Birmingham
Birmingham, Alabama, USA
www.healthinfonet.org

Contact: Catherine Hogan Smith
khogan@uab.edu and Steven L. MacCall, Ph.D., smaccall@bama.ua.edu

Health InfoNet of Alabama was created by University of Alabama, Lister Hill Library of the Health Sciences Librarian, Catherine Hogan Smith. It is a public library-academic library partnership to provide consumer health information. She was inspired by the Connecticut Healthnet (http://library.uchc.edu/departm/hnet) services. The Health InfoNet of Alabama Web site is just the most visible and important of the resources and services provided by the project.

The Health InfoNet e-library collection is intended to provide high quality health information for residents of the state of Alabama. It does not aim to duplicate information provided by national consumer health information projects such as MedlinePlus (www.medlineplus.gov) or the Mayo Clinic (www.mayoclinic.com) publishes on the Web. Rather, the goal is to provide links to the best of the best and to focus on local sources of support and information in Alabama communities.

Catherine Hogan Smith and Steven L. MacCall work on the Health InfoNet project as part of their regular assignments. UAB computer staff supply technical support as needed. At times they have had assistance from students of the Schools of Library and Information Studies at the University of Alabama. A student was hired to design the site for high accessibility. An advisory committee makes suggestions regarding site design, services, and resources to be included.

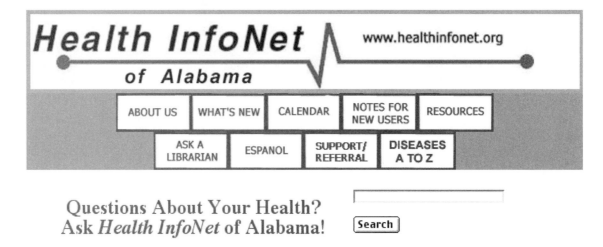

Questions About Your Health?
Ask *Health InfoNet* of Alabama!   [Search]

NEWS FLASH - Health InfoNet of Jefferson County is now Health InfoNet of Alabama! See "What's New" for more information.

Health InfoNet is a consumer health information service for the residents of Alabama. This service is a cooperative effort of the public libraries of Jefferson and Shelby counties and the Lister Hill Library of the Health Sciences of the University of Alabama at Birmingham. See About Us for more information.

Health InfoNet helps you answer your health questions by providing Resources that will:

- connect you with local Support groups;
- connect you with local and national medical and social service organizations for Referral;
- provide information on diseases and medical conditions from A to Z (or access to a Health Expert);
- provide a section of Easy to Read sources of medical information.

HOT TOPIC OF THE MONTH - Immunization Awareness Month

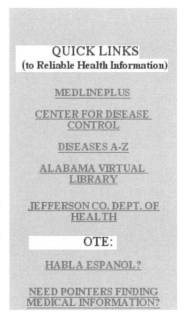

QUICK LINKS
(to Reliable Health Information)

MEDLINEPLUS

CENTER FOR DISEASE CONTROL

DISEASES A-Z

ALABAMA VIRTUAL LIBRARY

JEFFERSON CO. DEPT. OF HEALTH

OTE:

HABLA ESPANOL?

NEED POINTERS FINDING MEDICAL INFORMATION?

Figure 2.4.2 Health InfoNet of Alabama www.healthinfonet.org

"We are working with the input and collaboration of local health agencies, professionals in healthcare and other health information providers to provide the citizens of Alabama with easy access to high-quality health information resources, both print and electronic, as well as referrals to resources in the community. Members advising us for this year are listed at the link Advisory Committee." (http://hinfonet.lhl.uab.edu/about_us.htm)

FrontPage is used to create and edit the individual linked Web pages for Health InfoNet. The Web site runs on a Gateway E-4400 server running Windows 2000 and Internet Information Server 5.0 (IIS5).

The Clinical Digital Libraries Project (CDLP) supplies the "Diseases A-Z" medical encyclopedia section for Health Infonet:

"The Clinical Digital Libraries Project (www.cdlp.org) is a joint research, teaching and service effort of the Schools of Library and Information Studies at the University of Alabama (www.slis.ua.edu) and the University of North Texas (www.unt.edu/slis/>www.unt.edu/slis)."

The EBSCOHost Health source database is accessible through a link to the Alabama Virtual Library (http://hinfonet.lhl.uab.edu/AVL.htm). Future change to the Health InfoNet may include access to additional fee-based databases. Currently, the NORD Rare Diseases database is available at the UAB, Lister Hill Library physical location only.

Health InfoNet provides e-mail based librarian mediated searches and reference assistance through the "Ask-A-Librarian" link (http://hinfonet.lhl.uab.edu/asklibrarian.htm).

"A primary goal of Health InfoNet of Alabama is to provide consumers with a wide range of health and medical information. The Ask a Librarian Service is designed to help if you have trouble finding sources of medical information....Our aim is to promote individual responsibility for health and not to offer medical advice....Only a licensed health care practitioner, who has a complete medical history of an individual, can advise that person in health decisions...Thus, materials provided here do not necessarily imply approval or recommendation by Health InfoNet or by Lister Hill Library."

Future plans include the creation of a virtual reference service through the Lister Hill Health Science Library.

"It is anticipated that this service will eventually be made available on the Health InfoNet site for consumers to use as well as our professional/student users here at Lister Hill."

Individuals connecting from outside of Alabama are referred to their local health information libraries:

"If you are unsure of a resource library near you, go to the NN/LM Web site at www.nnlm.nlm.nih.gov and use the map or call 1–800–338–7657."

Although a formal written collection plan has not been developed for Health Infonet, it does work under a basic set of selection criteria (http://hinfonet.lhl.uab.edu/linkingguide.htm).

"Information should be both free and full-text (no links to pages of links with the exception of sites like MedlinePlus), noncommercial as well as authoritative, evidence-based and current."

As part of a major NN/LM (http://nnlm.gov) funded initiative during 2000–2001 the site was revised in partnership with Professor Steven MacCall, of the UA, School of Library.

Web resources included in Health InfoNet are not cataloged formally. Health InfoNet is continuously reviewed and revised. Link checking is done manually every few months or as link problems are identified in the course of using Health InfoNet.

Selection and collection of resources for this e-library involves communications with other organizations as well as identifying Web sites through reviews in print and e-journals. Health InfoNet also requires marketing and promotion of the service so as to encourage support group and agency participation:

"I try to keep up with local support groups and health events through local media, meetings I attend and word of mouth. Since a number of health organizations have been represented on our advisory board, I try to keep ongoing contact with those people as a means of getting info from that segment of health info providers. I also have the participating organization form on our site, and of course I promote Health InfoNet via exhibits at health fairs and other events (I inform as many local organizations about our existence and services at these events as potential users), and through presentations before different groups. Through my work on this project, I've been asked to serve on another health organization board providing health services to Latino immigrants. Naturally, a lot of my information on the Espanol page comes via this group. My colleagues here at Lister Hill and in the public libraries keep me posted on things, events, groups, resources that I might have missed as well. Serendipity, as well as search engines, definitely play a part."

Health Infonet serves as a means of coordinating information by and about local health organizations. The Support and Referral Page (http://hinfonet.lhl.uab.edu/contacts.htm) lists organizations that consumers can turn to for in-person or more locally focused support for specific illnesses, or other health related issues. Organizations that want to participate can complete a form (http://hinfonet.lhl.uab.edu/participatingorgform.htm) to be considered for inclusion.

Health Infonet is intended for the general public and also for health information providers. An "Easy to Read" page (http://hinfonet.lhl.uab.edu/easytoread.htm) is provided for the information providers that might be with healthcare consumers who have a reading difficulty, including nurses and others who provide patient education services.

"Another part of the mission of Health InfoNet is to educate users about how to find quality health information. Some of the pages you see on the site, such as the Notes for New Users page (http://hinfonet.lhl.uab.edu/newusers.htm) address this part of our mission."

Additional tutorials and handouts are planned for this phase of the project.

Feedback on the site has come primarily from participating health organizations.

"I solicit comments on the homepage, although the only responses I've received so far have been from participating health organizations, not users... I do appreciate any comments I receive, because it often provides a different perspective on certain aspects of the site...We also conducted a web usability study after the revisions were complete, and we do plan to conduct these studies on a (more or less) regular basis."

Future plans for Health InfoNet include acquiring Web analysis software to supply a clearer picture of who is using the site and what they are looking for as well as a more reliable search engine for the site. Because there is very little funding for this project, many decisions about software and hardware upgrades revolve around what is least expensive and has the most value.

CIAO [CLINICAL INFORMATION ACCESS ONLINE]

Department of Health, East Perth, Western Australia
www.ciao.health.wa.gov.au/index.cfm

Contacts: Marg Lundy, marg.lundy@health.wa.gov.au and Maureen Bradford maureen.bradford@health.wa.gov.au

CIAO [Clinical Information Access Online] was created by the Western Australian Department of Health to support clinicians working throughout Western Australia (WA).

The project was first conceived in 1992. There was much interest and support for the project but it was 1994 before funding was obtained to begin the project. CIAO evolved from a dial-up CD-ROM network in 1994 to the Web-based e-library in 2002. The history of the project demonstrates the commitment of librarians working to make essential information available to clinicians in Western Australia:

"In 1994, the Health Department of WA Library was successful in obtaining a RHSET (Rural Health Support, Education and Training) grant of $235,000 for the establishment of a stand-alone dial-up CD-ROM network to facilitate provision of information to rural health workers. This was well utilised."

In 1994, a working party was set up by the then CEO of King Edward Memorial Hospital/Princess Margaret Hospital (now the Women and Children's Health Service) to establish a single facility connected to the Health Department of WA's Wide Area Network (WAN). This would provide access to Medline and other databases, with provision for dial-up access for remote users and the potential for connection to the Internet. Again, the recommendations of the Working Party were well received, but the facility was not established."

The Committee of Librarians in Charge—Health Libraries (CLIC-HL) attempted to progress the Project again in 1997, but the project floundered due to budgetary cuts and restructuring of the Health Department of WA.

"In 1999, the CLIC-HL group prepared a business case for a WAN project called CHEK-UP (Clinical Health Evidence and Knowledge—Useful for Practitioners) which was successful in attracting funding for Phase 1. In place of Phase 2, however, the Department of Health decided to fund a Project based on a business case prepared by a consultant contracted by the Department's Executive Committee (DEC) at the time. The CIAO (Clinical Information Access

Online) Pilot managed by a Project Control Group (PCG) offered electronic products and support mechanisms to encompass all WA government health sector employees (via the Internet). 12 sites (metropolitan and rural) commenced trialling the Project in April 2000 and by June 2002, CIAO was available to all public health professionals in WA."

A written collection plan, online at www.ciao.health.wa.gov.au/about.cfm, was developed and used to make choices for electronic resources to include in the collection. Selection of resources is focused on the need to support clinical decision-making at the point of care, as well as to support the continuing medical education of clinicians. The information resources selected must provide immediate information that clinicians require at the point of diagnoses and treatment.

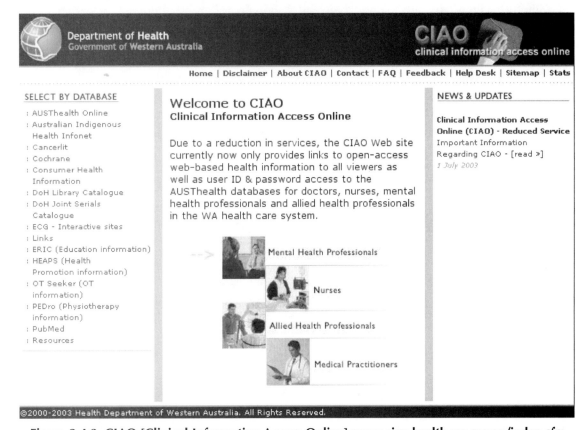

Figure 2.4.3. CIAO [Clinical Information Access Online] www.ciao.health.wa.gov.au/index.cfm

The collection includes several fee-based clinical information databases and full-text electronic journals including Ovid Journals Online, and other databases (e.g., Medline, CINAHL, PsycINFO, EBMR) and Micromedex. Online medical reference tools STAT!Ref, Therapeutic Guidelines, and Harrison's Principles of Internal Medicine are accessible as well. Several Australia specific medical resources are also included: MIMS Online—"Australia's most comprehensive and authoritative pharmaceutical database"—Australian Medicines Handbook and AUSThealth Online. AUSThealth Online provides access to "eight of Australia's leading medical research databases."

"The WA Department of Health funds these fee-based Web-accessible databases under licensing arrangements with Health Communication Networks (HCN)—the database service provider. UserID/password protected access is available to these databases for all WA public sector health clinicians via the internet (from workplace, home or wherever internet access is available, 27/7.)"

The Web resource links collection is extensive. CIAO links to OMNI: Organising Medical Networked Information (http://omni.ac.uk/), the UK's gateway to high quality biomedical Internet resources site as a source of further Web resources in addition to those selected for direct inclusion in CIAO. The Web resource collection is browseable and searchable.

"One half-time Librarian is employed exclusively to support CIAO. Also, a Manager manages CIAO as part of her full-time role as Information Resources Manager (Library, Records and Corporate Information Unit). Two support personnel give technical support as required. DoH librarians also provide ad hoc training on request."

Training of librarians and support personal is done through "shadowing" of experienced librarians. Knowledge and experience with medical and clinical information is considered important for librarians working with CIAO. The half-time librarian who works exclusively to support CIAO is the CIAO Project Officer.

The CIAO Project Officer did not have to have a library background.

"This person provides CIAO system administration, user support, marketing, education and training for WA Department of Health clinicians throughout the state."

The CIAO Project Officer and the manager have primary collection responsibilities but they look to other health librarians and Department of Health clinicians as needed. The CIAO Project Officer is responsible for adding new links to the collection.

"Links are checked manually as often as possible and feedback is sought from users to let us know if links are broken. Link-checking software is not utilised at this time."

The Web site is hosted on a Microsoft IIS server and uses Macromedia ColdFusion and MS Access.

"HCN, the suppliers of CIAO products hosts the databases on servers external to the Department. A fee is charged for this and other administrative and contract management services."

For the free Web-accessible resources, the collectors rely on serendipity informed by selection criteria and monitoring of electronic and print reviews of Web-accessible resources.

Fee-based resources are selected after evaluation of the resource by Department of Health librarians and clinicians.

"An informal policy currently exists that no trials will be conducted on the CIAO site. Products made available for trial are usually delivered through the Health Library site. Utilisation of products is considered at the time negotiations commence to renew the contract. No formal process is yet in place to initiate a full review, though this is planned for the future."

Ongoing maintenance of the collection is informed by "a sophisticated statistical gathering mechanism which allows comprehensive checking of their usage, by user groups and by areas within the state of WA."

Reference and document delivery services are offered through the Department of Health Library.

"'Virtual library' services as described in this question are offered by the Department of Health Library Services staff rather than CIAO support staff. This works successfully, but would be improved by integrating electronic resources with the library catalogue."

The CIAO Project Officer actively solicits and responds to user feedback. She makes any changes as quickly as possible if they are determined to be beneficial and if they do not require additional funding.

"Reviews and upgrades are on-going. The Support/Project Officer meets weekly with the Manager to discuss and review CIAO. Other management arrangements are currently under review (more input from clinicians, other health librarians within the Department of Health, etc.). The contract is re-negotiated, put to tender on an annual basis."

Future CIAO upgrades include an upgraded front screen and enhancement of searchability and accessibility of the collection:

"The CIAO Manager and management team have looked at USE (Universal Search Engine) software and are considering it for CIAO. Further enhancements (available shortly) will make this facility much more desirable Funding, of course, is always one of the main factors in decisions whether to include new services/databases/facilities and at what stage."

OSF St. Francis Medical Center Library and Resource Center

http://library.osfsaintfrancis.org
Decatur, Illinois, USA

Contact: Carol J. Galganski, Manager, Carol.J.Galganski@osfhealthcare.org

The OSF St. Francis Medical Center Library and Resource Center E-Library serves healthcare consumers, clinicians, pharmacists, nurses, hospital administration/management, as well as librarians and OSF St. Francis Medical Center affiliates.

Carol Galganski developed the original collection in the mid-1990s on an Intranet Web site for use by library staff in serving their patrons. The e-library has evolved into

"a public site useable for our OSF physicians, nurses, regional hospitals, as well as library staff. I continue to develop and maintain the website with assistance from our IT staff for publishing."

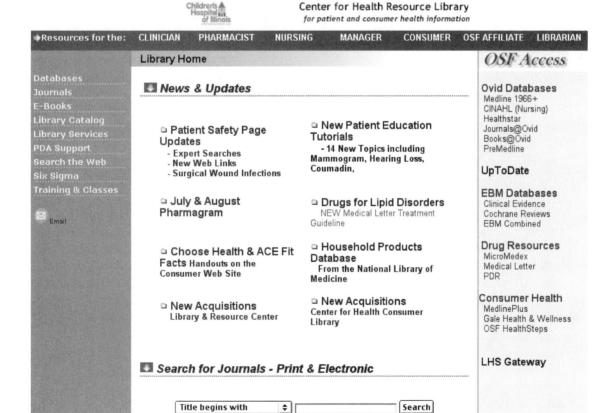

Figure 2.4.4. OSF St. Francis Medical Center Library and Resource Center
http://library.osfsaintfrancis.org

A written collection development plan was created and continues to evolve as choices are made regarding electronic resources and print resources.

"This has been an ongoing challenge, as we move from print to electronic access, with changing vendors, opportunities, and requests from our medical staff and patrons."

Carol Galganski's goals for creating the e-library were very clear and development of the collection has been shaped by these goals:

"We had multiple goals in developing the site:

1. to provide a gateway to the electronic resources we have available, both for staff, end users, and our regional affiliates.

2. to promote the use of electronic knowledge based resources to our physicians and nurses as a means to increase their computer skills in preparation for the implementation of our electronic medical record.

3. to increase awareness of evidence based resources."

Each intended patron group has a dedicated area of the e-library intended to serve its specific information needs. Library staff defined these specific patron groups, and uses their working knowledge and ongoing interactions with these groups to add, change, and evolve the e-library collection. For example, clinician refers to physicians, advanced nurse practitioners, midwifes, or those individuals who are healthcare professionals.

"These are the major user groups who utilize our knowledge based resources, so we wanted to provide subject specific resources for their use. Feedback from database training sessions indicated that users didn't know where to start in finding information—and they preferred pages that organized books, electronic journals, etc., on one page by their profession."

Detailed criteria are used in selecting new resources to add to the e-library or make other changes:

"1. User demand
2. Financial considerations—price breaks for system wide access
3. Licensing options—prefer both on campus and remote accessibility
4. Access options—IP validation vs. id and pw access.
5. Rights to Interlibrary loan for e-journals
6. Duplication of existing resources"

Fee-based Web-accessible databases are included in the OSF St. Francis e-library.

"The Library works collaboratively with our OSF Corporate Office in providing access to electronic resources. Products are licensed either for the entire system (coming from the corporate budget), or for OSF Saint Francis as an individual institution (through the Library's budget). Access to these resources are both from within the network, and remotely. Remote access is provided through another website named OSF Access, that is password protected."

The library manager works on the e-library an average of five hours per week adding, editing, and maintaining the collections. Information Technology staff publish updates each week and maintain the server and network. IT staff provide approximately thirty hours of support each year.

"at this point I am alone in doing this, fast realizing I need to add this to our medical librarian functions. Classes in beginning and advanced FrontPage will be scheduled, and they will be assigned portions of the web as their responsibility for updating and maintaining."

Collection is an ongoing process. Web resource reviews from medical metasites, publications such as Medicine on the Net (www.corhealth.com/MOTN) are all considered. They use the Ovid auto-alert feature to direct attention to articles that evaluate and describe good Web sites in the desired subject areas.

"New products are continually being reviewed for inclusion as we are made aware of them, depending on user need. For example, as a result of a PDA user survey, it was determined we need to evaluate products that can be utilized both at the desktop, but that also include a PDA component. We have been evaluating a number of products with that capability in the last 6 months."

The library creates catalog records for Web resources for which they have a print counterpart. In that way, the hyperlinks to the Web product are available through the catalog record.

Internally created patient education materials, wellness handouts, and other documents will be added in future to the appropriate areas of the e-library.

OSF St. Francis Medical Center library staff are involved with the Illinois Libraries' MyWebLibrarian Virtual Reference project http://myweblibrarian.com/index.html and the MyWebLibrarian service is available through their e-library.

"We currently staff the MyWebLibrarian virtual reference desk on Monday, Wednesday, and Friday, from 1–3 in the afternoon. Staffed hours will increase as additional librarians are trained in providing the service."

Frontpage is used in creating and editing the Web site and hosted on a Windows 2000 server. Frontpage links report is used monthly and manual checks are scheduled monthly as well. Serials Solutions is used for searching electronic and print journals. Cross-database search tools may be integrated in future.

"We are trying to consolidate our resources to one or two vendors so that patrons are not confused by so many choices. If we are not able to accomplish this, we will investigate products that cross-database search."

Although no formal evaluation has been conducted, the library staff routinely ask for user suggestions for new resources, navigation, or other changes to the collection. The e-library organization is reviewed continually and all library staff are asked for their feedback before major reorganizations are undertaken.

"A major revision with new design is planned by October 1, 2003. A simpler, less graphically intense design is planned with easier navigation."

The major revision will also include expansion of the collection and creating more subject specific areas within these target patron groups.

"New pages and sections are added in response to user requests—e.g., we will be applying for Magnet status in July 2004, our Nursing Department has requested a section on the nursing page for magnet resources and updates. In addition, we are planning a separate page on Patient Education resources."

Other future plans for the OSF St. Francis e-library include the development of Web-based training modules.

"We are actually developing modules for database training, with hopes to add a few more like PDA instruction, use of the catalog, etc. These will be offered through E-College, which is already available within OSF by our Colleges of Nursing in Peoria and Rockford. The Library and Resource Center has 20 seats available in E-College, and is currently hosting 2 consumer health journal clubs utilizing this software....Our plan is to offer the modules as the first choice for user education and training, particularly for our regionally affiliated hospitals, both in and out of the OSF Healthcare System. If patrons need more help beyond the module, then we will provide in person training."

4.6 REFERENCES AND WEB SITES CITED

(Note that some sites are included in the resource lists and webliographies in subsequent chapters, and therefore are not necessarily duplicated in this section.)

Fitzpatrick, J. J., C. A. Romano, and R. Chasek, eds. 2001. *The Nurses' Guide to Consumer Health Web Sites.* New York: Springer Verlag.

Grohol, J. M. 2002. *The Insider's Guide to Mental Health Resources Online.* New York: The Guilford Press.

Kim, P., et al. 1999. Published Criteria for Evaluating Health Related Websites: Review. *British Medical Journal* 318, no. 7184 (March): 647–49, www.bmj.com/cgi/content/full/318/7184/647.

Kovacs, D. K. Forthcoming. Electronic Collection Development for Consumer Health Information. *Journal of Consumer Health on the Internet* 7, no. 4.

Lord, J., and B. Ragon. 2001. Working Together to Develop Electronic Collections. *Computers in Libraries* 21, no. 5 (May): 40–45.

Smith, R. P. 2001. The Internet for Physicians. 3rd ed. New York: Springer Verlag.

CINAHL (Ovid). Available: www.ovid.com, or www.cinahl.com.

EbscoHost-All Health/Medical Databases. Available: www.epnet.com.

Gale Group Health Reference Center Academic. Available: www.galegroup.com.

Health on the Net Foundation (HON). Available: www.hon.ch.

HIPAA—Federal Health Privacy Rule integral to the Health Insurance Portability and Accountability Act of 1996. Available: http://aspe.hhs.gov/admnsimp/pl104191.html.

Internet Healthcare Coalition. Available: www.ihealthcoalition.org.

JMIR: Journal of Medical Internet Research. Available: www.jmir.org.

Medline (Ovid). Available: www.ovid.com, or see Ebscohost (above).

Netwellness. Available: www.netwellness.com.

PsycINFO (Ovid). Available: www.ovid.com.

The Web Quality Bibliography (For Medical Information) compiled by Steven L. MacCall, Ph.D., of the Clinical Digital Libraries Project, University of Alabama, School of Library and Information Science. Available: http://bama.ua.edu/~smaccall/qualitybib.html.

See Part III, Resource List 1: Collection Development Related Discussion Lists, Newsgroups, and Blogs for discussion lists, newsgroups, e-serials, and other resources cited in this chapter.

4.7 THE CORE WEB MEDICAL REFERENCE COLLECTION

MEDICAL METASITES

GeneralPediatrics.com

www.generalpediatrics.com

> Pediatric information for both healthcare consumers and professionals. The search tool searches fifty selected Web sites. Choose to search fifty selected Web sites for healthcare consumers or fifty selected Web sites for healthcare professionals. GeneralPediatrics.com is curated and maintained by Donna M. D'Alessandro, M.D. Available: www.uihealthcare.com/depts/med/pediatrics/pedsmds/dalessandro.html.

Mayo Clinic

www.mayoclinic.com

> Mayo Clinic staff provide full-text medical information for health care consumers. The A-Z index of in-depth articles is licensed by many other health care facilities. The "First Aid" section is very useful. The Mayo Clinic also provides annotated links to supporting Web sites in each health topic area as well as news and articles about current topics in health.

MEDLINEplus

www.nlm.nih.gov/MEDLINEplus or www.MEDLINEplus.gov

> National Library of Medicine's metasite for healthcare consumers. Includes NLM publications and articles as well as links to MEDLINE indexed materials. Great online drug information collection. Unique and valuable features include medical encyclopedias and dictionaries full-text, drug databases, medical information tutorials designed for consumers in both English and Spanish, and also searches PubMed.

Merck Medicus

www.merckmedicus.com

> Healthcare professionals resources including research news, medical encyclopedia, continuing medical education directory of both online and offline opportunities. Full text of many core medical reference texts and some databases available for registered healthcare professionals.

NOAH: New York Online Access to Health Home Page

www.noah-health.org

> Consumer health information sponsored by the New York Academy of Medicine and the New York Public Library. Although specifically designed for residents of the state of New York, this marvelous site compiles sites and resources that all health care consumers will find useful. The Spanish language version of the site is invaluable.

Intelihealth

www.intelihealth.com

> Good health and wellness information published under the auspices of the Harvard School of Medicine. The site includes articles as well as collections of annotated Web sites.

WebMD

www.webmd.com

> Good health and wellness information including original articles, encyclopedia, dictionary, and collections of annotated Web sites on multiple health topics.

Healthfinder®

www.healthfinder.gov

> This site is published by the U.S. Department of Health and Human Services, Office of Disease Prevention and Health Promotion. The site is simple and very accessible. The resources selected are few but excellent. Links to the DrugDigest site.

MedicineNet

www.medicinenet.com

> Medical resource in easy-to-understand language. Updated by board-certified physicians. Has good pharmacological/drug information and annotated collections of Web sites in specific health topic areas.

DIRECTORIES OF MEDICAL INFORMATION

(hospital and healthcare-professional contact information or licensing status, and drug information)

AMA Physician Select

www.ama-assn.org/aps/amahg.htm

> "Provides information on virtually every licensed physician in the United States and its possessions. All physician credential data have been verified for accuracy and authenticated by accrediting agencies, medical schools, residency training programs, licensing and certifying boards, and other data sources." AMA Web site also provides a complete list of state medical boards with Web sites and contact information (www.ama-assn.org/ama/pub/category/ 2645.html). State medical boards are frequently a great source for evaluative information about physicians and other health care professionals and their licensing status.

American Hospital Directory

www.ahd.com

The American Hospital Directory provides summary and detailed statistics for thousands of hospitals, clinics, and medical centers. Data may include Medicare/Medicaid cost reports, and other public use files obtained from the federal Health Care Financing Administration. Summary data is free. Subscription required for detailed statistics.

DIRLINE Search

http://dirline.nlm.nih.gov

Directory of Health Organizations Online. Listing with links to national and international health organizations.

Drug Digest

www.drugdigest.org

"DrugDigest is a noncommercial, evidence-based, consumer health and drug information site dedicated to empowering consumers to make informed choices about drugs and treatment options."

(JCAHO) Joint Commission on Accreditation of Health care Organizations

www.jcaho.com

JCAHO sets standards for health care organizations. The Web site is a directory of health care organizations that have been evaluated by JCAHO. They publish summary statistical and accreditation information as well as the guidelines for accreditation. The Web site is a challenge to navigate. Don't give up.

MEDLINEplus Drug Information

www.nlm.nih.gov/MEDLINEplus or www.MEDLINEplus.gov

National Library of Medicine librarians have collected and annotated thousands of high quality Web resources on many health and medical topics. The site includes the ADAM Encyclopedia of Medicine and a great online drug information collection. "A guide to more than 9,000 prescription and over-the-counter medications provided by the United States Pharmacopeia (USP) in the USP DI® Advice for the Patient®...copyright by Micromedex, Inc.," and a medical dictionary.

MEDICAL DICTIONARIES

MEDLINEplus Dictionaries

www.nlm.nih.gov/MEDLINEplus/mplusdictionary.html

MEDLINEplus partners with Merriam-Webster to provide a robust online dictionary that defines and expands on medical terminology.

Stedman's Medical Dictionary

www.stedmans.com

Stedman's publishes a very basic dictionary for free and a professional version by subscription.

ABSTRACTS, INDEXES, AND TABLE OF CONTENTS SERVICES FOR MEDICAL SERIALS

PubMed

www.ncbi.nlm.nih.gov/PubMed

The MEDLINE database is designed for keyword searching. Some full-text articles are available through links to publisher sites or may be acquired through interlibrary loan or fee-based document delivery service. PubMed is easy to search but health care consumers should be advised to take articles to their health care professionals for explanation as the reading level for most of the journals in this database require higher medical or biomedical educational attainment.

Free Journal Indexes and Databases

http://library.wustl.edu/subjects/life/free.html

Washington University Libraries has compiled this collection of free journal indexes, and full-text journals in the sciences. The concentration is on the biological and life sciences but there are also physical sciences resources.

National Library of Medicine Gateway

http://gateway.nlm.nih.gov

The NLM Gateway allows for searching of multiple National Library of Medicine databases including MEDLINE and the MEDLINEplus site. MEDLINEplus is intended for health care consumers. The other databases are intended for health care professionals and librarians. "Gateway searches MEDLINE/PubMed, OLDMEDLINE, LOCATORplus, MEDLINEplus, DIRLINE, AIDS Meetings, Health Services Research Meetings, Space Life Sciences Meetings, and HSRProj."

ENCYCLOPEDIAS OF HEALTH AND MEDICAL INFORMATION

(See also Medical Metasites above)

FamilyDoctor.Org

www.familydoctor.org

The American Academy of Family Physicians publishes this encyclopedic Web site with topics related to family medicine. Includes news and articles of current interest as well as in-depth discussion of a variety of diseases, behavioral issues, and injuries. The "Self-Care" guide is a marvelous tool. For example, given a "sore throat," click on "Throat Problems" and answer questions that direct you to additional questions. This is not intended as a substitute for a health care professional, but it will guide decisions to seek emergency care or make a regular doctor appointment.

KidsHealth

www.kidshealth.org/index.html

This Web-published medical encyclopedia focuses on children's health information. The Nemours Foundation sponsors the site. Physicians, nurses, and other health care professionals create and review the encyclopedia articles published on this site. It is written at three levels: Parents, Kids, and Teenagers.

MEDICAL E-SERIALS AND DATABASES

Public Library of Science (PLoS)

www.publiclibraryofscience.org

"PLoS" is a nonprofit organization of scientists and physicians committed to making the world's scientific and medical literature a freely available public resource." PLos is building a collection of e-serials, primary and other research and teaching related documents for the sciences (and education and related areas).

PubMed Central

www.pubmedcentral.nih.gov

Growing collection of full-text medical and biological sciences journals on the Web. PubMed Central is free and unrestricted access to "the U.S. National Library of Medicine's digital archive of life sciences journal literature."

MEDICAL NEWS

(All of the metasites discussed above provide current medical news on the Web site and through publication of e-newsletters, or e-journals.)

KEY PRIMARY DOCUMENTS
(medical and pharmaceutical research data, statistics, clinical trials, and clinical guidelines)

Clinical Trials.gov

http://clinicaltrials.gov

"The U.S. National Institutes of Health, through its National Library of Medicine, has developed ClinicalTrials.gov to provide patients, family members and members of the public current information about clinical research studies. Before searching, you may want to learn more about clinical trials and more about this Web site. Check often for regular updates to ClinicalTrials.gov." This is the most comprehensive listing of clinical trials published online. It is searchable and browsable by condition, treatment, sponsor, and other categories.

National Guideline Clearinghouse

www.guidelines.gov

"A public resource for evidence-based clinical practice guidelines. NGC is sponsored by the U.S. Agency for Healthcare Research and Quality (formerly the U.S. Agency for Health Care Policy and Research) in partnership with the American Medical Association and the American Association of Health Plans."

U.S. Food and Drug Administration

www.fda.gov

The USFDA directories not only inform about drugs and food, but also cosmetics, tobacco, medical devices, and products, toxicology. Other sections have specific information for patients, consumers, health professionals, state and local officials, even kids.

MEDICAL SPECIFIC SEARCH ENGINES

SUMSearch

http://sumsearch.uthscsa.edu

SUMSearch is a unique method of searching for medical evidence by using the Internet. SUMSearch combines meta-searching and contingency searching in order to automate searching for medical evidence. Searches PubMed, National Guideline ClearingHouse, DARE-CRD Databases, Cochrane Collaboration Library, and others. These resources are intended for healthcare professionals.

4.8 MEDICAL RESOURCE COLLECTION TOOLS

See also Part III: Web Collection Development Resources
See also Core Web Medical Reference Collection: Medical Metasites

The Alternative Medicine Homepage

www.pitt.edu/~cbw/altm.html

Charles B. Wessel, M.L.S., Librarian, Falk Library of the Health Sciences, University of Pittsburgh has evaluated and collected Web resources related to complementary and alternative medicine.

CAPHIS—Consumer and Patient Health Information Section of the Medical Library Assocation

http://caphis.mlanet.org/consumer

The CAPHIS top 100 "Web sites you can trust." Compiled by members of CAPHIS and organized by general health interest.

Doctors Guide to the Internet

www.docguide.com

Commercial site with news and annotated links to various medical and professional sites. Intended for physicians. Good collection of patient support sites.

Hardin Meta Directory

www.lib.uiowa.edu/hardin/md/index.html

Database of Web sites by category; size of site and connection rate is annotated. Also lists the Medical/Health Sciences Libraries on the Web.

The Harriet Lane Links (formerly Pediatric Points of Interest)

http://162.129.72.40/poi

"Maintained and edited at the Johns Hopkins University, this site attempts to catalog, review and score...existing links to pediatric information on the Internet." The majority of sites reviewed are intended for health care professionals, but the site maintains some collections with the "Target Audience" categories Laypersons: Parent/Caregiver, Teenager, Child, and Child Care Professionals.

HealthNet

http://library.uchc.edu/departm/hnet

This site was developed to "assist in the development of local public libraries as primary access points for consumer health information." Internet resources for consumer health, as well as print and local referrals for consumer health information are selected by the HealthNet librarians.

HealthWeb

http://healthweb.org

This site provides links to specific, evaluated information resources on the World Wide Web selected by librarians and information professionals at leading academic medical centers in the Midwest (the Greater Midwest Region of the National Network Libraries of Medicine). Selection emphasizes quality information aimed at assisting health care professionals, as well as consumers in meeting their health information needs.

Martindale's Health Science Guide

http://www-sci.lib.uci.edu/HSG/HSGuide.html

"A 'Multimedia Specialized Information Resource' currently containing over 55,500 teaching files; over 126,300 Medical Cases; 1,055 Multimedia Courses/Textbooks; 1,450 Multimedia Tutorials; over 3,430 Databases, and over 10,400 Movies." Very crowded and difficult to navigate but there is some good stuff here.

MedHist

http://medhist.ac.uk

Collection of medical history related Web sites. It is part of the BIOME project http://biome.ac.uk and is also WW Virtual Library www.vlib.org/Home.html or http://conbio.net/VL/DataBase

HISTORY SECTION

Medical Matrix

www.medmatrix.org

Fee-based peer-reviewed collection of medical Web sites. Search the database by specialties, disease, clinical practice, literature, education and more.

MedlinePlus

www.medlineplus.gov

Medical librarian evaluated and selected health and medical Web sites, as well as access to PubMed and many other National Library of medicine resources.

Mednets
www.mednets.com

Collection of Web sites of online medical journals, search engines of medical schools, international specialty and regional associations in medicine, nursing, physiotherapy, and dentistry.

MedWebPlus
www.medwebplus.com

This resource collects selected Web sites for both health care professionals and consumers. It is not annotated. There is a selection policy.

The Megasite Project
www.lib.umich.edu/megasite

A Web page with graphics that link to medical databases that have been identified as "the most useful sites for assisting with health sciences reference."

MLA—Collection Development Section
http://colldev.mlanet.org

The Medical Library Association Collection Development Section provides resources of interest to librarians doing health sciences collection development. A selective collection of Subject-Based Resource Lists (Print and Web-Based) is included on the site.

National Institutes of Health (NIH)
www.nih.gov

Huge Web site with links to all twenty-five of the National Institutes of Health, many of which produce databases of their specific health information and resources. NIH also has links to other government agency Web health resources (A-Z guide), NIH publications, funding, and scientific news.

Nutritional Navigator
http://navigator.tufts.edu

The Tufts University Nutrition Navigator Advisory Board of six nutrition researchers and educators evaluates and rates Web sites that provide information about nutrition. The Web sites are rated, annotated, and updated quarterly.

OMNI
http://omni.ac.uk

Collection of metasites, as well as individual specialty sites, in medicine, biomedicine, allied health, health management and related topics. Part of the BIOME project www.biome.ac.uk, OMNI resources are carefully evaluated, reviewed, and selected by information specialists and subject experts at the University of Nottingham Greenfield Medical Library. Although hosted in the UK, the scope of this collection is international.

E-JOURNALS AND E-NEWSLETTERS THAT PUBLISH REVIEWS AND EVALUATIONS OF MEDICAL WEB RESOURCES
(See also the metasites above)

Medicine on the Net
www.corhealth.com

It is subscription only full-text access to reviews of health and medicine related Web sites, marketing strategies, guides to health care issues and the Internet, and COR Electronic Journals and Newsletters. Some free news and analysis.

5:   Legal Information Resources

"The information contained in this web site, and its associated web sites, including but not limited to FindLaw, the CyberSpace Law Center, the LawCrawler, LegalMinds and the University Law Review Project, is provided as a service to the Internet community, and does not constitute legal advice. We try to provide quality information, but we make no claims, promises or guarantees about the accuracy, completeness, or adequacy of the information contained in or linked to this web site and its associated sites. As legal advice must be tailored to the specific circumstances of each case, and laws are constantly changing, nothing provided herein should be used as a substitute for the advice of competent counsel.

FindLaw Disclaimer (http://www.findlaw.com/info/disclaimer.html)

5.1 DEVELOPING THE COLLECTION PLAN FOR LEGAL INFORMATION RESOURCES

The FindLaw (www.findlaw.com) Web site disclaimer that introduces this chapter serves two purposes. First, it establishes the conditions under which the FindLaw metasite provides its legal resources e-library. Second, it exemplifies the conditions under which most Web-accessible legal information is supplied.

Just about every field of study has a legal aspect to it. For example, patent searching and trademark and copyright information are included in section 5.7 under the "Core Web Legal Reference Collection," because they all involve the legal identification of intellectual property ownership. However, these areas of law are also part of business, humanities, sciences and technology research as well. The interdisciplinary nature of legal research will help inform your selection process and the resources you choose. Each library will need to decide what areas of law they will support.

Many freely accessible law Web resources are published by governmental agencies, bar organizations, law schools, or law firms.

Some of the best U.S. Federal primary resources are those made freely available by the Government Printing Office through the GPO Access Web site (www.gpoaccess.gov/index.html). This site includes core resources such as the United States Revised Code—the law of the land—and the decisions of the United States Supreme Court.

The Cornell University Law School's Legal Information Institute Web site (www.law .cornell.edu) is an alternative site that provides a rich variety of legal materials, including links to state level materials. Much legal documentation on the Web is in a raw state, presented as plain ASCII texts without added value such as indexing, searchability, or significant formatting. The Legal Information Institute tries to make some of it more readily searched and readable.

Availability of legal documentation or primary resources, will vary from jurisdiction to jurisdiction. Some countries, states, provinces, municipalities, government, and nongovernment organizations have been more proactive in publishing their laws, regulations, and court decisions on the Web.

Freely accessible law Web resources typically lack the amenities, such as advanced search and report capabilities or hyper-linking between decisions, that make the big commercial legal vendors, such as Lexis/Nexis and Westlaw, so popular with lawyers. Both of those fee-based services are Web-accessible, and available in a number of variations depending on the user group they serve. However, they may be more expensive than the library can afford. They may also provide more data and information; and search and report capabilities than your patrons will ever need. Lawyers, paralegals, and law school students whoneed to do in-depth legal research, benefit greatly from access to the commercial services. For the average consumer or small businessperson, however, the open Web provides good and inexpensive access to basic legal information.

WHAT PURPOSE WILL YOUR LAW COLLECTION SERVE? FOR WHOM ARE YOU COLLECTING LEGAL WEB RESOURCES?

These two questions are strongly interrelated in any subject collection planning. In evaluating and selecting legal Web resources, they are virtually the same question since knowing who your users are will typically also tell you what the purpose will be. A collection built for lawyers and paralegals is substantially different from a collection built to serve journalism undergraduate students, or one built to serve the patrons of a small public library.

Much useful legal information is available on the Web. If you are serving a nonspecialist clientele, then a broad variety of materials, including U.S., international, state, and specialized legal codes, court decisions at all levels, as well as federal and state pending legislation will be beneficial. In an academic setting, those resources as well as full-text law review articles should serve most needs. Whenever possible, provide links to full-text searchable tools as those will be most useful.

Some Legal Web resources publish content that is highly complex and intended for law professionals. Other sites focus on legal information specifically aimed at professionals in particular fields, such as business, healthcare, or science and technology. Some information on the Internet is written for the consumer who wants "do it yourself" legal forms and advice. Some resources will be pertinent only to those in that jurisdiction. Legal information intended for children of various ages is difficult to find, although not impossible. For example, the Library of Congress, Thomas database (http://thomas.loc.gov) has guides and tutorials: "How Congress Makes Laws" and historical documents and the U.S. Office of the President provides the "White House for Kids" Web site with legal and political information intended for young people (www.whitehouse.gov/kids).

WHAT TYPES OF LEGAL WEB RESOURCES WILL YOU COLLECT?

Legal Web resources take the following forms that can be described in terms of traditional reference source types. The annotated "Core Web Legal Reference Collection" lists essential Internet reference tools organized by these reference source types:

- Legal Reference Metasites
- Directories of lawyers, law schools, and legal services.
- Dictionaries of legal terms (although Black's Law Dictionary, regarded as the core legal dictionary is not available on the Web)
- Abstracts, indexes, and table of contents services for legal serials—many of the best indexing tools are fee-based, although free options do exist
- Encyclopedias of legal information
- Legal e-serials and databases
- Legal news
- Key primary documents including international, U.S. Federal, state, and municipal codes, court reports, current legislation, and more

Legal reference metasites frequently contain information from all the reference types, and high-quality sites are freely available on the Web. Such metasites frequently provide all the legal reference tools that most public and general academic library patrons will need.

HOW WILL YOU ORGANIZE YOUR LEGAL WEB RESOURCE COLLECTION?

Many of the legal Web resources provided for nonpractitioners are metasites, and they have their own organization and search options. In organizing discrete resources implementing an organizational structure that stresses the kind of questions that the resource assists in answering might be useful. For example, arrange a collection of materials that provides information on divorce, bankruptcy, lemon laws, property laws, liability laws, adoption, landlord-tenant laws, and other legal problems with which people commonly cope as topical links. Cornell's Legal Information Institute site is organized in this style.

Law professionals and law school students might find it useful for a collection to be arranged first by type of law (judicial, legislative or administrative), then by jurisdiction with distinctions between primary and secondary materials, though a broad topical approach by area of law might work also.

5.2 IDENTIFYING AND COLLECTING LEGAL INFORMATION RESOURCES

WEB SITES THAT REVIEW AND EVALUATE LEGAL WEB RESOURCES: INCLUDING OTHER E-LIBRARIES OR SUBJECT COLLECTION GUIDES/WEBLIOGRAPHIES

The Law Library Resource Exchange (LLRX—www.llrx.com) is an outstanding collection of law resource announcements that not only publishes legal Web site reviews but also publishes articles discussing all aspects of legal information on the Web.

In terms of annotations, evaluations, and scope of subject coverage, the Internet Legal Resource Guide (www.ilrg.com) is exemplary. It is "designed for everyone," lay persons and legal scholars alike, it is quality controlled to include only the most substantive legal resources online." (Internet Legal Resource Guide, homepage—www.ilrg.com) The 'Lectric Law Library (www.lectlaw.com) is also a very useful site for identifying and collecting quality law Web resources (don't be put off by its less than serious attitude—the legal links provided there are of good quality).

DISCUSSION LISTS AND NEWSGROUPS WHERE INDIVIDUAL PARTICIPANTS REVIEW AND EVALUATE LEGAL WEB RESOURCES

Cornell Law Library provides a service called the "Big Ear" (http://barratry.law.cornell.edu :5123/notify/buzz.html), which

> "listens to a variety of law-related mailing lists and newsgroups. From each, it selects messages which contain references to Net documents, and constructs a convenient cumulative listing which shows the title of the document, a link to it, and a link to the message "announcing" it on the mailing list. At the end of a week's time, the old listing is scrapped and a new one started. It thus offers a (slightly distorted) view of what's new on the Net for lawyers, and of what people are talking about."

BigEar monitors LAWSRC-L, NET-LAWYERS, TEKNOIDS, LAW-LIB, LEGAL-WEBMASTERS, and INT-LAW.

The discussion list LAWSRC-L is devoted entirely to reviewing and discussing law Web resources. The core discussion lists for law librarians are Law-lib and Lawlibref-L. Both of these discussion lists encourage discussion of Internet legal information resources as well as many other topics of interest to law librarians. Use the Web Law Lists and Discussion Groups site at www.washlaw.edu/listserv.html to find additional legal discussion lists and newsgroups.

E-JOURNALS AND E-NEWSLETTERS THAT PUBLISH REVIEWS AND EVALUATIONS OF LEGAL WEB RESOURCES

LLRX distributes a current awareness e-newsletter that announces new resource reviews on their Web site, as well as articles on different legal Web resource topics.

InSITE "highlights selected law-related World Wide Web sites in two ways: as an annotated publication issued electronically and in print and as a keyword-searchable database." It is published by the Cornell Law Library (www.lawschool.cornell.edu/library/International_Resources/insitearch/insitesearch.html). There are dozens of other e-journals and e-newsletters with law-related Web resource reviews published by law schools, law organizations, and commercial information providers. The best way to locate them is by using FindLaw (www.findlaw.com).

PRINT BOOKS AND JOURNALS THAT REVIEW LEGAL WEB RESOURCES

Those law journals that publish book reviews also usually include Web resource reviews. Lawlibref-L subscribers identified the following three titles as particularly useful: *Law Practice Management*, *The Internet Lawyer*, and *Legal Assistant Today*. Library-oriented serials including *Choice, Library Journal, College and Research Libraries*, and *American Libraries*, also review law resource Web sites. Some examples of excellent articles in print journals include Jatkevicius (2003) and Cramer (2002).

Jatkevicius focuses on legal aggregator sites: "those sites that collect and organize databases of primary and secondary legal material." (Jatkevicius, 2003: 22) This excellent article points out the major sites, which include FindLaw (of course), but also some newer and lesser-known sites such as AllLaw (www.alllaw.com). Most useful is the chart comparing each of the sites on eight criteria: "Supreme Court Cases, Circuit Cases, State Court Cases, U.S. Code, Law Reviews, Legal News, Attorney Directory and Other." (Jatkevicius, 2003: 26)

The Cramer article is also an excellent tool for learning about legal resource sites. "This guide attempts to identify specific resources, show the scope of materials available, and discuss which sites offer extra features that enhance their usefulness." (Cramer 2002: 150) This article includes a wide variety of resources, both U.S. and International. A short annotation accompanies each listed resource. Cramer points out, quite correctly, that "while full retrospective collections of materials may never be available (exclusive of subscription services), it would serve patrons well to become familiar with the excellent electronic resources which are currently available." (Cramer 2002: 159)

Additional books are listed in the "References" section at the end of this chapter. They are a mix of general legal research guides, with discussions or tutorials on Web legal research, and texts that focus solely on doing legal research with law Web resources. All of them include annotated links to law Web resources.

5.3 EVALUATION GUIDELINES

As with business and medical information, legal information has the power, when misunderstood or misapplied, to affect library patrons' financial and physical well-being.

It is very important that librarians are aware, and make their patrons aware, that relying solely on legal Web resources for legal advice and information may result in negative consequences. Misinterpreting legal information or using bad legal information may result in patrons losing home, family (divorce, custody, adoption issues), and money. Taking bad legal advice or using bad legal information may even result in patrons being convicted of a crime. For example, some sites on the Web declare that the U.S. Federal government has no legal right to collect taxes, issue driver's licenses, or otherwise regulate our society. If a patron takes that advice and does not pay taxes or get a legal driver's license, they will have problems with law enforcement agencies. The Anti-Defamation League's Law Enforcement Agency Resource Network (www.adl.org/learn/ext_us/Militia_M.asp?xpicked=4&item=19) lists and describes the presence of these types of Web sites.

Librarians and library staff can only endeavor to choose high quality legal Web resources and should never, under any circumstances, offer legal advice. We can provide resources to answer a patron's questions but we cannot interpret those resources, nor should we attempt to solve their problems. Whenever a question goes beyond the scope of the resources we make available a librarian should refer patrons to legal counsel.

These factors make it imperative that e-library collectors make a special effort in evaluating Internet legal information. As librarians we cannot help patrons to interpret or apply the legal information they find. However, we can assist patrons in selecting appropriate resources that they might use to research their questions. Using the strategies described in Chapter 1 will help you to find the answers to the following questions about legal Web resources.

WHO PROVIDED THE INFORMATION? WHAT IS THEIR REPUTATION AS AN INFORMATION PROVIDER? DO THEY HAVE THE AUTHORITY OR EXPERTISE TO PROVIDE INFORMATION ON THAT TOPIC?

When dealing with legal information, knowing the source of that information is essential. Not only do the typical questions of authority and intent come into play, but also so does the question of jurisdiction. In the legal world, information can have boundaries that limit its usefulness. For example, a Google search on the phrase "law dictionary" retrieves more than one hundred forty thousand hits. One site retrieved is Duhaime's Law Dictionary (www.duhaime.org/dictionary/diction.htm). This is a law dictionary authored by a Canadian lawyer. He states that the dictionary is "Researched, written in plain language and provided free of charge by lawyer Lloyd Duhaime." There may not be large differences in legal usage between the United States and Canada, but depending on the terms, what difference exist can be significant. Also, this publication is one lawyer's definitions. This may be a perfectly useable site for individuals needing basic definitions of legal terms in the context of Canadian law. Attention to the source and authority of legal information providers is essential.

IS THE INFORMATION PROVIDED FOR CURRENT INFORMATION OR HISTORICAL PURPOSES? DOES CURRENCY AFFECT THE QUALITY OF THE INFORMATION? WHEN WAS THE LAST UPDATE OF THE INFORMATION?

All legal information is time sensitive. Existing laws expire and are amended, new laws are passed, some are found unconstitutional, while others are reinterpreted by the courts, and a few become obsolete every day. Decisions issued by courts are overturned by later courts or made moot by legislation. It is important that Internet legal information resources clearly state the version of legal codes and the dates of court decisions. If a resource is selected to serve as a historical record, make certain that is clearly stated. Resources that provide counsel or interpretation of law need to indicate a date of authorship—as advice can date very quickly.

IS SECURITY IMPORTANT IN INTERACTING WITH A GIVEN BUSINESS WEB SITE? IS A SITE LIKELY TO BE HACKED AND INFORMATION ALTERED? WILL PERSONAL OR FINANCIAL INFORMATION BE REQUESTED FROM PATRONS?

Security of legal information Web sites is very important. It is unlikely that freely accessible legal sites will request financial or personal information from patrons. Sites that charge a fee, such as the "by credit card" versions of Lexis and Westlaw, will naturally require personal information in completing the credit card transaction. Personal and financial information should never be submitted through un-encrypted e-mail or Web forms. Patrons should be advised to use Web browser functionality to determine the security certification of any Web site that requests personal or financial data. Never send personal or financial information through e-mail, unless you are using an e-mail encryption tool. If there is any doubt about security, they should consult with the Web site owner prior to providing any personal information.

Freely accessible sites usually lack the firewalls of corporate sites, making them slightly more vulnerable to hacking. Legal information sites from corporate entities, such as Nolo Press and Lexis, are less likely to be hacked, though they are not entirely immune. On the whole, however, patrons are in less danger from hacked legal sites than they are from inappropriate or misapplied information.

IS PRIVACY AN IMPORTANT FACTOR FOR YOU OR YOUR PATRONS?

Privacy is an issue of importance for all patrons, but most especially for those seeking legal information. If someone is looking for information about bankruptcy or how to contest a DUI, they probably don't want the whole world to know about it. So providing resources, which patrons can use without revealing all, and providing them in such a way that users may not even need to ask for assistance will be well-received.

5.4 SELECTION CRITERIA

In October 2002, as a follow-up to previous surveys done in May 1998, and again in May 1999, we posted the questions reproduced in the following survey results box to Lawlibref-L and several general reference lists. This survey results box also lists the core legal reference tools that respondents from the surveyed groups said they relied on. These tools, recommended by individuals who answer legal reference questions, influenced the sites listed in the "Core Web Legal Reference Collection" in this chapter and on the companion Web site.

Table 2.5.1. Core or Essential Law Reference Tools Survey

Asked on buslib-l@listserv.boisestate.edu, publib@sunsite.berkeley.edu, libref-l@listserv.kent.edu, and oplinlist@oplin.lib.oh.us:

• What are your 2–5 most used reference tools for Law Questions?

Asked on lawlibref@lists.washlaw.edu:

1. What are the top 5–8 print reference books that you can't work without?
2. What are the top 5–8 CD-ROM, Tape or Online databases that you can't work without?

Table 2.5.2. Core or Essential Law Reference Tools

a. Revised State Codes (the Code for the state in which the Library is located). NOTE: All state codes are available on the Web through the Legal Information Institute: www.law.cornell.edu/states/listing.html.
b. *Black's Law Dictionary*. Available: http://west.thomson.com.
c. Lexis-Nexis. Available: www.lexisnexis.com.
d. FindLaw. Available: www.findlaw.com.
e. Nolo handbooks (print and Web). Available: www.nolo.com.
f. *West's Encyclopedia of American Law*. Available: http://west.thomson.com.
g. *Code of Federal Regulations*. Available: www.gpoaccess.gov/cfr/index.html, or Legal Information Institute. Available: http://cfr.law.cornell.edu/cfr, and *U.S. Code*. Available: www.gpoaccess.gov/uscode/index.html, or Legal Information Institute. Available: http://www4.law.cornell.edu/uscode.
h. Cleveland Law Library Association. Available: www.clevelandlawlibrary.org.
i. Lawyers.com. Available: www.lawyers.com.

URLs provided are for the publisher's Web site.

The access and design of all these core law Web resources are based on standards of simplicity, international Web accessibility standards, and no special software required for access. Most of them are free of direct cost. Some have special fee-based products or services.

Working through the collection-planning process will lead you to develop the criteria to select for the variety of legal information resources that are best for your patrons. Another option would be to look to existing legal reference collections as a guidepost to developing your own collection. As you are building your collection, the needs of your patrons are the single most important factor. What another library may include in their collection may not be appropriate for your patrons. In compiling the resources for this chapter, the patron group includes librarians who are building legal reference Web pages and supporting consumers, law students, paralegals, or law professionals in answering brief simple legal reference questions.

5.5 E-LIBRARY SUCCESS STORIES

ROETZEL & ANDRESS, A LEGAL PROFESSIONAL ASSOCIATION

www.ralaw.com
222 South Main Street, Suite 400
Akron, OH USA 44308
Ohio offices: Akron, Cleveland, Columbus, Cincinnati, and Toledo
Florida offices: Fort Myers, Naples, and Tallahassee

> Contact: Bobbie Feigenbaum, Director, Research and Reference, bfeigenbaum@ralaw.com and Jolan A. "Lani" Mikalas, Research Librarian, jmikalas@ralaw.com

The Roetzel & Andress Research and Reference Department maintains two e-libraries. The Publicly accessible Law Links* at www.ralaw.com/library and an internal collection accessible only to Roetzel & Andress employees. Each of these e-libraries will be discussed in turn.

Roetzel & Andress Publicly Accessible Law Links E-Library

Law Links was designed and created to offer a high quality collection of selected law related Web resources for the general public, clients and employees of Roetzel & Andress. This is a robust e-library of over one thousand five hundred free legal resources available 24-7. Visitors

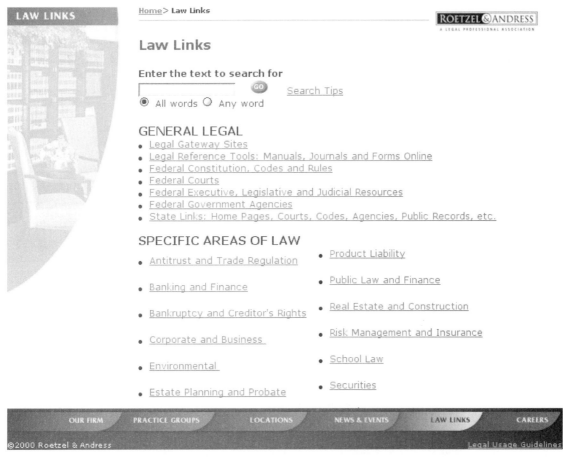

Figure 2.5.0. Roetzel & Andress Law Links www.ralaw.com/library

to the Web site have the option to search or browse Law Links. Although the Law Links collection is accessible to the general public, the Web sites are selected with the information needs of Roetzel & Andress employees in mind. Attorneys, paralegals, and law librarians will find this collection especially useful. No fee-based Web sites are included in the publicly-accessible Law Links collection.

Roetzel & Andress Law Links is organized into three main areas: General Legal, Specific Areas of Law, and Reference Shelf.

The "General Legal" area includes Web sites for federal and state legal information (court information, statutes, regulations, legal and public records sites), legal reference tools, forms, legal search engines and links to information for all fifty states.

The "Specific Areas of Law" section represents the practice areas of Roetzel & Andress. There are ten to twenty relevant links under each specialty.

The "Reference Shelf" includes links to dictionaries, maps, zip code lookup tools, libraries, experts/expert witness databases, verdict information, directories of arbitrators, mediators, and legislators, election information, news, public records, and miscellaneous statistics, standards sources and more.

Roetzel & Andress staff working with outside Web designers, created the firm's Web site. The Information Technology Department at Roetzel & Andress maintains the technical aspects of the site and handles any design modifications.

Roetzel & Andress' Research and Reference staff created the Law Links collection based on approximately five hundred Web sites they had already identified and were using on a daily basis. They added additional practice area Web sites, links for all fifty states, as well as other reference resources, to create a full complement of Web links. Initially it took many months to create Law Links. Now, general upkeep of Law Links involves approximately 1–2 hours per week. Bobbie Feigenbaum is responsible for upkeep of the Roetzel & Andress Law Links section. She is able to keep Law Links up-to-date by utilizing Web Trends software. Web Trends automatically checks all links weekly and identifies any "broken" Web addresses in a weekly report. Bobbie manually makes the necessary adjustments or identifies new Web sites to replace those that are no longer active.

The Research and Reference Department evaluates new resources and reviews current links on an ongoing basis. They evaluate each site for currency, accuracy and whether it is from a reliable and credible information source. They use a variety of collection development tools to select new Law Links. These tools include: recommendations from users, newsletters (such as, The Cyberskeptic's Guide to Internet Research, The Internet Lawyer), search engines, such as Google (www.google.com) and of course serendipity.

Roetzel & Andress Internal E-library

This collection includes web-accessible fee-based subscriptions to many services and over one hundred fifty individual titles. These are password protected and available only to Roetzel & Andress employees and in some cases only to specific individuals within the firm. These web-accessible subscriptions are organized on each Roetzel & Andress computer desktop within an application entitled: "Online Research Tools" for ease of access. Eventually, these will be accessible via the firm's Intranet.

Subscriptions are selected on the basis of the information needs of Roetzel & Andress attorneys and paralegals. Practice areas covered include business-corporate, bankruptcy, litigation, tax, medical, construction, risk management, environment, transportation, intellectual property law, and Federal practice, among others.

When attorneys want to purchase additional reference materials and do not have particular titles in mind, Research and Reference uses resources such as: *IndexMaster* (www.indexmaster .com) or *Legal Information Buyer's Guide and Reference Manual*, by Kendall F. Svengalis, referrals from other law librarians, especially *Law Library Resource Xchange (LLRX.com)* at www.llrx.com. LLRX.com has great topical material lists under their "Resource Centers" section. Also, review of other online law library catalogs and publisher's catalogs is helpful. Final decisions on subscriptions are based on attorneys' needs, budget considerations, and ease of access.

In many instances, the global accessibility of a web-based version of a print title, even when there is an increase in cost, is preferable because the title is virtually available to attorneys in any of the firm's eight offices (barring site license and user restrictions).

The Research and Reference Department handles specific issues generated by web-accessible fee-based subscriptions: They must negotiate license agreements, prepare instructions for navigating the web-based subscription services, train the users, and maintain a list of user ID's and passwords. Initially, it is more work to set up web-accessible fee-based subscriptions. However, once a subscription is negotiated, and instructions are prepared, the Research and Reference Department needs to provide very little upkeep.

It is important to note, if you cancel an electronic subscription, you have nothing to show for it. Whereas, if you have a print subscription, it can still be useful for several years. You can leave it on the shelf and label it "Upkeep Stopped."

Bobbie Feigenbaum, the attorneys and the firm's Library Committee evaluate and choose whether the reference resources should be web-accessible or in print. Roetzel & Andress management prefers electronic resources when these are feasible. However, not all practice-specific topical materials are available as Web subscriptions, or the subject matter may not lend itself to electronic ease of use. The goal is to offer electronic resources to allow 24-7 accessibility for the attorneys from any location. This has already been done with the case law. Roetzel & Andress has access to Lexis and Westlaw for legal research.

The Research and Reference Department in Roetzel & Andress' main office in Akron, Ohio, provides reference services for all eight offices by e-mail, fax, and telephone, as well as in person. Often attorneys request e-mails of the research results. They find it helpful to have the results in electronic format.

Each web-accessible fee-based subscription may include many titles from different practice areas. The Research and Reference Department creates separate catalog records for each title within the subscription. They use Total Library Computerization (TLC), a catalog program from On Point, Inc. (www.onpointinc.com) for all their holdings. They do original cataloging and use their own tailored classification system. For e-library subscriptions, they use a subject word as their classifier and add "Internet" in the title, type and location fields of the record. For print titles, they use a subject word as a classifier appended to a ten-digit number for accurate shelf placement. They have cataloged all web-based subscriptions, as well as all print materials in the firm's eight offices. Currently one library assistant handles cataloging and updating of catalog records. This requires approximately three hours per week.

Currently the catalog is only available to the Research and Reference Department. It is capable of being accessed by the entire firm and will be available through the firm's Intranet in the near future.

Growing the Roetzel & Andress internal e-library collection is an ongoing project. The Research and Reference Department works closely with the attorneys to identify and maintain high-quality cost-effective reference resources.

*This site is not offered as legal advice and anyone using it is advised to seek professional legal advice if they require further information or explanation of any information they find through this site.

5.6 REFERENCES AND WEB SITES CITED

(Note that some sites are included in the resource lists and webliographies in subsequent chapters, and therefore are not necessarily duplicated in this section.)

Ambrogi, R. 2001. *The Essential Guide to the Best (and Worst) Legal Sites on the Web*. New York: Alm Publications.

Biehl, K., and T. Calishain. 2000. *The Lawyer's Guide to Internet Research*. Lanham, MD: Scarecrow Press.

Chandler, Y. J. 2001. *Neal-Schuman Guide to Finding Legal and Regulatory Information on the Internet*. 2nd ed. New York: Neal-Schuman.

Cramer, J. 2002. Guide to Free Online Legal and Legislative Resources. *Reference Services Review* 30, no. 2: 150–59.

Elias, S., and S. Levinkind. 2002. *Legal Research: How to Find and Understand the Law*. 10th ed. Berkeley, CA: Nolo.

Jatkevicius, J. 2003. Free Lunch Legal Resources from Plain to Polished. *Online* 27, no. 2: 22–26.

Long, J. A. 2000. *Legal Research Using the Internet*. Albany, NY: West Legal Studies / Thompson Learning.

Ramy, H. N., and S. A. Moppett. 2000. *Navigating the Internet: Legal Research on the World Wide Web*. Littleton, CO: F.B. Rothman Publications.

Svengalis, K. F. 2003. *Legal Information Buyer's Guide and Reference Manual*. Westerly, RI: Rhode Island Lawpress.

The Anti-Defamation League's Law Enforcement Agency Resource Network. Available:www.adl.org/learn/ext_us/Militia_M.asp?xpicked=4&item=19.

Big Ear. Cornell Law Library. Available: http://barratry.law.cornell.edu:5123/notify/buzz.html.

FindLaw. FindLaw Disclaimer. Available: www.findlaw.com/info/disclaimer.html.

IndexMaster. Available: www.indexmaster.com.

Lexis-Nexis. Available: www.lexisnexis.com.

Thomas—Library of Congress. Available: http://thomas.loc.gov.

White House for Kids. Available: www.whitehouse.gov/kids.

See Part III, Resource List 1: Collection Development Related Discussion Lists, Newsgroups, and Blogs for discussion lists, newsgroups, e-serials and other resources cited in this chapter.

5.7 THE CORE WEB LEGAL REFERENCE COLLECTION

LEGAL REFERENCE METASITES

FindLaw

www.findlaw.com

This is arguably the most comprehensive source of Internet legal resources on the Web. The site is searchable and also organized by category. Resources are sorted by user group: Business; Public and Consumer; Student; Legal Professionals; Corporate Counsel. A "Services for Lawyers" section and a "Legal Market Center" are additional options. Organized similarly to Yahoo!

Internet Law Library

www.priweb.com/internetlawlib

This site provides full-text searchable access to thousands of legal documents on the Internet. Provided by Pritchard Law Webs, the site includes state, federal and international codes, constitutions, court decisions, and treaties. Links to legal research tutorials, legal organization directories, and many other legal reference tools on the Internet. See the "About" section of the site for an excellent listing of law and law librarianship discussion lists.

Internet Legal Resource Guide (ILRG)

www.ilrg.com

ILRG is very comprehensive and is especially useful source of international Internet legal resources. It is geared more for the legal profession and law student than for the consumer or small business. However, it includes a fine collection of law journals, forms, state and federal resources, and research assistance sites that will be invaluable for everyone.

LawGuru.com

www.lawguru.com

This site collects and organizes Internet legal resources on all topics. The strength of the collection is consumer legal support. The site links to LawyerTool.com a site that "search[es] over 550 free legal related databases from one easy interface." Eslamboly & Barlavi, the law firm that sponsors the site, also monitors and maintains a legal question and answer forum and an online attorney network. The legal question and answer forum archives are searchable and organized into an FAQ. Beware the pop-up ads.

Legal Information Institute—Cornell Law School
www.law.cornell.edu
Comprehensive and highly regarded site whose offerings include a full-text searchable version of the U.S. Code, Constitution of the United States, excellent state resources and a fine international law collection. Also available is BigEar, a current awareness service for new Internet legal resources.

Washburn University School of Law Internet Legal Resource Metasite
www.washlaw.edu
This was one of the first Internet legal resource collections. It is enormous but easily browsed. Includes general reference tools that would be useful for law school students and faculty as well as legal resources.
Directories of lawyers, law schools, and legal services.
(See also Legal Reference Metasites above)

Findlaw—West Legal Directory
http://lawyers.findlaw.com
Search options for law firm or lawyer in a particular zip code, state and area of practice. Can be browsed by state or area of practice. The "Finding and Hiring a Lawyer" section offers information on "Do you need a lawyer? What questions should you ask? and What about Legal Fees and Costs?"

Lawyers.Com
www.lawyers.com
Martindale-Hubbell's directory of lawyers in the U.S. and sources of legal advice on the Web. Articles about current legal issues in the U.S.

LawyersLocator
www.lawyerlocator.co.uk
Martindale-Hubbell's directory of lawyers in the UK and sources of legal advice on the Web. Articles about current legal issues in the UK.

Martindale.com
www.martindale.com/xp/Martindale/home.xml
From the publisher of the major print title for locating lawyers. "Use the locator to find a lawyer by name or…search by location/area of practice, by firm, or for lawyers in corporations, agencies of the US government, or law school faculty."

West Legal Directory
http://wireless.wld.com
Graphic-free search for lawyers, law firms, courthouses or legal vendors. Allows lawyer and law firm searches to be limited by area of practice. Courthouse option searches for federal, state or military courts.

DICTIONARIES OF LEGAL TERMS.
(See the Core Web Ready-Reference Collection)
(See also Legal Reference Metasites above)

ABSTRACTS, INDEXES, AND TABLE OF CONTENTS SERVICES FOR LEGAL SERIALS

LexisNexis by Credit Card
http://web.lexis.com/xchange/ccsubs/cc_prods.asp
Offers "pay as you go" searching of legal resources, including "Federal and State case law, Codes, legislative materials, law reviews." There is a set price option for days or weeks of access to business and new resources. Depending on your

needs, there are other versions of LexisNexis available. One variation is: LexisONE www.lexisONE.com a unique Web community designed to meet the day-to-day practice demands of solo and small-firm attorneys. The lexisONE service is loaded with free resources, including: case law, forms, headline legal news, expertly written articles on small-firm practice, and an extensive legal Web site directory providing links to thousands of law-related Web sites, including state online resources.

WestLaw by Credit Card

http://creditcard.westlaw.com/welcome/frameless/default.wl

"Westlaw by credit card is a document retrieval service provided by West Group that lets you easily retrieve legal documents on Westlaw® and check citations in KeyCite®" Other variations of WestLaw are available; go to http://west .thomson.com/products/westlaw/suboptions.asp for more information.

ENCYCLOPEDIAS OF LEGAL INFORMATION

(See also Legal Reference Metasites above)

Nolo.com Self-Help Law Center

www.nolo.com

This well-known publisher of print legal tools for consumers and small business, provides a Web site that goes beyond the traditional legal encyclopedia, although it does provide an online Legal encyclopedia. The site includes in-depth features in a "Law Centers" format. Topics include "Wills and Estate Planning," "Divorce and Child Custody," "Employment Law," "Independant Contractors," "Landlords and Tenants," and much more. A good basic law dictionary, a collection of "calculators," and a tutorial on how to conduct legal research—with links to important Internet legal research tools, rounds out this excellent site. Legal e-serials and databases.

(See also Legal Reference Metasites above)

Law Reviews Online

www.loc.gov /law/guide/lawreviews.html

Maintained by the Library of Congress, this site lists all of the law reviews on the Web that offer "free and complete access to the full text of articles and notes." Listings include school of origin and inclusive dates.

LEGAL NEWS

(See also Legal Reference Metasites above)

CNN

www.cnn.com/LAW

Full-text version of the CNN legal news reports and features. Updated continuously. Archives searchable.

Court TV Online

www.courttv.com

Full-text reports and archives on legal events covered by Court TV.

FindLaw Legal News and Commentary

http://news.findlaw.com

News from a legal perspective on the following topics: Business; Civil Rights; Crime; Environment; Immigration; Labor; Personal Injury; Politics; Product Liability; and Tech and IP. Also offers legal commentary.

KEY PRIMARY DOCUMENTS

(including International, U.S. Federal, state, and municipal codes, court reports, current legislation, and more)

(See also Legal Reference Metasites above)

Copyright Office of the U.S. Library of Congress

http://lcweb.loc.gov/copyright

> This site contains "key publications, including informational circulars; application forms for copyright registration; links to the copyright law and to the homepages of other copyright-related organizations; news of what the Office is doing, including business-process reengineering plans, Congressional testimony and press releases; our latest regulations; a link to our online copyright records cataloged since 1978; and much more."

GPO Access

www.gpoaccess.gov

> Searchable access to the Federal Register, Code of Federal Regulations, Congressional Documents, Directory and Index, the budget of the U.S. Government and more.

Municipal Codes Online

www.spl.org/govpubs/municode.html

> Compiled by the Seattle Public Library

U.S. Patent and Trademark Office Patent Databases

www.uspto.gov

> This Web site has news, laws, and information and also offers free, full-text, and image searchable database of patents and registered trademarks.

5.8 LAW RESOURCE COLLECTION TOOLS

See also Part III: Web Collection Development Resources
See also Core Web Legal Reference Collection: Legal Reference Metasites.

Cleveland Law Library Assocation.

http://clevelandlawlibrary.org

> The Cleveland Law Library site provides an excellent e-library of legal materials of national and state interest. Both the resources selected and the layout of the site can serve as a useful guide. Pay special attention to the FAQ section, which is laid out by area of law, and then lists resources that will answer those questions. NOTE: most of the resources listed in the FAQ are specific to Ohio.

Law Library Resource Exchange (LLRX)

www.llrx.com

> LLRX is a hybrid electronic legal research journal, legal encyclopedia and legal metasite. The articles are always timely and very helpful for the librarian or other legal researcher. Internet legal resources are organized in "Information Centers." Of special note is the LLRX collection of court rules, forms and dockets. The LLRX site is fully searchable.

Roetzel & Andress Law Links

www.ralaw.com/library

> This excellent collection is designed to support the research needs of law librarians, lawyers and paralegals—though it can also be of value to the general public. Evaluated by the Research and Reference Librarians at the firm for accuracy, currency and authority, all of the public Law Links are freely accessible resources. The front page of the site has a very clean look, with three divisions: General Legal, Specific Areas of Law, and Reference Shelf. The set of links available for each of the fifty states is especially impressive.

6: Biological Sciences Information Resources

"Scientists have always been skilled in retrieving data from distributed sources worldwide and synthesizing them into a logical whole. And, for hundreds of years, scientists have been communicating their ideas and knowledge in the form of a scientific paper, proposal, or presentation—to a forum of peers for comment, critical review, questioning, and judgement...Before the emergence of worldwide computer internetworks, scientists accomplished these tasks by applying the technologies of the day: postal delivery, phone, fax, printed media such as the science journal, and transportation to join colleagues in the lab, field, or conference. Now they use electronic mail, discussion groups, File Transfer Protocol, Telnet, Gopher, and the World Wide Web to accomplish the same...the Internet has enabled scientists to perform ordinary tasks more efficiently, quickly, and effectively."

Clements (1996: xvii)

Collecting, evaluating, and selecting scientific information resources is a relatively complex process. Much scientific information requires resource collectors to either have some subject expertise or to have access to someone else who has subject expertise. The collection of biological sciences, physical sciences, engineering, computer sciences, and technology Web resources are no different in this respect. Non-subject specialists will want to consult with subject specialists in the process of collecting, evaluating, and selecting scientific information resources from the Web.

6.1 DEVELOPING THE COLLECTION PLAN FOR BIOLOGICAL INFORMATION RESOURCES

Biological sciences resources include biomedical research sources as well as agriculture, botany, zoology, environmental science, fresh water biology, oceanography, and other biological or life science fields. The scope of biological science resources on the Web is as broad and diverse as the biosphere of the earth. There are thousands of biological sciences specializations.

Biological sciences Web resources include: general introductions to biological concepts, complete full-text databases in specialized biological research areas, peer-reviewed biological sciences e-serials, and other specialized archives in every biological sciences research area conceivable.

WHAT PURPOSE WILL YOUR BIOLOGICAL SCIENCES COLLECTION SERVE? FOR WHOM ARE YOU COLLECTING BIOLOGICAL SCIENCES WEB RESOURCES?

Before collecting biological sciences Web resources, begin by analyzing and listing the specific biological science specializations or subtopics that your patrons will need or want. Biological sciences information will probably be used primarily by students and researchers, both academic and professional. The important aspects to be aware of are age and educational level of the patrons. School librarians, as with other categories of scientific information, will probably want to collect biological sciences information resources designed for K–12 students.

Introductory biology resources might be needed in a K–12 library. Public librarians may decide to serve not only the K–12 students, but other members of the public who may want more or less complex information. Public libraries may wish to look at the biological science related industries or government agencies that are part of the communities they serve. Academic libraries will frequently collect for undergraduate, graduate, postdoctoral students, and biological science educators and researchers. Academic libraries will look for both basic college level biological science resources, as well as complex, scientific research based resources.

WHAT TYPES OF BIOLOGICAL SCIENCES WEB RESOURCES WILL YOU COLLECT?

Biological sciences Web resources take forms that can be described in terms of traditional reference source types:

- Directories of scientists, science organizations, and projects
- Dictionaries of scientific terminology
- Abstracts, indexes, and table of contents services for scientific serials
- Encyclopedias of scientific information
- Sciences e-serials and databases
- Science news services
- Key primary documents such as scientific research data and statistics

An annotated "Core Web Biological Sciences Reference Collection" at the end of this chapter lists selected Web reference tools organized by these reference source types.

HOW WILL YOU ORGANIZE YOUR BIOLOGICAL SCIENCES WEB RESOURCES?

Organizing by biological science field and subtopics under those fields is a good strategy. BIOME (www.biome.ac.uk), for example, has developed hierarchical subject headings to ease browsing within the different collections (called gateways). BIOME also creates for each resource a database record, which includes keywords and subject headings. INFOMINE organizes browsing by large category "Biological, Agricultural and Medical Sciences," and then by Library of Congress Subject Headings. As with BIOME, INFOMINE also creates a record for each resource in the iVia virtual library system and those records are searchable.

6.2 IDENTIFYING AND COLLECTING BIOLOGICAL INFORMATION RESOURCES

WEB SITES THAT REVIEW AND EVALUATE BIOLOGICAL SCIENCES WEB RESOURCES: INCLUDING OTHER E-LIBRARIES OR SUBJECT COLLECTION GUIDES/WEBLIOGRAPHIES

One central metasite called BIOME selects, evaluates, and annotates biological sciences resources. BIOME (www.biome.ac.uk) includes the BIORES, AGRIFOR, and OMNI collections of biological research, agriculture, food, and forestry, and medical and biomedical Web resources.

INFOMINE—Comprehensive Biological, Agricultural and Medical Internet Resource Collection (http://infomine.ucr.edu/reference/balref.html)—is also a great tool to use in identifying biological sciences Web resources for academic patrons.

Other biological sciences specialization metasites include the Agriculture Network Information Center (AgNIC) (www.agnic.org) and Envirolink (www.envirolink.org).

Additional metasites may be found in the "Bio-Sciences Resource Collection Tools: Metasites, E-library collections, etc." webliography in this chapter or on the companion Web site.

DISCUSSION LISTS AND NEWSGROUPS WHERE INDIVIDUAL PARTICIPANTS REVIEW AND EVALUATE BIOLOGICAL SCIENCES WEB RESOURCES

One of the first ever newsgroups to evolve on the Internet is BIOSCI Electronic Newsgroup Network for Biology (www.bio.net). The BIOSCI forums are on all biological science topics. Not only do they discuss good Web resources but they also collect them into a collection of "Useful Web sites for the biosciences." Most of core discussion lists and newsgroups for the biological sciences Web resources are part of the BIOSCI—Electronic Newsgroup Network for Biology.

Other biological sciences discussion lists may be identified using the tools discussed in Chapter 1.

E-JOURNALS AND E-NEWSLETTERS THAT PUBLISH REVIEWS AND EVALUATIONS OF BIOLOGICAL SCIENCES WEB RESOURCES

Many of the individual Web sites for biological science fields offer e-newsletters or e-journals, for example, the BIOME Newsletter (http://biome.ac.uk/whatsnew/newsletter/index.html). The greatest of all, the Internet Scout Project (http://scout.cs.wisc.edu) publishes "The NSDL Scout Report for the Life Sciences" that reviews biological and biomedical sciences Web sites.

Several scholarly journal open archive project sites are included in the "Medical Resource Collection Tools" webliography, found in section 4.8 of Part II, Chapter 4. Such sites list and link to freely available scholarly journals for the biological sciences DOAJ—The Directory of Open Access Journals (www.doaj.org) and the SPARC Institutional Member Repositories (www.arl.org/sparc) are typical.

PRINT BOOKS AND JOURNALS THAT REVIEW BIOLOGICAL SCIENCES WEB RESOURCES

Many print journals review Web resources within the scope of the journal's coverage. Use a good biological sciences index or abstract tool such as BIOSIS: Biological Abstracts (www.biosis.org/products_services/ba.html) or Biological and Agricultural Index (www.hwwilson.com) to identify journals that might review biological sciences Web resources in a field or subtopic that you wish to collect.

6.3 EVALUATION GUIDELINES

As with medical information, care must be taken to identify the authors of biological sciences information and to verify their qualifications and educational attainment, and research experience. Attention to their record of publishing may be important. That is, are they previously published in peer-reviewed journals? Do they have a clear record of scholarship and research that is traceable? Good biological science Web resource will clearly identify the authors, information providing organizations, and their records of scholarship and research. For example, Eurekalert! (www.eurekalert.org) science news service is published on the Web by the American Association for the Advancement of Science. Each biological science news item has an identified contact person, with their e-mail, telephone, and the museum, laboratory, school, or research organization they are affiliated with.

6.4 SELECTION CRITERIA

Each library will need to determine what their core biological sciences will include. The "Core Web Biological Sciences Reference Collection" (section 6.7 in this chapter, and on the companion Web site) consists primarily of general biological science reference tools and search tools and metasites that may be used by librarians to assist patrons to locate information in general biological science fields and common specialties. Emphasis in this core Web reference collection is on free Web resources. The access and design of all these core biological sciences Web resources are based on standards of simplicity, international Web accessibility standards, and no special software required for access. Most of them are free of direct cost. Some have special fee-based products or services.

6.5 E-LIBRARY SUCCESS STORY

INFOMINE SCHOLARLY INTERNET RESOURCE COLLECTIONS

University of California
Riverside, California, USA
http://infomine.ucr.edu

Contact: Steve Mitchell, smitch@ucrac1.ucr.edu

INFOMINE is an e-library collection created for academic faculty and students. The goal is to enable them to find important educational and academic resources quickly.

At the same time it also helps to simplify the Internet resource collection process for librarians anywhere in the world who are developing e-libraries for academic faculty and students, or for instructors who are trying to incorporate Internet resources into their courses.

INFOMINE was conceived by Steve Mitchell, Science Reference Librarian, and Margaret Mooney, Head of the Government Publications Department of the Library of the University of California, Riverside, in 1993.

INFOMINE began as an interprofessional collaboration between librarians in the University of California system. Ten years later it has grown to include institutional collaboration with Wake Forest University, California State University Fresno, and the University of Detroit (Mercy). INFOMINE is expanding to include other interested college and university libraries around the world.

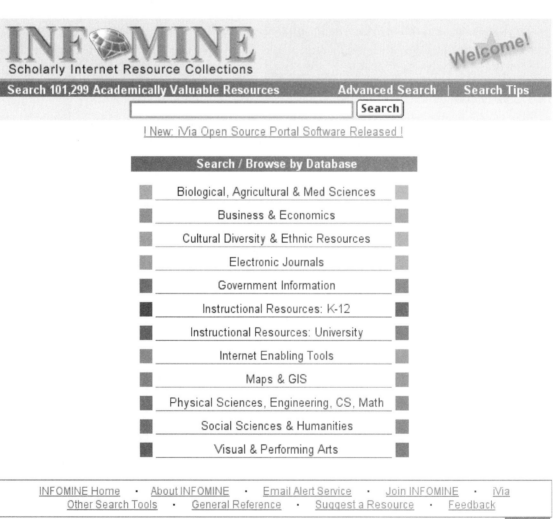

Figure 2.6.0. INFOMINE Scholarly Internet Resource Collections http://infomine.ucr.edu

The iVia Open Source Virtual Library System has been developed from the original INFOMINE project. This system functions as shareable, scalable, collection management database, cross-database search tool, and collection building tool.

"iVia is designed to help virtual library systems scale as the number of high quality resources on the Internet continues to rapidly grow. The labor costs required to provide both coverage of major subjects, if only in representative ways, and collection maintenance are becoming prohibitive. The large, critical mass of resources that would represent good coverage and enable fine granularity in searching, which users of Internet finding tools often expect, isn't present in most Internet virtual libraries, whether of single- or multi-subject focus. At the same time, commercial virtual libraries and finding tools continue to evolve at a rate that noncommercial virtual libraries have been unable to match." (www.dlib.org/dlib/january03/mitchell/01mitchell.html)

Web resource metadata records are created in INFOMINE as a function of their iVia Open Source Virtual Library System. In iVia, records can be added manually by experts, semi-automatically (crawler identified and librarian reviewed) or fully-automatically. Also included are converted MARC records from library catalogs.

More than twenty-five academic librarians with some faculty input, contribute to collection building and maintenance of INFOMINE.

"We have over 25 content builders equating to roughly 3 FTE. This should triple shortly as new alliances are formed. Approximately .25 FTE of staff time is required for support and maintenance of the INFOMINE system. Development of the system has involved 3.5 FTE. Management, coordination and planning involve another 2.5 FTE."

The iVia system includes crawler software that uses expert defined criteria to trawl through the Web, identify, locate, and deliver metadata information to the INFOMINE collectors for evaluation for inclusion in the e-library.

"A major value of our project is not only the information service we provide but the cutting edge systems development we've been involved in over the last 4 years. We are having some success at introducing machine assistance into e-library content building which will save significant resources and allow our type of project to better scale."

In order to be an INFOMINE collector, each librarian receives training from experienced collectors through the telephone and e-mail or in-person, if that is possible. Librarians collect as part of their jobs or as volunteers outside of working hours.

Librarians collect in the areas of their subject expertise and use the collection policy guidelines established for their subject areas in general.

Very streamlined collection plans have been written for INFOMINE given that goals are clear to librarian participants. Employing their in-depth training as subject bibliographers and selectors, they have worked together to collect all Web resources that will be valuable to academic faculty and students in multiple subject areas.

"We have general guidelines for collection. Because we're fortunate to have the participation of trained librarians (almost all of whom select print and electronic resources in other contexts) collecting roles are easily assumed. We have found that, as in any physical library, one collects the most significant resources in one's area of expertise, usually in order from broadest to most specialized in usage. Generally we emphasize selection of broader and core rather very specialized resources. Naturally, there are special concerns with Internet resources such as volatility, access concerns/restrictions, and credibility but most of these issues are of equal concern and/or have parallels in print collecting as well."

INFOMINE collectors use a variety of collection tools including print and electronic review sources, recommendations from users, subject metasites, and serendipity in addition to the information provided by the iVia crawler software.

The collection includes free and fee-based resources including some commercial database access. Each participating university library pays subscriptions or makes other licensing arrangements for their own faculty and staff. These faculty and staff must have login and password and/or proxy information from their campus in order to login but they can access the fee-based Web accessible databases through INFOMINE.

INFOMINE collectors work continuously on the project as they have time. Editors for each major subject area of the database review Web records before they are submitted and are responsible for adding the records to the iVia system through the content management page.

Links are checked at least once per year by collectors and database editors. The iVia system has link checking software that checks links and can also detect changes in the contents of the Web resource accessed.

INFOMINE has been integrated into distance learning courses offered by the University of California, Riverside and informally supports distance learning at all the participating academic institutions.

> "Several faculty have developed online materials for their classes that include access to INFOMINE content of relevance to their teachings. Additionally, indirectly, we work as an e-library to support distance learners by getting them to the important resources they need to do their work."

INFOMINE welcomes and encourages feedback from all users, academic faculty, students and librarian. Such feedback is valued although individual responses are not usually possible. A management team continually reviews the service and the system to identify areas for change and improvement.

> "We do periodic surveys of ALA librarians as one way of knowing. We also get dozens of suggestions daily from users on content and system features. This is priceless feedback and has helped us in our design work."

An important component for the future of INFOMINE is the continued development to the iVia system. This is very exciting. Using iVia, each participating library can customize INFOMINE for local access.

> "MyI and our Theme-ing software allow any institution or individual (such as WFU or a UC Davis faculty member) to develop their own view of our data (via MyI) and/or their own customized interface, emphasizing their brand and institutional "look and feel" (via Theme-ing), to INFOMINE."

Future development of the iVia system is being funded by the U.S. Institute of Museum and Library Services (IMLS), and the Library of the University of California, Riverside. Many other e-library projects, including the Librarian's Index to the Internet and BUBL, have contributed support to the development of this system.

6.6 REFERENCES AND WEB SITES CITED

(Note that some sites are included in the resource lists and webliographies in subsequent chapters, and therefore are not necessarily duplicated in this section.)

Clements, G. 1996. *Science and Technology on the Internet.* Berkeley, CA: Library Solutions Press.

BIOSIS: Biological Abstracts (www.biosis.org/products_services/ba.html)

Google (www.google.com)

InfoTrac (http://infotrac.thomsonlearning.com)

ISI Web of Science (www.isinet.com/isi/products/citation/wos)

Kirk-Othmer Encyclopedia of Chemical Technology (www.mrw.interscience.wiley.com/kirk)

SciFinder Scholar (www.cas.org/SCIFINDER/SCHOLAR)

See Collection Development Related Discussion Groups, E-serials and Guides, Evaluation Guides, and Workshops Webliography in Chapter One for discussion lists, newsgroups, e-serials and other resources cited in this chapter.

6.7 THE CORE WEB BIOLOGICAL SCIENCES REFERENCE COLLECTION

(See also Biological Sciences Resource Collection Tools)

DIRECTORIES OF BIOLOGICAL SCIENTISTS, SCIENCE ORGANIZATIONS, AND PROJECTS

The American Institute of Biological Sciences

www.aibs.org/core

> Web site includes such things as an online membership directory including organizational and society members, and links to their publications' tables of contents.

National Press Club's Directory of News Sources

http://npc.press.org/newssources

> Online directory of experts used as sources by reporters. Search by category, name, organization, or keyword to identify organizations and individual contacts for all areas of the sciences.

Open Directory Project—Science—Biology—Directories

http://dmoz.org/Science/Biology/Directories

> The Open Directory Project has collected multiple Web sites that are directories of biological scientists, organizations, and projects.

DICTIONARIES OF BIOLOGICAL SCIENTIFIC TERMINOLOGY

(See also the Core Web Ready-Reference Collection)

BIOSIS Resource Guides—Glossaries

www.biosis.org.uk/zrdocs/zoolinfo/glossary.htm

> BIOSIS has collected a number of biological science dictionaries, glossaries, and other biological sciences vocabulary guides that are freely available on the Web.

Open Directory Project—Reference—Dictionaries—Science

http://dmoz.org/Reference/Dictionaries/By_Subject/Science

> The Open Directory Project comes through again with a collection of science dictionaries freely available on the Web.

ABSTRACTS, INDEXES, AND TABLE OF CONTENTS SERVICES FOR BIOLOGICAL SERIALS

Entrez

www.ncbi.nlm.nih.gov/Entrez

> National Center for Biotechnology Information searchable bioscience databases. Includes Pubmed search, as well as Genbank, and other subsets of the NCBI's research programs.

Free Journal Indexes and Databases

http://library.wustl.edu/subjects/life/free.html

> Washington University Libraries has compiled this collection of free journal indexes, and full-text journals in the sciences. The concentration is on the biological and life sciences but there are also physical sciences resources.

ENCYCLOPEDIAS OF BIOLOGICAL SCIENTIFIC INFORMATION

(See Biological Sciences Resource Collection Tools: Metasites, and E-library collections)

BIOLOGICAL SCIENCES E-SERIALS AND DATABASES

DOAJ—The Directory of Open Access Journals (from the Budapest Open Archive Initiative)

www.doaj.org

Public Library of Science (PLoS)

www.publiclibraryofscience.org

"PLoS" is a nonprofit organization of scientists and physicians committed to making the world's scientific and medical literature a freely available public resource." PLos is building a collection of e-serials, primary and other research and teaching related documents for the sciences (and education and related areas).

PubMed Central

www.pubmedcentral.nih.gov

Growing collection of full-text medical and biological sciences journals on the Web. PubMed Central is free and unrestricted access to "the U.S. National Library of Medicine's digital archive of life sciences journal literature."

SPARC Institutional Member Repositories

http://www.arl.org/sparc

Scholarly journals archiving projects.

BIOLOGICAL SCIENCES NEWS SERVICES

Eurekalert!

www.eurekalert.org

Science news organized by subject including many different biological sciences. "Reference Desk" collection of scientific dictionaries and glossaries and special statistical resources in each subject area. This is a project of the American Society for the Advancement of Science.

KEY PRIMARY DOCUMENTS (SCIENTIFIC RESEARCH DATA AND STATISTICS)

(See Biological Sciences Resource Collection Tools: Metasites, and E-library collections)

BIOLOGICAL SCIENCES SEARCH ENGINES

California Digital Library Search Light—Sciences and Engineering

http://searchlight.cdlib.org/cgi-bin/searchlight?Science

Searches publicly available biological and physical sciences and engineering Web sites and databases.

UCSD—Database Advisor—Sciences

http://scilib.ucsd.edu/Proj/dba_public

University of California-San Diego's database advisor tool assists the searcher to decide which biological or physical science database will be most useful.

Yale Science Navigator

www.library.yale.edu/science/wizard.html

Yale University Science Libraries database advisor. Assists searchers by identifying the biological or physical sciences databases, both free and fee-based that might be most useful given their search.

6.8 BIOLOGICAL SCIENCES RESOURCE COLLECTION TOOLS

See also Part III: Web Collection Development Resources

Agriculture Network Information Center (AgNIC)

www.agnic.org

"Guide to quality agricultural information on the Internet as selected by the National Agricultural Library, Land-Grant Universities, and other institutions."

BioResearch

http://bioresearch.ac.uk

Reviewed and annotated collection of Web resources in multiple biological fields. Selected for academic faculty, students, and researchers. "BioResearch offers free access to a searchable catalogue of Internet sites covering the biological and biomedical sciences, including genetics, biotechnology, virology, biochemistry and molecular biology."

BIOME: The Hub for Internet resources in the Health and Life Sciences

http://biome.ac.uk

BIOME is a central database and search tool for the OMNI http://omni.ac.uk collection of medical Web sites, VETGATE http://vetgate.ac.uk collection of veterinary Web sites, BIORES http://bioresearch.ac.uk collection of biological and biomedical sciences Web sties http://nature.ac.uk, and the AGRIFOR http://agrifor.ac.uk forestry, food, and agriculture Web sites. All resources are carefully evaluated, reviewed, and selected by information specialists and subject experts at the University of Nottingham Greenfield Medical Library. Although hosted in the UK, the scope of these collections is international. BIOME is part of the Resource Discovery Network (RDN) (www.rdn.ac.uk), and is funded by the Joint Information Systems Committee (JISC) www.jisc.ac.uk.

BIOSCI Electronic Newsgroup Network for Biology

www.bio.net

Not only is this a "no fee" communications forum, this also contains a metasite for all categories of bioscience.

Catalog of U.S. Government Science and Technology Web Site Resources

www.scitechresources.gov

Comprehensive collection of U.S. Government sponsored or funded science and technology sites. This collection is collected for scientists, engineers, and "science aware" citizens. Biological and Physical Sciences sites collected.

Envirolink

www.envirolink.org

Extensive links to environmental sites along with a chat room, job center, and more.

INFOMINE—Biological, Agricultural and Medical Sciences Collection

http://infomine.ucr.edu

Large annotated collection of Internet resources related to biology, agriculture, and medicine. Resources have been determined to be "'of use' as a scholarly information resource in research or educational activities at the university level."

Internet Biologists

www.internetbiologists.org

Biology resource and information sharing site fosters "virtual connections between Biologistsat disparate locations, provide training opportunities for research scientists with the integration of Internet tools into their research, and provide networking and mentoring opportunities for the international Biological research community."

On The Web (formerly Web Spinning)

www.davincipress.com/ontheweb/index.html

> Archived online version of print column published in *Genetic Engineering News*, which reviews Web sites for biotechnology and bioengineering.

SciCentral

http://scicentral.com

> This searchable metadatabase includes all areas of science and their subcategories with directories, research and latest news.

Science.gov: FirstGov for Science—Government Science Portal

www.science.gov

> Directory of U.S. Government science programs on the Web, with special emphasis on science education. Physical and biological sciences are represented.

7: Physical Sciences, Engineering, Computer Sciences, and Technology Information Resources

"Science and technology impact our daily lives from new drug discoveries, to interest in the environment in our back yard, to the incorporation of new technologies into business and industry. This creates an enormous demand for scientific and technical information by a very large population with diverse backgrounds. To meet these needs, science.gov provides a gateway to information resources at the U.S. government science agencies. ...Science.gov contains reliable information resources selected by the respective agencies as their best science information. Two major types of information are included—selected authoritative science Web sites and databases of technical reports, journal articles, conference proceedings, and other published materials.

http://www.science.gov/about.html

7.1 DEVELOPING THE COLLECTION PLAN FOR PHYSICAL SCIENCES, ENGINEERING, COMPUTER SCIENCES, AND TECHNOLOGY INFORMATION RESOURCES

Physical sciences and technology are often grouped together for collection purposes. The physical sciences include fields such as chemistry, physics, geology, and mathematics. Technology generally includes engineering, computer science, and other related fields. For brevity we'll employ the simpler phrase "Physical Sciences and Technology" in place of "Physical Sciences, Engineering, Computer Sciences, and Technology."

Resources that support scientific study and education in the physical science and technologies were some of the first to appear on the Web. Specifically, computer science and high-energy physics information were the first kinds of scientific information distributed through the Web.

WHAT PURPOSE WILL YOUR PHYSICAL SCIENCES AND TECHNOLOGY COLLECTION SERVE? FOR WHOM ARE YOU COLLECTING PHYSICAL SCIENCES AND TECHNOLOGY WEB RESOURCES?

As with the other types of scientific information discussed in previous and subsequent chapters, users of physical scientific information will most likely be students, of various ages and educational attainment, and researchers both academic and professional. Technology information may be also be needed by consumers or by professionals (such as engineers or computing professionals).

Special libraries serving physical sciences and technology researchers will need to acquire resources that provide depth of coverage in a specific area of scientific or technological information. For example, they may need to collect resources for geology, nuclear physics, manufacturing engineering, chemical synthesis, environmental engineering, or computer engineering, and so on. Academic libraries may need to cover a broad range of physical sciences and technology topics for undergraduate and graduate students, and also to cover specific subtopics in-depth for researchers working in their parent institutions. Public libraries may need to serve K–12 students or even to support the businesses or government agencies in their community. For example, the Cleveland Public Library supports their communities' sciences and technology information needs through their Science and Technology Subject Department and Links e-library (www.cpl.org/ LinksLibrary.asp?FormMode=SDCategory&ID=12).

Each library should be aware of which scientific subject areas they support for researchers and students in their parent organizations or patron communities.

WHAT TYPES OF PHYSICAL SCIENCES AND TECHNOLOGY WEB RESOURCES WILL YOU COLLECT?

Robert McGeachin's 1998 article, "Selection Criteria for Web-Based Resources in a Science and Technology Library Collection," focuses on collection development for science and technology resources. He identifies:

> "Web-based materials that fit the needs of users of science and technology libraries include electronic journals and magazines, books and reference books, statistical sources and databases." (McGeachin, 1998: 2)

Physical sciences and technology Web resources take the same kinds of forms as the Biological sciences Web resource reference types described in Part II, Chapter 6.

An annotated "Core Web Physical Sciences, Engineering, Computer Sciences, and Technology Reference Collection" end of this chapter lists selected Web reference tools organized by these reference source types.

HOW WILL YOU ORGANIZE YOUR PHYSICAL SCIENCES AND TECHNOLOGY WEB RESOURCES?

Physical sciences and technology Web resources might be organized by main subject, and then by subfields and specialties. Some thought might be given to organizing the resources by level of education as well as by subject area. For example, different resources might be more suitable for undergraduates or for advanced researchers. Many good physical sciences and technology collections use a Web-accessible database to organize and access records for each selected resource. Some libraries will elect to organize physical sciences and technology resources by resource type or by both subject and resource type.

7.2 IDENTIFYING AND COLLECTING PHYSICAL SCIENCES, ENGINEERING, COMPUTER SCIENCES, AND TECHNOLOGY INFORMATION RESOURCES

WEB SITES THAT REVIEW AND EVALUATE PHYSICAL SCIENCES AND TECHNOLOGY WEB RESOURCES: INCLUDING OTHER E-LIBRARIES, SUBJECT COLLECTION GUIDES/WEBLIOGRAPHIES

EEVL: The Internet Guide to Engineering, Mathematics, and Computing (www.eevl.ac.uk), INFOMINE—Physical Sciences, Engineering, Computing and Math (http://infomine.ucr.edu), and SciCentral (http://scicentral.com) selectively compile Web resources in multiple areas of physical sciences, engineering, and computer science.

Several other physical sciences and technology subject collections, metasites, and e-libraries are included in the subsection called, "Resource Collection Tools: Metasites, E-library collections," of section 7.7, "The Core Web Physical Sciences, Engineering, Computer Sciences, and Technology Reference Collection," and on the companion Web site. Many of them deal with a narrow range of physical science specialization such as the Sheffield ChemDex (www.chemdex.org), AstroWeb (www.stsci.edu/science/net-resources.html), or the Physicsweb http://physicsweb.org metasites.

DISCUSSION LISTS AND NEWSGROUPS WHERE INDIVIDUAL PARTICIPANTS REVIEW AND EVALUATE WEB PHYSICAL SCIENCES AND TECHNOLOGY INFORMATION RESOURCES

The core discussion lists and newsgroups for physical sciences and technology Web resources in libraries are STS-L, discussion of physical sciences and technology librarianship; SLA-Dite, discussion for the Information Technology Division of the Special Libraries Association; ELDNET, discussion of the Engineering Libraries Division of the American Society of Engineering Education, and PAMnet, discussion list of the Physics-Astronomy-Mathematics (PAM) Division of the Special Libraries Association. All four discussion lists include discussion and review of physical sciences and technology related Web sites.

Examples of other subject specific discussion lists include: CHMINF-L, chemical information sources discussion list that posts announcements and reviews of chemistry related Web resources; and MATHQA a mathematics focused discussion list that includes reviews of mathematical Web sites.

Additional physical sciences and technology resource-related discussion may be found using the tools discussed in Chapter 1.

E-JOURNALS AND E-NEWSLETTERS THAT PUBLISH REVIEWS AND EVALUATIONS OF PHYSICAL SCIENCES AND TECHNOLOGY WEB RESOURCES

The Internet Scout Project (http://scout.cs.wisc.edu) serves science and engineering researchers and educators with the NSDL Scout Report for Physical Sciences that includes geology, chemistry, astronomy, physics, and other physical science Web sites (http://scout.wisc.edu/nsdl-reports/phys-sci/current). The Scout Report also distributes the NSDL Report for math, engineering, and technology, which includes industrial engineering, calculus, algebra, geometry, civil engineering, applied mathematics, environmental engineering, computer sciences, human factors, hardware, and software, and related Web sites (http://scout.wisc.edu/nsdl-reports/met/current). Both reports include an education section with resources intended for K–12 and undergraduate students as well as for teachers and professors to use in teaching science.

You may identify additional scholarly e-journals for the physical sciences and technology by searching DOAJ—The Directory of Open Access Journals (www.doaj.org) or the SPARC Institutional Member Repositories (www.arl.org/sparc).

WEB LOGS, A.K.A. BLOGS, THAT PUBLISH REVIEWS AND EVALUATIONS OF PHYSICAL SCIENCES AND TECHNOLOGY WEB RESOURCES

Engineering librarians in particular have begun blogs that include or even focus primarily on Web sites for the physical sciences and engineering fields.

John Dupuis edits Confessions of a Science Librarian (http://jdupuis.blogspot.com). Catherine Lavallée-Welch edits EngLib Blog (http://englib.info). Randy Reichardt edits The SciTech Library Question (www.podbaydoor.com/engine). All of these blogs include Web and other resource reviews and pointers, as well as news and discussion for the International community of academic physical sciences and technology and engineering librarians.

PRINT BOOKS AND JOURNALS THAT REVIEW PHYSICAL SCIENCES AND TECHNOLOGY WEB RESOURCES

Many physical sciences, engineering, and computer sciences journals include reviews of Web resources within the text of articles or in their review sections.

Use a good physical sciences or technology index such as those listed in the survey results box found on page 175 to locate additional print or electronic journals that publish Web resource reviews.

Although, in the past some books were published on this topic the majority of these are now badly out of date.

7.3 Evaluation Guidelines

The key criteria for evaluating physical sciences and technology information resources is to determine the source of the data, the research and statistical methodologies used in collecting the information, and the authority of the information provider. Scientific information is often difficult for the non-subject specialist to evaluate, especially information provided at the research or higher-education levels. Each scientific field (such astronomy, geology, computer science, all areas of engineering, chemistry, physics, anthropology, economics, botany, zoology, environmental sciences, and so on) has its own particular vocabulary and accepted research methodologies. The physical sciences, engineering, and computer sciences, in particular, use mathematical and symbolic notations or computer languages that are not easily interpreted by the non-subject specialist. It will be more difficult for the non-subject specialist to judge the information content without consulting a subject specialist. At the K–12 educational level, or with materials provided specifically for the nonspecialist, it will be important to verify that the information provider has the authority including educational attainment and research experience to write on a particular topic. It will also be important to determine if the information provider has experience in teaching K–12 level scientific subjects. As with most subject areas, the evaluation strategies for Web information resources described in Chapter 1 will work very well for evaluating Web physical sciences and technology information resources.

7.4 Selection Criteria

The critical element in efficiently collecting physical sciences and technology Web resources is to focus on the subject interests of your patron community. This is highly dependent on the exact physical sciences, engineering, computer sciences, or technology fields for which you are collecting resources. Selection must be made in the subject fields and subspecialties represented by the library's patrons. Furthermore, selection must be made at the education or complexity level required by those patrons. For example, high-energy physics research scientists studying the quark will need very different materials from the high school physics students studying they physics of flight.

The "Core Web Physical Sciences, Engineering, Computer Sciences, and Technology Reference Collection" included with this chapter is selected for a broad coverage of physical sciences, engineering, computer sciences, and technology fields.

During April and May 2003, a Web survey URL was sent to librarians subscribed to the discussion lists STS-L, LIS-SCITECH, LIS-LINK, Govdoc-L, Publib, Libref-L, OPLINLIST, Web4Lib, and Nettrain. The survey is reproduced in the following survey results box and is also online at www.kovacs.com/scitechcorevote.html. The results are also reproduced in the box following this paragraph. The survey response was small—twenty-five usable surveys. The majority of responses (64 percent) were received from academic libraries with graduate programs in computer science, engineering, or physical sciences. Four responses came from small or rural public libraries and four responses came from special libraries. These results are used as a model for the core Web reference collection but only a few of these resources are found freely available on the Web. The intended patron group is librarians who work with patrons who might be interested in ready-reference scientific research information at a postsecondary school educational level. The access and design of all these core physical sciences and technology Web resources are based on standards of simplicity and international Web accessibility, with no special software required for access. Some of these sites do offer special instructional or graphics software for download. Most of them are free of direct cost with some also offering fee-based services.

Table 2.7.1. Core or Essential Physical Sciences, Engineering, and Computer Sciences Reference Tools Survey

Survey URL sent to: STS-L, LIS-SCITECH, LIS-LINK, Govdoc-L, Publib, Libref-L, OPLIN-LIST, Web4Lib, and Nettrain.

1. Which library type best describes the library you work in/for/with?
2. If you chose "Other type of library" what type of library do you work in?
3. What are the essential 3–5 print reference sources that you can't work without in answering physical science reference questions (e.g., geology, physics)?
4. What are the essential 3–5 Web-accessible or other electronic databases that you can't work without in answering physical science reference questions?
5. What are the essential 3–5 print reference sources that you can't work without in answering engineering reference questions (e.g., structural/civil, electrical engineering)?
6. What are the essential 3–5 Web-accessible or other electronic databases that you can't work without in answering engineering reference questions (e.g., structural/civil, electrical engineering)?
7. What are the essential 3–5 print reference sources that you can't work without in answering computer science reference questions (including computer technology)?
8. What are the essential 3–5 Web-accessible or other electronic databases that you can't work without in answering computer science reference questions (including computer technology)?

Table 2.7.2. Core or Essential Physical Sciences Reference Tools

Core Physical Sciences Databases

1. INSPEC. Available: www.iee.org/Publish/INSPEC.
2. ISI Web of Science. Available: www.isinet.com/isi/products/citation/wos.
3. SciFinder Scholar. Available: www.cas.org/SCIFINDER/SCHOLAR.
4. GeoRef. Available: www.agiweb.org/georef/index.html.
5. Compendex/Engineering Index. Available: www.ei.org/eicorp/eicorp?menu=compendexmenu&display=compendex, through multiple vendors, and Kirk-Othmer Encyclopedia of Chemical Technology. Available: (www.mrw.interscience.wiley.com/kirk.
6. Google. Available: www.google.com.
7. Applied Science and Technology Abstracts. Available: www.hwwilson.com, and NASA Astrophysical Data Service. Available: http://adswww.harvard.edu.

Core Physical Sciences Print Reference

1. Merck Index. Available: www.merck.com/pubs/mindex.

URLs provided are for the publisher's Web site.

Table 2.7.3. Core or Essential Engineering Reference Tools

Core Engineering Databases

1. Compendex/Engineering Index. Available: www.ei.org/eicorp/eicorp?menu=compendexmenu&display=compendex, through multiple vendors.
2. INSPEC. Available: www.iee.org/Publish/INSPEC.
3. Applied Science and Technology Abstracts. Available: www.hwwilson.com.
4. ISI Web of Science. Available: www.isinet.com/isi/products/citation/wos.

Core Engineering Print Reference

1. ASM handbooks (www.asm-intl.org/Content/NavigationMenu/Bookstore/ASM_Handbooks/ASM_Handbooks.htm, and
   CRC handbooks. Available: www.crcpress.com.
2. ASTM Standards. Available: www.astm.org.
3. Perry's Chemical Engineers Handbook. Available: http://books.mcgraw-hill.com/cgi-bin/pbg/0070498415.html.
4. McGraw-Hill Encyclopedia of Science and Technology. Available: www.mhest.com.
5. Kirk-Othmer Encyclopedia of Chemical Technology. Available: www.mrw.interscience.wiley.com/kirk, and
   Machinery's Handbook. Available: www.industrialpress.com/mh.htm, and
   National Electric Code. Available: (www.nfpa.org/nec.

URLs provided are for the publisher's Web site.

Table 2.7.4. Core or Essential Computer Sciences Reference Tools

Core Computer Science Databases

1. IEEE/IEE Electronic Library—IEL. Available: (www.ieee.org/products/onlinepubs/iel/iel.html,
   and INSPEC. Available: www.iee.org/Publish/INSPEC.
2. ACM Digital Library. Available: www.acm.org, includes ACM Journals Portal and ACM database.
3. Compendex/Engineering Index. Available: www.ei.org/eicorp/eicorp?menu=compendexmenu&display=compendex, through multiple vendors.
4. InfoTrac. Available: http://infotrac.thomsonlearning.com, and
   ISI Web of Science. Available: www.isinet.com/isi/products/citation/wos.
5. MathSciNet. Available: www.ams.org/mathscinet.
6. Applied Science and Technology Abstracts. Available: www.hwwilson.com, and
   Books24X7. Available: www.books24x7.com.

Core Computer Science Print Reference

1. Encyclopedia of Computer Science. Available:
   www.wileyeurope.com/WileyCDA/WileyTitle/productCd-0470864125.html.
2. Encyclopedia of Computers and Computer History. Available:
   www.mosgroup.com/html/pub/computers.html.

URLs provided are for the publisher's Web site.

7.5 E-LIBRARY SUCCESS STORY

EEVL: THE INTERNET GUIDE TO ENGINEERING, MATHEMATICS, AND COMPUTING

Lead: Heriot-Watt University
Edinburgh, United Kingdom
www.eevl.ac.uk

Contact: Roddy MacLeod, R.A.MacLeod@hw.ac.uk

EEVL, the Internet guide to Engineering, Mathematics, and Computing, was created in 1996 as a simple subject-based gateway to engineering resources for academic faculty, students, and researchers. Michael Breaks, the University Librarian at Heriot Watt University initiated EEVL.

Since then, EEVL has grown steadily and now includes academic Web resources for mathematics and computer science, as well as links to a number of databases and search tools, plus various additional services.

"As we are funded by a body which serves the UK higher and further education community, students, staff and researchers at UK universities and colleges are our prime target audience. However, we see that by serving the needs of anyone (in academia anywhere, or industry, or just the general public) who is looking for information in the three subjects we cover, we will be better placed to serve our prime target."

EEVL is a collaborative project between Heriot Watt University (lead site), University of Birmingham, Cranfield University, and University of Ulster. All the partners provide staff to support EEVL, but the Heriot-Watt University Library staff provides centralized management. Technical support is provided through the Heriot-Watt University's Institute of Computer Based Learning. (www.eevl.ac.uk/org.htm).

"Heriot Watt manages the engineering part of EEVL. The Aerospace and Defence section of EEVL is developed by AERADE, based at Cranfield University.

The math section of EEVL is managed and developed by MathGate, a collaboration between Information Services at the University of Birmingham and the LTSN Maths, Stats and OR Network, formerly CTI Mathematics, and forms part of the University of

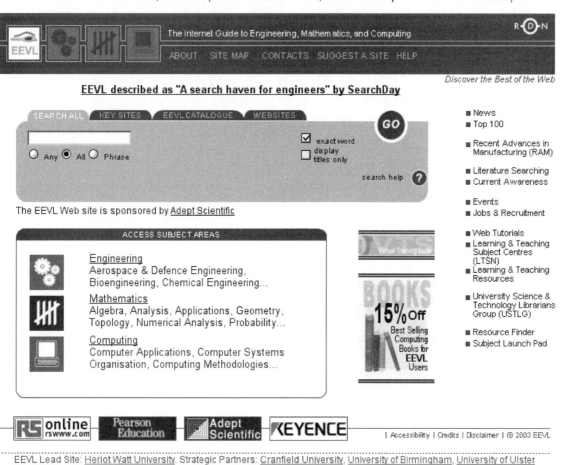

Figure 2.7.0. EEVL: The Internet Guide to Engineering, Mathematics, and Computing
www.eevl.ac.uk

Birmingham's contribution to the Resource Discovery Network (RDN), along with the Altis Hub for Sport, Leisure, Tourism and Hospitality, and the Eurostudies section of SOSIG, the Social Sciences Gateway.

Finally, the LTSN for Information and Computer Sciences, based at the University of Ulster, manages and develops the Computing section of EEVL." (www.eevl.ac.uk/org.htm)

Subject librarians in other partner institutions (The Nottingham Trent University, Imperial College London, Sheffield University and the University of Birmingham, University of Exeter and Bell College) contribute approximately 10 percent of their time to EEVL.

"There's currently a lot of development work going in to developing what are being called Subject Portals. See: www.portal.ac.uk/spp/ EEVL will develop considerably in the future as a result of this work. So, if you count our people involved in that, there are full time equivalents of about 11 people."

EEVL is freely accessible to anyone connected to the Internet. Although it is designed to support academics at UK universities and colleges, it does not directly support a distance learning program; however, it is used by instructors as a resource for distance learners. The EEVL collection includes online tutorials on basic Internet skills and on using the Internet for research in engineering, mathematics, and computing.

A detailed collection development policy was developed for EEVL and ongoing development of the collection follows that policy closely. As scope and types of resource available in the target subject areas has grown and changed, the collection development policy for EEVL has also been revised and updated. One aspect of this has been the emergence of Web-accessible fee-based databases.

"In fact, because engineering and computing are very much 'applied' subjects, commercial sites can be very important for EEVL. Also, some of the best resources available are subscription-based, and so we include many such resources—but we always highlight the subscription elements in our descriptions, so that those only looking for freely available resources are not inconvenienced."

EEVL doesn't license the databases for general access, but rather simply links to them so that those with logins may connect as they wish. The basics of the EEVL collection policy involve the identification, evaluation, and selection of resources based on the following criteria:

"1. Subject matter: Information of relevance to academics, researchers, professionals, information specialists and students in both higher and further education.
2. Acceptable sources: Information from academic, government, commercial, trade and industry, nonprofit and private sources are all eligible for inclusion in EEVL, providing that they meet the subject and quality criteria.
3. Level: Resources suitable for higher and further education, although on occasion, good resources of relevance to school students or the general public will be included.
4. Resource types: university departmental web sites, society and institution sites, commercial information, government sites, e-journals, international agencies, databases, mailing lists, resource guides, directories, courseware/training materials, reference materials, event announcements, job sites, patents, standards, research projects and centres, software, FAQs, full text documents, e-book, theses, conference documents, government documents, images/videos, publishers, contracts and procurements and library catalogues."

EEVL collectors (called Subject Consultants) look for resources that have substantial content.

"Resources consisting entirely of lists of links will normally be rejected unless their subject is very specific, they are particularly important for their subject area or there is substantial value-added information by means of annotations, etc."

The EEVL cataloguers identify and select resources daily. They use a variety of sources to identify new and appropriate Web resources.

"A couple of people use the Copernic search agent (www.copernic.com/en/index.html). We check numerous print sources. Plus various Web sites. A lot of the time the cataloguers 'happen across' sites."

Staff check links monthly using linkchecking software and revise and update URLs as required. Frequent manual checks supplement this automatic Web site review.

Feedback from EEVL users is actively solicited and is always responded to as quickly as possible. A formal evaluation survey was conducted as well.

"We take feedback very seriously. As a result of some feedback we developed the Keysite part of the service www.eevl.ac.uk/key.htm which limits searches to only the creme de la creme (top 10%) of the resources included in the catalogue."

The EEVL project has also made available bibliographic database projects such as *Recent Advances in Manufacturing* bibliographic database (thirty eight thousand items), and makes those available through the Web site.

EEVL uses a custom programmed Web-accessible database based on MySQL and PHP. Collectors add new records via a password protected Web-based admin interface. There are plans to upgrade this database software. The software is constantly being tweaked and improved. Efforts are being made to change the organizational structure so that librarians in the partner libraries can be more involved with the building and improvement of the EEVL collection.

"We feel that the Internet Resource Catalogue, by itself, is important, but not enough to sustain a subject-based service. Over the years we have added considerably to the IRC—introducing things like the Engineering E-journal Search Engine, which indexes the full text of about 100 freely available engineering e-journals; the RAM bibliographic database; subject-based full text search engines, and so on etc.

Now, however, we plan to considerably develop cross-searching and aggregation services, and allow one-step authentication, personalization, and current awareness services. A lot of the information about this is available at: www.portal.ac.uk/spp and also www.eevl.ac.uk/engineering/eng-portal-home.htm and www.mathgate.bham.ac.uk/mathsportal. We also hope to aggregate news, job, events and possibly product information."

7.6 REFERENCES AND WEB SITES CITED

(Note that some sites are included in the resource lists and webliographies in subsequent chapters, and therefore are not necessarily duplicated in this section.)

Applied Science and Technology Abstracts. Available: www.hwwilson.com.

ACM Digital Library. Available: www.acm.org, includes ACM Journals Portal and ACM database.

Biological and Agricultural Index. Available: www.hwwilson.com.

Books24X7. Available: www.books24x7.com.

Compendex/Engineering Index. Available: www.ei.org/eicorp/eicorp?menu=compendexmenu&display=compendex.

GeoRef. Available: www.agiweb.org/georef/index.html.

IEEE/IEE Electronic Library—IEL. Available: www.ieee.org/products/onlinepubs/iel/iel.html.

INSPEC. Available: www.iee.org/Publish/INSPEC.

ISI Web of Science. Available: www.isinet.com/isi/products/citation/wos.

MathSciNet. Available: www.ams.org/mathscinet.

NASA Astrophysical Data Service. Available: http://adswww.harvard.edu.

SciFinder Scholar. Available: www.cas.org/SCIFINDER/SCHOLAR.

7.7 THE CORE WEB PHYSICAL SCIENCES, ENGINEERING, COMPUTER SCIENCES, AND TECHNOLOGY REFERENCE COLLECTION

DIRECTORIES OF PHYSICAL SCIENTISTS, ENGINEERS, COMPUTERS SCIENTISTS, AND PHYSICAL SCIENCES, AND TECHNOLOGY ORGANIZATIONS AND PROJECTS.

National Press Club's Directory of News Sources

http://npc.press.org/newssources

> Online directory of experts used as sources by reporters. Search by category, name, organization or keyword to identify organizations and individual contacts for all areas of the sciences.

Open Directory Project—Science—Directories

http://dmoz.org/Science/Directories

> The Open Directory Project has collected multiple Web sites that are directories of scientists, organizations, and projects.

The Internet Public Library Directory of Science and Technology Associations

www.ipl.org/div/aon/browse/sci00.00.00

> Provides links to hundreds of association Web sites.

DICTIONARIES OF PHYSICAL SCIENCES, ENGINEERING, AND COMPUTER SCIENCES TERMINOLOGY

(See also the Core Web Ready-Reference Collection)

Open Directory Project—Reference—Dictionaries—Science

http://dmoz.org/Reference/Dictionaries/By_Subject/Science

> The Open Directory Project comes through again with a collection of science dictionaries freely available on the Web.

Internet Public Library: Calculation and Conversion Tools Reference

www.ipl.org/div/subject/browse/ref19.00.00

> There are so many options for conversion resources that it is hard to pick the quintessential site. IPL has listed and described the differences of many sites quite nicely.

Martindale's 'The Reference Desk'

www.martindalecenter.com

> A collection of reference tools, journals, databases, and miscellaneous Web resources for astronomy, chemistry, computer science, engineering, geosciences, materials science, mathematics, physics, bioscience and many other subject areas.

ENCYCLOPEDIAS OF PHYSICAL SCIENCES, ENGINEERING, OR COMPUTER SCIENCES

Eric's Treasure Troves of Science

www.treasure-troves.com

> Entries can be searched by keyword or browsed by the following categories: Astronomy, Biography, Books, Chemistry, Life, Math, Music, or Physics. Each category includes hundreds of terms, many well referenced.

Eric Weisstein's World of Science a.k.a. ScienceWorld

http://scienceworld.wolfram.com/info

> Publicly accessible science encyclopedias. Plenty of basic information in these reference tools for astronomy, chemistry, math, physics, and science biography. Still under development. "Technical Internet Encyclopedia Developer." Eric Weisstein is sponsored by Wolfram Research Products. He has a Ph.D. in planetary astronomy, as well as an undergraduate degree in physics. His encyclopedia

entries are clear and concise and appropriate for advanced middle-school science students and up.

How Stuff Works

www.howstuffworks.com

Collection of encyclopedia articles describing how various technologies work. These entries are simply and clearly written and will be appropriate for middle-school science students and up. The site is very commercial with a great deal of advertising. The site makes clear in each entry who wrote the article.

Tech Encyclopedia

www.techweb.com/encyclopedia

Over eleven thousand technology terms are included. Provides lengthy definitions, some articles have pictures available for free. Sometimes provides Web links. Lists terms that appear alphabetically before and after the search term.

ABSTRACTS, INDEXES, AND TABLE OF CONTENTS SERVICES FOR PHYSICAL SCIENCES AND TECHNOLOGY SERIALS

Elsevier Contents Direct

www.elsevier.nl/homepage/alert.htt?mode=direct

A "free e-mail service which delivers Elsevier Science book and journal tables of contents directly to your PC, providing you with the very latest information on soon-to-be published research."

Elsevier Contents Search

www.elsevier.nl/homepage/alert/?mode=contents&main=/homepage/about/estoc

"Working with the world's most respected scientists and researchers, Elsevier Science has set a high standard for quality. Its publications are written and edited by international scholars with excellent technical and scientific credentials, and wide research and teaching experience in their fields."

Free Journal Indexes and Databases

http://library.wustl.edu/subjects/life/free.html

Washington University Libraries has compiled this collection of free journal indexes, and full-text journals in the sciences. The concentration is on the biological and life sciences but there are also physical sciences resources. Physical Sciences and Technology E-serials and Databases.

Cheminfo

www.indiana.edu/~cheminfo/network.html

Hosted at Indiana University this site offers discussion and reference assistance on chemical sciences related topics. Contents include a collection of free chemical sciences databases on the Web, "Resource Guides," and "Instructional Materials." Cheminfo compiles and announces chemical sciences Web resources. Affiliated with the CHMINF-L discussion list.

DOAJ—The Directory of Open Access Journals (from the Budapest Open Archive Initiative

www.doaj.org

MathSciNet

www.ams.org/mathscinet

American Mathematical Society journals and mathematics reviews. Basic search free. Full search by subscription.

National Technical Information Service (NTIS)

www.ntis.gov/search.htm

Free searching of keywords in titles only. Results provide title, personal author, corporate author, NTIS number, cost and pagination of document. Online ordering is available. Full searching is fee-based.

New Scientist

www.newscientist.com

Current science and "hot topics," which include a cluster of articles about each subject. Also includes job listings, editorials, reviews, and letters.

Popular Science

www.popsci.com/popsci

Full-text access to news and feature stories as well as links to interesting science Web sites. Specific headings include: science, Internet, medicine and biotechnology, computers and consumer electronics, aviation and space, automotive and home tech.

SPARC Institutional Member Repositories

http://www.arl.org/sparc

Scholarly journals archiving projects.

PHYSICAL SCIENCES, ENGINEERING, OR COMPUTER SCIENCES NEWS SERVICES

Eurekalert!

www.eurekalert.org

Science news organized by subject. "Reference Desk" Collection of scientific dictionaries and glossaries, and special statistical resources in each subject area. This is a project of the American Society for the Advancement of Science.

ScienceDaily

www.sciencedaily.com

"A free, advertising-supported online magazine that brings you breaking news about the latest discoveries and hottest research projects in everything from astrophysics to zoology. The magazine's articles are actually news releases submitted by leading universities and other research organizations around the world." It is update daily.

TechWeb

www.techweb.com

This comprehensive IT directory provides "a distinctive combination of top-notch original content and one-stop, contextual access to the resources of CMP's network of industry-leading technology publications."

KEY PRIMARY DOCUMENTS (SCIENTIFIC RESEARCH DATA AND STATISTICS).

(See Physical Sciences: Engineering, Computer Sciences, and Technology

RESOURCE COLLECTION TOOLS: METASITES, E-LIBRARY COLLECTIONS

Swain Library: Patent and Technology Transfer Databases

http://www-sul.stanford.edu/depts/swain/patent/patdbases.html

Stanford University, Swain Chemistry and Chemical Engineering Library collection of patent and technology transfer tutorials, Web sites, and databases, both fee-based and free. This site is thorough in reviewing each resource collected. This site will be useful for both business and science and technology librarians.

USPTO Patent Databases

www.uspto.gov/patft/index.html

The U.S. Patent and Trademark Office (PTO) now offers Web access to bibliographic and full-text patent databases, covering January 1, 1976 to the most recent weekly issue date.

SCIENCE SEARCH ENGINES.

California Digital Library Search Light—Sciences and Engineering

http://searchlight.cdlib.org/cgi-bin/searchlight?Science

Searches publicly available biological and physical sciences and engineering Web sites and databases.

UCSD—Database Advisor—Sciences

http://scilib.ucsd.edu/Proj/dba_public

University of California, San Diego's database advisor tool assists the searcher to decide which biological or physical science database will be most useful.

Yale Science Navigator

www.library.yale.edu/science/wizard.html

Yale University Science Libraries database advisor. Assists searchers by identifying the biological or physical sciences databases both free and fee-based that might be most useful given their search.

7.8 PHYSICAL SCIENCES, ENGINEERING, COMPUTER SCIENCES, AND TECHNOLOGY INFORMATION RESOURCE COLLECTION TOOLS

See also Part III: Web Collection Development Resources

AstroWeb

www.stsci.edu/science/net-resources.html

Exhaustive metasite of astronomy and astrophysics of Internet resources.

Catalog of U.S. Government Science and Technology Web Site Resources

www.scitechresources.gov

Comprehensive collection of U.S. Government sponsored or funded science and technology sites. This collection is collected for scientists, engineers, and "science aware" citizens. Biological and Physical Sciences sites collected.

The Collection of Computer Science Bibliographies

http://liinwww.ira.uka.de/bibliography/index.html

Searchable metasite relating to computer science topic areas containing over 1.2 million references (reports, papers and articles); "More than 150,000 references contain URLs to an online version of the paper."

Confessions of a Science Librarian

http://jdupuis.blogspot.com

John Dupuis edits this discussion for academic engineering librarians. Web and other resource reviews and pointers as well as news and discussion of issue of interest to the International community of academic engineering librarians.

CyberStacks

www.public.iastate.edu/~CYBERSTACKS

A "centralized, integrated, and unified collection of significant World Wide Web (WWW) and other Internet resources categorized using the Library of Congress classification scheme." According to CyberStacks, "this is prototype demonstration service emphasizing the fields of Science and Technology."

EEVL: The Internet Guide to Engineering, Mathematics, and Computing

www.eevl.ac.uk

> EEVL is a metasite for engineering, mathematic, and computer information on the Web. See the e-library case story for EEVL in Chapter 7, section 7.5 of this book.

EELS—Engineering Electronic Library Sweden

http://eels.lub.lu.se

> "At present the Royal Institute of Technology Library and Lund University Libraries, Sweden are working on creating a new service, based on the original All Engineering service below, consisting of harvested records automatically selected from their relevance in accordance with the Engineering Index Thesaurus (EI)."

EngLib Blog

http://englib.info

> Catherine Lavallée-Welch edits this discussion for engineering school librarians. Web and other resources are reviewed as well as news and interests of engineering school librarians, including job announcements. International in scope.

Issues in Science and Technology Librarianship

www.library.ucsb.edu/istl

> Quarterly Publication which "serves as a vehicle for sci-tech librarians to share details of successful programs, materials for the delivery of information services, background information and opinions on topics of current interest, to publish research and bibliographies on issues in science and technology libraries."

Knovel—Online Interactive Books and Databases

www.knovel.com

> Publisher of online full-text engineering, physical science, and other technical books, manuals, and databases. Some sample materials are available for preview.

Math Archives

http://archives.math.utk.edu

> Searchable metasite of teaching materials for all areas and grade levels, archives and links to other math sites.

The Math Forum Internet Mathematics Library

http://mathforum.org/library

> With hundreds of links to mathematics Internet sites, this project of the Math Forum provides one easily navigable location for finding math content on the Web. The sites are organized by mathematics topics, teaching topics, resource types, and education levels.

Networked Computer Science Technical Reference Library (NCSTRL)

www.ncstrl.org

> View this international collection of computer science research reports and papers by year, institution or browse by subject.

PAM—Physics—Astronomy—Mathematics Division of Special Libraries Association (SLA)

www.sla.org/division/dpam/index.html

> SLA—PAM division Web site contains links to the PAMnet discussion list, bulletin, and a collection of highly selective Web resources for physics, astronomy, mathematics, and computer science.

Physicsweb

http://physicsweb.org

Collection of "Best of Physics Web" sites, as well as physics news, job information, and other pertinent data. Physics World e-journal is published here.

SciCentral

http://scicentral.com

This searchable metadatabase includes all areas of science and their subcategories with directories, research, and the latest news.

Science.gov: FirstGov for Science—Government Science Portal

www.science.gov

Directory of U.S. Government science programs on the Web, with a special emphasis on science education. Physical and biological sciences are represented.

The SciTech Library Question

www.podbaydoor.com/engine

Discusses news and reviews of Web and other resources for the science and technology, and engineering librarians. International in scope. Randy Reichardt is the blog editor.

Sheffield ChemDex

www.chemdex.org

Directory of chemistry related Web sites. An enduring site, this has been on the Web since 1993.

StatLab Index

http://lib.stat.cmu.edu

StatLab Index most clearly summarizes its purpose, as "a system for distributing statistical software, datasets, and information by electronic mail, FTP and WWW.

8:   Social Sciences and Education Information Resources

"Using the Internet in education is a global, grassroots phenomenon. Even though governments and major corporations are debating (and in some cases funding) the construction of the information super-highway, thousands of educators, parents, and community members are not waiting but are using what's available now to transform today's classrooms into global learning environments....Learning to harness Internet resources does not require you to become an expert in computers, networking, or advanced technology. The goal is still to create an effective learning environment; the Internet is just a tool to help you to achieve this goal.

The Internet has changed forever the way I teach, and the way my students learn. None of us is willing to ever go back to the way it was before, and we join with thousands of others waiting online to welcome you into this exciting process."

Serim and Koch (1996: 4)

8.1 DEVELOPING THE COLLECTION PLAN FOR SOCIAL SCIENCES AND EDUCATION INFORMATION RESOURCES

Social sciences subjects include anthropology, archaeology, economics, sociology, psychology, philosophy, and many other areas related to the study of human cultures, societies, ideas, and minds.

Most quality social sciences-related Web sites on the Internet are published by academic or research organizations. There are literally thousands of such Web sites.

WHAT PURPOSE WILL YOUR SOCIAL SCIENCES COLLECTION SERVE? FOR WHOM ARE YOU COLLECTING SOCIAL SCIENCES WEB RESOURCES?

Social sciences information resources will nearly always be needed for use in an educational or research context. The important questions for selecting social science Web resources are: Which subjects will be included in the collection? and To what age group and educational level is the collection targeted? A social sciences information collection for a school or public library is likely to be designed for K–12 students to use in support of their school curriculum—social studies, history, and so forth, as well as for other members of the community to use in an educational, professional, or business context. Academic libraries may need to collect resources both for college students and for the social scientists teaching and researching in their parent college or university. They will probably choose to collect resources specific to their curriculum and the research interests of their faculty. Special libraries may collect social sciences information that supports business or technology research in some way. Demographic data, marketing surveys, product testing, industrial design, and other social scientific information may be included.

WHAT TYPES OF SOCIAL SCIENCES WEB RESOURCES

Social sciences Web resources take forms that can be described in terms of traditional reference source types:

- Directories of social scientists, social science organizations, and projects
- Dictionaries of social scientific terminology
- Abstracts, indexes, and table of contents services for social scientific serials
- Encyclopedias of social scientific information
- Social sciences e-serials and databases
- Social science news
- Key primary documents such as research data and statistics

An annotated "Core Web Social Sciences and Education Reference Collection" at the end of this chapter lists selected general Social Sciences Web reference tools organized by these reference source types.

Education resources are defined, for discussion in this chapter, as resources that support teachers, administrators, schools, educational researchers, and provide practical support for the work of students.

Some higher-education resources are included in the "Core Web Social Sciences and Education Reference Collection" at the end of this chapter, but the focus will be on K–12 educational support. In the United States we say kindergarten through twelfth grade to denote the years before students go to college.

Education resources broadly defined (e.g., "homework help") could include any of the resources in any of the other chapters in this book. We will only briefly mention "homework help" resources in the "Core Web Social Sciences and Education Reference Collection College information resources are also included in this broad definition.

K–12 education-related information is easy to find on the Web. College information consists of Web sites provided by colleges, financial aid agencies, and educational organizations. This information includes everything from course and program descriptions and applications, to anecdotal descriptions by current and past students.

WHAT PURPOSE WILL YOUR EDUCATION COLLECTION SERVE? FOR WHOM ARE YOU COLLECTING EDUCATION-RELATED WEB RESOURCES?

Educational resources at the college or university level can literally be any information resource in any subject area. Does your library support teachers and school administrators? Education students or researchers? Define the group that the education collection will support and that will dictate the scope of education-related Web resources that you will collect.

Academic libraries may want to collect education Web resources to support teacher education and educational researchers in their colleges and universities. School and public librarians will want to collect the "homework help" resources that will be useful to students studying the subjects taught in their schools. Student teachers may also benefit from "homework help" resources in learning to plan instruction and teach.

WHAT TYPES OF EDUCATION-RELATED WEB RESOURCES WILL YOU COLLECT?

Education-related Web reference tools take forms that can be described in terms of traditional reference source types. An annotated "Core Web Social Sciences and Education Reference Collection" at the end of this chapter, and on the companion Web site, lists essential Web reference tools organized by the following reference source types, many of which are also part of any ready-reference collection:

- Directories of schools, colleges, universities, educational organizations, and programs
- Dictionaries
- Abstracts, indexes, and table of contents services for education-related serials
- Encyclopedias
- Education e-serials and databases

- Education news or any news site
- Education metasites (including "homework help")

Many of the education Web resource reference types overlap with ready-reference types. In fact most of the reference source identified in previous chapters, especially Chapter 4, will be valuable as sources for education-related reference.

How will you organize your Education Web resources?

Educational resources can obviously be organized by subject. It may also be useful to organize them by age appropriateness and/or educational level of the intended patron groups. Some libraries will find that organizing education-related Web resources by reference type will make them more accessible for education students and researchers.

8.2 Identifying and Collecting Social Sciences and Education Information Resources

Web sites that review and evaluate Social Science Web resources: including other e-libraries or subject collection guides/webliographies

SOSIG—Social Science Information Gateway (http://sosig.ac.uk/welcome.html) is the central clearinghouse for social sciences Web resources as well as a central communications tool for social scientists interacting on the Web. SOSIG reviews and compiles the best of the best social sciences Web sites. In fact, some libraries may choose to simply provide a link to the SOSIG site. The BUBL—Social Sciences catalogue (www.bubl.ac.uk/link/soc.html) is an excellent source of reviewed and annotated social sciences information resources. Both metasites link to several annotated collections of social sciences resources in specific subject areas as well.

Discussion lists and newsgroups where individual participants review and evaluate Social Sciences Web resources

There is no global social sciences Web resource discussion list or newsgroups. There are some groups that discuss social sciences Web resources by specific topic. For example, ASIA-WWW-MONITOR discusses Web sites for social science studies in and about Asia. Use The COOMBSWeb Social Sciences server at http://coombs.anu.edu.au/CoombsHome.html can help to find some specific social-science-related discussion lists.

SOSIG includes discussion lists or Web forums within their categories.

E-journals and e-newsletters that publish reviews and evaluations of Social Sciences Web resources

Many social sciences Web sites also have e-newsletter options. SOSIG for example invites people to register and subscribe to their current awareness newsletter. Literally thousands of social sciences related e-journals are available. Search SOSIG or NewJour to identify titles that would review social sciences Web resources. For example, a SOSIG search retrieves PSYCLINE: Your Guide to Psychology and Social Science Journals on the Web (www.psycline.org/journals/psycline.html). PSYCLINE can be searched by journal title or search multiple free indexes and table of contents services on the Web. PSYCLINE article search does a meta-search of those external services.

Print books and journals that review Social Sciences Web resources

Most social sciences journals publish Web resource reviews at some time. Use Sociological Abstracts (www.csa.com/csa/factsheets/socioabs.shtml), PsychInfo (www.apa.org/psycinfo), or another good social sciences index to identify articles that review social sciences Web sites.

Web sites that review and evaluate Education-related Web resources: including other e-libraries or subject collection guides/webliographies

The first place to look for education-related resources is in education metasites. The Eric Clearinghouse (www.eric.ed.gov) is one of the best collections. The Education Index (www.education index.com) which is an annotated collection of evaluated education resources organized by age, educational level, and subject is another good source to check. The Academic Info site (www.academicinfo.net) is a useful metasite for higher-education resources. The "Education Resource Collection Tools" webliography lists several other potentially useful metasites.

Kathy Schrock's Guide for Educators (http://school.discovery.com/schrockguide) is the premier source for education-related Web sites that support teacher's information needs. In fact some libraries may simply choose to link to these metasites.

Discussion lists and newsgroups where individual participants review and evaluate Education-related Web resources

The most important Web educational resources discussion list is LM_NET. This discussion group is for school library media specialists, or any librarian, teacher, or parent who is working with information intended for K–12 students in any format. The focus, however, is on Web resources, trouble-shooting, software choices, and similar topics for K–12 libraries.

Edresource is a discussion of the education resources available that benefit Web educators. Numerous additional discussion lists and newsgroups discuss and review Web education resources for different age groups, educational levels, and subject areas. You can locate most of them by searching the tools discussed in Chapter 1 or AskERIC maintains a directory and archives for several education-related discussion lists (www.askeric.org/Virtual/Listserv _Archives)

E-journals and e-newsletters that publish reviews and evaluations of Education-related Web resources

The Internet Scout project's *The Scout Report* (http://scout.cs.wisc.edu/scout/index.html) is the premier source of reviews of education-related Web resources.

AskERIC Update (www.askeric.org/NewNote/Updates) is a monthly e-newsletter to announce new sites or services added to the AskERIC site. Other education-related e-serials can be found listed in education metasites or by searching the NewJour archives. (http://gort.ucsd.edu/newjour)

Print books and journals that review Education-related Web resources

We list several education-related books at the end of this chapter. Most of these are actually tutorials, or project manuals for teachers, which also include annotated lists of educational Web sites.

Print education journals including *Educational Research*, *High School Journal*, *Journal of Adult Education*, *Journal of Education*, *Reading Research Quarterly*, and *Teacher Education and Practice*, and *School Library Journal* all publish reviews of education-related Web resources. Search ERIC (www.eric.ed.gov) or Education Index (www.educationindex.com) to identify specific articles or reports that review education-related Web resources.

8.3 Evaluation Guidelines

As with other scientific information, the key criteria for evaluating social sciences information resources is to determine the source of the data, the research and statistical methodologies used in collecting the information, and the authority of the information provider. Social sciences information can be a challenge for the nonsubject specialist to evaluate, especially statistical or qualitative research information. Each social sciences area will have its own particular vocabulary and accepted research methodologies. At the K–12 educational level, or with materials provided specifically for the nonspecialist, it will be important to verify that the information provider has the authority including educational attainment and research experience to write on a particular topic. It will also be important to determine if the information provider has experience in teaching K–12 level social science. As with most subject areas, the evaluation strategies for Web information resources described in Chapter 1 will work very well for evaluating social sciences Web resources.

Education resources vary greatly in content and the authority of the information provider. Some of them are provided by educational or research organizations, and others by teachers with varying degrees of expertise. Government and nongovernment agencies publish some important education resources. Other education Web resources are made available for commercial purposes. The best strategy to follow is the basic process of evaluating Web information resources described in Chapter 1. When evaluating educational resources related to business, medical, or legal subjects use the strategies for evaluating those types of information described in those specific chapters.

8.4 SELECTION CRITERIA

Obviously each library will want to select social science subject resources that will support its own patrons. During April and May 2003, a Web survey URL was sent to librarians subscribed to the discussion lists LIS-LINK, Govdoc-L, Publib, Libref-L, OPLINLIST, InfoOhio, and Nettrain. The survey is reproduced in the following survey results box and is also online at www.kovacs.com/socedcorevote.html. The results are also reproduced in the box following this paragraph. Responses were received from a nearly equal number each of academic, public, and high school libraries.

Table 2.8.1. Core or Essential Social Sciences and Education Reference Tools Survey

Survey URL sent to: LIS-LINK, Govdoc-L, Publib, Libref-L, OPLINLIST, InfoOhio, and Nettrain

1. Which library type best describes the library you work in/for/with?
2. If you chose "Other type of library" what type of library do you work in?
3. What are the essential 3–5 print reference sources that you can't work without in answering social sciences reference questions (e.g., History, Anthropology, Sociology, Social Geography, Social Psychology)?
4. What are the essential 3–5 Web-accessible or other electronic databases that you can't work without in answering social sciences reference questions (e.g., History, Anthropology, Sociology, Social Geography, Social Psychology)?
5. What are the essential 3–5 print reference sources that you can't work without in answering education reference questions (e.g., questions asked by teachers, school administrators, education researchers, NOT homework questions)?
6. What are the essential 3–5 Web-accessible or other electronic databases that you can't work without in answering education reference questions (e.g., questions asked by teachers, school administrators, education researchers, NOT homework questions)?

Table 2.8.2. Core or Essential Social Sciences Reference Databases

1. PsycInfo. Available: www.apa.org/psycinfo.
2. Sociological Abstracts. Available: www.csa.com/csa/factsheets/socioabs.shtml.
3. America: History and Life. Available: www.abc-clio.com.
4. Ebscohost. Available: www.epnet.com.
5. Encyclopaedia Brittanica . Available: www.britannica.com, and
   Historical Abstracts. Available: www.abc-clio.com, and
   InfOhio. Available: www.infohio.org.
6. Gale Resource Centers. Available: www.galegroup.com, and
   Google. Available: www.google.com, and
   InfoTrac . Available: http://infotrac.thomsonlearning.com, and

JSTOR. Available: www.jstor.org, and
Librarians Index to the Internet. Available: www.lii.org, and
SIRS. Available: www.sirs.com/products/rfeatures.htm, and
United States Census Bureau. Available: www.census.gov.

7. American Memory Project. Available:
    http://memory.loc.gov/ammem/amhome.html, and
    Facts on File. Available: www.factsonfile.com, and
    Library of Congress. Available: www.loc.gov, and
    MasterPlots. Available: www.salempress.com, and
    PAIS. Available: www.pais.org, and
    Social Sciences Abstracts/Social Sciences Index. Available: www.hwwilson.com,
    Social Sciences Citation Index. Available: www.isinet.com/isi/products/
    citation/ssci, United States Bureau of Labor Statistics. Available: www.bls.gov, and
    Yahoo. Available: www.yahoo.com.

URLs provided are for the publisher's Web site.

Table 2.8.3. Core or Essential Social Sciences Print Reference Tools

1. Any general encyclopedia; e.g., World Book Encyclopedia. Available:
    http://www2.worldbook.com, or Encyclopaedia Britannica. Available: www
    .britannica.com.
2. World Almanac/Almanac. Available: www.worldalmanac.com/index-n.htm.
3. Statistical Abstract of the United States. Available: www.census.gov/statab/www.
4. Biographical Sources (American National Biography, Current Biography,
    Dictionary of World Biography, Chambers Biographical Dictionary, biographical
    dictionary unspecified)
5. Culturegrams. Available: www.culturegrams.com, and
    Mental Measurements Yearbook. Available: www.unl.edu/buros.
6. Encyclopedia of Psychology. Available: www.oup-usa.org/sc/1557981876/
    k030editors.html, and
    Europa World Year Book. Available:
    www.europapublications.co.uk/titles/ewyb.html.
7. American Decades. Available: www.galegroup.com, and
    Day by Day series. Available: www.factsonfile.com, and
    Encyclopedia of Associations. Available: www.galegroup.com, and
    Encyclopedia of Sociology. Available:
    www.galegroup.com/macmillan/pressroom/jul01_sociology.htm, and
    Facts on File. Available: www.factsonfile.com), and
    Gale Encyclopedia of Multicultural America. Available: www.galegroup.com.

URLs provided are for the publisher's Web site.

Table 2.8.4. Core or Essential Education Reference Databases

1. ERIC—Educational Resources Information Center. Available: www.eric.ed.gov.
2. Ebscohost databases. Available: www.epnet.com, and
    InfOhio. Available: www.infohio.org, and
    State Department of Education/Board of Education sites.
3. Education Index. Available: www.educationindex.com.
4. PsycInfo. Available: www.apa.org/psycinfo, and
    SIRS. Available: www.sirs.com/products/rfeatures.htm, and
    United States Department of Education. Available: www.ed.gov.

5. Education Abstracts/Education Full Text. Available: www.hwwilson.com, and
   Google. Available: www.google.com, and
   National Center for Education Statistics. Available: http://nces.ed.gov.

URLs provided are for the publisher's Web site.

Table 2.8.5. Core or Essential Education Print Reference Tools

1. Digest of Educational Statistics. Available: http://nces.ed.gov/pubsearch/major-pub.asp, and
   Encyclopedia of Educational Research. Available: www.galegroup.com, and
   Mental Measurements Yearbook. Available: www.unl.edu/buros.
2. Association for Supervision and Curriculum Development (ASCD) publications. Available: www.ascd.org.
3. Peterson's Guides. Available: www.petersons.com.
4. World Almanac. Available: www.worldalmanac.com/index-n.htm.
5. College Blue Book. Available: www.galegroup.com, and
   Encyclopedia of American Education. Available: www.factsonfile.com, and
   International Encyclopedia of Education. Available: www.elsevier.com/locate/iee2, and
   Teacher Magazine. Available: www.teachermagazine.org, and
   World of Learning. Available: www.europapublications.co.uk/titles/wol.html.

URLs provided are for the publisher's Web site.

The "The Core Web Social Sciences and Education Reference Collection" in this chapter was collected for librarians who will be supporting general social sciences reference questions from their patrons. The survey results were used to guide selection of resources. The emphasis is on resources with broad social sciences coverage. The access and design of all these core social sciences Web resources are based on standards of simplicity, international Web accessibility standards, and no special software required for access. Most of them are free of direct cost. Some have special fee-based products or services.

Selection criteria for education-related information resources are derived from the answers arrived at during the collection-planning process. The survey and results reproduced in the box preceding this paragraph also queried librarians for their choices of core education reference tools. The "The Core Web Social Sciences and Education Reference Collection" included below was compiled with results of the survey in mind. The intended patron group is librarians working with teachers or other educators or with students looking for educational information. The access and design of all these core education-oriented reference Web resources are based on standards of simplicity and international Web accessibility. All of them are free of direct cost. Archival access is varied in these resources.

8.5 E-LIBRARY SUCCESS STORIES

UNIVERSITY OF CANTERBURY WEB E-LIBRARY

University of Canterbury
Christchurch, New Zealand
http://library.canterbury.ac.nz/

Contact: Tim Stedman, Web Librarian, timothy.stedman@canterbury.ac.nz and Teresa Horn, Collection Services Manager, teresa.horn@canterbury.ac.nz

The University of Canterbury Library Web e-library was conceived **in the 1994/1995 academic year.** Over the past ten years this original idea has evolved into the University of Canterbury Library Web-accessible information and resources collection.

Web-accessible resources are selected to serve the academic faculty, research assistants, fellows, visiting scholars, students, and staff at all of the University of Canterbury's campuses.

Although the e-library is not designed specifically to support distance learning it does provide off-campus access to both fee-based and free Web resources.

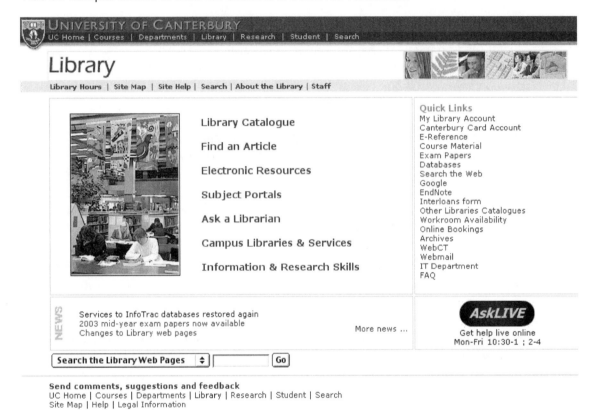

Figure 2.8.0 University of Canterbury Web E-library http://library.canterbury.ac.nz/

University of Canterbury faculty, students, and staff can access the site and with appropriate logins and passwords from home, office, or even overseas on sabbatical. EZProxy is used to proxy access to databases and journals.

"We have many database subscriptions (the library pays the subscriptions) but we provide free access to legitimate users, as per license agreement stipulations. We don't offer a fee-based service as the license agreements require users our genuine University of Canterbury staff and students. We provide remote access (see q2) using EZProxy, legitimate staff and students must authenticate to gain access."

"Proxying access to ejournals using EZProxy is a bigger long term job which we're working on, an ongoing basis. Databases excluded from remote access include locally hosted CDROMs, and databases where special software is required and thus restricted to certain campus computers only."

The University of Canterbury does provide online learning opportunities at http://library.canterbury.ac.nz/tutorial/leo.shtml. The University of Canterbury Library developed the e-library collection policy as part of the overall library collection development policy, which is currently being updated and revised. The Library's strategic plan also includes policies regarding the e-library (http://library.canterbury.ac.nz/about/vision_2002.doc). Policies and guidelines for development of the Web site were also developed, essentially:

"The content of all pages on the Library's Web site shall be related to the function and mission of the Library and the University. The Mission of the Library is: 'To Guide People to the Creation and Discovery of Knowledge' This statement should be considered the underlying policy governing the Library's Web site. It can be used as a measure of whether a document or link should be included."

Librarians who collect resources or edit the Web site also follow a Web site style-guide. They identify, evaluate, and select both fee and free Web accessible resources. Fee-based resources are chosen based on the value of the content to the primary users of the University Canterbury library, the scope and coverage, formats of information (e.g., monographis, journal articles) the price, functionality (e.g., search and browse options), and accessibility.

Before including free Web resources, librarians carefully evaluate each one. When it comes to metasites (e.g., Web resource directories, e-libraries, resource guides) primary considerations include the reputability of the information supplier, source of information, coverage, access restrictions, number of dead links, and frequency of updates.

"We encourage people to be mindful of the guidelines outlined in *College and Research Libraries News* 59 (7) July/Aug 1998).

Accuracy

Check to see if the page lists the author and institution that published the page and provides a way of contacting him/her.

Authority

Does the page give the credentials of the author (as opposed to the 'webmanager') and check the Internet domain of the Web page (e.g., dot-gov, dot-org, dot-edu), is it suitable for academic audience?

Objectivity

Are any opinions expressed on this page, and is it a mask for advertising? Could the information be biased?

Currency

Are there any dead links on the page, is it current and updated regularly, is the information outdated?

Coverage

Range of Subjects and Subtopics, Dates covered, Balance of text and images. Is there a fee to obtain information? Does the page require any special software to view the information, how much are you missing if you don't have the software?"

The Web Librarian, Tim Stedman, works on the e-library and other electronic resource related tasks full time. A half-time Web support staff person also works on the library Web site. In addition, most of the subject/information librarians work on the Web in selecting, evaluating, and collecting new resources to add to the collection. Some subject librarians dedicate significant time to the development and maintenance of specific subject collections on the Web site.

"In September 2001 a person from our Information Services department (me) was moved into the Web Librarian position and a member of the Library IT department was moved to half time web support. We basically train ourselves, and then we train others in turn. Minimum qualifications are undergraduate degree and tertiary library qualification, with detailed understanding of the web in libraries and several years experience developing and maintaining web pages."

Subject librarians use many tools for selecting resources including the list of collection tools specified on their "Keeping up to date with new Academic Web Resources" page (http://library.canterbury.ac.nz/art/libr/sources.shtml). Subject librarians also use Blackwell's Collection Manager (http://cm.blackwell.com), various professional or subject related discussion lists, as well as reviews and recommendations from faculty.

Collection for the e-library is integrated with overall library collection activities. The growth of the e-library is:

"Ongoing, not really much different to print resources. We often participate in consortial deals and undertake trials and evaluations as required. Collection Services and Subject librarians identify sites to be added to the Library catalogue and/or web pages."

A Web team reviews links to be added and updates and maintains the Web pages. The Web server is Apache running on Unix.

"Most pages are static html pages, created using Dreamweaver 4, Dreamweaver MX, and Frontpage 2002. Frontpage 2002 is free with our campus Microsoft license, purchasing individual copies of Dreamweaver costs. Staff submit new pages and edits to the web team in Library IT, who proof check the pages for stylistic and other issues, and flick them up onto the server."

Web resources are routinely cataloged and included in the University of Canterbury Library catalog. Catalogers, all of whom received training in cataloging Web and other electronic resources, create and add these records as part of their regular duties. Catalogers and Web support staff check links regularly. Locally developed link checking software is used to check for dead links, but content changes and redirection of links are handled by staff.

The library is also building a collection of digitized local reserves including, exam papers and some high use photocopies of course readings, assignments, tests, and some archival materials.

"Quite a lot of it is copyrighted so we restrict access by EZProxy and/or IP to legitimate users as permitted by the copyright owner."

University of Canterbury librarians offer the AskLIVE online reference service, which is growing in popularity with faculty and students, E-mail Web form reference is also offered. These services are restricted to faculty and students (http://library.canterbury.ac.nz/ask/index.shtml).

Interlibrary loan requests can be made through the Web site and some document delivery is provided through Ariel desktop delivery.

Feedback from users is solicited for trial evaluations of fee-based databases through feedback forms (e.g., http://library.canterbury.ac.nz/forms/trials/bsp.shtml, or http://library.canterbury.ac.nz/forms/trials/sdeval.shtml).

"Their responses help us greatly in our decision making about what products to purchase. In May 2002 we conducted surveys and we have also done usability testing and built the results into our new 2003 page design."

Usually once a year during the summer, staff reviews and evaluates the Web site.

Future plans for the University of Canterbury Library include migrating to a Web-accessible database for e-resource collection management (http://webapps.libr.canterbury.ac.nz/webdb/database.php?page=alpha-h).

"The data is extracted from catalogue records in our ALS and displayed on our web pages on the fly using MySQL and php. Cataloguers maintain the actual content on cataloguing records, and this updates the web pages automatically...The setup costs include the Library's IT department and Collection Services staff time to do the work in setup (eg programmers time, etc)."

The library is evaluating cross-database search tools. Integration of the e-library into the catalog, and development of z39.50searching options, as well as usability testing of the e-library are priorities.

TAFT LIBRARY/MEDIA CENTER

Marion, Ohio, USA
www.infotaft.marioncity.k12.oh.us

    Contact: Deb Logan jd3logan@bright.net

Deb Logan built the Taft Library/Media Center e-library to help make the Internet more manageable for the students and teachers of Taft Middle School in Marion, Ohio. Her principal, Mr. Born, felt it was a good idea and encouraged her to build the Taft Library/Media Center Web Site.

Deb Logan's collection plan was unwritten but simple.

"My primary goal in creating Taft Library Media Center Web Site was to create a starting place on the Internet for my students and faculty. In our building very few individuals had direct experience with the Internet. Also, my middle school students did not have the sophistication to look at information found on the Internet with an adequate level of discrimination. Consequently, I felt that I needed to teach them how to navigate on the 'Information Super Highway' and to assist them with locating usable, accurate and reliable information resources that support the curriculum and/or teach Internet skills. In a manner of speaking, Taft Library Media Center Web Site was my method of creating an index to recommended resources for my users. Also, I wanted to make the Internet approachable and attractive for reluctant or uncomfortable users."

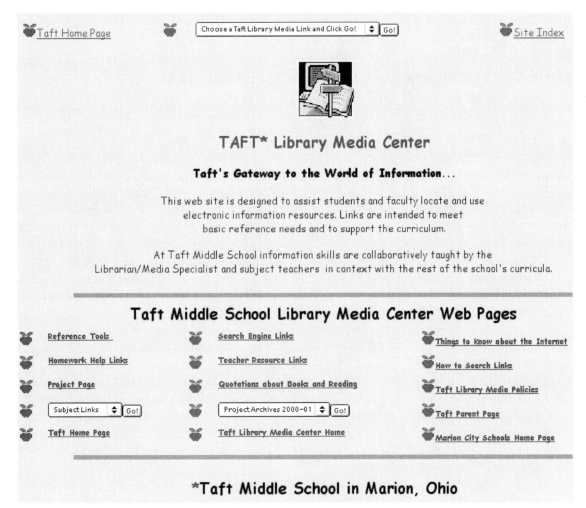

Figure 2.8.1 Taft Library/Media Center www.infotaft.marioncity.k12.oh.us

She began by collecting lists of recommended sites and organizing them in a notebook by subject and bookmarking sites as she found them. This was over a year before her school had access to the Internet. Since using the lists and bookmarks was cumbersome for her library users, she decided to create a Web site containing her collected resources. When the school was connected to the Internet, the e-library was ready for use within a month.

In the library, students and teachers access the Internet and the e-library on nineteen personal computers (PCs). Deb Logan did most of the work building the e-library at home on her personal PC. The Web site is published on the Web server of the district's DA site.

Deb Logan was the only person to work directly on the Taft Middle School Library/Media Center's e-library. She learned HTML by taking a workshop and reading books on the topic outside of her regular working hours. Since Logan changed school districts, no one is working on the Taft Library Web site.

> "My primary resource was the class I took at Kent State from Diane Kovacs. I wrote the page in HTML on WordPad. I have several HTML books and class notes that I consulted. The main books that I used were: *HTML 4 for the World Wide Web: Visual QuickStart Guide* (1997), by Elizabeth Castro (Peachpit Press); ISBN: 0201696967...*HTML: The Definitive Guide* (1997), 2nd. ed., by Chuck Musciano, Mike Loukides (ed.), and Bill Kennedy (O'Reilly and Associates); ISBN: 1565922352"

The costs of the books and training were her only direct costs. However, she spent considerable amounts of her own personal unpaid time building the e-library. She initially spent over five hundred hours working on the Web site. Her library aide assisted with some of the graphics.

Deb Logan has since moved to a new library but the Web site she created continues to serve the Taft Middle School.

MIAMI VALLEY EDUCATIONAL COMPUTER ASSOCIATION/INFOHIO

http://www2.mveca.org/infohio/default.htm
Yellow Springs, OH, USA

   Contact: Jim Pesch, INFOhio Support Specialist, PESCH@mveca.org

The MVECA/INFOHio electronic collection Web site (e-library) was conceived by Jim Pesch. He wanted to create for MVECA member school library media specialists a central location for the links they needed to use the INFOhio (the Information Network for Ohio Schools) resources, MVECA member resources, as well as other Web resources of general interest. This site is not designed specifically for patrons, but rather for librarians to use in developing sites and strategies to use with their patrons.

> "The original intention was to give the librarians I support a stepping stone to INFOHio services (Electronic Resources, Union Catalog, etc.) and to the services MVECA provides them as member schools and as INFOhio automated schools. Many schools use it as the homepage for their library computers if the library does not have it's own web page. I also wanted to provide links to the districts public libraries as well as organizations that deal with librarianship and the school library media specialist profession at the local, state and national level."

Rather than creating a formal collection plan, Jim Pesch used his working knowledge of the information needs of school library media specialists to make choices regarding what to include in the collection. He solicits suggestions from the school library media specialists for additions or changes. The central criteria is that the resources added to the collection give the school library media specialists the tools they need to do their job. However, the collection is not intended to be "everything to everyone."

> "I will be looking at adding additional links to sites that will be more help to students and teachers, but there are a lot of those type sites out there and I don't want the page to become an unmanageable list of sites."

A central part of the MVECA e-library is its links to the INFOHio project databases and services.

> "Of course you can tell that we are part of INFOhio so the databases are paid for out of the state budget...INFOhio has a task force that decides which databases to purchase. We have partnered with Ohiolink and OPLIN to get discounts."

The INFOhio system is funded by the state of Ohio to automate school and other state libraries and to provide a core collection of electronic resources for Ohio students and teachers. INFOhio has automated more than half of Ohio's school libraries and maintains a statewide database of more than a million catalog records.

> "INFOhio is working with the State Library of Ohio and Ohio's academic network (OhioLINK) and public library network (OPLIN) to obtain further resources to add to this core collection, resources available to all Ohio citizens. For more information about INFOhio, visit www.infohio.org."

The MVECA e-library links only to the fee-based Web accessible databases that are available to all members.

> "Some schools have purchased additional databases for their schools. We do not include them on our website as all other districts would not be able to access them. Students, teachers and parents have access to the electronic databases from school and from home. Home use requires a password."

Search
MVECA
Libraries

Libraries

* Greene County Public Library
* Clark County Public Library
* New Carlisle Public Library
* Blanchester Public Library
* Sabina Public Library
* Wilmington Public Library
* Carnegie Public Library WCH
* Highland County District Library
* Dayton Metro Library
* State Library of Ohio

LSTA Grant Info
* Library of Congress
* OPLIN
* OhioLINK

Associations

* GMVETC
* OELMA
* Ohio Library Council
* American Library Association
* SOITA

Initatives

* MORE for Ohio
* Web Accessibility

MVECA Services

Transition to Sirsi K-12
MVECA is working with your district staff and INFOhio to make a smooth transition to the new software. Check here often for updates.

Library Automation - MVECA works with you and various vendors throughout your automation to get you up and running on SIRSI MultiLIS.

Electronic Resources - MVECA provides you with access to the INFOhio-provided electronic resources as well as those purchased by your school directly.

Union Catalog - MVECA provides access to the INFOhio Union Catalog which contains more than 1 million unique MARC records. Records in the Union Catalog can be exported to other automation systems.

Media Booking - MVECA is your gateway to scheduling media delivery from any of the INFOhio Medianet sites in the state. Medianet is a product of Dymaxion.

Training - MVECA offers training for all INFOhio services throughout the school year and provides online documentation for users.

Instructional Development - MVECA supports the INFOhio Instructional Development program and the many services and resources available through it.

Barcode and Spine Label Printing - In order to print barcode labels you must install the Code39 barcode font for your platform (PC or MAC) in the appropriate directory of your PC or MAC. Installation directions available here.
See Also

Electronic Resources

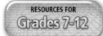

Figure 2.8.2. Miami Valley Educational Computer Association/InfoOhio
http://www2.mveca.org/infohio/default.htm

Jim Pesch is the main person building and maintaining the MVECA collection with support from other MVECA staff persons. He was hired to support INFOhio.

"I think my experience in libraries and with automation software was important. Most of my training since has come from the INFOhio support site in Lima, Ohio. (NOACSC)"

Jim Pesch does all of the link checking, changes, and additions, to the collection, as they are required.

The site is hosted on a Win2002 server.

Individual MVECA member libraries may create catalog records for Web resources if they choose to do so.

"MVECA loads vendor provided records into the Sirsi Multilis system. Districts that are automated through us are able to copy catalog records from each other, the INFOHIO Union Catalog, and the Library of Congress. They are welcome to create their own records for web resources. Records enhanced with 856 tags are available from several vendors but licensing usually restricts the copying of the 856 tag info as they generally link to a paid service. Those companies maintain the links. There is no tracking of those records at MVECA if they indeed exist."

Although MVECA has no plans for creating digital collections, some of the member schools do maintain digital collections of local materials. MVECA may host those library's Web sites but do not make their digital collections generally available.

MVECA does not offer virtual reference sources, but the Sirsi Multilis catalog software does enable some interlibrary loan between schools in the same district.

"As an INFOhio site, MVECA supports the MORE program for MOVING OHIO RESOURCES EVERYWHERE across the state, but as yet no MVECA districts have joined."

MORE is a program for resource sharing throughout the state of Ohio.

Future plans for the MVECA collection are focused on distance learning resources. MVECA plans to expand distance learning opportunities through the site. This will initially take the form of archives of video learning programs developed locally.

"MVECA has a distance learning coordinator. Nearly all of the schools in our area purchased video conference equipment with a grant a few years ago. The distance learning coordinator works primarily with the teachers to link them to content, schedule video conferences, train on equipment use and. Since most of the video conference equipment is housed in the school libraries, the librarians have become the defacto contact people for video conference scheduling and testing, etc. Last year we held a special training for librarians to show them ways to find content, (free and fee based) how to schedule with the provider and how to schedule the conference on the state system. We did manage to conduct one session of library software training this year where we had 2 remote sites attending. We are planning to expand this next year as budgets shrink— making travel to our site more difficult. Next year we plan to offer most training sessions with a distance learning component. This will be library software training, some MARC training, and electronic resource training. My audience will be the library staff. Others at MVECA will train in their areas—again primarily school staff. We are also looking at doing some video streaming for short topic training."

8.6 REFERENCES AND WEB SITES CITED

(Note that some sites are included in the resource lists and webliographies in previous or subsequent chapters, and therefore are not necessarily duplicated in this section.)

America: History and Life. Available: www.abc-clio.com.

American Memory Project. Available: http://memory.loc.gov/ammem/amhome.html.

Ebscohost. Available: www.epnet.com,

Education Abstracts/Education Full Text. Available: www.hwwilson.com.

Education Index. Available: www.educationindex.com.

Encyclopaedia Brittanica. Available: www.britannica.com.

Facts on File. Available: www.factsonfile.com.

Gale Resource Centers. Available: www.galegroup.com.

Google. Available: www.google.com.

Historical Abstracts. Available: www.abc-clio.com.

InfOhio. Available: www.infohio.org.

InfoTrac. Available: http://infotrac.thomsonlearning.com.

JSTOR. Available: www.jstor.org.

Librarians Index to the Internet. Available: www.lii.org.

Library of Congress. Available: www.loc.gov.

MasterPlots. Available: www.salempress.com.

National Center for Education Statistics. Available: http://nces.ed.gov.

PAIS. Available: www.pais.org.

PsycInfo. Available: www.apa.org/psycinfo.

Serim, F., and M. Koch. 1996. *NetLearning: Why Teachers Use the Internet.* Sebastopol, CA: O'Reilly.

SIRS. Available: www.sirs.com/products/rfeatures.htm.

Social Sciences Abstracts/Social Sciences Index. Available: (www.hwwilson.com), and Social Sciences Citation Index. Available: www.isinet.com/isi/products/citation/ssci, and United States Bureau of Labor Statistics. Available: www.bls.gov.

Sociological Abstracts. Available: www.csa.com/csa/factsheets/socioabs.shtml.

United States Census Bureau. Available: www.census.gov.

United States Department of Education. Available: www.ed.gov.

Yahoo. Available: www.yahoo.com.

8.7 THE CORE WEB SOCIAL SCIENCES AND EDUCATION REFERENCE COLLECTION

DIRECTORIES OF SOCIAL SCIENTISTS, SCIENCE ORGANIZATIONS, AND PROJECTS

National Press Club's Directory of News Sources

http://npc.press.org/newssources

Online directory of experts used as sources by reporters. Search by category, name, organization or keyword to identify organizations and individual contacts for all areas of the sciences.

Open Directory Project—Science—Social Sciences—Directories

http://dmoz.org/Science/Social_Sciences/Directories

The Open Directory Project has collected multiple Web sites that are directories of social scientists, organizations, and projects.

DICTIONARIES OF SOCIAL SCIENTIFIC TERMINOLOGY

(See also the Core Web Ready-Reference Collection)

Nelson/Thomson Learning Online Dictionary of the Social Sciences

http://socialsciencedictionary.nelson.com

Compiled for undergraduate social sciences students by Gary Parkinson, Ph.D., and Robert Drislane, Ph.D. Scope includes basic concepts in: anthropology, sociology, criminology, Canadian studies, political science and women's studies.

SOSIG:Social Science Information Gateway

http://sosig.ac.uk

SOSIG includes various dictionaries for social sciences subfields.

ABSTRACTS, INDEXES, AND TABLE OF CONTENTS SERVICES FOR SOCIAL SCIENCES SERIALS

SOSIG:Social Science Information Gateway

http://sosig.ac.uk

> SOSIG is the best source to look for free Web abstracts, indexes, and toc's for journals in the social sciences subfields.

ENCYCLOPEDIAS OF SOCIAL SCIENTIFIC INFORMATION

SOSIG:Social Science Information Gateway

http://sosig.ac.uk

> SOSIG includes various encyclopedias for social sciences subfields.

SOCIAL SCIENCES E-SERIALS AND DATABASES

(See also SOSIG http://sosig.ac.uk)

PSYCLINE: Your Guide to Psychology and Social Science Journals on the Web

www.psycline.org/journals/psycline.html

> Searches external collection of social science e-journals on the Web. Also browse by title and publisher.

SOCIAL SCIENCES NEWS SERVICES

(see SOSIG http://sosig.ac.uk)

KEY PRIMARY DOCUMENTS (SCIENTIFIC RESEARCH DATA AND STATISTICS)

(See Social Sciences Resource Collection Tools)
(see SOSIG http://sosig.ac.uk)

AnthroBase: A Searchable Database of Anthropological Texts

www.anthrobase.com

> Collection of field notes, and other anthropological data collections. Currently under development, this site is growing and adding new tools including a dictionary of anthropology.

SOCIAL SCIENCE SEARCH ENGINES

California Digital Library Search Light—Social Sciences and Humanities

http://searchlight.cdlib.org/cgi-bin/searchlight?SSH

> Searches publicly available social science and humanities Web sites and databases.

UCSD—Database Advisor—Social Sciences

http://scilib.ucsd.edu/Proj/dba_public

> University of California, San Diego's database advisor tool assists the searcher to decide which social sciences or humanities database will be most useful.

(See also the Core Web Ready-Reference Collection, and all other Core Collections)

DIRECTORIES OF SCHOOLS, COLLEGES, UNIVERSITIES, EDUCATIONAL ORGANIZATIONS, AND PROGRAMS.

American School Directory

www.asd.com

> The Internet guide to all one hundred four thousand K–12 schools in the U.S. providing information about enrollment, administration, contacts, number of homerooms, type of school, mascot, colors, history and technology capabilities. Provides links to school homepages when available.

Peterson's Guide Online

www.petersons.com

> Calling itself "the Education supersite" Peterson's offers free searching of school and program information from grade school through graduate studies, with special subjects such as College Choice for African Americans, Summer camps and programs, study abroad programs, and lots more. Basic information including contact numbers and addresses is offered for free on all programs, with reference to the print Peterson publication containing full information.

DICTIONARIES

See Core Web Ready-Reference Collection

ABSTRACTS, INDEXES AND TABLE OF CONTENTS SERVICES

ERIC Database Search

www.eric.ed.gov

> This version of the ERIC Database provides access to ERIC Document citations from 1966 and ERIC Journal citations from 1966. Updates are about to the previous 3–4 months. At this writing (8/25/03) the future of ERIC is in doubt. Currently ERIC (Educational Resource Information Center) is funded by the U.S. Department of Education.

ENCYCLOPEDIAS

See also Core Web Ready-Reference Collection

Encyberpedia

www.encyberpedia.com/cyberlinks/links/index.html

> Rather than being a resource for educators, it is a resource for students. This encyclopedia is actually a collection of Web sites. Some entries lead to full encyclopedic entries, others provide a list of links, which subdivide the topic. While in the end it is a bit of a metasite, it does provide an interface that looks encyclopedia-like and is easy for students to use.

EDUCATION E-SERIALS AND DATABASES

(see SOSIG http://sosig.ac.uk)

American School Board Journal

www.asbj.com/about.html

> "Chronicles change, interprets issues, and offers readers—some 40,000 school board members and school administrators—practical advice broad range of topics pertinent to school governance and management, making, student achievement, and the art of school leadership." The online version offers full text access to some articles, abstracts of some articles, and full table of contents of the print version.

EDUCATION NEWS (CURRENT EVENTS)

Education Vital Signs

www.asbj.com/evs

> A publication of the American School Board Journal, this site provides annual statistics that evaluate the state of education. Includes statistics such as violence, standards and attainments, indicators of school success, and facts and figures about schools and children.

Education Week on the Web

www.edweek.org

> Includes the Daily News Section with "best education articles from around the country." Also includes full text of special reports and feature stories.

Eurekalert!

www.eurekalert.org

> Science news organized by subject including "Education" and "Reference Desk" Collection of scientific dictionaries and glossaries and special statistical resources in each subject area. This is a project of the American Society for the Advancement of Science.

Chronicle of Higher Education

http://chronicle.com

> Some free and some fee based articles. Online subscription accompanies a print subscription. Daily news about higher education with lots of feature stories. A subscription entitles you to daily news reports via email.

U.S. Department of Education

www.ed.gov

> Provides access to news on education legislation, loans and student aid information and forms (including FAFSA forms), funding opportunities, statistics from the NCES, and more.

EDUCATION METASITES (ALSO "HOMEWORK HELP" METASITES)

(See also the Education Resource Collection Tools: Metasites, E-library collections)

Berit's Best Sites for Children

www.beritsbest.com

> Compiled by librarian Berit Erickson, this site reviews, evaluates, and selects Web sites that will interest, educate, and entertain younger students. Berit's criteria state that sites are selected for children through age twelve—which corresponds roughly to seventh or eighth grade. Under the "Serious Stuff" link homework help and serious educational sites are collected.

High School Hub

http://highschoolhub.org/hub/hub.cfm

> A "noncommercial learning portal to high-quality free online educational resources for high school students. It features interactive learning games, puzzles, and quizzes. It also includes subject guides for English, foreign languages, math, science, and social studies."

Kids Click!

http://sunsite.berkeley.edu/KidsClick!

> Everything kids will be interested in. All selected for age/grade appropriateness and organized by subject—over six hundrfed specific subjects.

KidSpace @ The Internet Public Library

www.ipl.org/div/kidspace

> Collection of homework and other learning sites on subjects from art and music to science and history. Especially useful for secondary school students in science and literature.

8.8 SOCIAL SCIENCES AND EDUCATION RESOURCE COLLECTION TOOLS

See also Part III: Web Collection Development Resources

SOCIAL SCIENCES RESOURCE COLLECTION TOOLS

Administration of Justice Web Guide—George Mason University

http://library.gmu.edu/resources/socsci/criminal.html

> This phenomenal site provides indexes, directories, and links to information relating to the law enforcement, the legal system and justice.

American Studies Web: Reference and Research

http://cfdev.georgetown.edu/cndls/asw

> "The American Studies Web is the largest bibliography of web-based resources in the field of American Studies." The twenty-eight general categories range from American Studies to Working Class and Labor Studies.

Anthropology Resources

www.qozi.com/anthropology

> Collection of anthropology related Web resources, as well as news and other anthropology related information.

Archaeology on the Net

www.serve.com/archaeology

> Selective but comprehensive collection of Archaeology resources on the net. Hosts ArchPub, a mailing list for keeping up with publications in the fields.

Argos—Limited area Search of the Ancient and Medieval Internet

http://argos.evansville.edu

> Although the search tool has been discontinued. Argos is still a fine directory of ancient and medieval studies sites.

Arts and Humanities Data Service

http://AHDS.AC.UK

> "The AHDS is here to help you create, deposit, preserve or discover and use digital collections in the arts and humanities"

INFOMINE—Social Sciences and Humanities

http://infomine.ucr.edu/sshinfo.html

> Browsable and searchable index of thousands of sites "of use as a scholarly information resource in research or educational activities at the university level."

Philosophy Around the Web

http://users.ox.ac.uk/~worc0337/phil_index.html

> Humorous site with fourteen main categories of philosophy databases (e.g., organizations, papers, philosophers, education).

Philosophy in Cyberspace

http://www-personal.monash.edu.au/~dey/phil

> This searchable site is organized in five categories: branches of philosophy (including philosophers), text-related materials, organizations, forums and miscellaneous.

Political Resources on the Net

www.politicalresources.net

> "Listings of political sites available on the Internet sorted by country, with links to Parties, Organizations, Governments, Media and more from all around the world."

SocioSite—Subject areas

http://www2.fmg.uva.nl/sociosite

> Created in the Netherlands, this site has a European emphasis on sites, but has an extensive listing of subjects and sites covered.

SOSIG: Social Science Information Gateway

http://sosig.ac.uk/welcome.html

> "SOSIG is a freely available Internet service which aims to provide a trusted source of selected, high quality Internet information for students, academics, researchers and practitioners in the social sciences, business and law."

Voice of the Shuttle

http://vos.ucsb.edu

> What began as "static webpages" has evolved into a huge searchable database of all humanities topics and their subcategories.

Women's Studies/Women's Issues Resource Sites

http://www-unix.umbc.edu/~korenman/wmst/links.html

> "selective, annotated, highly acclaimed listing of web sites containing resources and information about women's studies / women's issues, with an emphasis on sites of particular use to an academic women's studies program."

EDUCATION RESOURCE COLLECTION TOOLS

American Association of School Librarians (AASL) Resource Guides for School Library Media Program Development

www.ala.org/Content/NavigationMenu/AASL/Professional_Tools10/ Resource_Guides

AASL_Resource_Guides_for_School_Library_Media_Program_Development.htm

> Web-based information guides for school library collection development, programs, technology issues, and more.

Academic Info

www.academicinfo.net

> Compilation of Web resources for college or advanced high school. "Each subject guide is an annotated listing of the best general Internet sites in the field, as well as a gateway to more advanced research tools."

AskERIC

http://ericir.syr.edu

> This marvelous site includes a collection of Internet resources that the Network Information Specialists at AskERIC have found valuable when responding to teacher's questions.

Blue Web'N—Knowledge Network Explorer

www.kn.pacbell.com/wired/bluewebn

> Sponsored by SBC Pacific Bell, this is a huge collection of evaluated, annotated, education related Web sites. Organized by content area, subject, and grade level.

Education Index

www.educationindex.com

> An "annotated guide to the best education-related sites on the Web. They're sorted by subject and lifestage, so you can find what you're looking for quickly and easily." Lists more than three thousand sites in sixty-six categories. Includes a chat room. Offered by CollegeView, and publishers of educational software.

Educational CyberPlayGround

www.edu-cyberpg.com/TOC.asp

> Gleason Sackman and Karen Ellis have collected many resources of interest to K–12 school teachers, librarians, and administrators.

Educause Information Resources

www.educause.edu/ir/ir.html

> "Provides access to collections of materials related to managing and using information resources in higher education."

EdWeb—Exploring Technology and School Reform

www.edwebproject.org

> Collection of international Web sites that support education. Specific resources for educational technology and school reform issues.

Eisenhower National Clearinghouse for Mathematics and Science Education

www.enc.org

Search for mathematics and science education materials.

ERIC Clearinghouse and Eric Resources

www.eric.ed.gov

Educational Resource Information Center collections of Web resources, ERIC documents and reports, reference sources collected by subject experts. Links to resources for parents as well as question and answer service.

Internet Scout Project

http://scout.wisc.edu

Librarians and educators filter announcement each week looking for online resources most valuable to the education community.

Kathy Schrock's Guide for Educators

http://school.discovery.com/schrockguide

Selective categorized collection of Web sites "useful for enhancing curriculum and professional growth." It is intended for teachers, administrators, and researchers.

OH! Kids

http://oplin.lib.oh.us/products/oks

Ohio Public Library Information Network's special e-library collection for kids.

Mid-continent Regional Educational Laboratory

www.mcrel.org/programs/rel

Reports, articles, standards, and benchmarks for K–12 education.

National School Network Exchange Web Site Evaluation

http://nsn.bbn.com/webeval/site1.htm

Searchable database of reviewed educational Web sites or enter a review of your own.

ThinkQuest Internet Challenge Library

www.thinkquest.org/library/IC_index.html

Collection of more than five thousand education-related Web sites that have been entered and won the ThinkQuest Internet Challenge contests.

Virtual Reference Desk—Ask A+ Locator

http://vrd.org/locator

Provides resources and links to experts (criteria explained) of different subjects relating to academics.

Virtual Search Engines

www.virtualfreesites.com/search.html

Offers the most popular search engines and many specialized search engines (many annotated).

Yahooligans!

www.yahooligans.com

Yahoo!'s special collection of homework and recreational Web sites for kids.

9: Using the Web for Reader's Advisory and Collection Development Information Resources

"From their initial inception and implementation, readers' advisory services have sought to link users with relevant books and other information materials, and books with users. With the proliferation of digital resources in recent years, libraries and librarians have begun to facilitate access and use of the diversity of electronic resources available from a variety of vendors using advanced database advisors, truly "saving the time of the reader" and fulfilling the intent of this principle."

McKiernan (2002)

9.1 DEVELOPING THE COLLECTION PLAN FOR READER'S ADVISORY AND COLLECTION DEVELOPMENT INFORMATION RESOURCES

WHAT PURPOSE WILL YOUR READER'S ADVISORY AND COLLECTION DEVELOPMENT RESOURCES COLLECTION SERVE? FOR WHOM ARE YOU COLLECTING READY-REFERENCE WEB RESOURCES?

Libraries collect reviews of books, Internet and multimedia resources in order to help both the librarians and the library patrons to make choices about specific information sources.

Reader's advisory and print collection development information resources are two sides of the same coin. Reader's advisory tools are the resources we use to help us recommend books to our patrons that they may want to read for educational, recreational, or other reasons. Print collection development tools are the resources we use to decide which books to acquire and include in the library collection to serve our patrons' educational, recreation, and other information needs. These same tools can be used for the collection of books, videos, and other locally held materials for our libraries.

These types of information are especially useful for library staff making recommendations to patrons, or selecting print materials for acquisitions. The organization of these resources in the e-library should enhance access by library staff. Library patrons will also want access to reader's advisory related Web sites.

Nisonger (1997), Bybee, et al. (1999), Rabine and Brown (2000), Schneider (1999), and Shook (2000) have written some of the most interesting of the many articles about the use of the Web as a collection development tool.

Nisonger (1997) was one of the first to write about the use of the Internet for support of collection development activities of all sorts. He identifies and describes in detail the:

"relationship between the Internet and collection management in libraries on three levels: (1) use of the Internet to perform traditional functions for traditional materials (for example, using the Internet to help select books and serials or evaluate the collection), (2) the application of traditional collection development functions to the Internet (evaluation and selection of Internet resources), and (3) the impact the Internet's existence will have on traditional functions and materials (selecting fewer print resources because they can be accessed electronically on the Internet)." (Nisonger, 1997: 29)

Bybee et al. (1999), see the Web as a tool to use among other collection tools. They identify key Web sites, discussion lists (called listservs), and e-mail. One of the most important benefits they describe is the use of the Web to work more efficiently through being able to see or ask about the collection policies and procedures of other libraries. The use of the Web to learn about and communicate with vendors is another major asset.

WHAT TYPES OF READER'S ADVISORY AND COLLECTION DEVELOPMENT WEB RESOURCES WILL YOU COLLECT?

Schneider (1999) and Shook (2000) review Web sites that are useful tools for collection development of print resources. Although some of the reviews are out of date (e.g., Bookbrowser is now integrated with the Barnes and Noble bookstore site (www.barnesandnoble.com/bookbrowser) the evaluations and strategies for using these tools remain valid.

Many useful collection development Web sites are new and used bookstores. Amazon.com (www.amazon.com), Barnes and Noble (www.barnesandnoble.com). Book "jobbers" also have a reliable Web presence. YBP Library Services (www.ybp.com)—Baker and Taylor, Lindsay and Howe—and Blackwell (www.blackwell.com) are well-known book jobbers with reliable Web services for libraries. Publishers are also maintaining catalogs and stores where libraries can review and purchase their publications. Neal-Schuman (www.neal-schuman.com), ALA Publications (www.ala.org), and Scholastic (www.scholastic.com) are typical examples.

HOW WILL YOU ORGANIZE YOUR READY-REFERENCE WEB RESOURCES?

Tools designed specifically for the selection of reading matter should be placed where library patrons will find them easily. For example, you might create a category called "What Books to Read?" which is then suborganized by nonfiction, fiction, fiction genres, and children's resources.

Rabine and Brown (2000) recommend that a special collection development Web site be added to the library's e-library for the particular use of library staff. They also describe the kinds of tools that will be useful and recommend several specific sites.

9.2 IDENTIFYING AND COLLECTING READER'S ADVISORY AND COLLECTION DEVELOPMENT RESOURCES

WEB SITES THAT REVIEW AND EVALUATE READER'S ADVISORY AND COLLECTION DEVELOPMENT WEB RESOURCES: INCLUDING OTHER E-LIBRARIES OR SUBJECT COLLECTION GUIDES/WEBLIOGRAPHIES

ACQWEB (http://acqweb.library.vanderbilt.edu) is the best and most complete collection development resource site.

Gerry McKiernan (2002) suggests that in addition to using the Web for Reader's Advisory in the sense of bringing books and reader and readers and books together, that we also provide library database advisory services. He also lists a number of great reader's advisory and database advisory services available on the Web.

DISCUSSION LISTS AND NEWSGROUPS WHERE INDIVIDUAL PARTICIPANTS REVIEW AND EVALUATE READER'S ADVISORY AND COLLECTION DEVELOPMENT WEB RESOURCES

Collection development discussion lists include COLLDV-L, discussion of collection development issues; and CONSDIST, discussion of collection and preservation. COLLDV-L is particularly active and useful for Web resource collection development issues.

Publib is a discussion list that, among other useful topics, encourages the sharing and reviewing of materials in all formats of interest to public librarians including specifics and strategies for reader's advisory services.

Many discussion lists that focus on specific genres, authors, or even specific books can be identified using the tools discussed in Chapter 1. For example, the authors moderate DOROTHYL, a discussion list for people who read and write mystery books and related topics. Many librarians subscribe to DOROTHYL for reader's advisory purposes. Recently, Suzanne Pontius, Coordinator of Collection Development, Preble County District Library, posted a query to the DOROTHYL group asking for recommendations for good mystery reference books. Here is the list of books recommended in the order that they were received:

- *Encyclopedia of Murder and Mystery*, by Bruce Murphy
- *Make Mine a Mystery*, by Gary Niebuhr
- *Detecting Men and Detecting Women*, by Willetta Heising
- *Oxford Companion to Crime and Mystery Writing*, by Rosemary Herbert
- *Mammoth Encyclopedia of Modern Crime Fiction*, by Mike Ashley
- *What Mystery Do I Read Next?*, by Steven Stittwell
- *By a Woman's Hand*, by Jean Swanson and Dean James
- *20th Century Crime and Mystery Writers*
- *Murder Ink*, by Dilys Wynn
- *Mystery Lover's Companion*, by Art Bourgeau
- *Whodunit*, by H.R.F. Keating
- *The Fine Art of Murder*, by Ed Gorman
- *Omnibus of Crime*, by Dorothy L. Sayers

(Posted to DOROTHYL@listserv.kent.edu, Fri, 22 Aug 2003)

E-JOURNALS AND E-NEWSLETTERS THAT PUBLISH REVIEWS AND EVALUATIONS OF READER'S ADVISORY AND COLLECTION DEVELOPMENT WEB RESOURCES

E-serials that publish book reviews, written by librarians or other readers are also published on the Web. Some of the bookstore and publisher Web sites include book reviews as well. Several of these are included in the webliography "Collection Development and Reader's Advisory, and Misc." at the end of this chapter and on the companion Web site.

9.3 EVALUATION GUIDELINES

Evaluation of reader's advisory and print collection development information is a simple matter. The main criteria will be to identify who is writing the reviews and whether their credentials as a reviewer are acceptable in the context of the kinds of materials being reviewed. For example, a sixth grader may be a qualified reviewer of the books of Madeline L'Engle or J.K. Rowling. The information required for evaluating may be discovered about Web reader's advisory and print collection development information by following the same strategy for evaluating Internet resources used throughout this book and described in Chapter 1.

9.4 SELECTION CRITERIA

Selection criteria for reader's advisory and collection development Web sites will be entirely dependant on the type of library making the selection and the community of patrons for whom they are selecting. As a result the webliography for this chapter is a general collection of Web resources related to "Collection Development and Reader's Advisory, and Miscellany."

9.5 E-LIBRARY SUCCESS STORIES

CYBERSTACKS[SM]

Iowa State University Ames, IA USA
www.public.iastate.edu/~CYBERSTACKS

Contact: Gerry McKiernan
gerrymck@iastate.edu

CyberStacks(sm) was initiated in 1995 by Gerry McKiernan, Science and Technology Librarian and Bibliographer, Iowa State University, Ames, to explore the value of the application of a traditional library classification scheme as a framework for facilitating access to select science and technology Web resources. From the outset, CyberStacks(sm) was intended as a Web-based e-library, organized within the conceptual structures of a print-based classification system.

The CyberStacks(sm) project also served as a foundation for exploring alternatives to established access and organizational schemes. Such studies, in turn, stimulated interest in nonconventional and novel digital technologies and their potential value for navigating Internet resources. These investigations and their associated literature reviews have led to the preparation and publication of original articles that describe emerging digital technologies and their library applications.

The CyberStacks(sm) has not been maintained as an e-library Web site; it grew instead into several new projects and e-resource collections that are described below. The following text is provided by Gerry McKiernan:

Beyond Bookmarks: Schemes for Organizing the Web

www.public.iastate.edu/~CYBERSTACKS/CTW.htm

> Beyond Bookmarks is a clearinghouse of World Wide Web sites that have applied or adopted standard classification schemes or controlled vocabularies to organize or provide enhanced access to Internet resources. Beyond Bookmarks was designated a Scout Report Selection in June 1996.

The Big Picture(sm): Visual Browsing in Web and non-Web Databases

www.public.iastate.edu/~CYBERSTACKS/BigPic.htm

> The Big Picture(sm) is a clearinghouse of projects, research, products and services that describe or apply information visualization technologies for enhancing use and access to Web and selected non-Web databases. The clearinghouse is arranged by the name of the university, corporation, or other organization with which the principal investigator of a project is affiliated. Selected significant reports, papers, and articles are also provided for each profiled activity. A general bibliography of applicable works is also provided.

Just-In-Time (sm): Electronic Article Delivery Services

www.public.iastate.edu/~CYBERSTACKS/Just.htm

> Just-In-Time(sm) is a clearinghouse of projects, research, products and services which are investigating or provide desktop access, on an "As Needed" basis, to individual journal, magazine, newspaper, or other serial publication article, chapter, or paper for which an individual or institution does not have a formal subscription. Entries have been organized in categories that characterize the scope of service; within each category, entries are arranged alphabetically by the name of the service, project, or publisher.

EJI(sm): A Registry of Innovative E-Journal Features, Functionalities, and Content

www.public.iastate.edu/~CYBERSTACKS/EJI.htm

> EJI(sm) is a categorized registry of electronic journals, journal services, or 'knowledge environments' that offer or provide innovative or novel access, organization, or navigational features, functionalities, or content.

M-Bed(sm): Embedded Multimedia Electronic Journals

www.public.iastate.edu/~CYBERSTACKS/M-Bed.htm

> M-Bed(sm) is a registry of electronic journals that have integrated multimedia within the text of their associated articles. Common types of multimedia include

CyberStacks(sm) Main Main

Select A Subject Group

G	Geography, Anthropology and Recreation	
H	Social Sciences	
J	Political Science	
K	Law	
Q	Science	
R	Medicine	
S	Agriculture	
T	Technology	
U	Military Science	
V	Naval Science	

CyberStacks(sm)

Figure 2.9.0. Cyberstacks www.public.iastate.edu/~CYBERSTACKS

audio and video files as well as two-dimensional and 3-D models, and supplemental datasets.

The Next WAVe^{SM}: Auditory Browsing in Web and non-Web Databases
www.public.iastate.edu/~CYBERSTACKS/Wave.htm

The Next WAVe^{SM} is a clearinghouse of projects, research, products and services that describe or apply auditory interfaces, displays or interactive technologies to enhance use of and access to Web and selected non-Web databases.

Onion Patch^{SM}: New Age Public Access Systems
www.public.iastate.edu/~CYBERSTACKS/Onion.htm

Onion Patch^{SM} is a clearinghouse devoted to projects, research, products and services that support or demonstrate alternative approaches to Second Generation OPACs and other current online public catalogs and indexes.

Project Aristotle^{SM}: Automated Categorization of Web Resources
www.public.iastate.edu/~CYBERSTACKS/Aristotle.htm

Project Aristotle^{SM} is a clearinghouse of projects, research, and products and services that are investigating, or which demonstrate, the automated categorization, classification or organization of Web resources. A working bibliography of key and significant reports, papers and articles, is also provided. Projects and associated publications have been arranged by the name of the university, corporation, or other organization with which the principal investigator of a project is affiliated. Project Aristotle^{SM} was designated a Scout Report Selection in July 1999.

All That JAS: Journal Abbreviation Sources
www.public.iastate.edu/~CYBERSTACKS/JAS.htm

All That JAS is a categorized registry of Web resources that list or provide access to the full title of journal abbreviations or other types of abbreviated publication titles (e.g., conference proceedings titles). Selected OPACs that offer abbreviated title searching have also been included. In addition, All That JAS includes select lists and directories that provide access to the unabbreviated titles of serial publications.

LiveRef^{SM}: A Registry of Real-Time Digital Reference Services
www.public.iastate.edu/~CYBERSTACKS/LiveRef.htm

LiveRef^{SM} is a categorized listing of libraries that offer real-time library reference or information services using chat software, live interactive communications utilities, call center management software, Web contact center software, bulletin board services, or related Internet technologies. LiveRef^{SM} was designated a Scout Report Selection in July 2001.

IDEALS^{SM}: A Registry of Emerging Innovative Augmented Digital Library Services
www.public.iastate.edu/~CYBERSTACKS/IDEALS.htm

IDEALS^{SM} is a categorized registry of emerging innovative library services that enhance patron access, use, or manipulation of information resources made available by a library or similar organizational unit within a digital framework.

9.6 References and Web Sites Cited

Note that some sites are included in the resource lists and webliographies in previous chapters, and therefore are not necessarily duplicated in this section.

Bybee, H. et al. 1999. Working the Web: WWW Strategies for Collection Development and technical Services. *Technical Services Quarterly* 16, no. 4: 45–61.

Fowler, D. C. 2000. Information Technology and Collection Development Departments in the Academic Library: Striving to Reach a Common Understanding. In *Electronic Collection Management*, ed. S. D. McGinnis, 17–36. Binghamton, NY: Haworth Information Press.

McKiernan, G. 2002. Library database advisors—emerging innovative augmented digital library services. *Library Hi Tech News* 19, no. 4, http://cherubino.emeraldinsight.com/vl=2053493/cl=24/nw=1/rpsv/journals/lhtn/eprofile1.htm.

Rabine, J. L., and L. A. Brown. 2000. The Selection Connection: Creating an Internal Web Page for Collection Development. *LRTS* 44, no. 1 (January): 44–49.

Shook, G. 2000. Web Acquisitions and Collection Development. *The Christian Librarian* (April): 52–53.

Schneider, K. G. 1999. Internet Librarian: Let Your Fingers Do the Collection Development—Online. *American Libraries* 30, no. 5 (May): 100.

ACQWEB. Available: http://acqweb.library.vanderbilt.edu.

ALA Publications. Available: www.ala.org.

Neal-Schuman. Available: www.neal-schuman.com.

Scholastic. Available: www.scholastic.com.

9.7 Collection Development and Reader's Advisory, and Miscellany

See also Part III: Web Collection Development Resources
(For more e-books—text and audio—see Part I, Chapter 1, section 1.8: Ready-Reference Resource Collection Tools)

ACQLink
http://link.bubl.ac.uk/acqlink

UK based Web site, which supports acquisition and collection development library activities.

ACQWEB
http://acqweb.library.vanderbilt.edu

Web site that supports acquisition and collection development librarians. Includes a listing of Web-based tools for non-Internet resource collection.

AllReaders.com Home Page
www.allreaders.com

Reader's advisory tool recommends books by plot, theme, character, and other options.

Amazon.com
www.amazon.com

Online bookstore that has searchable database of over two-and-a-half million books in-print and out-of-print. Reviews from professional review sources as well as reviews by readers.

American Libraries Association
www.ala.org/alonline/index.html

Visit the online version of the ALA's news publication. Besides providing all the news on libraries and librarians, articles about trends in spending and costs of publications appear here regularly.

Ariadne—The Web Version
www.ariadne.ac.uk

This quarterly newsletter reports "on information service developments and information networking issues worldwide, keeping the busy practitioner abreast of current digital library initiatives."

Booklist

www.ala.org/booklist

> This is the "digital counterpart of the American Library Association's Book List magazine. It reviews thousands of the latest books (adult, children, reference), electronic reference tools and audiovisual materials.

Booktv.org

www.booktv.org

> A great site for interviews with authors, summaries of books, and information on the publishing industry. "Each weekend, Book TV on C-SPAN2 will feature 48 hours of nonfiction books from 8 a.m. Saturday to 8 a.m. Monday. This web site will enhance information on those books, provide an opportunity to watch or listen to programs you might have missed, and provide additional information not available on the cable network."

Choice—Current Reviews for Academic Libraries

www.ala.org/acrl/choice

> "Timely," "Concise," "Authoritative" and "easy-to-use" reviews by experts of books and electronic media.

Collection Development Training for Arizona Public Libraries

www.dlapr.lib.az.us/cdt/index.htm

> Web-based collection development training published by the Arizona Department of Library, Archives and Public Records.

College and Research Libraries News

www.ala.org/acrl/c&rlnew2.html

> Online version of magazine, some articles available online.

Copyright Clearance Center

www.copyright.com

> CCC assists libraries and individuals in obtaining permissions for use of copyrighted material and clarifying the process.

David Magier's Library World Bookmarks

www.columbia.edu/~magier/libworld.html

> Categorized (Outline format) links to all kinds of sites related to libraries and librarians.

EContentMag.com

www.econtentmag.com/EContent100

> Web magazine that publishes research and news about digital content.

Educause / Cornell Institute for Computer Policy and Law

www.educause.edu/icpl

> "The Institute incorporates experts from a wide variety of fields, including chief information officers, judicial-system administrators, librarians, attorneys, policy advisors and many others. The Institute supports the professional development of information technology, policy and legal professionals within higher education to facilitate the creation and administration of effective information technology policies. It also monitors and analyzes changes in technology and law to assess the impact of those changes on academic information technology policy."

Glossary of bibliographic information by language

http://stauffer.queensu.ca/techserv/biblang.html

> Terms are divided by language and do not appear in alphabetical order, but with the use of your browser's "find in page" feature this should be easy to use.

Glossary—Abebooks

http://dogbert.abebooks.com/docs/HelpCentral/Glossary/buyerIndex.shtml

This comprehensive list of book-related terms relating to book sizes, book condition, common abbreviations, and a general glossary is included, as well.

Government Information Quarterly/ Journal of Government Information

www.lib.auburn.edu/madd/docs/giq/conlink.html

This is a table of contents for these government journals, which contains information relating to the government's information policies.

InFoPeople Project

www.infopeople.org

What started as a project to provide public access in the library has evolved into training opportunities for information specialists as well as online guides and links to information technology, "improves the quality of information access to the people of California by upgrading the skills, resources and tools available through libraries."

International Federation of Library Associations: Metadata Resources

www.ifla.org/II/metadata.htm

Digital Libraries: Metadata resources, articles and discussions about many topics relating to metadata—meta search, meta gateway, meta server, meta repository, metadata entry.

Internets

www.internets.com

"Largest filtered collection of useful search engines and newswires."

The Isaac Network Project

http://scout.wisc.edu/research/isaac

Information Seeker's Avenue to Authoritative Content; this project proposes to link geographically distributed collections of metadata into a virtual collection searchable as a unified whole.

Library Journal

http://libraryjournal.reviewsnews.com

"LJ combines news, features, and commentary with analyses of public policy, technology, and management developments. In addition, some 7500 evaluative reviews written by librarians help readers make their purchasing decisions: reviews of everything from books, audio and video, CD-ROMs, websites, and magazines."

Library Web Manager's Reference Center

http://sunsite.berkeley.edu/Web4Lib/RefCenter

Directories, programs, tutorials, discussion topics, and links to digital library maintenance, tools and updates.

Metadata

www.ukoln.ac.uk/metadata

Reviews "current approaches to resource description and looks at future options for metadata in the wider context of resource discovery."

Neat New Stuff We Found This Week

http://marylaine.com/neatnew.html

Listing of links of various choice sites with a comment about each—most sites listed are informational—few may considered "just for fun."

New York Public Library Reader's Advisory Service.

www.nypl.org/branch/recread.html

Book recommendations from the NYPL.

OCLC Office of Research and Special Projects

www.oclc.org/research

> Conference listings, research projects, and publications relating to resource management.

Overbooked

www.overbooked.org

> Reader's advisory tool specializes in literary and genre fiction information. Includes author Web pages, annotated lists of nonfiction, fiction and mystery book reviews.

Phoaks

www.phoaks.com/phoaks2

> Filtering project that looks through collection of Usenet newsgroups to find and extract messages about Internet resources—opinions are read, classified and tallied automatically. This site is getting a bit dated but is an interesting historical artifact.

Publist

www.PubList.com

> "Undergoing technical improvements at this time. Site is still searchable free in-depth information relating to 150,00 periodicals worldwide."

Prepub Alert

http://libraryjournal.reviewsnews.com/index.asp?layout=sectionsMain&verticalid=151&industry=PrePub%20Alert

> Lists publishing information and provides a synopsis for upcoming fiction and nonfiction in the months ahead.

The Reader's Robot: A Reader's Advisory Service

www.tnrdlib.bc.ca/rr.html

> Visually attractive collection of genre fiction and nonfiction book reviews. Search by a concept called "appeal." Select a genre, then a mood, style, or plot theme.

ROADS (Resource Organisation And Discovery in Subject-based Services)

www.ilrt.bris.ac.uk/roads

> "The software allows you to set up a subject gateway." No longer maintained, but is still useful.

ResearchBuzz—Internet Research News

www.researchbuzz.com

> "ResearchBuzz is designed to cover the world of Internet research. To that end this site provides almost daily updates on search engines, new data managing software, browser technology, large compendiums of information, Web directories—whatever." Archived.

Search Engine Watch

http://searchenginewatch.com

> Database of search engine facts, guides and resources to various categories of search engines, such as kids search engines, specialty, and meta-search.

Special Libraries Association

www.sla.org

> "(SLA) is the international association representing the interests of thousands of information professionals in over seventy countries. Special librarians are information resource experts who collect, analyze, evaluate, package, and disseminate information to facilitate accurate decision-making in corporate, academic,

and government settings. The Association offers a variety of programs and services designed to help its members serve their customers more effectively and succeed in an increasingly challenging environment of information management and technology."

Technical Processing Online Tools

http://tpot.ucsd.edu

Library technical processing Web resources; some restricted areas.

A Tool Kit of Links and Documents for Collection Development and Management Librarians

http://ublib.buffalo.edu/libraries/units/lml/colldev/cdinternet.html

The librarians at the State University of New York at Buffalo have collected resources of interest to collection development and management librarians.

W3C Web Accessibility Initiative

www.w3.org/WAI/References

"Highlights the work of organizations around the world in improving accessibility for people with disabilities."

Webrary®—Search MatchBook

www.webrary.org/rs/matchbooksearch.html

Morton Grove Public Library reader's advisory tool to match the reader with the books they will find interesting.

What's New Archives

http://archive.ncsa.uiuc.edu/SDG/Software/Mosaic/Docs/whats-new.html

Archive of early Web sites (1993–1996).

whichbook.net

www.whichbook.net/sounded/index.html

Choose books by mood, style, or other detail.

Wired for Books

http://wiredforbooks.org

Ohio University-sponsored site that publishes book reviews and RealAudio readings.

University Library HTML Standards

http://library.csun.edu/htmlstds.html

This page has standards, lectures and workshops relating to HTML standards.

PART III

WEB COLLECTION DEVELOPMENT RESOURCES

Resource List 1: Collection Development Related Discussion Lists, Newsgroups, and Blogs

DIRECTORIES OF DISCUSSION LISTS, NEWSGROUPS, BLOGS

Association of Cancer Online Resources
www.acor.org/mailing.html

Directory of patient support and medical research related mailing lists.

LibDex—Library Weblogs
www.libdex.com/weblogs.html

Index of Web logs relating to librianship and information specialists.

Library Weblogs
www.libdex.com/weblogs.html

Index of Web logs relating to librianship and information specialists

CataList—the official catalog of Listserv® Lists
www.lsoft.com/lists/listref.html

Nearly one hundred thousand public discussion lists run on the Listserv® software all over the world.

Directory of Scholarly and Professional Electronic Conferences
www.kovacs.com/directory

Directory of discussion lists, newsgroups, mailing lists, chats and MUDS, which have a scholarly or professional topic. Also published annually in print with the *ARL Directory of Electronic Journals* as the *ARL Directory of Electronic Journals and Academic Discussion Lists*.

FreeLists
www.freelists.org

Free mailing list host site with directory of hosted lists.

NewList
www.edu-cyberpg.com/Community/newlist.html

The first and still one of the best sources to learn about new discussion lists. Subscribe to the distribution, post a new list announcement, or search the archives for previously announced lists. Edited by Gleason Sackman.

Topica/Liszt List of Lists
www.topica.com

Topica hosts discussions and has incorporated the directory that was Liszt's List of Lists.

Yahoogroups

www.yahoogroups.com

Yahoogroups new incorporates the discussion lists hosted by several smaller services (e.g., egroups.com). Search for the discussions in which you are interested.

GENERAL INTERNET RESOURCE ANNOUNCEMENT LISTS

Library Hot Five

Announcements of new Web sites.

Subscribe and Archives: http://listserv.classroom.com/archives/hot5.html

Contact: cybrarian@classroom.com

Net-Happenings

Announcements of new Web sites and other Internet resources including excerpts from various discussions of Internet-related events.

Archives: www.edu-cyberpg.com/Community/NetHappenings.html

Subscribe: Send e-mail to nethappenings-request@freelists.org

Contact: Gleason Sackman nethappenings-request@freelists.org

NewJour

Distribution list for the announcement of new electronic journals and newsletters.

Archives: http://gort.ucsd.edu/newjour

Subscribe: submit the form at http://gort.ucsd.edu/newjour/subscribe.html

Contact: owner-newjour@ccat.sas.upenn.edu

GENERAL REFERENCE, COLLECTION DEVELOPMENT AND E-LIBRARY RELATED DISCUSSIONS

ACQNET

Discussion for acquisitions and collection development librarians.

Archives: www.library.vanderbilt.edu/law/acqs/acqs.html

Subscribe: Send email to listproc@listproc.appstate.edu with the message:

Subscribe acqnet YourFirstName YourLastName

Contact: EleanorCook cookei@appstate.edu

BACKSERV

Focuses entirely on the informal exchange of serial back issues and books among libraries.

Archives: http://lists.swetsblackwell.com/pipermail/backserv

Subscribe: http://lists.swetsblackwell.com/mailman/listinfo/backserv

Contact: listadmin@us.swetsblackwell.com

COLLDV-L

Moderated: discussion for library collection development officers, bibliographers, and selectors plus others involved with library collection development, including interested publishers and vendors.

Subscribe: Send email to listserv@vm.usc.edu with the message:

subscribe colldv-l YourFirstName YourLastName

Contact: Lynn Sipe lsipe@calvin.usc.edu

COLLIBS

Discussion of collection development in Australian academic and research libraries.

Archives:http://palimpsest.stanford.edu/byform/mailing-lists/cdl

Subscribe: Send email to LISTSERV@IS.SU.EDU.AU with the message:

SUBSCRIBE COLLIBS Your-first-name Your-last-name

Contact: Walter Henry consdist-request@lindy.stanford.edu

CONSDIST

Discussion of collection and preservation of library, archives and museum materials.

Archives: http://palimpsest.stanford.edu/byform/mailing-lists/cdl

Subscribe: Send email to consdist-request @lindy.stanford.edu

Contact: Walter Henry consdist-request@lindy.stanford.edu

DIG_REF

Discussion of digital reference/virtual reference services.

Archives: http://groups.yahoo.com/group/dig_ref

Subscribe: Send email to LISTSERV@LISTSERV.SYR.EDU with the message:

SUBSCRIBE DIG_REF Your-first-name Your-last-name

Contact: Joann Wasik jmwasik@ericir.syr.edu, Blythe Bennett blythe@ericir.syr.edu , Jeremy Morgan richlist@ericir.syr.edu

ERESOURCESTUDY-L

Discussion for the discussion of e-resources content and management, research and study.

Archives: www.library.yale.edu/ecollections/eresstudy/maillist.html

Subscribe: Send email to listproc@cornell.edu with the message:

Subscribe eresourcestudy-l YourFirstName YourLastName

Contact: Adam Chandler , alc28@cornell.edu and Tim Jewell, tjewell@u.washington.edu

ERIL-L

Discussion of electronic resource issues, especially for electronic resource librarians.

Archives: http://listserv.binghamton.edu/archives/eril-l.html

Subscribe: Send e-mail to listserv.binghamton.edu with the message:

subscribe ERIL-L YourFirstName YourLastName

Contact: Abigail Bordeaux, bordeaux@binghamton.edu or ERIL-L-request@LISTSERV.BINGHAMTON.EDU

EUROBACK

Focuses on the informal exchange of serial back issues and books among libraries in Europe.

Subscribe: Send e-mail to majordomo@lists.ulg.ac.be with the message:

Subscribe euroback

LIBLICENSE-L

"moderated list for the discussion of issues related to the licensing of digital information by academic and research libraries. Increasingly, libraries are being inundated with information created in digital format and transmitted and accessed via computers. This list is designed to assist librarians and others concerned with the licensing of information in digital format in dealing with some of the unique challenges faced by this new medium. Information providers (creators, publishers and vendors) who deal with libraries are welcomed as members of LIBLICENSE-L."

Subscribe and Archives: www.library.yale.edu/~llicense/mailing-list.shtml

Contact: Ann Okerson, www.library.yale.edu/~llicense/email.shtml

Library Link

http://matilde.emeraldinsight.com/vl=15946431/cl=63/nw=1/rpsv/librarylink

The online information and discussion forum for Librarians and Information Professionals worldwide.

Libref-L

Discussion of library reference concepts, issues and service.

Archives: http://listserv.kent.edu/archives/libref-l.html

Subscribe: Send e-mail to listserv@listserv.kent.edu with the message: subscribe Libref-L YourFirstName YourLastName

Contact: Diane K. Kovacs diane@kovacs.com

LIS-LINK

Discussion of library and information science issues, e-libraries, and related topics. UK based but global in scope. Announces new BUBL resources and changes.

Archives: www.jiscmail.ac.uk/lists/lis-link.html

Subscribe: Send e-mail to listserv@jiscmail.ac.uk with the message: subscribe LIS-LINK YourFirstName YourLastName

Contact: LIS-LINK-request@jiscmail.ac.uk

LiveReference

Discussion group on live reference services for librarians.

Subscribe and Archives: http://groups.yahoo.com/group/livereference

PACS-L

The Public-Access Computer Systems Forum (PACS-L) is a mailing list that deals with end-user computer systems in libraries. Utilizing PACS-L, subscribers discuss topics such as digital libraries, digital media, electronic books, electronic journals, electronic publishing, Internet information resources, and online catalogs. PACS-L was founded in June 1989 by http://info.lib.uh.edu/cwb/bailey.htmCharles W. Bailey, Jr., who moderated the list until http://info.lib.uh.edu/news/news2n11.txtNovember 1991.

Subscribe and Archives: http://info.lib.uh.edu/pacsl.html

Contact: Diane Gwamanda, DGwamanda@UH.EDU, Anne Mitchell, AMitchell@UH.EDU, and J. Michael Thompson, JMThompson@UH.EDU

PACS-P

Announcement list for notification of new issues of Current Cites (complete issue) http://sunsite.berkeley.edu/CurrentCites, D-Lib Magazine (publication announcement) www.dlib.org/dlib.html, Issues in Science and Technology Librarianship (publication announcement) www.library.ucsb.edu/istl, and Scholarly Electronic Publishing Bibliography (publication announcement) http://info.lib.uh.edu/sepb/sepb.html

Subscribe and Archives: http://info.lib.uh.edu/pacsp.html

PUBLIB

Discussion of issues relating to public librarianship. "Particularly appropriate issues for discussion on PUBLIB include, but are not limited to: Collection development, acquisitions, management and weeding, including traditional and new media Reference services."

Archives: http://sunsite.berkeley.edu/PubLib/archive.html

Subscribe: Send the message "subscribe PUBLIB YourFirstName YourLastName" to

listserv@sunsite.berkeley.edu
Contact: Sara Weissman weissman@main.morris.org or
Karen Schneider kgs@bluehighways.com

PUBLIB-NET

A sublist of PUBLIB where discussion is devoted strictly to the Internet in public libraries.
Archives: http://sunsite.berkeley.edu/PubLib/archive.html
Subscribe: send e-mail to listserv@sunsite.berkeley.edu with the message: subscribe PUBLIB-NET YourFirstName YourLastName
Contact: Sara Weissman weissman@main.morris.org or
Karen Schneider kgs@bluehighways.com

SERIALST

Serials discussion covers collection management of serials.
Archives: http://list.uvm.edu/archives/serialst.html
Subscribe: send e-mail to LISTSERV@LIST.UVM.EDU with the message: subscribe SERIALST YourFirstName YourLastName
Contact: SERIALST-REQUEST@LIST.UVM.EDU; Birdie MacLennon, birdie.maclennan@uvm.edu; Marcia Tuttle, tuttle@email.unc.edu; Ann Ercelawn, ercelawn@library.vanderbilt.edu; Stephen Clark, sdclar@mail.wm.edu

Web4Lib

Discussion of the practical use and philosophical issues of the World Wide Web in library contexts.
Archives: http://sunsite.berkeley.edu/Web4Lib
Subscribe: send e-mail to listproc@sunsite.berkeley.edu with the message:
subscribe web4lib yourfirstname yourlastname
Contact: Roy Tennant rtennant@library.berkeley.edu or Thomas Dowling tdowling@ohiolink.edu

BUSINESS RESOURCE DISCUSSIONS

Buslib-L

Moderated electronic forum that addresses all issues relating to: the collection, storage and dissemination of Business Information within a library setting—regardless of format.
Archives and Subscribe: http://listserv.boisestate.edu/archives/buslib-l.html
Contact: Daniel Lester dlester@boisestate.edu

MEDICAL/BIOSCIENCES RESOURCE DISCUSSIONS

ACCRI-L

Discussion of Internet resources for anesthesiology and critical care.
Archives: Contact the moderator for details.
Subscribe: Send email to listserv@uabdpo.dpo.uab.edu with the message:
Subscribe accri-l YourFirstName YourLastName
Contact: A.J. Wright meds002@uabdpo.dpo.uab.edu

BIOSCI

Group of bioscience discussion lists and newsgroups.
Subscribe: www.bio.net
Contact: biosci-help@net.bio.net

BACKMED

Focuses entirely on the informal exchange of medical and health serial back issues and books among libraries.

Archives: http://lists.swetsblackwell.com/pipermail/backmed

Subscribe: http://lists.swetsblackwell.com/mailman/listinfo/backmed

Contact: listadmin@us.swetsblackwell.com

CAPHIS

Consumer health information discussion.

Archives: www.hslc.org/archives/caphis.html

Subscribe: Send e-mail to listserv@hslc.org with the message:

Subscribe caphis YourFirstName YourLastName

MEDLIB-L

Discussion list for medical librarians, which includes discussion of Internet resources for medical e-library collections. Official Medical Libraries Association, medical libraries discussion list.

Archives: http://listserv.acsu.buffalo.edu/archives/medlib-l.html

Subscribe: Send e-mail to listserv@listserv.acsu.buffalo.edu with the message:

Subscribe medlib-l YourFirstName YourLastName

Contact: Valerie Rankow, MEDLIB-L-request@listserv.buffalo.edu

MEDWEBMASTERS-L

"E-mail discussion group for healthcare Internet webmasters, listserv owners, moderators, content developers, site designers, etc., who are interested in the application of computer-based technology for developing and disseminating medical information and services on the Internet, Intranets, or other computer networks."

Archives: http://listserv.acor.org/archives/medwebmasters-l.html

Subscribe: Send e-mail to listserv@listserv.acor.org with the message:

Subscribe medwebmasters-l YourFirstName YourLastName

Contact: John Mack, johnmack@virsci.com

MMATRIX-L

Internet Medical Resources Announcement List.

Archives: http://listserv.acor.org/archives/mmatrix-l.html

Subscribe: Send e-mail to listserv@listserv.acor.org with the message:

Subscribe mmatrix-l YourFirstName YourLastName

P-SOURCE Psychiatry Resources List

Discussion list for review and recommendation of Psychiatry information resources of and off the Internet.

Archives: http://maelstrom.stjohns.edu/archives/p-source.html

Subscribe: To subscribe, send e-mail to LISTSERV@MAELSTROM.STJOHNS.EDU with the message:

subscribe P-SOURCE YourFirstName YourLastName

Contact: Myron Pulier, pulierml@umdnj.edu, m.pulier@verizon.net or Beverly Jamison, bjamison@RADIX.NET

LAW RESOURCE DISCUSSIONS

Insyte

An e-serial that reviews and annotates Internet legal information Web sites. It is published by the Cornell Law Library.

Subscribe and Archives: www.lawschool.cornell.edu/library/Finding_the_Law/insite.htm

Law-Lib

Discussion for law librarians.

Archives: http://lawlibrary.ucdavis.edu/LAWLIB/lawlib.html
Subscribe: Send email to listproc@ucdavis.edu with the message:
subscribe law-lib YourFirstName YourLastName
Contact: Judy Janes, jcjanes@ucdavis.edu

The Law Library Resource Exchange

(www.llrx.com)
> An outstanding current awareness 'webzine' which not only publishes legal Web site reviews but also publishes articles discussing all aspects of legal information on the Internet.

Lawlibref-l

> Discussion for law reference librarians working in all types of libraries.

Subscribe and Archives: http://lists.washlaw.edu/mailman/private/lawlibref
Contact: lawlibref-owner@lists.washlaw.edu

LawSource (formerly LAWSRC-L)

> Internet Law Resources List.

Subscribe Archives: http://groups.yahoo.com/group/LawSource

PHYSICAL SCIENCES, ENGINEERING, COMPUTER SCIENCES, AND TECHNOLOGY RESOURCE DISCUSSIONS

CHMINF-L

> The Chemical Information Sources Discussion List.

Archives: http://listserv.indiana.edu/archives/chminf-l.html
Subscribe: Send e-mail to listserv@listserv.indiana.edu with the message:
subscribe chminf-l YourFirstName YourLastName

ELDNET

> Discussion of the Engineering Libraries Division of the American Society of Engineering Education.

Subscribe: Send e-mail to listserv@ukans.edu with the message:
subscribe eldnet YourFirstName YourLastName
Contact: desart@falcon.cc.ukans.edu

LIS-SCITECH

> "Forum for science and technology librarians in all types of organisation to discuss common problems, swap experience, pose questions and generally work more closely. It is also the main means of communication for the UK Universities Science and Technology Librarians Group (USTLG). www.leeds.ac.uk/library/ustlg)"

Archives: www.jiscmail.ac.uk/lists/lis-scitech.html
Subscribe: Send e-mail to listserv@jiscmail.ac.uk with the message: subscribe LIS-SCITECH
YourFirstName YourLastName
Contact: LIS-SCITECH-request@jiscmail.ac.uk

Mathqa

> Discussion list that includes reviews of mathematical Web sites.

Archives: Contact the moderator for details.
Subscribe: Send e-mail to majordomo@lists.oulu.fi with the message:
Subscribe mathqa your e-mail address
Contact: Nick Halloway snowe@rain.org

PAMnet/SLA-PAM

> Discussion list of the SLA Physics, Astronomy, and Mathematics Division.

Archives: http://listserv.nd.edu/archives/pamnet.html

To subscribe, send a message to the list owner: David Stern, Yale University, david.e.stern@yale.edu

SLA-Dite

Discussion for the Information Technology Division of the Special Libraries Association.

Subscribe: Send e-mail to listserv@listserv.sla.org with the message:

subscribe sla-dite YourFirstName YourLastName

Contact: Hope N. Tillman hope@tiac.net

STS-L

Discussion of science and technology librarianship.

Subscribe: Send e-mail to listserv@listserv.utk.edu with the message:

subscribe sts-l YourFirstName YourLastName

Contact: Jeanine Williamson, jwsts@aztec.lib.utk.edu or Margaret Mellinger mmsts@aztec.lib.utk.edu

SOCIAL SCIENCES AND EDUCATION RESOURCE DISCUSSIONS

ASIA-WWW-MONITOR

Discusses Web sites for social science studies in and about Asia.

Archives: http://coombs.anu.edu.au/asia-www-monitor.html

Subscribe: Send e-mail to majordomo@coombs.anu.edu.au with the message:

subscribe asia-www-monitor youremailaddress

Contact: Dr. T. Matthew Ciolek tmciolek@coombs.anu.edu.au

Edresource

Discussion of the Education Resources available that benefit Internet Educators.

Subscribe and Archives: http://groups.yahoo.com/list/edresource

Contact: Arun Tripathi, tripath-@amadeus.statistik.uni-dortmund.de

LM_NET

Discussion for school library and media services librarians.

Archives: www.askeric.org/Virtual/Listserv_Archives/LM_NET.shtml

Subscribe: Send email to listserv@listserv.syr.edu with the message:

subscribe lm_net YourFirstName YourLastName

Contact: Mike Eisenberg mike@ericir.syr.edu or Peter Milbury pmilbury@cusd.chico.k12.ca.us

MISCELLANEOUS SUBJECT REFERENCE RESOURCE DISCUSSIONS

Genealib Discussion List

"Librarians Serving Genealogists." This discussion list is great. There is much sharing of all kinds of genealogical information and the Web site not only has subscription instructions but links to many good resources.

Subscribe and Archives: www.cas.usf.edu/lis/genealib

Contact: Drew Smith, drewsmithusf@aol.com

GOVDOC-L

Discussion of government documents issues begun in 1991.

Archives: http://docs.lib.duke.edu/federal/govdoc-l/index.html or http://lists1.cac.psu.edu/archives/govdoc-l.html

Subscribe: Send e-mail to listserv@lists.psu.edu with the message:

subscribe Govdoc-L YourFirstName YourLastName

Contact: Ann Miller, aemiller@duke.edu, Aimee Quinn, quinna@nevada.edu, Amy West westx045@tc.umn.edu, and Cassandra Hartnett, casshart@u.washington.edu

DOROTHYL

Discussion of mystery literature—good reader's advisory discussions. Begun in 1991.

Archives: http://listserv.kent.edu/archives/dorothyl.html

Subscribe: Send e-mail to listserv@listserv.kent.edu with the message: subscribe Libref-L YourFirstName YourLastName

Contact: Diane K. Kovacs, diane@kovacs.com

RRA-L

Discussion of romance fiction—good reader's advisory discussions. Begun in 1993.

Archives: http://listserv.kent.edu/archives/dorothyl.html

Subscribe: Send e-mail to listserv@listserv.kent.edu with the message: subscribe Libref-L YourFirstName YourLastName

Contact: Leslie Haas, lhaas@alex.lib.utah.edu

LIBRARY BLOGS

(Note some additional library blogs are included in the subject collection tools, rather than in this page; e.g., Confessions of a Science Librarian is in the Physical Sciences and Technology Collection Tools.)

LIS-News

www.lisnews.com

Blake Carver's current awareness blog for all library and information science related news.

Peter Scott's Library Blog

http://xrefer.blogspot.com

News, projects, and Web resources of interest to the international community of librarians.

The Shifted Librarian

www.theshiftedlibrarian.com

Jenny Levine's current awareness blog for all e-library, digital library, and other related library and information science news, new publications, grants, and ideas.

Resource List 2: Evaluation Guides

Bobby
http://bobby.watchfire.com

Bobby is a tool that allows you to submit any URL and evaluates its accessibility to everyone regardless of physical handicaps. It is also an HTML validation tool.

Criteria for Assessing the Quality of Health Information on the Internet
http://hitiweb.mitretek.org/docs/policy.html

Criteria for Evaluating Information Resources
www.usc.edu/isd/locations/science/sci/pubs/criteval.html

Contact: Julie Kwan, nhanel@usc.edu

Questions to ask in order to assess sources and analyze the results; no links.

Evaluating Web Resources
http://www2.widener.edu/Wolfgram-Memorial-Library/webevaluation/webeval.htm

Contact: Jan Alexander, Janet.E.Alexander@widener.edu or Marsha Ann Tate, Marsha.A.Tate@widener.edu

Provides materials to assist in teaching how to evaluate the informational content of Web resources.

Evaluating Internet Sites
www.lib.purdue.edu/InternetEval

Contact: Ann Scholz, scholz@sage.cc.purdue.edu

Evaluation of Information Resources
http://www2.vuw.ac.nz/staff/alastair_smith/evaln/evaln.htm

Contact: Alastair Smith, Alastair.Smith@vuw.ac.nz

Criteria for evaluating information resources, particularly those on the Internet.

Evaluating Internet Resources
http://web.wn.net/~usr/ricter/web/valid.html

Contact: Richard Terass, ricter@wn.net

Part of the Medical Radiography Web site. This has annotated links to Internet resources of evaluation—many listed on this chart.

Evaluating Web Sites for Educational Uses: Bibliography and Checklist
www.unc.edu/cit/guides/irg-49.html

Contact: Carolyn Kotlas, carolyn_kotlas@unc.edu

This site contains a bibliography of Internet evaluation articles online and in print. The page also includes a checklist of questions to ask when evaluating Internet sites.

The Good, The Bad and The Ugly: or, Why It's a Good Idea to Evaluate Web Sources

http://lib.nmsu.edu/instruction/evalcrit.html

Contact: Susan E. Beck at susabeck@lib.nmsu.edu

   The title speaks for itself.

Information Quality WWW Virtual Library

www.ciolek.com/WWWVL-InfoQuality.html

Contact: Dr. T. Matthew Ciolek , tmciolek@ciolek.com or Irena M. Goltz, irena.goltz@brs.gov.au

   "This set of pages keeps track of online resources relevant for evaluation, development and administration of high quality factual/scholarly networked information systems."

Internet Detective

http://sosig.ac.uk/desire/internet-detective.html

Contact: Emma Worsfold, emma.worsfold@bristol.ac.uk

   Interactive tutorial on evaluating the quality of Internet resources.

Publisher's Wanted, No Experience Necessary:Information Quality on the Web

www.llrx.com/columns/quality.htm

Contact: Genie Tyburski, tyburski@hslc.org

   Column from the *Law Library Resource Exchange*. Methods for identifying information quality on the Web.

Teaching Students to Think Critically about Internet Resources

http://faculty.washington.edu/zald/neteval.htm

Contact: Andrea Bartelstein , andi@u.washington.edu or Anne Zald, zald@u.washington.edu

   A Workshop for Faculty and TAs.

Ten C's for Evaluating Internet Resources

www.uwec.edu/library/Guides/tencs.html

Contact: Betsy Richmond at richmoeb@uwec.edu

   Ten easy criteria guide evaluations.

Testing the Surf: Criteria for Evaluating Internet Information Resources

http://info.lib.uh.edu/pr/v8/n3/smit8n3.html

Contact: Alastair Smith, Alastair.Smith@vuw.ac.nz

   Article from the Public-Access Computer Systems Review (PACS Review), which compares evaluation criteria for print and CD-ROM resources with the criteria needed to evaluate Internet resources; bibliography and links.

Thinking Critically About World Wide Web Resources

www.library.ucla.edu/libraries/college/help/critical

Contact: Esther Grassian, estherg@library.ucla.edu

   For collection development librarians or for use in teaching patrons, this is a good basic overview of evaluation criteria for Web resources.

Thinking Critically about Discipline-Based World Wide Web Resources

www.library.ucla.edu/libraries/college/help/critical/discipline.htm

Contact: Esther Grassian, estherg@library.ucla.edu

Resource List 3: Multiple Subject Resource Collection Tools

ACQNET/ACQWEB
http://acqweb.library.vanderbilt.edu
> Web site and discussion for acquisitions and collection development librarians.

The Argus Clearinghouse
www.clearinghouse.net
> Sites are annotated, reviewed and rated by subject experts (librarians). Search or browse the hierarchically arranged directory. No longer being actively maintained. Links are gradually being integrated into the Internet Public Library.

Bartlesville Public Library
www.bartlesville.lib.ok.us
> Good collection of resources with policies and mission statement for the community of patrons served.

Beaucoup
www.beaucoup.com
> Over two thousand five hundred search sites, including topics of parallel/Meta, Reviewed/What's New, Music, Science, Health, and Employment.

Beyond Bookmarks: Schemes for Organizing the Web
www.public.iastate.edu/~CYBERSTACKS/CTW.htm
> Overview of different ways that Web-based information might be organized.

Beyond the Black Stump
http://home.mira.net/%7Elions/anew.htm
> Fun searchable Web site that lists the latest/newest Web sites in reverse chronological order. It also has a categorized page.

BUBL / 5:15
http://bubl.ac.uk/link
> Highly selective, relevant, librarian-evaluated resources in all academic subject areas.

California Digital Library
www.cdlib.org
> An integrated Web gateway to digital collections, services, and tools.

Choice—Current Reviews for Academic Libraries
www.ala.org/Content/NavigationMenu/ACRL/Publications/CHOICE/Home.htm
> "Timely," "Concise," "Authoritative" and "easy-to-use" reviews by experts of books and electronic media.

CyberStacks

www.public.iastate.edu/~CYBERSTACKS

"Centralized, integrated, and unified collection of significant World Wide Web (WWW) and other Internet resources categorized using the Library of Congress classification scheme." This service emphasizes the fields of Science and Technology, but other topics are now available, such as Geography, Medicine, Social Science, and Law.

Detroit Public Library

www.detroit.lib.mi.us

Artwork was developed from actual bits of the library architecture, which is a way to connect the physical location to their comprehensive virtual services.

Digital Librarian

www.digital-librarian.com

Selected "best of the Web" resources maintained by Margaret Vail Anderson, a librarian in Cortland, New York.

Directory of Online Resources for Information Literacy

www.cas.usf.edu/lis/il

Database of sources regarding locating, evaluating and using information.

Directory of Networked Resources

www.niss.ac.uk/subject2

Search alphabetically, by subject or by "UDC" (library shelf classifications). Many subject gateways available through this site.

DOAJ—The Directory of Open Access Journals (from the Budapest Open Archive Initiative

www.doaj.org

Electronic Library Programme

www.ukoln.ac.uk/services/elib

Project, writings and program areas that deal with digital/electronic library initiatives with the main objective to provide a body of tangible, electronic resources, and services. LAST UPDATED OCTOBER 2001.

Encyclopedia Britannica Internet Guide

www.britannica.com

This subscription-based learning portal provides atlas, encyclopedia, dictionary resources, as well as research tools and guides in an advertising-free environment.

Gales Reference Reviews

www.gale.com/free_resources/reference/index.htm

Reviews of traditional and Internet resources for reference by various columnists, including archives of James Rettig's "Rettig on Reference column," Péter Jacsó's "Péter's Digital Reference Shelf," and Blanche Woolls' and David Loertscher's "Reference for Students" K–12 print reference reviews.

Gelman Library Research Guides

www.gwu.edu/gelman/guides/index.html

This resource has annotated lists of important information sources (including subject-oriented Web pages) in specific subject areas.

Infomine: Scholarly Internet Resource Collections

http://infomine.ucr.edu

"INFOMINE contains over 14,000 links. Substantive databases, electronic journals, guides to the Internet for most disciplines, textbooks and conference proceedings are among the many types of resources."

Internet Library for Librarians

www.itcompany.com/inforetriever

E-library collection for librarians. Includes links to many sites of interest to librarians in all areas and all types of libraries.

Internet Public Library

www.ipl.org

This easy-to-navigate site "is a public service organization and a learning/teaching environment at the University of Michigan School of Information."

Internet Resources Newsletter

www.hw.ac.uk/libWWW/irn/irn.html

"A free newsletter for academics, students, engineers, scientists and social scientists." Published by Heriot-Watt University Library.

Internet Reviews Archive

www.bowdoin.edu/~samato/IRA

College and Research Libraries News articles reviewing various Web sites.

Internet Scout Project

http://scout.wisc.edu/indextxt.html or http://scout.wisc.edu

Annotated links to the different activities of the Internet Scout project, including the Scout Report (and it's archive), toolkits and blog.

The Internet Tourbus

www.tourbus.com

"TOURBUS is a free email newsletter published twice a week, and read by about 100,000 people in 130 countries around the globe," which provides "in-depth reviews of the most useful, fun and interesting sites on the Net. Archived.

JSTOR—The Scholarly Journal Archive

www.jstor.org

Librarian's Index to the Internet

http://lii.org

Evaluated, annotated and searchable collection of Internet Resources (academic and popular) organized by subject. LII News e-newsletter announces newly added sites and other news about LII. http://lii.org/search/file/mailinglist

Librarians' Resource Centre

www.sla.org/chapter/ctor/toolbox/resource/index.html

The place to start searching. Selective collection of reference resources, subject-specific resources, and library and information professional resources.

Library Link of the Day

www.tk421.net/librarylink

John Hubbard's blog features a review of a new library link each day.

The Library of Congress

www.loc.gov/library

Services for Researchers, Publishers, Educators; Many collections of digital resources.

Library Spot

www.libraryspot.com

> Link to law, medical, musical libraries as well as online libraries; other features include archives, reading room and librarians' shelf (tools, humor, career info and more).

Morrisville College Library

www.morrisville.edu/library

> General and specialized (authorization needed on some) and periodical databases.

MEL—Michigan Electronic Library

http://mel.org

> Selective, high-quality colleciton of Web resources, reviewed and selected by librarians in Michigan libraries.

National Library of Australia: Pathways to Information

www.nla.gov.au/pathways/pthw_library.html

> Selective collection of evaluated Web resources that are easy to browse and search. Also contains subject lists of email discussion groups, online newspapers by country, and reference materials.

National Library of Canada—Electronic Collection

http://collection.nlc-bnc.ca/e-coll-e/about-e.htm

> Comprehensive site directory, which contains electronic published Canadian books and articles.

Needle in a CyberStack—The InfoFinder

http://home.mchsi.com/~albeej

> Use the "needle navigator" to locate the database(s) needed from a large selection of options (both academic and popular); also includes separate boxes for multi-research, research tools and business/career tools.

NewJour Archives

http://gort.ucsd.edu/newjour

> NewJour is a database of serials that are published on the Internet, either through e-mail or on the Web. NewJour has been compiling e-serials since 1993. The NewJour mailing list announces new e-serials as they are made available. Ann Shumelda Okerson Associate University Librarian, Yale University, and James J. O'Donnell, Provost, Georgetown University developed the NewJour project. The archive Web site is hosted courtesy of the Libraries of the University of California at San Diego.

North Carolina State University Library—Electronic Resources by Subject

www.lib.ncsu.edu/eresources

> Listing and links to research, reference, databases, and journals.

OPCIT (The Open Citation Project—Reference Linking and Citation Analysis for Open Archives

http://opcit.eprints.org/explorearchives.shtml

Ohio Public Library Information Network (OPLIN)—Web Site

http://oplin.lib.oh.us

> Annotated subject organized collection of Web-accessible resources.

Pinakes: A Subject Launchpad

www.hw.ac.uk/libWWW/irn/pinakes/pinakes.html

> This Web site is a set of "graphic" links (easy to use) to the major subject meta-sites for the sciences, education, art, architecture, engineering, and many multidisciplinary metasites.

Ramapo Catskills Library System

www.rcls.org

> Electronic Library with good research page which includes search tools (kids search tools), directories, and multiple subject database listings.

The ResourceShelf

http://resourceshelf.blogspot.com

> Annotated Web reference tools collection compiled and maintained by Gary Price. Also includes library news and current events.

The Scout Report

http://scout.wisc.edu/report/sr/current

> "The Scout Report is the flagship publication of the Internet Scout Project. Published every Friday both on the web and by email, it provides a fast, convenient way to stay informed of valuable resources on the Internet. Our team of professional librarians and subject matter experts select, research, and annotate each resource." Archived.

Scout Select Bookmarks: Subject-based Metasites

http://scout.wisc.edu/addserv/toolkit/bookmarks/index.html

> Very selective list ("chosen for selectivity, breadth, and depth of coverage scope and authority") of metasites in seven academic fields.

Seattle Public Library—Selected Web Sites and Databases

www.spl.lib.wa.us/selectedsites/selectedsites.html

> Full-service library with online databases, quick information center, and reference. Good public library community oriented collection of high quality Web sites. Librarian selected and reviewed. Selection criteria are described.

SPARC Institutional Member Repositories

http::/www.arl.org/sparc

> Scholarly journals archiving projects.

The Spire Project Australia

http://cn.net.au

> The Spire Project is uniquely not a library-based project. It is a subject guide to information research, released as FAQ, shareware, Web site and for publishing on other Web sites. The information is organized as a collection of research strategy articles covering topics like patent research and country profiles. The work is prepared by David Novak, a professional researcher and manager of Community Networking (Australia), with his wife Fiona.

Contact: David Novak david@cn.net.au

ResourceShelf

www.resourceshelf.com

> Gary Price's blog for reviewing Web resources, sharing news of interest to e-library collectors.

ResearchBuzz

www.researchbuzz.com

> Tara Calishain's blog for reviewing Web search tools, resources, and sharing news on these topics.

Virtual Visit of the Multimedia Library

http://xenakis.ircam.fr/infos/vrml/index-e.html

> Need to download special software to view/use the "virtual" Library. Can access without this, though. Heavy emphasis on music.

WebExhibits

http://webexhibits.org

> Novel collections of art, culture and science Web sites. Hundreds of exhibits. Sponsored by the U.S. Dept. of Education, National Gallery of Art, Brandeis University, and others.

WebWatch

http://libraryjournal.reviewsnews.com

> Monthly online review of the best Web sites dealing with monthly (usually social or information issues) subject.

World Wide Web Virtual Library

www.vlib.org/Home.html or http://conbio.net/VL/DataBase

> Individuals maintain the separate collections of this library at separate locations. Contact person listed at each site. Oldest catalog on the web. High quality, annotated collection of searchable Internet resources arranged by subject. The entire central database may be downloaded for use by other e-library collectors.

INDEX

ABOUT THE AUTHORS

Kara L. Robinson has been an Information Services Librarian at Kent State University since 1992. Her areas of specialization include History, Law and Political Science.

Kara received her M.L.S. from Kent State University's School of Library Science in 1989. She has a B.A. in History from Wright State University. Currently, she is working on her Law degree at the University of Akron.

Diane K. Kovacs has more than ten years of experience as a Web Teacher and Consultant as President of Kovacs Consulting—Internet & Web Training. She wrote her first book (*Internet Trainer's Guide*) in 1995 and her most recent book (*Genealogical Research on the Web*) in 2002.

Diane Kovacs is the 2000 recipient of the "Documents to the People" award from the Government Documents Roundtable of the American Library Association. She was also the recipient of the Apple Corporation Library's Internet Citizen Award for 1992 and was the University of Illinois Graduate School of Library and Information Science Alumni Association's first recipient of the Young Leadership Award in 1996.

Diane received an M.S. in Library and Information Science from the University of Illinois in 1989 and an M.Ed. in Instructional Technology from Kent State University in 1993. She has a B.A. in Anthropology also from the University of Illinois, 1985.